CASES ON
ENTREPRENEURSHIP
AND INNOVATION

ELGAR CASES IN ENTREPRENEURSHIP

Elgar Cases in Entrepreneurship offer an instrumental resource to fulfil the needs of instructors in entrepreneurship. Spanning numerous discrete fields, Elgar Cases cover state-of-the-art developments in real-world entrepreneurial endeavours, providing expert analysis with an international focus. Casebooks are edited by leading instructors, who bring together experienced and knowledgeable case writers to illustrate and analyse contemporary entrepreneurial scenarios. Each case offers a strong foundation for constructive discussion and includes learning objectives and summary questions to guide classroom discussion. Teaching notes for each case provide opportunities for instructors to further develop understanding and promote class engagement. An invaluable boon to course leaders and students alike, Elgar Cases in Entrepreneurship combine practicality, student engagement and international expertise to bring entrepreneurship alive!

For a full list of Edward Elgar published titles, including the titles in this series, visit our website at www.e-elgar.com.

CASES ON ENTREPRENEURSHIP AND INNOVATION

UNEXPLORED TOPICS AND CONTEXTS

EDITED BY

JANA SCHMUTZLER

Assistant Professor, Delft Centre of Entrepreneurship, TU Delft, the Netherlands, Affiliated Associate Professor, Business School, Universidad del Norte, Colombia, and Affiliated Researcher, Jackstädt Center of Entrepreneurship and Innovation Research, Bergische Universität Wuppertal, Germany

LORENA A. PALACIOS-CHACÓN

Professor of International Business, Department of International Business and Logistics, Tecnologico de Monterrey, Guadalajara, Mexico

SAMANTHA BURVILL

Associate Professor, School of Management, Swansea University, UK

VENETA ANDONOVA

Dean and Professor of Strategy and Entrepreneurship, School of Management, Universidad de Los Andes, Colombia

ELGAR CASES IN ENTREPRENEURSHIP

Cheltenham, UK • Northampton, MA, USA

Published by
Edward Elgar Publishing Limited
The Lypiatts
15 Lansdown Road
Cheltenham
Glos GL50 2JA
UK

Edward Elgar Publishing, Inc.
William Pratt House
9 Dewey Court
Northampton
Massachusetts 01060
USA

A catalogue record for this book
is available from the British Library

Library of Congress Control Number: 2024936443

This book is available electronically in the **Elgar**online
Business subject collection
https://dx.doi.org/10.4337/9781802204537

ISBN 978 1 80220 452 0 (cased)
ISBN 978 1 80220 453 7 (eBook)

Printed and bound by CPI Group (UK) Ltd, Croydon, CR0 4YY

CONTENTS

ABOUT THE EDITORS

Jana Schmutzler is Assistant Professor at the Delft Centre of Entrepreneurship at TU Delft (the Netherlands), Affiliated Associate Professor at Business School of Universidad del Norte in Barranquilla, Colombia and Research Fellow at the Jackstädt Center of Entrepreneurship and Innovation Research, Bergische Universität Wuppertal, Germany. From 2022 to 2023 she served as Director of the Entrepreneurship Center of Universidad del Norte, Colombia. She holds a PhD in economics from the Schumpeter School of Business and Economics at the Bergische Universität Wuppertal, Germany. Her research interests center on innovation processes and entrepreneurial behavior with a focus on developing countries. Specifically, she explores the role context plays in fostering (or hindering) these vital economic behaviors. She has published in internationally recognized journals in the field of entrepreneurship and innovation such as *Entrepreneurship: Theory and Practice, International Entrepreneurship and Management Journal,* and *Industrial and Corporate Change*. She co-edited the books *Innovation in Developing and Transition Countries* (2017) and *Entrepreneurial Ecosystems Meet Innovation Systems* (2020) and is on the Editorial Review Board of *Entrepreneurship Theory and Practice*. She is part of the Scientific Committee of Globelics and the Latin American Division of Regional Studies Association.

Lorena A. Palacios-Chacón is Assistant Professor of the International Business and Logistics Department at Tecnologico de Monterrey, Business School, Guadalajara Campus in Mexico. She earned her PhD in management from the University of Puerto Rico, and her two bachelors in economics and finance and international trade from the Sergio Arboleda University. One of her main interests is the writing of teaching cases and she has participated in a number of conferences, having won multiple best case awards. Lorena co-authored the case *FIFA 2010: Choosing the Best Coach in the World* through the CALDEA-BALAS case consortium. She is President of the Latin American Case Association. She has written books and articles in the areas of internationalization of the firm, financial deepening in Colombia, the processes of offshore and outsourcing of companies, and international economic integration between countries.

Samantha Burvill is Associate Professor at Swansea University School of Management in Wales and is Employability Lead for the Faculty of Humanities and Social Sciences. She holds a PhD in business growth from the University of South Wales. Her research interests focus on regional development, purposeful ecosystems, small to medium-sized enterprises, and the Well Being of Future Generations Act (Wales, 2015). Specifically, she explores the role of well being, sustainability, and ecosystems in regional development. She has published in numerous academic and pedagogic journals and has published teaching cases through the case center. Her work on regional development and purposeful ecosystems has won numerous awards including the Regions E-Zone Article of the Year 2022. She is a regular higher education and business consultant and works with colleagues both nationally and internationally.

Veneta Andonova is Dean and Associate Professor of Business Strategy and Entrepreneurship at Universidad de los Andes School of Management, Colombia. She obtained her doctoral degree in management from Universitat Pompeu Fabra, Spain. Her research has been published in top-ranked international journals in economics and management with a focus on emerging and growing economies such as *Entrepreneurship Theory and Practice, Journal of Development Economics*, and *Journal of Development Studies*. Her research on the topic of multilatinas and the Latin American business environment is collected in the edited volume *Multilatinas: Strategies for Internationalization* (2017) and is regularly updated at her Coursera MOOC, available in English and Spanish. Her book on the topic of entrepreneurship, entrepreneurial ecosystems, and new business models is *Entrepreneurial Ecosystems in Unexpected Places* (2019). She is a startup mentor and promoter of university-based entrepreneurship. She serves at the AACSB Latin America and Caribbean Advisory Council, Association of MBA Latin America Council, Global Business School Network Board, and the Universitat Pompeu Fabra International Advisory Board, where she advocates in favor of much-needed acceptance and legitimacy of high-quality research from the Global South.

CONTRIBUTORS

Rick Aalbers is a full Professor in Corporate Restructuring and Innovation at the Department of Business Administration of Radboud University. He has been a visiting scholar at Imperial College London and National University of Ireland at Galway and the Tokyo Institute of Technology. Rick's research focuses on organizational restructuring and innovation and revolves around corporate reorganization and innovation. His work on these themes has been accepted for publication by leading international journals, including *Research Policy, Long Range Planning, Journal of Product Innovation Management, Harvard Business Review*, and *MIT Sloan Management Review* (winner of MIT's Richard Beckhard award). He serves on the editorial review board of the *Journal of Management Studies*.

Zainab Almukhtar is Assistant Professor in Management Science at Cape Breton University. She concluded her PhD studies in management science at the Sobey School of Business, Saint Mary's University, Canada. She completed a master's in entrepreneurship and innovation from Saint Mary's University, a master's in engineering, and a bachelor in engineering. Her research interest spans healthcare modeling and policy with a particular focus on mental health. This includes the application of quantitative methods to address issues in healthcare and plan healthcare strategies. Other research interests include diversity, immigration and related policies, and integration. She is a research associate in the Canadian Centre for Policy Alternatives.

Helena Brito de Freitas graduated from the business administration program at Federal University of São Paulo and is now doing a post-graduate course in commercial management and sales. She works at Edenred with digital products.

Laura Sofía Buitrago Vidal is a political scientist from Pontificia Universidad Javeriana. She holds a master's in development studies. She was a research assistant at the International Institute of Social Studies and her research interests are in the areas of economic development and rural development in post-conflict scenarios. She works for the DISTRICT AGENCY FOR HIGHER EDUCATION, SCIENCE AND TECHNOLOGY – ATENEA in Bogotá, Colombia.

Jurgita Butkevičienė is Assistant Professor in the Faculty of Economics and Business Administration at Vilnius University, Lithuania. She holds a PhD in management and her research focuses on FinTech and blockchain, institutional change, collective institutional entrepreneurship, institutional innovations, and the development of entrepreneurial ecosystems – national and regional as well as physical and digital. She cultivates interdisciplinary knowledge and has experience in business, education, and policy domains. Before her tenure at Vilnius University, she served as an Associate Professor of Practice at the School of Economics and Business at Kaunas University of Technology in Lithuania and managed an information technology company. Jurgita also has multidecade experience in governmental export promotion organization. She contributed to the development and implementation of policies aimed at improving the national economy's competitiveness and international trade. Being a skilled professional, she utilizes her experience in business, academia, and non-governmental and governmental sectors to reach impactful outcomes.

Marcia Carvalho de Azevedo is Associate Professor at the Federal University of São Paulo. She is a psychologist with master's and doctoral degrees in business administration, both from Getulio Vargas Foundation in São Paulo. Her research interests are human resources, aging workers, entrepreneurship, and research methodology. Marcia has published papers in academic journals, such as *Personnel Review*, *International Journal of Entrepreneurial Behaviour & Research*, and *Knowledge and Process Management*. Her career includes working as a project manager and consultant in both private and public sectors.

Lourdes Casanova is Senior Lecturer and Gail and Rob Cañizares Director Emerging Markets Institute at Cornell University. She is co-author with Anne Miroux of *The Era of Chinese Multinationals* (2019) and *Emerging Market Multinationals Reports* (2016–2024). Lourdes is also co-author of *Financing Entrepreneurship and Innovation in Emerging Markets* (2018) and co-editor in Chief of the *Journal of Evolutionary Studies*.

Susanna Chui teaches for and conducts research in areas related to sustainability, entrepreneurship, and leadership at Leicester Castle Business School of De Montfort University. Her research interests include entrepreneurship, leadership and identity, social entrepreneurship, and social impact measurement. Her research experience also extends to examining social impact measurement, corporate social responsibility, stakeholder management, and human resources issues in organizational contexts. She has completed social impact research projects for two non-profit organizations: Dialogue in the Dark Foundation and Teach Unlimited in Hong Kong.

Cinzia Colapinto is Associate Professor of Entrepreneurship and Strategy at the Department of Management, Ca' Foscari University of Venice, Italy. Her research interests focus on entrepreneurship, innovation, and strategy. She is interested in the role played by digital technologies on business model transformations and on their impact on the achievement of sustainable development goals by small to medium-sized enterprises. Her main publications are in *R&D Management*, *Management International Review*, and *Management Decision*. She is the author of several monographs, including *Adaptive Decision Making and Intellectual Styles* (2013). Cinzia is a member of the Commission for the Enhancement of Knowledge at Ca' Foscari University and Scientific Director of the B2B Marketing Observatory.

Luis Hernan Contreras Pinochet is Professor at the University of São Paulo. He holds a doctorate from the School of Business Administration of São Paulo of the Fundação Getulio Vargas, a master's in administration from the Pontifícia Universidade Católica do Paraná, and a specialist degree in information and communication technology from FAE Centro Universitário. Luis has research experience in the following areas: behavior and technology, artificial intelligence and data science, smart cities and government, and operational research and mathematical decision models. He is a member of the ANPAD and AIS Chapter scientific societies.

Beth Cummings is Senior Lecturer in Marketing at Swansea University School of Management in Wales and is Employability Lead for the school. She holds a master's in marketing from the University of Wales. Beth is a chartered marketer and Vice Chair on the Chartered Institute of Marketing Wales regional board, responsible for education and professional pathways. Her research interests focus on employability and developing pedagogical practices that support this. Her most recent research has concentrated on regional development, purposeful ecosystems and the Well Being of Future Generations Act (Wales, 2015). Her professional marketing interests focus on sustainability, consumer insights, branding, and social media. She is particularly interested in the impact of social media on body image and well being.

Claudia De Fuentes is Professor of Innovation and Entrepreneurship at the Sobey School of Business at Saint Mary's University. Her research experience includes innovation in organizations and contributions to place-making, systems of innovation, the creation and use of knowledge in a globalized economy, new forms of academia–industry collaboration, and science, technology, and innovation policy. She has done research and lectured internationally in Mexico, Canada, Sweden, Vietnam, and Peru on topics such as innovation systems, innovation policy, innovation management, global innovation, and entrepreneurship. Claudia has supervised PhD and master's theses on related topics. She is an editorial board member of the *International Journal of Technological Learning, Innovation, and Development*, and has guest-edited special issues.

Zulima Fernández is Professor of Strategic Management and Director of the Institute for Entrepreneurship and Family Business at Universidad Carlos III de Madrid. She was formerly Director of the National Agency for Quality Assessment and Accreditation of Spain, Vice Chancellor of Academic Organization at Universidad Carlos III de Madrid, and President of Spanish Academy of Management. Her research interests are family business, internationalization, innovation, digital technologies, competitiveness, and strategy, topics on which she has published in leading international academic journals, such as the *Journal of International Business Studies, Journal of World Business*, and *Family Business Review*. Her research has produced more than 100 articles and book chapters.

Vladi Finotto is Associate Professor in Entrepreneurship and Strategy at the Department of Management, Ca' Foscari University of Venice, Italy. His research and teaching explore business model innovation in firms and value chains and the impacts of innovation on organizations, with a particular focus on the agri-food sector. He is a co-founder and researcher of the Agrifood Management and Innovation Lab and co-directs the master's program in Marketing and Strategies for the Food and Wine sector at Ca' Foscari University of Venice. Vladi is the Rector's delegate for technology transfer, entrepreneurship, and industrial liaisons, coordinates a variety of industry–university initiatives, and advises regional and national policy makers and industry associations on matters related to innovation.

Jonas Geisen is a PhD fellow of the Marie Curie ITN Program FINDER, a competitive research grant by the European Commission working in strategy and innovation at Radboud University Nijmegen, the Netherlands. As part of the team of the Radboud Centre for Organization Restructuring, Jonas' work is conducted in alignment with industry partners.

His research centers on high-tech industries and the effect of temporality on the performance outcome of corporate strategy, leveraged through acquisitions and divestitures.

Isabella Gomati de la Vega is a PhD candidate in neuroscience from the Pontificia Universidad Javeriana. She holds a master's in creativity and change leadership from Buffalo State University and has a BA in anthropology from the Universidad de los Andes, Colombia. She is a creativity and social innovation adjunct professor at the Colegio de Estudios Superiores de Administración. Her research focuses on the underlying processes of complex behaviors and their impact on socio-behavioral change.

Georgina M. Gómez is Associate Professor in Institutions and Local Development at the International Institute of Social Studies of Erasmus University Rotterdam. She has published widely on monetary systems with complementary currencies, solidarity and informal finances, grassroots economies, local economic development, and institutions.

Vanessa Itacaramby Pardim is Professor at the University Nove de Julho, São Paulo. She is actively engaged in projects related to undergraduate and post-graduate distance education, as well as extension programs and MOOCs affiliated with the Open University of Brazil at the Federal University of São Paulo. Her research and professional focus areas encompass online education, gamification, instructional design, teacher training, teaching and learning processes in administration, virtual learning environments, and intelligent tutoring systems.

Kenneth K. Kwong is a marketing faculty of the Business School at the Hang Seng University of Hong Kong. On the research side, his interests are on workplace well being, internal marketing, and family succession and governance. He uses case-based approaches for his consultancy work, teaching, and learning.

Mario A. Manzi-Puertas is Assistant Professor in the Department of Business Administration at Pontificia Universidad Javeriana in Bogotá, Colombia. He is a PhD candidate in advanced management of organizations and social economy at Mondragon University, Spain and holds a master's in creative studies and change leadership from Buffalo State University, USA. His research interests focus on entrepreneurship and innovation under resource constraints, as well as frugal innovation. He also has an interest in writing teaching cases, which have been published, awarded, and used in several universities. Mario is a co-founder and coordinating member of the Latin American Network for Frugal Innovation. His consulting work includes helping startups and companies create innovation cultures based on their own capabilities and resources, in order to generate solutions focused on shared value with their stakeholders.

Luis Martínez-Cháfer is Associate Professor in Management at Universitat Jaume I, Spain. His research is focused on social network analysis, innovation, knowledge transmission, social capital, and industrial clusters. His work has been published in leading journals such as *Journal of Business Research*, *Growth and Change*, and *European Planning Studies*. Luis' research has also been presented in several national and international congress proceedings.

Killian McCarthy is Associate Professor at Radboud University Nijmegen and Visiting Professor at the Kyiv School of Economics. His research focuses on the use and effect of corporate tools, such as corporate venture capital, strategic alliances, divestitures, and, especially, mergers and acquisitions, on firms' financial and innovation performance. His research has been published in journals such as *Harvard Business Review, Research Policy*, and the *Journal of Product Innovation Management*.

Alan Mella is a lawyer who specializes in intellectual property and technology transfer. He was a research assistant at the Innovation Observatory of the Faculty of Economics and Business at the University of Chile. He was a legal advisor at the Licensing Office of the University of Santiago de Chile. Alan is an associate lawyer in intellectual property at Alessandri Abogados. His research interests focus on the areas of innovation and corruption.

Anne Miroux is Faculty Fellow at the Johnson School of Management at Cornell University, former Director of the Division on Technology in the United Nations Conference on Trade and Development and Head of the Secretariat of the United Nations Commission on Science and Technology for Development. She has over 30 years of experience in international trade and finance, technology and innovation, and development policies. For several years, she directed the World Investment Reports. Her books include *The Era of Chinese Multinationals* (2019) and *From Copycats to Leaders: Innovation from Emerging Markets* (2021). Anne is also a member of the Editorial Board of the *Journal of International Business Policies*.

F. Xavier Molina-Morales is Professor at the Universitat Jaume I de Castelló, Spain. He has a doctorate in management from the Universitat Jaume I de Castelló. He has been a visiting scholar at the Maastricht School of Management, Copenhagen Business School, and Università Ca' Foscari, among others. His research interests include effects proximity in clusters and districts, social capital dimensions, and implications on innovation. His papers have appeared in journals such as *Strategic Management Journal, Environment and Planning A*, and *Research Policy*. He is Coordinator of the AERT research group and the doctorate program of Local Development and International Cooperation of the Universitat Jaume I de Castelló.

Nicolás Moncaut is Associate Professor at Universidad Nacional de San Martín, Argentina. He has a degree in economics and a master's in economic development. He is finishing his PhD in economic development at Universidad Nacional de Quilmes. Nicolás is working on his doctoral thesis on university–industry links oriented towards technological innovation. He has worked as an analyst and researcher in the Ministry of Economy and Public Finance, Argentina, United Nations Economic Commission for Latin America and the Caribbean, and Center for Economic Development Studies.

Cynthia O'Driscoll is an experienced leader currently pursuing her doctorate in business administration at Saint Mary's University in Halifax, Nova Scotia, Canada. She has a multidisciplinary background that includes masters from Bournemouth University, UK and Memorial University in Newfoundland and Labrador and an executive MBA from Saint Mary's University.

Frédéric Ooms is Assistant Professor and Researcher in Innovation and Entrepreneurship at HEC Liège, Belgium. He is a certified expert in design sprint, design thinking, lean startup, and business model innovation and has supported many startups, small to medium-sized enterprises, and large companies for more than 15 years in the incubation, development, and financing of their innovation projects. His research conducted at the frontiers of neuroscience and entrepreneurship focuses on the entrepreneurial mindset, i.e. how entrepreneurs think and act. The lab uses psychometric, neuroimaging, and naturalistic approaches to understand how people identify opportunities and create high-growth venture start-ups.

Jahan Ara Peerally is Associate Professor of International Business and Innovation at HEC Montréal, Canada. Her research encompasses the activities of multinational versus domestic and social enterprises in developing and emerging economies. Her publications focus on the sustainable and other socio-economic development effects of these enterprises' innovative technological capabilities, social innovations, and inclusive innovations, and their policy implications for innovation systems. Jahan has published scientific articles in several peer-reviewed books and journals.

Jesús Peiró-Palomino is Associate Professor in Economics at the University of Valencia, Spain. His research focuses on social capital, economic development, and social progress and the results have been published in prestigious journals occupying relevant positions in the ABS Academic Journal Guide and Journal Citations Report. He regularly participates in scientific meetings (congresses, workshops, and invited conferences), having also been an organizer on many occasions.

Fabrice Pirnay received his PhD from the University of Lille 2, France. Following his PhD studies, Fabrice was appointed as Senior Researcher at HEC Liège, Belgium. He has several publications in the field of high-tech startups and managing the growth of these companies. His ongoing research interests include impact entrepreneurship and family businesses.

Antonio Revilla is Associate Professor in Business Organization at Carlos III University of Madrid, Spain, where he is a member of the Institute for Entrepreneurship and Family Business and part of the management team of the MA in Entrepreneurship and Business Venturing. He holds a PhD in business strategy from Carlos III University and a master's in social research methods from the London School of Economics and Political Science. His research interests include open innovation, the internationalization of technology value chains, corporate entrepreneurship in family firms, and the links between digitalization and sustainability. He has published in journals such as *British Journal of Management*, *Family Business Review*, and *Technovation*. He regularly teaches courses on strategic management, innovation management, and entrepreneurship. He has lectured at Bath Spa University, UK and worked as a consultant at the Boston Consulting Group.

Ben Reynolds is Founder and Managing Director of Urban Foundry (www.urbanfoundry .co.uk) – one of Wales' first certified BCorps. He is an expert in creative urban regeneration, with a doctorate and 25 years of experience. He is a member of the Market Research Society and Fellow of the Royal Society of the Arts, has served as executive and non-executive director/trustee of various social businesses and charities, and is 'entrepreneur in residence' at Swansea University. He is also an invited member of the Regeneration Swansea partnership and has served as a commissioner for the Swansea Poverty Truth Commission and the Welsh Government's Cooperatives and Mutuals Commission. Ben has written on the cultural regeneration of urban centers and contributed to published works on community work. He co-supervises a European Social Research Council-funded regeneration PhD at Swansea University.

Jason Rhinelander is is a licensed Professional Engineer (PEng) and Associate Professor in the Division of Engineering at Saint Mary's University in Halifax, Nova Scotia, Canada. He is the inaugural Head of Technology and Innovation at the David Sobey Retailing Centre, where he seeks to apply machine learning and artificial intelligence solutions to real-world challenges. His research interests include artificial intelligence ethics, retail applications of machine-learning technologies, and computer vision. Jason holds a PhD in electrical and computer engineering from Carleton University, Ottawa, Canada. He also holds an MEng and BEng in electrical engineering from Memorial University in St. John's, Newfoundland and Labrador, Canada.

Verónica Robert has a PhD in economics and a master's in economics and industrial development. She is a specialist in the fields of innovation economics, technological change, and economic development. She is a dedicated CONICET researcher and she is a Full Professor at the National University of San Martín, Argentina. She is the proud recipient of the Annual Prize of Economic Research Dr. Raúl Prebisch, awarded by the Central Bank of the Argentine Republic, as well as an award from the Faculty of Economic Sciences at the University of Buenos Aires for her PhD thesis. She has published several articles in national and international journals and played a pivotal role in the publication of several books.

Alicia Rodríguez is Associate Professor at the University Carlos III of Madrid, Spain where she is Co-Director of the Master in Entrepreneurship and Business Venturing. She holds a PhD in strategic management from this University. Her research interests include sustainability, digitalization, internationalization strategies, innovation management, and entrepreneurship. Her research has been published in leading journals such as the *Journal of International Business Studies, Strategic Management Journal*, and *Long Range Planning*. She has also published her research in several book chapters.

Beatriz Rodriguez-Satizabal is Assistant Professor and Researcher in Economic and Business History at Universidad del Pacífico, Perú. Her research focuses on the evolution of the business system during the twentieth century in Latin America, with a special emphasis on Colombia and Perú. Her projects include analysis of the changes and transformations of advertisements, women entrepreneurs, entrepreneurial families, and business groups under the perspective of business history.

Francisco Sánchez is an Assistant Professor in Accounting at the University of Chile. He teaches accounting at the bachelor's and master's levels. He has published teaching cases in *Cladea Balas Case Consortium, Multidisciplinary Business Review*, and *Estudios de Administración*. His research interests are in the areas of accounting and finance. Francisco has published his research in international journals such as *Academia Revista Latinoamericana de Administración* and *Baltic Journal of Management*. Additionally, he is the author of the book *Fundamentos de Contabilidad Financiera*.

Sebastian Schäfer is an experienced entrepreneur and ecosystem builder. As Co-Founder and Managing Director of TechQuartier and the former head of the business incubator at Goethe University, he has spent the last 10+ years building up the startup scene in the Frankfurt Rhine-Main metropolitan region. He is also involved as an advisor, business angel, and co-partner of Pitch Club GmbH. Sebastian's academic background includes degrees in economics and Japanese studies from the University of Tuebingen and a doctoral degree in behavioral economics from the University of Frankfurt. He is associated with the Center for Leadership and Behavior in Organizations and the Frankfurt Laboratory of Experimental Economics at Goethe University. He continues to lecture at the Goethe Business School, Frankfurt School of Finance and Management and on event stages around the globe.

Francine Schlosser is Professor of Entrepreneurship and Odette Research Chair at the Odette School of Business, University of Windsor in Canada. Her research considers how educators, employees, migrants, and employers can stimulate entrepreneurial readiness and engagement in innovation and manage career transitions. She held the University of Windsor's Golden Jubilee Professorship in Business for research excellence and was the founding Executive Director of the Entrepreneurship, Practice and Innovation Centre from 2016 to 2019. Francine established three successive campus entrepreneurship centers that engaged students with the business community through multidisciplinary venture teams and consulting projects.

Aušrinė Šilenskytė is Program Manager and Ambassador for Internationalization at the University of Vaasa, Finland. She also serves as Chair at the Academy of International Business Teaching and Education Shared Interest Group and is a member of the Governing Board at the AIB-CIBER Doctoral Academy. Šilenskytė holds a PhD in the area of international management and her research centers around strategy implementation, blockchain adoption in international business management, and innovations in business education, particularly related to social sustainability. Aušrinė teaches various topics related to international management for undergraduates, master's students, as well as professionals in continuous education. She is an alumnus of the prestigious Nord-IB program. Aušrinė received several international awards for her research and as an educator. Before joining academia, she worked in managerial positions in Lithuania and Egypt, and throughout her academic career, she has consulted for international Finnish firms and engaged in project work aimed at achieving socio-economic sustainability through industry-academia collaborations.

Marte C.W. Solheim is Professor of Innovation Studies and Pro-Rector for Innovation and Society at the University of Stavanger. Holding a PhD in management, her research combines insights from organizational theory, innovation studies and economic geography. She is particularly interested in understanding how innovation is inspired when a variety of diverse knowledge intersect, and the contextual factors affecting this association.

Juan Pablo Soto is Associate Professor of Supply Chain Management and Technology and Vice Dean of Corporate Relations at Universidad de los Andes School of Management, Colombia. He holds a master's and a PhD in economics and business from Pompeu Fabra University in Barcelona, Spain. He has worked as a consultant for companies in the public and private sectors. His research interests are in sustainable supply chain management, closed-loop supply chains, reverse and green logistics, and retail logistics.

Mary Suen is Founder and Chief Executive of the Chief Happiness Officer Association in Hong Kong.

Julio Cesar Zuluaga is Assistant Professor at the School of Business and Economics, Universidad Icesi, Colombia and Visiting Professor at the IAE-Pau University, School of Management, France. He holds a PhD in management, a master's in organizational studies, and a BA in history. His primary teaching and research areas are organizational theory and strategy, innovation, and family business. He has researched innovation strategies, intellectual property rights and value-capturing mechanisms, the role of innovation intermediaries in technological change, and family businesses' socially responsible strategies. Julio Cesar is researching business elites' role in the emergence and evolution of developmental ecosystems. Previously, he worked as an Assistant Professor at Pontificia Universidad Javeriana, Senior Lecturer at the Management and Marketing Department at Westminster International University in Tashkent, and was Visiting Researcher at the Schumpeter School of Business and Economics, University of Wuppertal, Germany and University of Barcelona, Spain.

ACKNOWLEDGEMENTS

The editors Jana Schmutzler, Lorena A. Palacios-Chacón, Samantha Burvill, and Veneta Andonova would like to thank Yeri Tordecilla-Ávila for her invaluable work during the editing process. Without your dedicated work, this endeavor would have been much harder to complete.

SUPPLEMENTARY MATERIALS

Supplementary materials for this book can be found online at:
https://dx.doi.org/10.4337/9781802204537

1
Teaching cases in unexplored topics and contexts: why do we need such a book?

Jana Schmutzler, Lorena A. Palacios-Chacón, Veneta Andonova, and Samantha Burvill

1.   CONTEXT MATTERS

The teaching case method has gained in popularity across business and management schools all over the world, lately expanding towards other fields such as economics, public policy, law, not-for-profit management, and the like. Teaching cases are "a vehicle by which a chunk of reality is brought into the classroom … [and a] record of complex situations that must be literally pulled apart and put together again before the situations can be understood" (Lawrence, 1951, p. 215). They are thus a pedagogical tool that promotes critical thinking skills (Salemi, 2002; Michel, Carter, & Varela, 2009), creativity (Salemi, 2002), and collaboration (Morse & Stephens, 2012) among students by bringing them closer to decision-makers and thus fostering the application of theory to real-world problems (Christensen & Carlile, 2009; Michel et al., 2009). Being an effective teaching tool, case studies are a simplified and summarized version of reality. But what happens if reality for students is very different from the one presented in the teaching case studies?

The underlying assumption when using teaching cases is that managers, governmental authorities, or other decision-makers face similar problems around the world. However, research in both entrepreneurship and innovation has shown that context matters (e.g., Welter, 2011; Andonova, Nikolova, & Dimitrov, 2019; Tsvetkova, Schmutzler, & Pugh, 2020). Contexts differ tremendously among countries at different stages of economic development (Schmutzler, Suarez, Tsvetkova, & Faggian, 2017), between urban and rural places (Gaddefors & Anderson, 2019), or between well-off and forgotten or left-behind regions (Rodríguez-Pose, Wilkie, & Zhang, 2021). Relying therefore on case studies that are predominantly situated in thriving regions in the Global North may be detrimental to one of the main goals of teaching with cases: zooming in on relevant real-world examples.

In traditional classrooms, entrepreneurship and innovation are often taught through a universal lens. However, its practice is highly contingent upon the socio-economic, cultural, and geopolitical landscape (Tsvetkova et al., 2020). Context is not merely a backdrop; it is an active player shaping opportunities, risks, and outcomes while at the same time being shaped by entrepreneurial and innovative behavior (e.g., Welter, 2011; Erez, Van De Ven, & Lee, 2015; Ben-Hafaïedh et al., 2023). For example, starting a technology-based startup in Silicon Valley comes with its own set of rules and expectations, driven by an ecosystem rich in venture capital and science and technology expertise as well as business-related prowess. Although Berlin is located in a similar context to other well-developed entrepreneurial ecosystems, Scheidgen and Brattström (2022) show how networking in Silicon Valley and Berlin differs significantly. More importantly, networking within an emerging entrepreneurial ecosystem in a developing country is shaped by institutional factions that have generated a lack of trust, where governments are looked upon suspiciously (Porras-Paez & Schmutzler, 2019) and where specific informal institutions heavily influence social interactions (Porras-Paez, 2023).

The agriculture sector, often perceived as traditional or even archaic, is an area where innovation and entrepreneurship initiatives are making significant inroads. Particularly in developing economies, agricultural entrepreneurship serves as a cornerstone for rural development and offers a rich case base for sustainable business practices; and while peripheral[1] and rural regions are often used synonymously (and confusingly) (Pugh & Dubois, 2021), entrepreneurship research in both contexts has been of recent interest to scholars, shaping their development in spite of their lacking resources (e.g., Mayer & Baumgartner, 2014; Muñoz & Kimmitt, 2019). It has even given way to new concepts, such as slow innovation (Shearmur 2015, 2017; Shearmur & Doloreux, 2016). Challenges and opportunities in these places differ greatly from those of a developed entrepreneurial ecosystem such as Silicon Valley, and as such, entrepreneurs likely embark on different journeys. These examples show that not only does context matter; in fact, context shapes human interaction (North, 1991), and teaching cases that zoom in on (individual) behavior, asking that students analyze and evaluate decision-making processes, can only be complete if contextual details are an essential part of this evaluation. Additionally, diverse geographical settings of entrepreneurship, from bustling urban centers to peripheral and rural contexts as well as left-behind regions, provide a contrasting canvas for entrepreneurial action. In these varied contexts, entrepreneurship often transcends its business purpose to become a catalyst for community development and social inclusion. Teaching cases in those regions can shed light on the unique dynamics of entrepreneurship in underserved areas.

A large diversity of contexts in teaching cases is thus essential for educators, students, and practitioners alike. It not only makes the educational experience more relatable but also equips future entrepreneurs with the versatility to adapt to different settings and make contextualized decisions. Therefore, this book seeks to enrich the academic discourse by introducing case studies from a myriad of contexts to highlight how entrepreneurship is both universal and incredibly specific. The collection of our cases therefore covers not only geographical settings in the Global South, often overlooked by academic research on innovation and entrepreneurship (Tsvetkova et al., 2020; Cahen, Casanova, & Miroux, 2021), it also includes cases in regions that, albeit located geographically in the Global North, are not the common setting of teaching cases: peripheral and rural areas or transition economies of the former communist bloc. Yet, our book goes further than that: most of our cases touch upon emerging topics in entrepreneurship and innovation and thus combine not only relatively unexplored geographical contexts but also new topics where teaching cases are still rare.

2. UNVEILING THE UNCHARTED TERRAIN: TOPICS LESS TRAVELED IN ENTREPRENEURSHIP AND INNOVATION

2.1 Entrepreneurial equilibrium: Striking a balance between business and impact

Entrepreneurship and innovation are multifaceted concepts that encompass diverse phenomena, are influenced by a wide range of human factors, and manifest differently across a range of contexts. While entrepreneurship and innovation have traditionally been tied to the vision of a profit-driven enterprise, today, we see innovative entrepreneurial ventures operating at the intersection of societal change and commercial viability. The purpose of many is to balance their financial goals with impact, striving to create value for specific stakeholders and the broader community alike. This phenomenon is reflected in new topics emerging in the academic literature and the rise of concepts that defy conventional categorization. Social entrepreneurship[2] focuses on creating social impact alongside financial sustainability (Phillips, Lee, Ghobadian, O'Regan, & James, 2015; Le Grand & Roberts, 2021), representing a significant departure from the traditional dichotomy of for-profit versus not-for-profit activities. Social innovation,[3] defined as "innovative activities and services that are motivated by the goal of meeting a social need" (Mulgan, Tucker, Ali, & Sanders, 2007, p. 146), follows a similar focus. The entrepreneur or innovator acts not only as a businessperson but also as a social change agent committed to tackling complex societal problems.

From an organizational perspective, social enterprises sit between non-profits and traditional for-profit businesses as hybrid entities that aim to achieve specific social, environmental, or political outcomes while relying on market mechanisms for financial sustainability. Profit generation that is not pursued at the expense of society has given rise to yet another concept: responsible innovation.[4] It is through the transparent interaction of societal actors that "ethical acceptability, sustainability and societal desirability of the innovation process and its marketable products" (Von Schomberg, 2013, p. 50) are arguably ensured. As delineated by Alter (2007), this hybrid spectrum is characterized by market encroachment, which involves proactive revenue generation efforts and the incorporation of management practices characteristic of the private sector into the social realm, a situation that necessitates a careful balance weighing non-market goals and market-driven pressures. As Battilana (2018) notes, this duality challenges organizations to validate both their economic and social value creation to diverse stakeholders.

The pledge that businesses should not focus solely on profit maximization and shareholder value but instead take on responsibility for societal processes has also extended to the environmental domain (Parrish, 2010). Since the emergence of the sustainability goals in the 1970s, which call for the need to improve human well-being and halt (or even reverse) ecological degradation, the question as to the role entrepreneurs and corporations play has become central. Thus, not only the integration of social impact and an improvement of quality of life but fostering a net positive environmental impact has been proposed as a motivation for entrepreneurs and innovators (Schaltegger & Wagner, 2011). With the roots of sustainability-oriented entrepreneurship going back to the 1950s and its link to the concept of corporate social responsibility (Haldar, 2019), defined as "the idea of social responsibilities supposes that the corporation has not only economic and legal obligations but also certain responsibilities to society which extend beyond these obligations" (McGuire, 1963, p. 144), the concepts of entrepreneurship and innovation touch upon an organization's strategic impact on social and environmental performance.

The curated cases assembled in Part I of our book – *Entrepreneurial equilibrium: striking a balance between business and impact* – focus on those topics and allow students to embark on a profound journey into the heart of entrepreneurship that melds financial objectives with societal impact. Through analyzing the entrepreneurial journey of those who seek a balance between profit and societal impact, students gain a deep understanding of the transformative power of entrepreneurship in various contexts, comprehending the nuances and intricacies of establishing and scaling businesses that aim for more than just profit and become aware of the risks and complexities of such models.

Chapter 2, *Open Hands For You: empowering immigrants through social entrepreneurship in Norway*, introduces students to Aline Kamudege, a migrant and social entrepreneur in Norway who has dedicated her life to supporting the integration of immigrants in the Stavanger region through her organization Open Hands for You. Aline's journey from a refugee fleeing war-torn Burundi to a beacon of compassion and support for immigrants in Norway serves as a compelling narrative that challenges traditional business school case studies, which often feature predominantly white male protagonists. The case delves into the complexities of both social and migrant entrepreneurship in a multicultural context. Aline and her team are confronted with the challenge of financial sustainability, pondering how to stabilize their revenue streams to enable long-term planning. It presents an excellent opportunity for students to explore strategic decision-making, focusing on how to secure stable funding while maintaining the mission of societal integration. It underscores the ethical considerations and compassion that drive Aline's mission, as well as the resilience she has demonstrated as a migrant entrepreneur in overcoming personal and organizational challenges. Through Aline's inspiring story, students are encouraged to consider the broader impact of entrepreneurship beyond financial gains and the important role it can play in fostering social integration and diversity.

While the setting of the teaching case in Chapter 3, *Comproagro: transforming small farming in Colombia with an app*, changes to rural Colombia, with its troubled history and vast socio-economic challenges, the Vergara family's entrepreneurial journey similarly embodies the struggle to balance social impact with securing the financial resources for growth. In this case, a strategy has emerged: an investment round. Yet, the owner of the startup, the Vergara family, is having second thoughts about how a possible investor might influence what matters to the founders: community empowerment and social value. Both elements have so far been at the forefront of their entrepreneurial decisions. The digital platform of the Vergara family, Comproagro, aims to connect local agricultural producers directly with consumers, bypassing traditional middlemen and fostering economic growth in impoverished areas. While the platform has gained recognition and governmental support, it struggles with technological limitations and financial constraints. The Vergaras also run a profitable social enterprise, La Peladora, whose revenue has been crucial in supporting Comproagro. The case presents the Vergaras at a pivotal moment, faced with a venture capital offer that could infuse much-needed funds into their projects but could also compromise their social mission. Students are invited to engage in complex decision-making around balancing social impact with business sustainability, accompanying the Vergaras as they evaluate multiple avenues for sustaining their dual ventures without sacrificing their social goals. This teaching case serves as a rich exploration of the dilemmas that social entrepreneurs often face, particularly in economically challenged contexts.

While in the case of Comproagro the Vergara family is deciding whether or not an investment in its startup could pave the way towards financial sustainability, our case in Chapter 4, *Brazil's rising social enterprise star Ribon: the challenge of quantifying social impact*, focuses on a social enterprise startup that is readying for an investment round. Ribon has developed a novel mobile application to foster philanthropy. The app employs a unique business model that allows users to donate to social causes without spending their own money, converting their "time" into virtual currency, which is then transformed into financial donations by platform sponsors. Ribon stands at a decisive moment as it prepares to enter an investment round in January 2022. To do so successfully, it needs to quantify and communicate its social impact to various stakeholders, including organizational donors, sponsors, and user subscribers. The case serves as a rich example of how innovation and social entrepreneurship can coalesce into a disruptive business model. It presents students with the challenge of understanding this multifaceted entrepreneurial venture through the lens of stakeholder analysis and the business model canvas, specifically designed for social enterprises. In addition, students are expected to formulate a system of indicators based on the Krocil and Pospisil method to measure Ribon's social impact effectively. This case invites students to delve into the complexities of creating a sustainable, impactful, and investable social enterprise in a rapidly evolving philanthropic landscape.

Going back to Europe, the case in Chapter 5, *Urban Foundry: a purposeful business model*, is centered on a small to medium-sized enterprise registered as a B-Corp that finds itself struggling during the COVID-19 pandemic and the geopolitical instability caused by the war in Ukraine. The case urges students to inquire into the concept of B-Corp, comparing and contrasting it with corporate social responsibility and social enterprises. As such, it is a fantastic complement to the first case studies. Students are tasked with imagining themselves as the owner of Urban Foundry, faced with the challenge of justifying whether to maintain their B-Corp principles during the global crisis. By addressing the unique challenges and opportunities that come with being a B-Corp in a volatile global environment, this case provides a rich context for students to understand how external factors can impact an organization's mission and operations. Students will learn to weigh the pros and cons of maintaining B-Corp principles during a crisis, challenging them to think critically about the trade-offs between financial sustainability and social responsibility. They will also have to consider the interests of multiple stakeholders, adding another layer of complexity to their decision-making process. This case study serves as an excellent resource for students to study entrepreneurship, corporate social responsibility, and business ethics and to evaluate the intersection of these concepts.

While our case in Chapter 6, *Sustainable innovation and 3D printing: Comme des Machines' digital craftsmanship in Spain*, does not focus on a social entrepreneur, the protagonist finds itself at a similar crossroads where potential opposing objectives need to be aligned: Comme des Machines needs to navigate the intersection of technology, sustainability, and fashion and needs to make difficult but necessary decisions to stay afloat. This Spanish venture has harnessed the power of 3D printing to revolutionize the fashion industry, creating a value chain that is as efficient as it is environmentally friendly. As of late 2021, the entrepreneurs behind the venture find themselves at a strategic crossroads: should they stay true to their current business model focused on manufacturing and technology or should they pivot to align with the preferences of potential external investors? The case provides an in-depth look at the complexities of business model choices in high-tech entrepreneurship. It invites students to grapple with the trade-offs between sticking with a proven technology – 3D printing with rigid materials – and venturing into the uncertain but promising realm of digital fabrics and flexible materials. Students are encouraged to weigh the importance of the company's original ethos focused on sustainability in the fashion industry against the changing demands of the market and the direction potential investors might expect. Through the lens of Comme des Machines, students will explore the dynamics of sustainability, innovation, and decision-making in a rapidly evolving industry.

In essence, these cases arm students with the knowledge, tools, and perspectives needed to champion a new wave of entrepreneurship – one that is not just profit-driven but also purpose-driven. As they traverse through these stories, they will be better equipped to explore aspects such as the identification of social problems, the development of innovative yet ethically responsible solutions, the mobilization of resources, and the measurement of social impact, while protecting economic value creation and long-term sustainability. Students will learn the complexities involved in stakeholder management, from donor expectations to investor demands. They will be exposed to diverse business structures, ranging from B-Corps to purposeful businesses, understanding the frameworks and principles that guide them. Yet, this collection of cases spans more boundaries as many of the cases underline the importance of inclusion, connectivity, and the challenges that come along with being an underrepresented entrepreneur or operating in an environment that is not characterized by a fully developed entrepreneurial ecosystem. Aline, the protagonist of Chapter 2, for example, enters the entrepreneurial arena as a black migrant female entrepreneur, armed with a unique set of skills and cultural insights yet facing her own set of challenges, from social integration to regulatory constraints. At the same time, the Vergara family case in Chapter 3 shows how, despite the promise of technology to bridge economic divides, technological advancements come with limitations, particularly in rural contexts in emerging economies where the digital divide and lack of connectivity pose a huge barrier to digital transformation. In conclusion, the collection of cases in Part I serves as a repository of insights, challenges, role models, and breakthroughs illustrated by entrepreneurs who have dared to envision beyond traditional business paradigms. Through their stories, we are reminded that the essence of entrepreneurship is not just about the creation of financial wealth but also about creating value for society at large. By immersing in these real-world narratives, students are challenged to think critically, engage with diverse perspectives, and foster a mindset that embraces both business acumen and social responsibility.

2.2 Growth pathways: Dissecting entrepreneurial decision-making along the continuum of startups, corporations, and public policy makers

While Part I focuses on the creation of a dynamic equilibrium of financial sustainability and societal impact, the cases assembled in Part II – *Growth pathways: dissecting entrepreneurial decision-making along the continuum of startups, corporations, and public policy makers* – dive deep into the entrepreneurial process showcasing the multiple facets and challenges of entrepreneurial decision-making. The landscape of entrepreneurship is vast, ranging from bootstrapped startups in nascent markets to mature firms looking to pivot or diversify and even public actors that, through their entrepreneurial decisions, seek to foster economic growth. These settings, each with its own unique characteristics, cast varying shades of ambiguity and uncertainty on the fast-paced entrepreneurial decisions throughout the entrepreneurial process. While a startup entrepreneur in an emerging market might grapple with questions surrounding market validation and first-mover advantages, an established business owner in a mature market might wrestle with the challenges of disrupting existing value chains or the integration of novel technologies. Yet, at the heart of these disparate scenarios lies the unifying theme of decision-making under conditions of incomplete information. The entrepreneur must consistently weigh the perceived desirability of an opportunity – influenced by external socio-economic conditions, competition, and market demand – against their perceived capability to act upon a short-lived opportunity. This dynamic interplay, dictated by individual beliefs, resources, and the workings of the broader ecosystem, shapes the trajectory of entrepreneurial ventures across the spectrum.

The academic literature on entrepreneurship is dominated by four domains: opportunities, individuals and teams, the mode of organizing, and, finally, the specificities of the environments (Busenitz et al., 2003; Busenitz, Plummer, Klotz, Shahzad, & Rhoads, 2014). *Opportunities* often arise from the dynamic interplay between markets and environments, leading to the establishment of new pathways and objectives. The *individuals and teams* dimension explores the traits of individuals and groups, the growth of their intellectual and human capital, and contrasts between various entrepreneurs and non-entrepreneurs. The *mode of organizing* entrepreneurial ventures encompasses management practices, resource allocation and utilization, and the creation of systems and strategies that transform identified opportunities into tangible products or services. Lastly, the specificities of the *environmental* aspect focus on the overall rate of startup creation on a broader scale and the blend of cultural, economic, and market influences that either foster or hinder entrepreneurial endeavors. Each one of these elements plays a differential role alongside the entrepreneurial process, which encapsulates multiple phases, from exploring entrepreneurial ideas to scaleups to solidifying ventures (Reynolds & White, 1997).

The entrepreneurial journey begins with the very act of identifying business opportunities, a domain that demands a unique blend of cognitive and personality traits. The essence of entrepreneurial spirit – encompassing, among other factors, creativity, self-efficacy, and a penchant for risk-taking – lays the very foundation for recognizing the seeds of potential ventures. A century-long stream of literature has been evaluating the "traits of an entrepreneur." Frank Knight's book *Risk, Uncertainty and Profit* (1921) marks a key starting point of rigorous research on the entrepreneurial personality, evaluating those elements of a personality that prompt individuals to initiate an entrepreneurial journey as well as those that keep them going (Åstebro, Herz, Nanda, & Weber, 2014). Academic research has revealed that there is not one entrepreneurial personality, just as there is not one standard type of entrepreneur; instead, the entrepreneurial personality varies depending on the entrepreneurial activity (Kerr, Kerr, & Xu, 2018). Founders of startups differ from those of small businesses, intrapreneurs, or corporate entrepreneurs,[5] and from institutional entrepreneurs.[6] And while Shane (2000) and Shane and Venkataraman (2000) argue that opportunities exist autonomously, regardless of individuals or companies, we argue – alongside other authors such as Kerr and colleagues (2018) – that such opportunities only realize their potential through the distinct insights, viewpoints, and interpretations of the founders embedded in a specific context. Moreover, these opportunities do not convert to wealth without specific organizational efforts independently from the wider context in which they evolve. This implies that the juncture where opportunities meet entrepreneurially minded and skilled individuals, organizational methods, or environments, or a combination thereof, is fundamental to the understanding of the entrepreneurial process.

However, identifying an opportunity is but the first step. For any organization, establishing and maintaining its foothold requires a robust strategy to break into established markets. Faced with a lack of specific resources and capabilities that established firms can count on (Stinchcombe, 1965),[7] entrepreneurial founders must identify strategies to penetrate industries often dominated by established and sizable businesses (Cooper, Willard, & Woo, 1986). McDougall and Robinson (1990) identified in their empirical research eight different growth strategies, differentiating between aggressive, controlled average, and limited growth. Increasing returns based on learning by doing, scale economies, network effects, information contagion, and the accumulation of complementary assets have long been identified as a source of competitive advantage (Sterman, Henderson, Beinhocker, & Newman, 2007). The recognition of these positive returns sparked the emergence of a "get big fast" strategy to gain a competitive advantage among principally digital startups. Yet, in the fevered rush to gain dominance, startups often find themselves at a crossroads. The potential of excess capacity, as laid out by Sterman et al. (2007), is just one of the potential risks of such a strategy. Thus, the dilemma of a new (digital) venture's growth strategy becomes palpable: should they sprint and rapidly capture the market or opt for a slower-paced, sustainable trajectory?

Such dilemmas segue into another strategic conundrum in a setting that is quite different: to navigate the treacherous waters of sustaining current operations while simultaneously innovating is no small feat. The interest in organizational ambidexterity,[8] that is, "the ability to simultaneously pursue both incremental and discontinuous innovation … from hosting multiple contradictory structures, processes, and cultures within the same firm" (Tushman & O'Reilly, 1996, p. 24) has exploded (O'Reilly & Tushman, 2013). Intimately linked to this is the topic of corporate entrepreneurship and entrepreneurial activities, such as innovation, venturing, and strategic renewal, within existing firms (Zahra, 1996). At first sight, corporate entrepreneurship seems to juxtapose what entrepreneurship entails: the identification and exploitation of opportunity in the face of resource constraints as businesses are equipped with a plethora of resources and capabilities (Phan, Wright, Ucbasaran, & Tan, 2009). Yet, corporations face the same risk as business founders in exploiting opportunities: innovation outcomes are difficult to predict, and thus, corporate entrepreneurship, the process of organizational renewal (Guth & Ginsberg, 1990), is equally uncertain. Corporate entrepreneurship comprises two elements: innovation through corporate-venturing activities and renewal activities that aim to foster the corporation's risk-taking ability to enable it to remain competitive in the long run (Phan et al., 2009). The way organizations develop effective structures, processes, and cultures to activate corporate entrepreneurship is arguably one of the most pressing questions in academic research (Dess et al., 2003). Two pivotal strategic dilemmas emerge here: whether or not innovations should be developed by a closed process, that is, within the organization relying on classic research and development processes, or by an open process[9] through the acquisition of knowledge external to the organization (Chesbrough, 2003; Chesbrough & Crowther, 2006). While the former prioritizes home-grown, often slower, expansion, the latter presents opportunities for swift expansion, albeit with yet another strategic decision – how to acquire the knowledge needed – as well as potential pitfalls such as overvaluation or post-acquisition integration challenges.

Such inward-focused organizational dilemmas must be resolved under very specific conditions of the environment that shape innovation and entrepreneurship activities. Two important overarching concepts have emerged to provide useful frameworks for the holistic analysis of environmental conditions – innovation systems and entrepreneurial ecosystems. The first, relying on the "assumption that the pattern of innovation differs between countries and that such differences can be explained by systemic features" (Lundvall, 2015, p. 2), understands innovation as a systemic and interactive process (McCann & Ortega-Argilés, 2013). Along a similar line of thought and rooted in the same academic literature (Pugh, Schmutzler, & Tsvetkova, 2021), entrepreneurial ecosystems are understood as "a set of interdependent actors and factors coordinated in such a way that they enable productive entrepreneurship within a particular territory" (Stam & Spigel, 2016, p. 1). Against this background, examining both the formal and informal actors of ecosystems, multifaceted dimensions of capacity building and development can be discovered, and multiple successes and failures can be traced to very specific institutional details. Such an approach is especially illuminating when observing the role of entrepreneurs in rural innovation. Entrepreneurs, whether they are young, local, newcomers, or returnees, significantly impact rural areas, injecting innovation and development into these regions (OECD, 2019). Immigrants and entrepreneurs returning to their rural roots bring with them valuable experiences and knowledge, especially in agriculture (Bosworth, 2006). Therefore, the importance of policy measures that concentrate on drawing more innovative entrepreneurs to rural areas (Bosworth, 2006; Stockdale, 2006) emerges as a core driver of the entrepreneurial ecosystems, whereas the specific policy initiatives can vary significantly. In certain contexts, it is essential to ensure that rural enterprises tap into distant relational resources (Bosworth, 2006; Argent, Tonts, Jones, & Holmes 2013), while under other circumstances, the priority is entrepreneurial finance (Eid, 2006). Thus, policy actors need to act as entrepreneurs to infuse high-impact actions into resource-deprived regions.

When students immerse themselves in this collection of teaching cases centered on the foundational pillars of entrepreneurship, they journey through "opportunity" recognition, enabling them to learn about the delicate and fast-paced interplay between dynamic market opportunities and environmental enablers that hold the potential to spawn novel entrepreneurial pathways. Through the lens of individual and team characteristics, the spotlight is on distinguishing characteristics and growth trajectories of entrepreneurs in a range of settings. Furthermore, the organizational design aspect of entrepreneurship and innovation pulls back the curtain on how potential opportunities are channeled into tangible products or services, providing insights into resource management and strategic formulation. Lastly, by exploring the overarching concept of environments, students gain a macro perspective, analyzing the factors that either catalyze or impede innovation and entrepreneurial ventures on a grander scale. Interwoven through these domains is the journey of entrepreneurship itself, starting from the spark of recognizing an opportunity to the culmination of bringing a venture to fruition. This comprehensive collection of case studies provides students with a variegated understanding of the challenges, risks, gains, and strategies inherent in the entrepreneurial journey.

Our first case in Part II, in Chapter 7, *Three Colombian entrepreneurs in search of the next great business opportunity*, focuses specifically on entrepreneurial personalities. The case revolves around three Colombian entrepreneurs who have applied to the Zoom-Up entrepreneurship mentorship program. Carolina Trujillo leads GoTok Music, a digital music distribution startup; Gustavo de la Vega runs NativApps, a software development service; and Javier Villota manages Probionar, which produces biodegradable cleaning products. The management team of Zoom-Up must evaluate the entrepreneurs in order to select a winner for their program. This case delves into how early-stage entrepreneurs seek external resources, mentorship, and opportunities to grow and how they do so in very different ways, playing to the strengths of each personality. Students are tasked with role-playing as the management, challenging them to think critically about what makes an entrepreneurial venture scalable and ready for new market opportunities. This requires them to consider multiple aspects, including the entrepreneurial personality and the team each entrepreneur has set up but also the market needs addressed, the validation of the business model, and the long-term vision of the entrepreneur. The case provides a comprehensive overview of the challenges and opportunities that early-stage entrepreneurs face and how individuals with different personalities and resources act upon these, making it a valuable learning resource for students interested in entrepreneurship, venture selection, and business scaling.

In the case in Chapter 8, *Playground energy: fun, health, and education on the playground*, we changed the setting and the challenge faced by the protagonists. This case study unfolds during the early growth of Playground Energy, an innovation-driven startup located in Bulgaria aiming to revolutionize playgrounds. By transforming children's kinetic energy into electricity that powers sound, lights, and other interactive features, the company addresses multiple global trends: the fight against child obesity, the need for renewable energy solutions, and the competitive landscape of digital entertainment. This case explores the multifaceted aspects of entrepreneurship, spotlighting the founders' journey from opportunity recognition to securing pre-seed and seed financing. After completing two acceleration programs, they now confront the critical challenge of scaling their venture to reach and surpass the break-even point. Students are encouraged to engage with the complexities of product–market fit and sustainable growth strategies, analyzing the complexity of scaling a startup while not forgetting about the broader societal and environmental issues that Playground Energy aims to address. Through this case, students are invited to consider how entrepreneurial ventures can not only be financially successful but also socially impactful.

Set against the backdrop of the burgeoning e-commerce landscape in Africa, the case in Chapter 9, *Jumia, the Amazon of Africa: its quest for combining growth and profitability*, zeroes in on Jumia, the continent's largest e-commerce player headquartered in Lagos, Nigeria. Despite its remarkable growth and pioneering status as Africa's first unicorn, Jumia faces the quintessential startup dilemma: growth versus profitability. Operating in a region fraught with challenges like underdeveloped infrastructure and a nascent middle class, the case poses a critical question – how can Jumia transition from being a high-growth venture to a profitable enterprise? This case offers a unique lens into entrepreneurship in emerging markets, particularly Africa. It provides students with a nuanced understanding of the opportunities and challenges that come with technological innovation in less-developed contexts. While the core focus is on business strategy and profitability in emerging markets, the case also touches upon technology-based entrepreneurship. Students are invited to dissect Jumia's growth trajectory and consider various strategic paths the company could take to finally turn a profit. Through the lens of Jumia's experience, students will explore the complex interplay of market potential, operational challenges, and strategic decision-making in one of the world's most dynamic yet challenging environments for e-commerce.

The case in Chapter 10, *Social capital and corporate growth strategies in the Spanish ceramic cluster*, focuses on TerraCas, a medium-sized ceramic tile manufacturing firm located in Castelló, Spain, which has carved a niche for itself with its commitment to quality, innovation, and sustainability. TerraCas is at a crucial juncture, faced with intensified competition and industry changes that necessitate a strategic pivot. The founder, Javier Montoro, must choose between multiple corporate strategies, each with its own set of ethical and financial considerations. These options include organic growth, acquisitions, or selling the company to an investment fund or corporate group. This case delves into the complexities of entrepreneurship in a specific regional context, illustrating how regional clusters can facilitate knowledge-sharing and innovation while at the same time highlighting the founder's ethical considerations and commitment to social capital and community well-being. Students are invited to step into the shoes of Montoro to navigate the intricacies of making a decision that not only has implications for the firm's financial viability but also its ethical commitments. They are prompted to consider how TerraCas can continue to leverage its social capital and innovative capabilities while adapting to a rapidly changing industry landscape. This case offers a multidimensional view of entrepreneurship, underscoring the significance of context, ethical considerations, and strategic choices in shaping entrepreneurial trajectories.

Similar to the previous case, in the case in Chapter 11, *POKEMON: Ethias' corporate entrepreneurship initiative*, we focus on a traditional industry that is rapidly transformed by digital disruption. Here, traditional companies like Ethias need to adapt and stay competitive. This case study centers on Nicolas Dumazy, the chief strategy and data officer, and Fabian Delhaxhe, an unconventional employee with a disruptive idea: they are convinced that collaborating with emerging startups is the only way to stay competitive in the changing industry landscape. Yet, both grapple with a vital question: How can an established company successfully integrate a disruptive business model into its existing structure? The case serves as a rich learning opportunity in corporate entrepreneurship, emphasizing the need for fostering an entrepreneurial culture within traditional settings. It offers students a chance to explore the complexities involved in validating business assumptions and managing digital transformation strategically. The challenges presented by emerging insurtech startups provide the contextual backdrop, urging students to consider how legacy companies can evolve without losing their core competencies. Through Ethias' journey, students will gain valuable insights into the intricate balance needed between innovation and tradition in today's competitive landscape.

In the case in Chapter 12, *Corporate intrapreneurship through start-ups: Atos' innovation ecosystem*, we turn our focus to corporate entrepreneurship. At a critical juncture in its corporate journey, Atos, a leading player in the global information technology service industry, is faced with the challenge of reimagining its innovation strategy to stay ahead in a fiercely competitive market. The case spotlights the company's strategic pivot towards collaboration with startups and the consequential decisions that top management must make: How to drive an entrepreneurial spirit within an established corporation? Relying on open innovation by collaborating with startups, top management needs to tackle the second question: How do you select the right startups to partner with and determine the governance models for these collaborations? This case is situated within the realm of corporate entrepreneurship as it explores how established companies can foster innovation by aligning with younger, more agile organizations. However, it is not just about the "what" but also the "how." Students will dig into the complexities of strategic alignment, scouting motives, and the costs and risks associated with such partnerships. While primarily focusing on elements of corporate entrepreneurship, the case also extends its reach into the human dimension. It offers a rich context for exploring the intricacies of decision-making dynamics and how they shape an organization's innovative capabilities. Through Atos' lens, students gain a nuanced understanding of how an established entity can adapt, innovate, and grow in a constantly evolving landscape.

The case in Chapter 13, *Reversing Nova Scotia's declining rural agri-food sector*, is set in the struggling agri-food sector of rural Nova Scotia, Canada. This case study follows Marah Schneider, a junior policy analyst with a master's in innovation and development. Tasked with her first solo assignment, Marah must identify solutions to pressing challenges, including labor shortages and declining agri-food processing capabilities. The case introduces an intriguing proposition: could newcomers with agricultural expertise be the key to revitalizing this sector? The case offers a unique exploration of entrepreneurship and innovation within the context of rural development and immigration. Students will engage with Marah's two-fold assignment – first, to gather data using the system of innovation framework, and second, to deliver an integrated analysis outlining actionable initiatives for the Department of Agriculture. The case prompts students to think critically about the roles that different stakeholders, both local and foreign, can play in fostering innovation and sustainability in rural communities. It touches upon the pressures and challenges faced by individuals like Marah in their quest to bring about meaningful change. Through this lens, students will appreciate the complex web of factors that must be navigated to develop effective, impactful policies in a rural setting.

Chapter 14, the last case in Part II, *A pioneer without followers: a case of productive diversification from rice to aquaculture in Chaco, Argentina*, focuses on the agriculturally dominated province of Chaco, Argentina, where a crucial question looms: Can a single pioneer in sustainable entrepreneurship stimulate an entire industry? George, recently appointed as the head of the productive development office of the Chaco province, grapples with this challenge as he aims for job creation and diversification of the local economy. At the heart of this inquiry is Edward, an experienced rice farmer who transitioned into a diversified and sustainable model, focusing on pacú fish farming and franchising. Edward's venture not only addresses environmental concerns but also presents an innovative approach to local economic development. Yet, despite his success, no other entrepreneurs have followed suit. This teaching case explores the barriers that prevent other potential "followers" from entering the burgeoning industry. It encourages students to critically examine the complexities of capacity building, market entry barriers, and the implications for public policy aimed at fostering local development. This case offers a vivid snapshot of the opportunities and challenges that come with fostering entrepreneurship in low-income, agriculturally dependent regions. It also touches upon the influence of the state and the ethics behind policy intervention by questioning whether a policy focus on individual pioneers is sufficient or if broader, systemic interventions are needed to break down the barriers to entry for potential followers.

2.3 Navigating crises: Entrepreneurial resilience, well-being, and ethical imperatives

Adding to the importance of balancing financial strength and social impact addressed in Part I, Part II focuses on the decision-making process about creation and growth shaped by the market and macro forces, and more specifically on the ecosystem parameters, the type of business model, internal organization, and the personal aptitudes of founders. Finally, Part III – *Navigating crises: entrepreneurial resilience, well-being, and ethical imperatives* – includes cases that illustrate the resilience of different businesses towards the COVID-19 pandemic and the growing relevance of topics such as well-being, ethics, and responsible entrepreneurship and innovation as core in any entrepreneurial endeavor. The unpredictable event of the COVID-19 pandemic has had a profound impact on the minds of humans, the global economy, and the entrepreneurial landscape. The drastic measures of governments lowering social interaction through lockdowns marked an acute and unexpected crisis; it put high pressure on all economic actors (Kuckertz et al., 2020). Crises, in general, threaten the functioning of businesses and thus their performance (Williams, Gruber, Sutcliffe, Shepherd, & Zhao, 2017); in the case of COVID-19, the fact that the crisis was not only global (instead of much more localized earlier crises such as natural disasters) but sudden (instead of developing over a more extended time period such as the financial crisis) made it even more challenging (Kuckertz et al., 2020).

Entrepreneurs had to pivot their business models, leverage technology, and respond to shifting market demands; they had to be resilient. However, few academic studies had examined the way firms, and particularly entrepreneurs, can be and are resilient. COVID-19 has changed this, and a plethora of studies has emerged since then.[10] Teaching cases on COVID-19 and entrepreneurial resilience provide students with an opportunity to explore how entrepreneurs have navigated and adapted to the unprecedented challenges brought about by the pandemic, highlighting the role of collaboration, innovation, and social impact in addressing the crisis. By studying entrepreneurial resilience in the context of COVID-19, students gain insights into the importance of adaptability, agility, and innovation as part of the entrepreneurial journey. These cases foster critical thinking skills and provide students with lessons on how to navigate and thrive in the face of unexpected crises and disruptions.

The existential threat of COVID-19 has not only interrupted business functioning; it has also brought about change in many aspects of professional and personal lives. Particularly, it has brought new attention to the topic of well-being. Although entrepreneurship is often associated with high levels of stress, burnout, and work–life imbalance, entrepreneurial well-being (or solutions to ill-being) has been an understudied topic. Yet, in part as a response to the COVID-19 crisis,[11] entrepreneurial well-being, understood as the "experience of satisfaction, positive affect, infrequent negative affect, and psychological functioning in relation to developing, starting, growing, and running an entrepreneurial venture" (Wiklund, Nikolaev, Shir, Foo, & Bradley, 2019, p. 579; see also Shir, 2015) arose as a critical dimension (Ross, Strevel, & Javadizadeh, 2021). High levels of stress and uncertainty, coupled with the relentless pursuit of tangible results, take a toll on the mental health of entrepreneurs irrespective of the context (Torrès et al., 2022). Additionally, cultural elements influence the dominant coping mechanisms for this critical global problem (Backman, Hagen, Kekezi, Naldi, & Wallin, 2023). Investigating the well-being of entrepreneurs brings the discussion back to the human element, highlighting the need for a balanced approach to entrepreneurial success. Teaching cases on entrepreneurial well-being explore the challenges entrepreneurs face in maintaining their mental, physical, and emotional health while pursuing their entrepreneurial ventures. Moreover, work conditions during and after COVID-19 should be reviewed in order to strike a balance between quality of life and work. By looking closely at entrepreneurial well-being, students gain insights into the personal challenges and sacrifices that entrepreneurs often face. Such cases promote self-awareness, personal growth, empathy, and a holistic understanding of a profoundly intimate side of entrepreneurship beyond financial success and social status.

Alongside this focus on well-being and inextricably linked to it is the consideration of ethics, a theme that is critical regardless of context. In the face of technological changes, learning algorithms, and the emergence of technology-enabled instruments that exceed the limits of current regulations and the terms of the existing social contract in most jurisdictions (Moor, 2006), ethics acquires greater preponderance as a consideration for entrepreneurial decision-making as such technologies have become the core of successful entrepreneurial ventures (Shepherd & Majchrzak, 2022). Although financial incentives are widely accepted as powerful drivers of entrepreneurial decision-making, regulatory gaps and legal gray areas raise the stakes of ethical considerations in entrepreneurial dilemmas. For example, it is essential to identify under what circumstances the consequences of the depletion of resources on human health and the wider environment can lead to the creation of responsible ventures, many of which rely on technologies to reduce the long-term negative impact. In addition, robotization and machine learning can be seen under a specific set of rules as tools to create a more lasting and prosperous future rather than a menace for jobs. The cases presented in Part III expose entrepreneurial dilemmas to which ethics is central and empower students to reflect on how technology, ethics, organizational culture, and entrepreneurial decision-making crosscut fundamental issues in diverse economic sectors and geographical regions.

When a platform business model catapults an Italian startup into rapid growth, it is a cause for celebration; but what happens when an unforeseen crisis like the COVID-19 pandemic grinds everything to a halt? This is the narrative arc of Chapter 15, *Pivoting to face COVID-19 in the mobility industry: the BusForFun case*, an innovative venture that connected independent bus owners with concert and event attendees across Italy and parts of Europe. Leveraging a public funding program and a robust data-driven approach, the founders, Luca and Davide, expanded their business into a mobility solutions provider for both consumers and municipalities. They even spawned a second entity, ParkForFun, to manage bus-parking facilities. This teaching case serves as a rich exploration of startup lifecycle phases, emphasizing the concept of effectuation or how entrepreneurs build ventures through a series of stakeholder engagements and commitments. It also underscores the firm's resilience and adaptability in responding to the crippling impact of the pandemic. Students are invited to dissect the strategies employed by BusForFun and ParkForFun as they pivot and adapt, offering a comprehensive look at the entrepreneurial journey in the face of uncertainty and challenges.

Set against the same background of a crippling economy due to COVID-19, the case in Chapter 16 is set in the volatile landscape of the Colombian fast-food industry. *Feeding with love: Frisby's quest for a successor to preserve its legacy in times of sudden change* focuses on a fast-food company that stands as a beacon of quality and tradition. However, the family-run firm is at a crossroads, grappling not only with the challenges posed by the COVID-19 pandemic but also with the passing of one of its founders. At the heart of this case study is a pressing question: Who should take the helm as the new chief executive officer to both honor the company's legacy and adapt to evolving market conditions? This case delves deep into the human dimensions of entrepreneurship, explicitly focusing on decision-making, organizational culture, and legacy preservation in family businesses. Students are tasked with evaluating potential successors within the family, each with their own capabilities and viewpoints, to lead the company into a new era without compromising its foundational values. Through Frisby's story, students gain a nuanced understanding of how to balance the need for innovation and adaptation with the equally important need to uphold a company's long-standing cultural and operational ethos while focusing on individual entrepreneurial profiles.

As the world grapples with the "new normal" in the wake of the COVID-19 pandemic, Mary Chin, the human resources director at Gray China, faces a pressing challenge: How to create an enabling work environment that addresses not just employee motivation but also well-being. This is the central topic in Chapter 17, *Sustainable talent development at Gray Global: deployment of corporate entrepreneurship for developing employee well-being in China*. As an international professional consultancy firm, Gray China finds itself at a pivotal juncture where traditional methods of talent management no longer suffice, particularly as the workplace landscape undergoes significant changes introducing hybrid work models and a new-found focus on mental health, both as a direct result of the COVID-19 pandemic. The case sheds light on the complexities involved in navigating the evolving expectations and values of the workforce, not only as a result of changing values post-pandemic but also through the rising influx of Gen Z professionals. Mary is tasked with devising a talent strategy that transcends conventional hygiene factors and embraces an entrepreneurial approach to employee well-being. This case provides an in-depth look at the human dimensions in entrepreneurial contexts, emphasizing elements such as decision-making, ethical behavior, and well-being. It serves as an excellent platform for students to explore the intricacies of human resources management in an era marked by rapid change and heightened awareness of employee mental health and in which an entrepreneurial spirit within an established corporation can make way for new inputs to stay afloat.

The case study in Chapter 18, *Yogome's dramatic fall for alleged fraud*, revolves around a Mexican edtech startup that designed educational mobile games for children but shut down due to allegations of fraud by its co-founder, Manolo Díaz. The case is presented from the perspective of a Chilean angel investor who is considering investing in another Mexican startup, also in the edtech space. The investor becomes concerned after hearing about the alleged fraudulent activities at Yogome and starts to investigate the case to understand how to detect and prevent similar incidents in the future. Specifically, the case deals with themes around ethics and fraud as it explores the complexities and challenges investors face when trying to discern the ethical integrity of startups they are considering for investment. It also delves into the issue of how startup founders might manipulate financial data and what red flags investors should look out for. The case study offers students a comprehensive view of the complexities of due diligence in startup investing, especially in sectors where financial transparency is critical for both business success and ethical integrity. The investor's dilemma serves as a compelling narrative to engage students in discussions about ethical decision-making, the challenges of detecting fraud, and the potential consequences of unethical behavior on a startup's stakeholders. This case study is a valuable resource for students studying entrepreneurship, business ethics, and venture capital, offering key insights into the complexities and ethical considerations inherent in startup investing.

The story of Chapter 19, *Clearview AI: ethics and artificial intelligence technology*, serves as a cautionary tale about the collision of technology, ethics, and entrepreneurship. Emerging from the partnership of tech-savvy Hoan Ton-That and well-connected Richard Schwartz, Clearview AI developed a facial recognition technology that soon found itself at the center of a public debate on privacy and ethics sparked by a revealing *New York Times* article. The case offers a deep dive into ethical behavior and decision-making. Students are encouraged to grapple with complex questions about the boundaries of technological innovation and the ethical imperatives that come with it. How should entrepreneurs navigate the murky waters of privacy concerns while pushing the envelope of what is possible? The case also examines how venture capital and influential backing can shape the ethical considerations of a startup. It serves as an engaging platform for students to apply frameworks of responsible innovation and ethics, exploring the intricate balance that entrepreneurs must maintain between technological advancement and societal impact.

The last case, in Chapter 20, *Bridging cryptocurrency and traditional finance businesses: the case of SpectroCoin–Pervesk*, explores the convoluted landscape that digital entrepreneurs in emerging sectors like FinTech face, especially when regulations and norms are in flux. Located in Lithuania, a country with a pro-FinTech environment, SpectroCoin and its regulated counterpart, Pervesk, aimed to bridge the gap between the crypto economy and traditional financial services. However, a sudden change in regulatory stance posed significant challenges (financial and ethical), forcing the chief executive officer, Vytautas, to make critical strategic choices under conflicting institutional pressures. In this case, students examine how entrepreneurs navigate external challenges and make strategic choices. It engages directly with the theme of how regulatory, social, and technological factors intersect to create a complex environment for entrepreneurial decision-making. Students are tasked with evaluating a range of strategic responses, each with its own set of consequences and trade-offs. For instance, focusing solely on the crypto market could be lucrative but potentially unsustainable given its volatility and evolving norms, while sticking to the regulated market would mean forgoing exciting opportunities in the crypto economy. By emphasizing the importance of understanding and navigating conflicting institutional pressures, this case challenges students to think critically about how entrepreneurs can make informed decisions that balance compliance with institutional norms and the exploitation of market opportunities.

3.   CONCLUSION

Case-based research has been at the center of legitimate new theory development in new topic areas (Eisenhardt, 1989). The objectives of this book are to broaden the scope of knowledge in underresearched contexts from the Global South and neglected contexts in the Global North, such as rural or peripheral regions as well as in niche domains of innovation and entrepreneurship by offering a diverse and unique collection of teaching cases. As such, we see this book as a platform and as an invitation for collaborative research with scholars from all over the world with whom we can undertake an iterative and data-driven process for testing new theories of innovation and entrepreneurship.

The dominant theories on innovation and entrepreneurship are built on assumptions that are rarely tested outside the Global North, whose behavior patterns, institutional design, cultural preferences, and metrics are seen as the ultimate equilibrium conditions. Such an approach is consistent with a rather linear convergence trajectory, where resilience in the face of global uncertainty and historical accidents are not accounted for as triggers of reversal of fortunes and hope for improved well-being in many developing regions of the world. This line of thought is not only simplistic; it is also damaging to our collective understanding as it does not take into account the fast-paced and unpredictable outcomes of innovation and entrepreneurship as a phenomenon that can bring about unexpected outcomes.

Claiming the protagonistic role that innovators and entrepreneurs from unexpected places deserve and granting the legitimacy of scholarly research built on their experiences are pending tasks. The increasing level of internal instability and conflict in developed economies, the growing levels of inequality in once prosperous societies, and the climatic disasters that expand beyond the tropics are unfortunate current trends that make the experiences and lessons coming from the innovators and entrepreneurs from the Global South more relevant than ever. Building a collective research agenda to pursue these objectives is urgently needed, and we hope many of the instructors and students who will be transformed by the teaching cases in this book will join us in this endeavor.

ACKNOWLEDGEMENT

The first author would like to acknowledge the financial support by Alianza 4U for the project "Prácticas empresariales en la economía informal: una perspectiva interseccional de los ecosistemas de emprendimiento en regiones colombianas".

NOTES

1. Periphery can be defined as follows: "The core–periphery paradigm has been constructed as an opposition in terms of development potential between central places, such as global cities and national metropolises" (Pugh & Dubois, 2021, p. 268).
2. For recent literature reviews on the topic, please refer to Gupta, Chauhan, Paul, and Jaiswal (2020) and Ranville and Barros (2021).
3. For recent literature reviews on the topic, please refer to Phillips et al. (2015) and do Adro and Fernandes (2020).
4. In most cases, the concept is referred to as responsible research and innovation. For recent literature reviews on the topic, please refer to Burget, Bardone, and Pedaste (2017) or Thapa, Iakovleva, and Foss (2019).
5. For literature reviews on the topic, please refer to Phan et al. (2009) and Urbano, Turro, Wright, and Zahra (2022).
6. For an overview on the topic of institutional entrepreneurs, please refer to Hardy and Maguire (2008).
7. For an overview on various liabilities new ventures face and how these influence the venture's survival chances, please refer to Soto-Simeone, Sirén, and Antretter (2020).
8. For a recent literature review on the topic, please refer to Tarba, Jansen, Mom, Raisch, and Lawton (2020).
9. For a review on open innovation, please refer to Bogers et al. (2017).
10. For recent literature reviews on the topic, please refer to Castro and Zermeño (2020) and Kuckertz and Brändle (2022). Additionally, a book on the topic has been launched: Audretsch and Kunadt (2022).
11. The interest in entrepreneurial well-being had started to attract attention among researchers prior to COVID-19 (e.g., Stephan, 2018; Wiklund et al., 2019). However, the crisis has spurred a huge potential for empirical research and has thus contributed substantially to new insights on the topic.

REFERENCES

Alter, K. (2007). Social enterprise typology. *Virtue ventures LLC, 12*(1), 1–124.

Andonova, V., Nikolova, M. S., & Dimitrov, D. (2019). *Entrepreneurial Ecosystems in Unexpected Places*. Springer.

Argent, N., Tonts, M., Jones, R., & Holmes, J. (2013). A creativity-led rural renaissance? Amenity-led migration, the creative turn and the uneven development of rural Australia. *Applied Geography, 44*, 88–98.

Åstebro, T., Herz, H., Nanda, R., & Weber, R. A. (2014). Seeking the roots of entrepreneurship: Insights from behavioral economics. *Journal of Economic Perspectives, 28*(3), 49–70.

Audretsch, D. B., & Kunadt, I. A. (2022). *The COVID-19 Crisis and Entrepreneurship*. Springer.

Backman, M., Hagen, J., Kekezi, O., Naldi, L., & Wallin, T. (2023). In the eye of the storm: Entrepreneurs and well-being during the COVID-19 crisis. *Entrepreneurship Theory and Practice, 47*(3), 751–787.

Battilana, J. (2018). Cracking the organizational challenge of pursuing joint social and financial goals: Social enterprise as a laboratory to understand hybrid organizing. *M@n@gement, 21*(4), 1278–1305.

Ben-Hafaïedh, C., Xheneti, M., Stenholm, P., Blackburn, R., Welter, F., & Urbano, D. (2023). The interplay of context and entrepreneurship: The new frontier for contextualisation research. *Small Business Economics*, 1–12.

Bogers, M., Zobel, A. K., Afuah, A., Almirall, E., Brunswicker, S., Dahlander, L., ... & Ter Wal, A. L. (2017). The open innovation research landscape: Established perspectives and emerging themes across different levels of analysis. *Industry and Innovation, 24*(1), 8–40.

Bosworth, G. (2006). Counterurbanisation and job creation: Entrepreneurial in-migration and rural economic development. *Centre for Rural Economy Discussion Paper Series, 4*(4), 16.

Burget, M., Bardone, E., & Pedaste, M. (2017). Definitions and conceptual dimensions of responsible research and innovation: A literature review. *Science and Engineering Ethics, 23*, 1–19.

Busenitz, L. W., West III, G. P., Shepherd, D., Nelson, T., Chandler, G. N., & Zacharakis, A. (2003). Entrepreneurship research in emergence: Past trends and future directions. *Journal of Management, 29*(3), 285–308.

Busenitz, L. W., Plummer, L. A., Klotz, A. C., Shahzad, A., & Rhoads, K. (2014). Entrepreneurship research (1985–2009) and the emergence of opportunities. *Entrepreneurship Theory and Practice, 38*(5), 1–20.

Cahen, F., Casanova, l., & Miroux, A. (eds) (2021). *Innovation from Emerging Markets: From Copycats to Leaders*. Cambridge University Press.

Castro, M. P., & Zermeño, M. G. G. (2020). Being an entrepreneur post-COVID-19 – resilience in times of crisis: A systematic literature review. *Journal of Entrepreneurship in Emerging Economies, 13*(4), 721–746.

Chesbrough, H. (2003). *Open Innovation: The New Imperative for Creating and Profiting from Technology*. Harvard Business Press.

Chesbrough, H., & Crowther, A. K. (2006). Beyond high tech: Early adopters of open innovation in other industries. *R&D Management, 36*(3), 229–236.

Christensen, C. M., & Carlile, P. R. (2009). Course research: Using the case method to build and teach management theory. *Academy of Management Learning & Education, 8*(2), 240–251.

Cooper, A. C., Willard, G. E., & Woo, C. Y. (1986). Strategies of high performing new and small firms: A reexamination of the niche concept. *Journal of Business Venturing, 1*(3), 247–260.

Dess, G. G., Ireland, R. D., Zahra, S. A., Floyd, S. W., Janney, J. J., & Lane, P. J. (2003). Emerging issues in corporate entrepreneurship. *Journal of Management, 29*(3), 351–378.

do Adro, F., & Fernandes, C. I. (2020). Social innovation: A systematic literature review and future agenda research. *International Review on Public and Nonprofit Marketing, 17*(1), 23–40.

Eid, F. (2006). Recasting job creation strategies in developing regions: A role for entrepreneurial finance. *Journal of Entrepreneurship, 15*(2), 115–143.

Eisenhardt, K. (1989). Building theories from case study research. *Academy of Management Review, 14*, 532–550.

Erez, M., Van De Ven, A. H., & Lee, C. (2015). Contextualizing creativity and innovation across cultures. *Journal of Organizational Behavior, 36*(7), 895–898.

Gaddefors, J., & Anderson, A. R. (2019). Romancing the rural: Reconceptualizing rural entrepreneurship as engagement with context(s). *International Journal of Entrepreneurship and Innovation, 20*(3), 159–169.

Gupta, P., Chauhan, S., Paul, J., & Jaiswal, M. P. (2020). Social entrepreneurship research: A review and future research agenda. *Journal of Business Research, 113*, 209–229.

Guth, W. D., & Ginsberg, A. (1990). Guest editors' introduction: Corporate entrepreneurship. *Strategic Management Journal*, 5–15.

Haldar, S. (2019). Towards a conceptual understanding of sustainability-driven entrepreneurship. *Corporate Social Responsibility and Environmental Management, 26*(6), 1157–1170.

Hardy, C., & Maguire, S. (2008). Institutional entrepreneurship. In: Greenwood, R., Oliver, Ch., Saline, K., & Suddaby, R. (eds), *The Sage Handbook of Organizational Institutionalism*, 198–217. Sage.

Kerr, S. P., Kerr, W. R., & Xu, T. (2018). Personality traits of entrepreneurs: A review of recent literature. *Foundations and Trends® in Entrepreneurship, 14*(3), 279–356.

Kuckertz, A., & Brändle, L. (2022). Creative reconstruction: A structured literature review of the early empirical research on the COVID-19 crisis and entrepreneurship. *Management Review Quarterly, 72*(2), 281–307.

Kuckertz, A., Brändle, L., Gaudig, A., Hinderer, S., Morales, A., Prochotta, A., Steinbrink, K., & Berger, E. S. (2020), Startups in times of crisis: A rapid response to the COVID-19 pandemic. *Journal of Business Venturing Insights, 13*, 1–13.

Lawrence, P. (1951). The preparation of case material. In: Andrews, K. R. (ed.), *The Case Method of Teaching Human Relations and Administration: An Interim Statement*. Cambridge, MA: Harvard University Press, pp. 215–224.

Le Grand, J., & Roberts, J. (2021). Hands, hearts and hybrids: Economic organization, individual motivation and public benefit. *LSE Public Policy Review, 1*(3).

Lundvall, B. Å. (2015, September). The origins of the national innovation system concept and its usefulness in the era of the globalizing economy. 13th Globelics Conference, Havana, 23–26.

Mayer, H. & Baumgartner, D. (2014). The role of entrepreneurship and innovation in peripheral regions. *disP – The Planning Review, 50*(1), 16–23.

McCann, P., & Ortega-Argilés, R. (2013). Transforming European regional policy: A results-driven agenda and smart specialization. *Oxford Review of Economic Policy, 29*(2), 405–431.

McDougall, P., & Robinson, Jr., R. B. (1990). New venture strategies: An empirical identification of eight "archetypes" of competitive strategies for entry. *Strategic Management Journal, 11*(6), 447–467.

McGuire, J. W. (1963). *Business and Society*. New York: McGraw Hill.

Michel, N., Carter, J., III, & Varela, O. (2009). Active versus passive teaching styles: An empirical study of student learning outcomes. *Human Resource Development Quarterly, 20*, 397–418.

Moor, J. H. (2006). The nature, importance, and difficulty of machine ethics. *IEEE Intelligent Systems*, 4(July–August), 18–21.

Morse, R. S., & Stephens, J. B. (2012). Teaching collaborative governance: Phases, competencies, and case-based learning. *Journal of Public Affairs Education, 18*(3), 565–583.

Mulgan, G., Tucker, S., Ali, R., & Sanders, B. (2007). *Social Innovation: What It Is, Why It Matters, How It Can Be Accelerated*. Skoll Centre for Social Entrepreneurship.

Muñoz, P., & Kimmitt, J. (2019). Rural entrepreneurship in place: An integrated framework. *Entrepreneurship & Regional Development, 31*(9–10), 842–873.

North, D. C. (1991). Institutions stör. *Journal of Economic Perspectives, 5*(1), 97–112.

O'Reilly III, C. A., & Tushman, M. L. (2013). Organizational ambidexterity: Past, present, and future. *Academy of Management Perspectives, 27*(4), 324–338.

OECD (2019). *Business Development and Growth of Rural SMEs*. OECD.

Parrish, B. D. (2010). Sustainability-driven entrepreneurship: Principles of organization design. *Journal of Business Venturing, 25*(5), 510–523.

Phan, P. H., Wright, M., Ucbasaran, D., & Tan, W. L. (2009). Corporate entrepreneurship: Current research and future directions. *Journal of Business Venturing, 24*(3), 197–205.

Phillips, W., Lee, H., Ghobadian, A., O'Regan, N., & James, P. (2015). Social innovation and social entrepreneurship: A systematic review. *Group & Organization Management, 40*(3), 428–461.

Porras-Paez, A. (2023). "Take it easy": How informal institutions shape an emerging economy entrepreneurial ecosystem. *Regional Studies, Regional Science, 10*(1), 581–591.

Porras-Paez, A., & Schmutzler, J. (2019). Orchestrating an entrepreneurial ecosystem in an emerging country: The lead actor's role from a social capital perspective. *Local Economy, 34*(8), 767–786.

Pugh, R., & Dubois, A. (2021). Peripheries within economic geography: Four "problems" and the road ahead of us. *Journal of Rural Studies, 87*, 267–275.

Pugh, R., Schmutzler, J., & Tsvetkova, A. (2021). Taking the systems approaches out of their comfort zones: Perspectives from under explored contexts. *Growth and Change, 52*(2), 608–620.

Ranville, A., & Barros, M. (2021). Towards normative theories of social entrepreneurship: A review of the top publications of the field. *Journal of Business Ethics*, 1–32.

Reynolds, P. D., & White, S. B. (1997). *The Entrepreneurial Process: Economic Growth, Men, Women, and Minorities*. Westport, CT: Quorum Books.

Rodríguez-Pose, A., Wilkie, C., & Zhang, M. (2021). Innovating in "lagging" cities: A comparative exploration of the dynamics of innovation in Chinese cities. *Applied Geography*, 132, 102475.

Ross, J., Strevel, H., & Javadizadeh, B. (2021) Don't stop believin': The journey to entrepreneurial burnout and back again. *Journal of Small Business & Entrepreneurship*, 33(5), 559–582.

Salemi, M. K. (2002). An illustrated case for active learning. *Southern Economic Journal*, 68(3), 721–731.

Schaltegger, S., & Wagner, M. (2011). Sustainable entrepreneurship and sustainability innovation: Categories and interactions. *Business Strategy and the Environment*, 20(4), 222–237.

Scheidgen, K., & Brattström, A. (2022). Berlin is hotter than Silicon Valley! How networking temperature shapes entrepreneurs' networking across social contexts. *Entrepreneurship Theory and Practice*, 47(6).

Schmutzler, J., Suarez, M., Tsvetkova, A., & Faggian, A. (2017). Introduction. A context-specific two-way approach to the study of innovation systems in developing and transition countries. In: Tsvetkova, A., Schmutzler, J., Suarez, M., & Faggian, A. (eds), *Innovation in Developing and Transition Countries*. Edward Elgar Publishing, 1–12.

Shane, S. (2000). Prior knowledge and the discovery of entrepreneurial opportunities. *Organization Science*, 11(4), 448–469.

Shane, S., & Venkataraman, S. (2000). The promise of entrepreneurship as a field of research. *Academy of Management Review*, 25(1), 217–226.

Shearmur, R. (2015). Far from the madding crowd: Slow innovators, information value, and the geography of innovation. *Growth and Change*, 46(3), 424–442.

Shearmur, R. (2017). Urban bias in innovation studies. In H. Bathelt, P. Cohendet, S. Henn, & L. Simon (eds), *The Elgar Companion to Innovation and Knowledge Creation*. Cheltenham, UK and Northampton, MA, USA: Edward Elgar Publishing, pp. 440–456.

Shearmur, R., & Doloreux, D. (2016). How open innovation processes vary between urban and remote environments: Slow innovators, market-sourced information and frequency of interaction. *Entrepreneurship & Regional Development*, 28(5–6), 337–357.

Shepherd, D., & Majchrzak, A. (2022). Machines augmenting entrepreneurs: Opportunities (and threats) at the nexus of artificial intelligence and entrepreneurship, *Journal of Business Venturing*, 37(4), 106227.

Shir, N. (2015). *Entrepreneurial Well-Being: The Payoff Structure of Business Creation*. Stockholm: Stockholm School of Economics.

Soto-Simeone, A., Sirén, C., & Antretter, T. (2020). New venture survival: A review and extension. *International Journal of Management Reviews*, 22(4), 378–407.

Stam, F., & Spigel, B. (2016). Entrepreneurial ecosystems. Utrecht School of Economics Working Paper Series 16(13).

Stephan, U. (2018). Entrepreneurs' mental health and well-being: A review and research agenda. *Academy of Management Perspectives*, 32(3), 290–322.

Sterman, J. D., Henderson, R., Beinhocker, E. D., & Newman, L. I. (2007). Getting big too fast: Strategic dynamics with increasing returns and bounded rationality. *Management Science*, 53(4), 683–696.

Stinchcombe, A. L. (1965). Social structure and organizations. In: March, J. G. (ed.), *Handbook of Organizations*. Chicago, IL: Rand-McNally, 142–193.

Stockdale, A. (2006). Migration: Pre-requisite for rural economic regeneration? *Journal of Rural Studies*, 22(3), 354–366.

Tarba, S. Y., Jansen, J. J., Mom, T. J., Raisch, S., & Lawton, T. C. (2020). A microfoundational perspective of organizational ambidexterity: Critical review and research directions. *Long Range Planning*, 53(6), 102048.

Thapa, R. K., Iakovleva, T., & Foss, L. (2019). Responsible research and innovation: A systematic review of the literature and its applications to regional studies. *European Planning Studies*, 27(12), 2470–2490.

Torrès, O., Benzari, A., Fisch, C., Mukerjee, J., Swalhi, A., & Thurik, R. (2022). Risk of burnout in French entrepreneurs during the COVID-19 crisis. *Small Business Economics*, 58, 717–739.

Tsvetkova, A., Schmutzler, J., & Pugh, R. (eds) (2020). *Entrepreneurial Ecosystems Meet Innovation Systems: Synergies, Policy Lessons and Overlooked Dimensions*. Edward Elgar Publishing.

Tushman, M. L., & O'Reilly, III, C. A. (1996). Ambidextrous organizations: Managing evolutionary and revolutionary change. *California Management Review*, *38*(4), 8–29.

Urbano, D., Turro, A., Wright, M., & Zahra, S. (2022). Corporate entrepreneurship: A systematic literature review and future research agenda. *Small Business Economics*, 1–25.

Von Schomberg, R. (2013). A vision of responsible research and innovation. In: Owen, R., Bessant, J., & Heintz, M. (eds), *Responsible Innovation: Managing the Responsible Emergence of Science and Innovation in Society*. Wiley, 51–74.

Welter, F. (2011). Contextualizing entrepreneurship: Conceptual challenges and ways forward. *Entrepreneurship Theory and Practice*, *35*(1), 165–184.

Wiklund, J., Nikolaev, B., Shir, N., Foo, M. D., & Bradley, S. (2019). Entrepreneurship and well-being: Past, present, and future. *Journal of Business Venturing*, *34*(4), 579–588.

Williams, T. A., Gruber, D. A., Sutcliffe, K. M., Shepherd, D. A., & Zhao, E. Y. (2017). Organizational response to adversity: Fusing crisis management and resilience research streams. *Academy of Management Annals*, *11*(2), 733–769.

Zahra, S. A. (1996). Governance, ownership, and corporate entrepreneurship: The moderating impact of industry technological opportunities. *Academy of Management Journal*, *39*(6), 1713–1735.

PART I
ENTREPRENEURIAL EQUILIBRIUM: STRIKING A BALANCE BETWEEN BUSINESS AND IMPACT

2

Open Hands For You: empowering immigrants through social entrepreneurship in Norway

Marte C.W. Solheim

1.   SETTING THE SCENE

Aline Kamudege is a social entrepreneur who started her life in Norway alone at the age of 26. She came as a resettlement refugee and after several years studying and working in Stavanger, Norway, she started her own business, the not-for-profit organization Open Hands For You (OHY), at the beginning of 2015.[1] The organization embodied the core principles of social entrepreneurship, defined as 'an entrepreneurial activity with an embedded social purpose' (Austin et al., 2006: 1).

The vision of the organization had remained unchanged since its inception, namely: 'Open Hands works to increase tolerance, cultural understanding and integration for younger and older refugees and immigrants'.[2] Due to the increasing migration worldwide and within the Scandinavian context (in Norway, 15.98 per cent of the population were immigrants in 2023, up from 9.46 per cent in 2010),[3] the need for integration of immigrants was brought to the fore. The goals of OHY were to function as a link between immigrants, the public and civil society, familiarizing immigrants with Norwegian culture and language, organizing meetings and activities that promoted cultural understanding and focused on health and health-promoting activities (Open Hands For You, 2021a). The organization offered several social activities for the broader immigrant community, such as skiing trips, after-school activities, social clubs and sports. The activities at OHY had been extended in recent years, due to the increasing demand for its activities and to its improved understanding of the needs of its users. Moreover, the COVID-19 pandemic and the war in Ukraine shifted the organization's focus and activities. Their growth led to increased operating costs and thus the necessity of evaluating income streams that would enable short-term and long-term economic sustainability.

OHY's business model depended on seeking money from public agencies, investors and crowdfunding. The organization achieved a financial surplus during the financial assessment in 2021, mainly through managing the income and reviewing costs to ensure ongoing operations (Open Hands for You, 2021b). The board of the organization emphasized that they planned cautiously for the future to ensure the sustainability of the business and that in the longer term they expected improved financial circumstances in line with industry indicators predicting economic recovery. In their 2021 financial report, the board members emphasized that their conclusions were based on the state of current operations, good communication with donors and a conservative estimate of future income.

In 2023 the organization was at a turning point. While it offered a range of activities and was well known and relied upon by the broader community, Aline faced the challenge of maintaining its income streams. The critical tasks were to maintain a stable offer for its users and secure its premises. Most of its income came from direct fundraising as well as through ad hoc support from the municipality and national government. Aline had plans for how she might increase income to provide more stability for the organization's programmes. These plans followed the principles of social entrepreneurship such as users producing goods or creating entrepreneurial spin-offs. Aline was also contemplating the acquisition of a van to expand the existing food delivery programme and which could also be used to offer a taxi service.

2. LOCATION AND CONTEXT

OHY is physically located in Hillevåg, Stavanger, Norway (see Figures 2.1 and 2.2). Stavanger is the third-largest city region in Norway and is a place where immigrants make up around 20 per cent of the population, with most coming from Poland, the United Kingdom and other Nordic countries. In 2022, Hillevåg held the highest percentage of immigrants in the city (around 22 per cent), comprising substantial communities originating from Somalia, Poland and Pakistan. In relation to entrepreneurial ventures, globally there is an overrepresentation of immigrants engaging in entrepreneurial activity. Norway is no exception: in 2022, 15 per cent of its population was foreign-born, while a quarter of its entrepreneurs were immigrants (Statistics Norway, 2020; Wong & Solheim, 2022).

3. THE PROTAGONIST

In 2007, Aline arrived as a resettlement refugee in Stavanger, bringing an entrepreneurial orientation and mindset that she had already developed while in her home country. After studying and working in Norway, she started OHY.

Aline is from Burundi, a small country in East-Central Africa that 'has suffered from waves of violence at various times throughout its post-independence period, often expressed along ethnic lines. Democratic elections were held in 1993, but the newly elected president was killed three months after taking office, leading to a civil war' (Burihabwa & Curtis, 2021: 1222).[4] Aline experienced the trauma of growing up during wartime and was especially troubled by the sight of refugees living in poor conditions. She sought to provide as much assistance as she could. A particular occasion stands out in her mind, when she fetched clothes and a duvet from home to give to children residing in her neighbourhood who owned nothing (Kamudege, interview, 2022).

Source: © norgeskart.no.

Figure 2.1   Norway, showing the location of Hillevåg

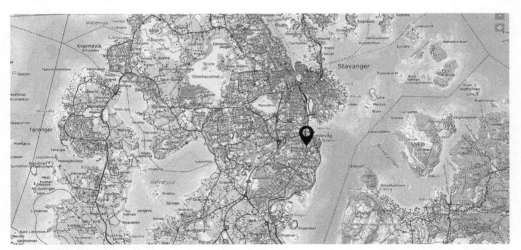

Source: © norgeskart.no.

Figure 2.2   Hillevåg, Stavanger

In 2004 after studying in Kenya, Aline moved back to Burundi to work with street children and women. Through an internship programme, she learned how to make shampoo, conditioner and oils, and started a business producing these items. The business was successful and profitable enough that she was able to provide for herself, leading her to want to enable others to do the same. She envisioned others being able to start their own shops selling hair and beauty products, which were scarce in Burundi. However, the instability caused by war, as well as the uncertainty of the political situation, made life there not only difficult but dangerous. Fearing for her life, Aline fled, first to Kenya and then to Ethiopia, before coming to Norway. She explains:

> It was not easy to come to Norway. There are many difficult issues you are faced with when coming as an immigrant to Norway, as a young person and with great hopes for the future, and you suddenly become a refugee, and you realize that a lot of your vision is completely turned off. You will have to start from zero. (Kamudege, interview, 2022)

When she arrived in Norway, there were many seemingly small aspects of life to which she had to adjust. While facing these challenges, Aline noticed that she was not alone in struggling to adapt and settle in. Continuing with her commitment to helping others, she started assisting with what she referred to as 'the smaller things', which meant helping others with practical issues such as shopping, using credit cards, logging onto the NAV system (necessary for registering as a job seeker, finding jobs and navigating the variety of state benefits and schemes).[5] Aline also helped other refugees with the basic facets of everyday life, such as organizing events and social networking.

Aline (Figure 2.3) got in touch with the municipal department working with refugees, realizing that newly arrived refugees needed both networks and information. She invited them to her home for meals and went out with them socially. During Easter 2014, there was a large unofficial gathering in Aline's house with 35 people from different countries in her small apartment to celebrate together. Friends had helped with what they could, but it was so crowded that people were sitting on the floor throughout her home. Her friends told her that she should consider making the work she was doing official and try to find a place where she could better organize her activities. She was not enthusiastic about the idea as setting up an organization would require a substantial effort. Many ideas emerged about how such an endeavour could be organized, what the relevant regulations would be and what activities it could develop. Despite her trepidations, once the seed of the idea was planted, Aline started planning the establishment of a formal organization.

4.   THE ESTABLISHMENT OF OPEN HANDS FOR YOU

In January 2015, Aline registered her company. With the papers in order and the initial requirements settled, she thought to herself: 'Where should I take it from here?' She was able to move into an office in the Hillevåg area provided by the Stavanger municipality in October 2016 for what was referred to as a 'trial period', for a few hours twice a week.

Aline received negative comments, with many telling her: 'This is impossible. Welcome to Norway! … You will die with your vision'. Aline herself thought: 'Ok, if this was my vision, let it die … but if I was born to do this work, it will work' (Kamudege, interview, 2022). Despite these discouragements, Aline persisted with her vision. Concomitantly, the migrant crisis of 2015 began, which brought Aline and OHY a large volume of work. Aline and her

Source: Aline Kamudege, used with her permission.

Figure 2.3   Aline Kamudege

group of volunteers started testing many different concepts, motivated by the opportunity to help others, as she explained: 'Money did not motivate me … it was the work that was in my heart … if this cannot be my job, I will work alongside somebody else whilst also doing this' (Kamudege, interview 2022).

5.   THE DEVELOPMENT OF THE BUSINESS MODEL: SOCIAL ENTREPRENEURSHIP

From the start, Aline applied for funding from both public and private institutions. Her approach was to test out her idea before applying for funding. At one time she observed that many children from unprivileged economic backgrounds did not have much to do at the end of the school day and hence did not have enriching ways to spend their time. During the organization's trial of a junior club, more than 100 children showed up to the opening session. This initial demand led to excitement regarding whether the project could receive further support, which the organization had applied for.

Aline's *modus operandi* was that she never applied for funding without having tested an initiative beforehand. In her own words: 'If it works, you sell this as something you know will work … if we don't get support, it's because they don't understand what we do. So, we always try to emphasize this. That is also why I always do pilot projects first' (Kamudege, interview, 2022).

In 2021, OHY had income streams as it was successful in receiving funding from private sources, such as the Gjensidigestiftelsen and Sparebankstiftelsen banks and public organizations such as the municipality of Stavanger, the Directorate of Integration and Diversity and other institutions, as well as through its own crowdfunding initiatives (Open Hands for You, 2021b). The organization's board highlighted its focus on sustaining current activities as well as securing more stable income streams, while Aline herself had several ideas for future projects tapping into other areas of the business model.

6.　　THE CORE OFFERINGS OF OPEN HANDS FOR YOU

Aline quickly realized that learning Norwegian was vital for refugee integration, something she had reinforced in the organization's existing projects through the hosting of language cafes, physical exercise programmes, a sewing club and activities for young people, in which refugees and migrants met Norwegians for idea exchanges and socialization. The organization also ran a food delivery programme for underprivileged families.

From the beginning, Aline had the perception that many saw the need for more efforts focused on children and adolescents in terms of integration and value creation. After running the organization for several years, she also noticed the needs of senior citizens, including the retired and those who had come to Norway as adults with limited networks and contacts outside their households. Many were spending their time at home, which Aline highlighted as having deleterious consequences for integration. One issue was that some of these residents were moved from their homes to accommodations for the elderly without sufficient language knowledge and skills. OHY ran language cafes and taught older generations how to exercise, brought people out of their homes and made them feel at ease using different types of fitness apparatus. This initiative required tackling cultural issues, with a need to identify barriers to participation in physical exercise and encouraging a focus on both the physical and mental benefits of exercise. In 2018, the organization received an 'immigrant integration award' from the Stavanger municipality for its efforts.

The organization also responded to developing international situations, including the COVID-19 pandemic and the war in Ukraine. Aline explained that the pandemic brought tough times, during which they had their hands full: 'refugees coming do not have the right information; they have misinformation that they then spread' (Kamudege, interview, 2022).

OHY quickly saw that there was a need to disseminate accurate information regarding the pandemic and received funding from the government to assist in this work. The organization also offered support by engaging people from many different countries as 'ambassadors'. People in these roles helped provide a sense of security and assisted people in their communities with practical issues during the difficult and uncertain times of the pandemic.

For Ukrainian refugees arriving in Stavanger during the spring of 2022, OHY organized meeting places in Flintegata 2 (as shown in Figure 2.4) and continued to provide frontline responses, delivering items such as clothing, sanitary towels, toiletries and more. They also organized gatherings for youth who were not in school and similar social events. Some were organized as part of OHY's ordinary activities and some were targeted specifically at new Ukrainian refugees, who attended events at Flintegata to meet their compatriots in the local area. During the gatherings urgent response materials and products were displayed, ensuring that refugees could pick up key items during their visit.

Figure 2.4   The Pådriv building in Flintegata 2, Hillevåg, Stavanger

7.   BALANCING THE SOCIAL AND THE ECONOMIC

OHY's business model was fuelled by Aline's vision and success in securing funding from various sources. Funds were often sourced at different and irregular points in time, demanding a constant pipeline of funding applications. Aline explained: 'You must apply for funding all the time. But you don't know how much you'll get. It is mostly philanthropic donations. You must be good at applying for funding and donations. I believe that the key is to get ownership of something that you can produce' (Kamudege, interview, 2022).

There were many loose ends and areas of potential that Aline planned to explore. A longer-term goal was for employees to be able to produce goods, and as such enabling more regular streams of income. OHY had significant regular expenses but very little recurrent funding. This situation was not atypical for social entrepreneurs such as Aline who had a high level of willingness to take risks. Aline and her team had mitigated these risks through the piloting of projects and their ability to innovate. Starting new projects based on immigrants' skills and needs, such as the sewing project, was an innovative attempt that had the potential to be self-sustainable and was fed with the motivation to achieve a social impact while creating economic value (Schätzlein et al., 2023: 178).

Consequently, Aline and her team have been considering different modes of operation, moving towards a model that would enable their 'social mission while engaging in commercial activities that sustain their operations' (Battilana & Lee, 2014: 399). This included evaluating options to situate the business between for- and non-profit models (Shepherd et al., 2019; Schätzlein et al., 2023). Two concrete directions were identified in this respect: the first revolves around the creation of entrepreneurial spin-offs based on the organization's current activities, to create workplaces and jobs for the participants; the other was concerned with the expansion of non-profit activities into profitable ventures.

Regarding the former model, Aline considered the development of the nascent sewing project. Immigrant women joining this project would learn to sew, before moving on to start their own businesses selling the resulting products. In 2022, approximately ten women are involved in the project and are learning to sew. The ambition was that with time and training they could develop their skills into entrepreneurial spin-offs, selling their work online or in stores. The sewing project served both as a social arena and as a means for integration and business development within the creative crafts. The project focused on learning and mastery in sewing and Norwegian language learning while providing a space in which participants and volunteers could spend time together and interact. The sewing project moved into the co-creation hub På-Driv Project in Hillevåg towards the end of 2020, which provided premises for the sewing workshops and social gatherings (see Figure 2.4). In its start-up phase, the focus was on teaching participants to sew and repair clothes, with a strong emphasis on sustainability (Open Hands For You, n.d.).

Aline hoped that those who found themselves at home with little to do could become productive if they were properly motivated and could produce goods that they could then sell for themselves. She had already contacted a store owner who had offered shelves that could be rented to project participants to exhibit their creations. Online sales were another possibility.

For the latter model of entrepreneurial development, Aline considered ways in which OHY could utilize its resources in new ways to create revenue. One such example was for OHY to offer services to people who needed to be picked up from home and to deliver food to the homes of people in need. By purchasing a vehicle, OHY could use it for its own needs as well as a taxi when it was not in use. Owning a vehicle meant that the organization could develop a new income stream while being more self-sufficient in its activities.

8.   MOVING FORWARD

Striving to balance the social and economic aspects of OHY, Aline and her team considered how they could best move forward. They needed to reflect on the next steps to be presented to the forthcoming board meeting. They needed to strategize to stay true to their vision of enabling immigrants to thrive as well as prioritizing their financial stability. The key questions they asked themselves were: (1) What is the path to robust self-sufficiency? (2) How can OHY best balance its vision with ensuring steady income?

ACKNOWLEDGEMENTS

I am grateful to Aline Kamudege in making this case study possible.

NOTES

1. www.udi.no/en/word-definitions/resettlement-refugees/
2. www.openhands.no/ and Kamudege (2022).
3. Statistics Norway, Immigrants and Norwegians born to immigrants, www.ssb.no/en/befolkning/innvandrere/statistikk/innvandrere-og-norskfodte-med-innvandrerforeldre and www.ssb.no/en/statbank/table/09817/tableViewLayout1/
4. Melchior Ndadaye.
5. NAV administers schemes such as unemployment benefits, work assessment allowance, pensions, child benefit, etc.: www.nav.no/en/home

REFERENCES

Austin, J., Stevenson, H., & Wei-Skillern, J. (2006). Social and commercial entrepreneurship: Same, different, or both? *Entrepreneurship Theory and Practice*, 30(1), 1–22.

Battilana, J. & Lee, M. (2014). Advancing research on hybrid organizing: Insights from the study of social enterprises. *Academy of Management Annals*, 8, 397–441.

Burihabwa, N.Z. & Curtis, D.E.A. (2021). Postwar state-building in Burundi: Ruling party elites and illiberal peace. *International Affairs*, 97(4), 1221–1238.

Open Hands for You (2021a). Annual report. https://usercontent.one/wp/www.openhands.no/wp-content/uploads/2022/09/Arsrapport-Open-Hands-For-You-2021.pdf

Open Hands for You (2021b). Financial report. Brøynnøysund Register Centre.

Open Hands for You (n.d.). www.openhands.no/

Schätzlein, L., Schlütter, D. & Hahn, R. (2023). Managing the external financing constraints of social enterprises: A systematic review of a diversified research landscape. *International Journal of Management Reviews*, 25, 176–199.

Shepherd, D.A., Williams, T.A. & Zhao, E.Y. (2019). A framework for exploring the degree of hybridity in entrepreneurship. *Academy of Management Perspectives*, 33, 491–512.

Statistics Norway (2020). Statistics Norway datasets 07358 and 09038. www.ssb.no/virksomheter-foretak-og-regnskap/statistikker/etablerere

Wong, N. & Solheim, M.C.W. (2022). Cultivating and fighting at the same time: An immigrant's innovative entrepreneurial journey in the agricultural scene in Norway. In Wigger, K.L., Aaboen, L., Haneberg, D.H., Lauvås, T. & Jakobsen, S. (eds), *Reframing the Case Method for Entrepreneurship Education: Cases from the Nordic Countries*. Edward Elgar Publishing.

3

Comproagro: transforming small farming in Colombia with an app

Laura Sofía Buitrago Vidal, Georgina M. Gómez, and Lorena A. Palacios-Chacón

1. LIFE IN RURAL COLOMBIA AND THE VERGARA FAMILY

The armed conflict in Colombia started in the late 1940s, and a peace agreement with the largest guerrilla group FARC was signed in 2016. It left 450,000 confirmed dead, 80 percent of whom were civilians, and 7.75 million forcefully displaced, according to an exhaustive official report in 2022 that counted confirmed cases only (IDPC, 2022). This seven decade-long conflict's intensity and geographical coverage varied in time and space but affected rural areas and farmers the most. At the risk of oversimplifying, the Colombian case was essentially a conflict about land, and rural areas were destroyed and decimated because many farmers had to escape or were killed. A study synthesized the situation as "Farmers without land and land without farmers" (Patiño, 2012). In 2016, after six years of negotiations and a referendum, a peace agreement was signed between the FARC guerrillas and the Colombian Government, led by Juan Manuel Santos. Since then, the implementation process had started, including one of the largest land restitution programs in history to support farmers' return to agriculture, but the harsh conditions of farming clashed with these goals. Making a decent income on small farming in many parts of Colombia was extremely difficult because of low yields, no technical assistance, no access to loans, deficient infrastructure, abusive intermediaries, and cartelized markets in Bogotá and the other main cities.

Comproagro was conceived in these hardships, which the Vergara family experienced along with everyone else in their community. The head of the Vergara household was Rosalba Vergara, born and raised in rural Toca, located four hours' drive from Bogotá and 45 minutes from Tunja, the capital city of the department[1] of Boyacá. This is one of the 32 departments in Colombia and one of the least affected by the violence of the armed conflict. Boyacá had a population of over 1.2 million in 2015, half of them scattered around hilly rural areas. Toca is located 2.810 meters above sea level, and its main economic activities were agriculture, livestock, and the cultivation of flowers. Toca was recognized in 2012 as the safest town in

Colombia. However, facing poverty and lack of access to public services were part of everyday life for the people of Toca. Furthermore, public transportation was infrequent, and rural dwellers depended on costly private transport to move around.[2] Rosalba had lived in the district's urban and rural areas. Her parents inherited the 3.22 hectares of land from her grandparents, and all generations had always lived in poverty, growing corn, onions, and potatoes.

In 1997, Rosalba gave birth to her twins Ginna and Bryan, and her partner abandoned her three months later. She then became a single mother living with her parents and her children. One year later, in 1993, she found a job as a salesperson in the city and decided to move there with her children. In 1999, a severe financial crisis hit the Colombian economy and Rosalba had to return to her parents' home. In 2001, she was able to find a job in the only source of employment in Toca, the flower growers, where she worked for 11 years. She had always wanted to become a teacher, and she completed a degree program in teaching while working full time and raising her two children. Those years working in the flower sector helped her to understand the tough gender issues that women face when involved in forms of work that are regarded as men's work. On the positive side, work in the flower sector allowed Rosalba to save every possible cent to buy a property in Toca and start the painfully slow house construction. She was able to build the main structure of the house but could not afford windows or doors. Rosalba's parents then decided to distribute their farm between their two children, Rosalba and her brother Alfredo, who continued farming in poverty.

In 2011, after a crisis in the flower company, Rosalba decided to quit and compete for a job as a primary school teacher in Boyacá. She was offered a position in a remote rural area located three hours from Toca. She left her children with her parents to take the job in the school, which she accessed on horseback daily. She could only talk to her children, Bryan and Ginna, once a week because the nearest reception point was about one hour from the school on foot. For three years (2011–2014) the family was separated, and Ginna behaved as a mother to Bryan, who suffered from Rosalba's absence and got sick regularly. In turn, the twins clashed with their grandparents and moved to the unfinished family house.

The life of the family changed drastically in 2014. Rosalba was granted a transfer to a small rural school in Toca, and she could finally reunite with her children and head for a fresh start with a minimum but stable wage. Rosalba was one of a handful of rural women in Toca who had accessed higher education, so she was highly recognized for that achievement. Locals spoke of her as a "good woman" and called her "*la profe*," meaning teacher.

The socioeconomic situation of farmers in the region was particularly strenuous that year. A frost season damaged many of the crops around Toca and other towns. Farmers could only manage to harvest a few sacks that did not cover the costs of bringing the products to the marketplace. These hardships led many small farmers to take loans to keep the farms, which created further financial pressures. The Vergara family saw how some of their neighbors went hungry, and Rosalba had to support her parents and relatives with her minimum wage. The Vergaras wished they could do more to help their community and became determined to "do something."

2.   THE BEGINNING OF COMPROAGRO

Ginna came back from school one day with an idea. By coincidence, a delegate of the Ministry of Technology and Communications (MINTIC) visited the school to promote a program that aimed at boosting digital entrepreneurship among students across the country. The program specifically targeted youth, assuming they would be more open to digital technologies and business. The delegate promoted the program App.co, created in 2012 with the aim of generating new business ideas based on technology. App.co aimed at "helping to transform ideas into a sustainable business, promoting digital entrepreneurship in Colombia through the creation of information technology and communication." The program had supported over 100,000 digital startups by 2019 with training, marketing, networking, technological capabilities, and other services (MINTIC, 2018).

Following the information session of App.co at school, Ginna went home and shared details of the session with Rosalba and Bryan. "What if these new technologies can help farmers connect to buyers directly and eliminate the middlemen? Farmers would get more money," she thought. That was the conception moment of Comproagro, because the Vergaras identified the trading and market structure of agricultural products in Colombia as the key problem. Small farmers in the area could not afford to take their own products out of their farms, so local middlemen bought the crops at the farm's gate for a low price. The middlemen transported the products to the central market in Bogotá or sold them to other intermediaries. After three to five traders, products reached the Central Market of Bogotá (Corabastos), which was the main market for fresh fruit and vegetables and the key price maker in the country. The owners of the products had no influence on the prices they obtained for their products, the selling conditions, or even the identity of the buyers. A farmer who transported his goods to Bogotá described what happened next: "Once you enter Corabastos, the product is no longer yours because they take the product into a closed space and market it based on their criteria ... they set the prices and find the buyer. Basically, the farmer becomes a spectator of this game."

The Vergara family often heard this story and experienced it with their products. They looked at a trading application as an opportunity to connect the two ends of the chain and eliminate the intermediary system separating producers in Toca from consumers in Bogotá. They imagined that trade of agricultural products could occur after a simple connection in the app, an email, or a call so that farmers could get higher profits. The complicated reality of launching a trading platform escaped them at that point, so the Vergara family went through a long learning process on digital technology. They had to prepare a business proposal for App.co, describing the idea and its potential social impact. For instance, the project design did not include information on future income flows or business feasibility. Still, it was a valuable experience to learn to persuade others of the potential of Comproagro. They were granted further entrepreneurial training offered by MINTIC, where they also met technology experts, MINTIC officers, different governmental agents, and consultants who were enthusiastic about their idea. They passed through different stages of this government support program for digital startups and were met with great enthusiasm. Ginna, especially, developed skills to engage with the audience and to share what Comproagro could be and do for farmers in Colombia.

The concept of a platform to trade agricultural products came at a time when MINTIC was promoting digital technologies and access to the internet to tackle social inequalities. "Our responsibility is to promote internet access in order to help to reduce poverty," stated Diego Molano, Minister of Technology and Communications. The leaders of App.co emphasized in a public interview that Comproagro was exceptional in its potential to work at different levels for the benefit of small farmers with incomes under the poverty line. They described the platform as a fresh startup that could improve the livelihoods of thousands of small-scale farmers in Colombia. Comproagro was considered a revolutionary innovation. However, the government did not contribute fresh funds but other kinds of support, such as training, so it did not follow up the evolution of the financial sustainability of Comproagro.

Comproagro rapidly received attention across Colombia. A non-governmental organization posted a video on Facebook (in Spanish but with subtitles in English) titled "The network that has saved an entire agricultural community."[3] The video included aerial images of rural Toca and pictures of tired farmers, diverse in gender and age, with the quote "Farmers work hard." In another video on the MINTIC YouTube channel, Rosalba claimed that "Comproagro starts its first steps to dignify Colombian farmers, to let them show their products."[4] By 2019, there were more than 30 promotional videos on YouTube that advertised the potential of Comproagro to change the market dynamics of small-scale farming in Colombia. The Vergaras were active in supporting the platform on social media, and the construction of their concept was remarkably consistent across the different videos and presentations: Comproagro was an app created by their family in a rural household with the support of a government program that promoted digital technologies for agribusiness. Comproagro was "the local initiative that works for farmers in Colombia." One of the most appealing statements was the number of users: the videos reported that more than 7,000 users, including producers and consumers across the country, had signed up by 2018, and this was increasing fast. The app was open source and free for everybody; an account could be opened in minutes and did not require advanced technical skills. Buyers were a mix of consumers and small local stores nationwide.

Despite the enthusiasm around Comproagro, a closer look revealed a less glittering reality. Rural areas in Colombia had minimal access to information and communication technology. In 2012, MINTIC reported that only 200 of the 1,102 municipalities in Colombia had fiber optic networks, and internet connections were unstable or limited everywhere outside the main cities (MINTIC, 2012). In order to accelerate connectivity development, in 2010, the Colombian government started implementing a public policy to extend information and communication technologies. The program was called Vive Digital, and it sought to expand access and use of the internet across the country.

The progress of Vive Digital had not reached rural Toca by 2014, when Comproagro was launched, and in 2018 Toca had only one public internet point offered by the Vive Digital program. It was open a total of 35 hours a week, and the Wi-Fi network was shared with the public library. Toca was both home to Comproagro and one of the "unconnected places" in the connectivity map of Colombia. Besides inadequate connectivity, many small farmers, especially the poorest and oldest, were illiterate or semi-illiterate, too poor to own smartphones or tablets, and not all farmers had electric power. For instance, almost none of the farmers in Toca used social media, and even fewer were users of digital platforms or could remotely imagine selling their crops online.

Against this background, the dream that digital technologies could transform the lives of small farmers in Colombia failed to materialize, at least in places like Toca. Of the approximately 14,000[5] inhabitants in Toca, by 2018, only three had become users of Comproagro. Two of them were young family members helping the older generation of farmers, but their main occupation was not related to agriculture, and their primary residential address was not in Toca. The expectation of information and communication technology as a game-changing tool in rural development was out of touch with the local context of places like Toca.

Still, the Vergaras were committed to the project, membership kept climbing, and the government was confident that connectivity would expand eventually. Moreover, the Vergara children were determined to stay in Toca, and as they finished school, they had more time but were also pressed by the need to generate an income. They centered their attention on increasing household income so that they could support themselves. They also realized they had to cover the costs of the app, as the government technological and managerial support was about to phase out.

3.   THE STRUGGLE TO GENERATE INCOME

The app was never conceived with a profitable business model in mind, but as a public service to farmers in rural Colombia; almost a school experiment that fitted well within some policy circles. While it was attracting thousands of farmers and much public support, it generated zero revenue for the family but recurrent expenses. The app required more support and development than the package offered in the App.co program and it was beyond what the family could afford. All the technological input, as well as marketing, was based on a voluntary scheme. They tried to charge a yearly membership fee to use Comproagro, and later they attempted to charge per transaction closed via the app, but these initiatives did not work. Users resisted the extra costs, would try to trade outside the platform, and would even deregister. Besides, payments were made directly between traders, not via the app, so they could not retain part of the money.

To make a living for themselves and maintain the virtual life of Comproagro, they needed a regular income besides Rosalba's minimum wage as a teacher. While Bryan and Gina refused to migrate to the cities in search of jobs, they could not see how they could increase the revenues from growing onions and potatoes on their farm. So, the Vergaras kept on thinking about how to make a living and, in 2016, two years into the life of Comproagro, they came up with a separate business idea. The Vergara family launched La Peladora, a social enterprise that sorts, cleans, and peels onions and potatoes for supermarkets and other major retailers in urban centers in Colombia. Gina thought that by offering ready-to-eat onions, they could add value to the products that they were growing on the farm and the farms around them. They set up the processing plant in an old and cracked house that Rosalba had received from her maternal grandmother, which they used as the storage warehouse for Comproagro. Although half of the house had collapsed, it was still a good place to start. They covered the roof and a wall with plastic to endure the hardships of winter and rain.

While the plan was to sell the onions in supermarkets and to larger retailers, they realized again that their entrepreneurial knowledge and connections were more limited than their vision. The family expected that the media exposure received with Comproagro would benefit La Peladora, especially considering that La Peladora was launched to cross-subsidize Comproagro. However, the brick-and-mortar and the virtual worlds of agricultural value chains were separated, so mentioning Comproagro did not help to open any doors. A middleman eventually got the Vergaras an interview with a supermarket manager for a fee, which they could barely afford but considered a meaningful investment. Rosalba later explained that "only companies with strong financial background get to that level. We were a small company, and we had to pay a middleman to get us an interview with the manager." It paid off, and they were eventually successful in becoming a supplier of a large supermarket chain nationwide, with other chains following later.

Unlike its digital cousin Comproagro, which generated expenses but no revenues, La Peladora quickly started generating profit, and fixed costs were low. It became the family's main income source, allowing them to keep the app running. Still, La Peladora was not a regular business aiming to maximize profits but a social enterprise that simultaneously pursued social goals, which implied "foregoing some profits some of the time," as Rosalba explained. Social enterprises are businesses for which the social and political impact matters as much as the economic goals (Seelos and Mair, 2017). The social goals of La Peladora were multiple. It only hired local rural women who were heads of households and offered them better employment conditions than other jobs in Toca (higher wages, more flexible hours, and facilities for childcare). It supported two dozen rural women's financial independence and their efforts to keep their children at school. In turn, La Peladora processed only vegetables grown by local small farmers, whom the Vergaras paid higher prices and gave better trading conditions than regular middlemen. For example, it paid farmers the official prices of Corabastos and picked them up at farms' gates at no extra cost because transportation was one of the main obstacles for farmers to market their products outside Toca. In short, La Peladora provided for the Vergara household and the basic maintenance of the app, and at the same time, it employed a few women and supported small farmers in their community. It seemed that the social businesses of the Vergaras and their personal financial needs were secured by 2018.

Comproagro could have continued running at a basic level but was unable to grow because it depended completely on the profits of La Peladora, which became the households' main business and absorbed all their energy and time. Comproagro needed investment to expand and generate a healthy stream of revenue in the longer run. In addition, La Peladora required investment to grow, for example, to improve the storage and processing structures so they could expand the scale, boost productivity, and reach more buyers. In May 2018, the family took a five-year loan (2018–2022) of USD 5,000 from the public Agrarian Bank to improve the building of La Peladora, hence relegating Comproagro for the future. The Vergaras decided that the redevelopment and expansion of the app would have to wait while they concentrated their efforts on La Peladora, which in turn generated income and employment for others in the community.

The family still dreamed of transforming the app into Colombia's biggest digital market-place for agricultural products and thought of Comproagro as the springboard to get small farmers out of poverty. However, that dream seemed beyond the economic possibilities of the Vergara family because it required a more sophisticated web design and a more advanced level of technical support than what they could do at home or could get from the App.co support package. The Vergaras estimated that they needed USD 2,200 a year to keep the platform running and updated. Besides, positioning the app needed financial muscle to run an active publicity campaign that could attract more members. In turn, Comproagro needed to do more than provide a point of contact between producers and consumers; it also needed to manage the transportation, packaging, and delivery of agricultural products at small, medium, and large scales. They estimated they needed a cash injection of USD 50,000 for upgrading, updating, and expansion of the app.

When the plan seemed clear, another opportunity sprang up. Shark Tank (2018) was a reality television show where aspiring entrepreneurs could present their business ideas to a group of investors hoping to attract venture capital. It was originally a Japanese show that had been reproduced in different formats in more than 30 countries around the world. It arrived in Colombia through a partnership with INNpulsa Colombia (2018), a government agency to support innovation and entrepreneurship development. INNpulsa was responsible for programs to promote entrepreneurship, innovation, and productivity as an axis for business development and competitiveness in Colombia. INNpulsa connected Shark Tank with the Vergara family and got them a first interview that assessed whether Comproagro was sufficiently interesting for the show and for the potential investors. They passed three filters, and in August 2018, they were notified that they had been selected to pitch in front of the Colombian Sharks.

This was perhaps the opportunity that the Vergara family had been waiting for, which could boost Comproagro for good. The show started with a statement made by Ginna, "With hard work, everything we want is achievable." Subsequently, Ginna and Bryan explained to the potential investors (four men and a woman) the difficulties of farming in Colombia. The presentation lasted a total of three minutes. Ginna and Bryan looked nervous but confident. They were pitching their family's dream once again. The investors looked engaged with the family story, the twins' presence in the studio, and the two twenty-year-old siblings with the immense aspiration of transforming rural Colombia with an app. Two of the potential investors appeared in the show wiping away tears, clearly emotional, and giving compliments to the Vergara twins. Then they made their offer.

It was a venture capital offer that differed substantially from their expectations. Four of the five investors believed in the project and were willing to invest in it. The family sought an investment of USD 85,000 for 5 percent of the app's ownership. The amount would allow them to upgrade, update, and revamp the design of the platform and would also leave them with capital to invest in the infrastructure and distribution facilities of La Peladora. The sum of USD 85,000 was agreed upon but for 50 percent of Comproagro. That meant that the family would share the management decisions to define the future of Comproagro, and maybe the new managers would have different ideas in mind. The Vergaras needed to think carefully if they would reject or accept the offer because Comproagro was much more than a business for them. Bryan was positive. "I know that big things will come with them. They will design the platform well. They will make it possible for Colombians to join and sell their harvests. To trade with fixed prices, regardless of other conditions. It will really make a difference for us and all small farmers." But the family also wondered if they were faithful to the dream and its trajectory to offer a free open platform to benefit all small farmers in Colombia. They had configured the platform as a public service, not as a business. Comproagro was linked to a government program that supported digital entrepreneurship for all; taking the offer felt like they had betrayed the principles they had committed to.

In the meantime, most neighbors in Toca knew the family of La Peladora and only referred to Comproagro when they were specifically asked about it. They did not express any interest, no support, or criticism; they were indifferent to the platform and did not understand how it could transform their lives as farmers. The growing membership of Comproagro did not fit the expected profile that the Vergaras had in mind when they had created the app. The actual users of Comproagro were not poor small farmers excluded from the digital world. The local community of Toca was rather indifferent to the future of Comproagro, in contrast to their positive assessment of La Peladora as a successful social enterprise.

4.   STRATEGIC OPTIONS

The Vergara family had to make a decision that would balance the business and social goals that they had pursued for years. Five years after the launch and considerable media exposure of Comproagro, the moment of truth had come for the family's digital platform. The app needed maintenance and upgrading, which implied resources that the Vergaras did not have, and the combination of the various government programs did not provide Comproagro with the necessary conditions to develop and achieve financial sustainability. Moreover, the household needed to generate an income to support themselves, especially the twins who were now adults. The investors would not only inject capital into the app but would bring a rich network of connections and entrepreneurial knowledge. If the Vergaras rejected the offer, they could leave the app waiting until they could secure capital by different means, and they would not have to share the management of Comproagro. Perhaps Comproagro needed to wait until connectivity spread widely across the Colombian territory and more farmers could join the platform and pay a fee for its use. Should they keep it in their hands as a public service until they could return to invest in Comproagro? Or should they share the management of the initiative to be able to develop it further? Do they have any other options?

NOTES

1. In Colombia states are called departments.
2. Toca, Boyacá: https://en.wikipedia.org/wiki/Toca,_Boyac%C3%A1
3. The title in Spanish was: *La red que ha salvado a toda una comunidad agrícola*: www.publico .es/videos/633511/la-red-que-ha-salvado-a-toda-una-comunidad-agricola
4. Rosalba's statement on video footage: www.youtube.com/watch?v=Mk8eLudISOM

5. Official census 2005 reports 10,157 habitants in Toca.

REFERENCES

IDPC. (2022). Call for a great peace declaration of the commission for the clarification of truth, coexistence and non-repetition. https://idpc.net/publications/2022/08/call-for-a-great-peace-declaration-of-the-commission-for-the-clarification-of-truth-coexistence-and-non-repetition

INNpulsa Colombia. (2018). www.innpulsacolombia.com/es/nuestra-organizacion

MINTIC. (2012). Informe de gestión al Congreso de la República. https://mintic.gov.co/images/documentos/informes_congreso/mintic-informe-congreso-2012.pdf

MINTIC. (2018). App.co Es Una Oportunidad. https://App.co/acerca/appsco/#que-es

Patiño, L.C.A. (2012). Campesinos sin tierra, tierra sin campesinos: territorio, conflicto y resistencia campesina en Colombia. *Revista Nera 16*, 81–95.

Seelos, C. and J. Mair (2017). *Innovation and Scaling Impact: How Effective Enterprises Do It*. Stanford University Press.

Shark Tank. (2018). Sobre Shark Tank Colombia. https://la.canalsony.com/programas/sharktankcolombia

4

Brazil's rising social enterprise star Ribon: the challenge of quantifying social impact

Marcia Carvalho de Azevedo, Francine Schlosser, Luis Hernan Contreras Pinochet, Vanessa Itacaramby Pardim, and Helena Brito de Freitas

1. RIBON: AN INNOVATIVE SOCIALTECH APPLICATION

Ribon is an app (https://app.ribon.io/) that enables users to allocate money to social projects with virtual donations. The Ribon app is distinct because it allows users to donate without spending their own money; essentially, they donate their "time" in a virtual way, and the "time donated" is transformed into cash donations financed by platform sponsors. While using the app, users can simultaneously practice an online activism while they perform tasks related to social issues, such as reading news or wellness advice. By reading articles or watching videos, users increase their personal knowledge of global social issues and earn the virtual currency, called "ribon" (Figure 4.1). News is posted daily on the app and users can convert, at any time, their ribons to donations to social projects carried out by non-governmental organizations (NGOs) listed on the app. Users can convert their ribons (Ribon currency) to donations to support these social projects at any time. The money for the donations is financed by sponsors whose names are associated with the donations. Ribon users can also become voluntary donors themselves through a paid subscription. The Ribon platform retains a fixed percentage of the money received by its sponsors (the major source of the organization income) and its subscriber base to finance its operation costs.

When Ribon's owners decided to start the business in 2016, their purpose was to have a business that would make the world a better place. They believed that Ribon's business model achieved this goal as it promoted two complementary objectives: (1) to support organizations that develop social initiatives and (2) to promote philanthropy behavior among its users. Since the start of Ribon operations in 2016, the company has been recognized as an innovative socialtech. Consequently, it has attracted a lot of attention in the media. Through the years it

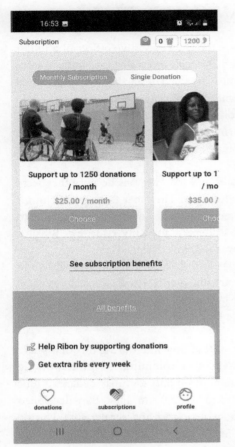

Source: Ribon Foundation (version 5.1.4). Google Play Store. Authorized by Ribon Foundation.

Figure 4.1 The app's initial screen and subscription screen

grew its user base and was able to attract venture capital. However, to have long-term sustainable growth the company needed to retain and continually increase its user and donor bases. This goal was complicated because Ribon's users and sponsors didn't have direct contact with the individuals, communities, and organizations who benefited from their donations.

The company is owned by three partners who realized the need to measure Ribon's impact on the social projects it supported. This requires a structured way to evaluate the impact of the social projects promoted and supported by the donations managed by Ribon. With this information, Ribon is able to better inform its different stakeholders about organizational achievements. Ribon's entrepreneurial team decided to hire a consulting company to propose indicators to be used in an evaluation structure adapted to Ribon's profile. Ribon is intending to participate in a new investment round in six months and the evaluation structure will need to be ready in this time frame.

2. THE BEGINNING: A DREAM COMES TRUE

Rafael Rodeiro, a production engineering student, was the chief executive officer of a junior enterprise at the Universidade de Brasilia in Brazil. He was deeply interested in helping to solve social problems and promoting philanthropy, and he also dreamed of starting a business based on social innovation. His initial idea was to launch a mobile application on which users could donate without spending their own money. Donations would be financed by sponsors and users would receive resources for donations by performing some socially-related tasks. Rafael decided to look for partners with complementary competencies by seeking potential venture co-founders with programming and design expertise.

Rafael Cordeiro already knew Carlos Menezes (Juju) and João Moraes because they were all members of different university-related junior enterprises. They met through the Junior Enterprise Movement, a program that encouraged and prepared undergraduate students to become entrepreneurs. They were also undergraduate students at the Universidade de Brasilia, where Juju was studying computer science and João was studying design.

In 2016, Rafael, Juju, and João had several meetings and realized that they would like to work together as business partners. They believed their competencies and personalities complemented each other. Ribon was created in June 2016 in Brasilia, with the objective of creating a solution that would support social projects and popularize the giving habit among young people, mainly Generation Z and Millennials.

All three co-founders had other activities going on at that time and during this first phase of the company things evolved slowly. They kept their other commitments while working together to develop the business. All of them woke up at dawn and routinely dedicated four hours every day exclusively to the business from 5:00 a.m. to 9:00 a.m. First, they developed the app's prototype and started conversations with angel investors and accelerators. During this time a friend of Juju, who believed in Ribon's project, arranged a loan that would pay two months' salaries so that the entrepreneurs would be able to work full time on their startup.

In the founders' view the app promoted a culture of volunteering. Its virtual operation was very appealing to Millennials and fostered strong donation behavior among younger people (70 percent of the users had performed their first donation through the Ribon platform). It was not a "Millennials-only" app, as anybody could download it, but this group made up 89 percent of its users. Using the Ribon app, users were able to donate virtually, performing online activism when they read news or performed some social-related task. By reading this news (about global social issues) or performing tasks on other platforms through integration, such as watching a video or going to the gym, they increased their personal knowledge of global social issues or improved their well-being. In this process users earned a virtual currency, called "ribon." This currency could later be exchanged at any time by users for donations to the organization of their choice in the application base. The money for the donations was financed by sponsors whose names were associated with the donations (Gentil, 2020).

The process of choosing which NGOs to include in the app was based on a few main criteria. Ribon would reach out to new organizations if the organization or the project matched the values and interests of Ribon and if the charity had a strong position in established charity rankings such as Give Well and The Life You Can Save, that certified and evaluated the impact of NGOs worldwide.

Ribon increased the amount of money for donations received by sponsors as users could voluntarily donate their own money. Some users liked the business model and became donors themselves, with the majority of the users that made donations with their own money becoming monthly subscribers. Subscribers could choose between four different values to donate every month (US$5, US$7, US$10, or US$20). Ribon retained a fixed percentage of the money received from the sponsors and users to finance its operation costs. From sponsors, 70 percent of the value was directed to donations and the remaining 30 percent was directed to finance Ribon operations. When it came to user donations, almost everything (93 percent) was directed to donations, with the company retaining only a small percentage of the amount received to cover basic operational costs. The value of a ribon was not disclosed by the owners because they wanted to take the focus away from the monetary value and wanted to emphasize instead the impact resulting from the donation.

When an organization or project was chosen by Ribon, they set a goal of how much money the organization was going to receive, usually associated with a specific project or target. This meant that most NGOs were only listed in the app for a certain amount of time and then were replaced by new organizations, in a type of rotation. The inclusion of new organizations and rotation of others enabled Ribon to help many different projects over time and broadened the user experience. After users donated their chosen amount of ribons to their preferred organization, Ribon converted the virtual coins to Brazilian currency, so the funding could be utilized by the NGOs.

The company received venture capital from the outset of its operation. The first investment of US$3,000 was made at the beginning of the project in 2016 by an angel investor who was a friend of one of the owners. The money was used to finance the development of the application, paying one month's salary for the partners (Rafael, Juju, and João). In 2016, the first year of its operation, Ribon was selected by a startup accelerator to participate in an investment round. In 2017 they received funds of approximately US$32,000. At this time the owners started to work full time at Ribon but, by the end of 2017, the company had run out of cash and almost closed. At this point, the owners started to work part time in other places and stopped receiving an income from Ribon.

This situation was overcome thanks to another investment of US$41,000 made by a government research support fund in 2018. The year of 2019 was very important for the company, as Ribon participated in its first round of investment, raising US$300,000. In the same year it participated in a second round of investment, raising about the same amount of venture capital. The capital enabled Ribon to invest in technology development that resulted in the implementation of a blockchain system (Gentil, 2020).

Although Ribon had initiated operations in 2016, it wasn't until 2018 that Ribon made the first donation to four NGOs. Since then, its impact has been steadily growing. In 2019 it reached 1 million donations. Over the next few years the company received many prizes related to startups, and was selected to participate in business competitions around the world. Ribon and its owners were also listed in some rankings. For example, the company was included in the 100 Startups To Watch list from Globo (Gomes, 2019), and Rafael was included in the Forbes 2019 list as a promising young founder (30 and under) in the innovation and technology category.

The onset of the COVID-19 pandemic challenged most organizations, and for Ribon it was no different. COVID-19 forced the company to change its business model. At the beginning of its operations Ribon contributed to four NGOs that were located outside of Brazil. Over the years, the number of assisted NGOs increased and during the course of the year 2020 Ribon began to include Brazilian NGOs in its platform. By 2021, Ribon was donating money to 18 different NGOs for feeding (4), health (9), education (3), and inclusion initiatives (2). Of these, 13 were Brazilian and 5 were not.

Ribon reached 2021 with a new beta version that enabled the integration of its interface with any digital platform, and it also included philanthropists in its donor base and adopted blockchain technology. In 2021 its business model received recognition by the Bill and Melinda Gates Foundation as one of the ten most creative and innovative solutions in the world in the philanthropy area. It was the only Latin American and non-English-speaking startup to be included in the final list of the 400 projects evaluated (Ingizza, 2021; Pompeo & Simonds, 2021). The Ribon headquarters was still based in Brasilia and by the beginning of 2022 the team was composed of 18 people working in development, design, growth, communication, sales, business, and finance. The website of Ribon explains how the company operated (https://ribon.io/en/).

3.   VOLUNTEERING IN THE DIGITAL ERA

Ribon was unique in that it offered users the potential to donate money to social projects without spending its own funds. Users could provide funds to organizations that helped individuals and communities in a variety of initiatives related to food, health, education, and inclusion. It functioned on computers, tablets, and mobile phones, but it was accessed mainly through mobile phones. The app had versions in two languages, Portuguese (official language of Brazil) and English, and the option to change the language setting was available on all the webpages. The app was easy to operate and had gamification features that increased user engagement.

There were other applications available on the internet through which individuals could donate money to social projects. But the business model of these other applications was based, at least in part, on the donation of money from the users themselves. The possibility for users to donate their own money to social projects was also available in the Ribon app through subscriptions or one-time donations, but it was not mandatory and only a small percentage of app users chose to make use of this feature (Gentil, 2020). Ribon differentiated itself from other donation apps because the business model emphasized the promotion of philanthropic behavior, and not only the donations themselves, in order to create a more holistic impact on users and society.

4.   COMPETITIVE ENVIRONMENT

Ribon had no direct competitors in the traditional sense, meaning organizations that offered a similar product or service. A search for information about Ribon's competitors, on Similarweb, a website that identifies industry competitors based on web analytics and data mining, revealed that the four closest competitors were in completely different segments (orthotoolkit – orthopedic tools; Bigwhite – ski resort facility; Mirait Group – engineering and service company; 3D Sex Galleries – free 3D adult cartoons) (Similarweb, n.d.).

From a broader perspective, it was clear that Ribon was competing for users' attention and time, especially in the mobile phone app segment. Since it was an online free app, all Brazilians could be acknowledged as potential clients for the Portuguese app version, a group of 212 million people (IBGE, n.d.). For the English version of Ribon, all native English speakers could also be considered potential clients, a population of 400 million people worldwide (Melo, 2021).

The online environment was very competitive regarding the number of existing mobile apps and the number of new entrants. The number of apps available in Google Play Store rose steadily until March 2018 when it reached its peak with 3.60 million. The quantity of available apps has since been fluctuating. This churn happened because Google Play Store was highly competitive and some of the players weren't able to stay in the market. Regarding apps in Apple Store, the number rose steadily until July 2020 and since then has remained stable. By 2021 Google Play Store had 3.48 million apps available for download and Apple Store had 2.22 million. It is important to note that there was a high turnover rate in the app market, so that even when the number of existing players appeared stable, there were many apps being discontinued, while at the same time, many new ones entered the market. Another important figure was the increasing number of downloads, which grew from 140 billion downloads in 2016 to 230 billion in 2021 (Buildfire, 2021; Statista, 2021).

Ribon was classified as a lifestyle app among 35 different categories in Google Play Store. Named "Ribon – Charity donation without spending money," the app was accompanied by a video named "Ribon – Creating the habit of good deeds." This sentence was not chosen at random; it was deeply connected with Ribon's philosophy and reason for existence. As defined by the Ribon owners, the company's goal was to revolutionize the way Brazilians practiced philanthropy. The philanthropy habit was well established in other countries, but this had not been the case in Brazil.

5.   RIBON'S PHILOSOPHY AND GOALS

As Millennials themselves, the Ribon founders were keen to build a business aligned with their principles and world vision. They wished to create an organization that held significant meaning for them. They developed a unique business model that combined people, who were sensitive to social problems but were not regular donors, and organizations, who already wanted to contribute to social projects. They knew that their target market of Generation Z and Millennial groups were very involved in the discussion of issues related to social justice and the importance of collectively facing social challenges. The Ribon team also recognized that these groups were not comfortable with the traditional structure and process used by charity organizations, which caused them to resist donating to charities and limited their engagement as donors. Additionally, Millennials were born in an interconnected world and were identified as digital natives. They grew up in an environment surrounded by mobile phones and learned to perform daily activities through information technology tools, regularly using mobile apps.

Based on their personal ideals and perceptions, Rafael, Juju, and João identified a business opportunity to develop a system that was aligned with Millennials' digital environment. This would enable individuals concerned with social causes to donate money to social projects by volunteering their time to perform virtual tasks. The Ribon application was born from this vision. The use of the app could also enable users to have a positive experience and, as a result, sensitize them to the impact that their donations could have on people's lives. With this information, some voluntary users might convert to regular subscribers. The business model that combined sponsors and individual donors made it possible for Ribon to increase institutional donations up to 60 percent. By 2022, the version of the Ribon app enabled the owners of the company to achieve their initial goals: to help social projects, to contribute to the construction of individual donation culture among users, to increase the amount of money made available by sponsors to social projects, and to enable people without financial means to donate to causes they cared about. Ribon's operational model is represented in Figure 4.2.

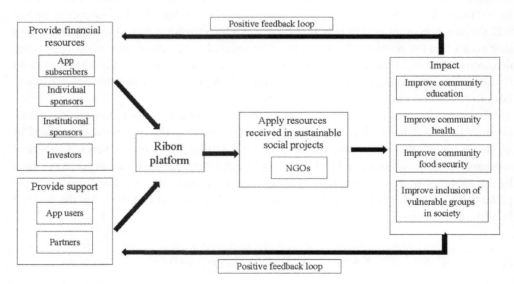

Figure 4.2   Ribon's operational model

6.   NEW CHALLENGES: COMMUNICATING IMPACT IN AN ONLINE ENVIRONMENT

Like any organization, Ribon's existence relied on the stability of its client base and support of its stakeholders. In Ribon's case, the client base was composed of three different groups: sponsors, users, and the organizations that received the funds donated. Ribon needed to be able to attract, maintain, and engage its clients, with engagement being a central element regarding user behavior. The three groups of clients were closely connected and impacted by each other. When Ribon attracted more users, it became more attractive to sponsors and was able to increase the number of organizations attended by donations, feeding a virtuous circle of philanthropy. The management of Ribon needed to consider all its stakeholders, not only users, for the planning and functioning of the organization. Stakeholders provided different kinds of resources and were impacted by Ribon's activities in different ways. Evan and Freeman (1988) and Mitchell et al.'s (1997) stakeholder theories are a good reference for the mapping and understanding of the stakeholders that are relevant for Ribon.

One very sensitive aspect for the organizations that made donations was the communication of their donations' impact on the target audience. For Ribon, with a business model based on an application that operated with virtual donations, this aspect was even more important. The loyalty of sponsors and users was influenced by multiple variables, for example, the engagement of both groups was impacted by the perceived effect of their donations on people's lives. Transparency and confidence in Ribon's operational decisions, with respect to (1) the criteria Ribon used to select charities to be part of their platform and (2) the impact evaluation of the donations received by the charities, were also important to both stakeholders.

Another aspect that was important specifically for users was the app's stability and ease of use. The existence of gamification elements positively impacted the user experience, particularly among Millennials. Gamification features that provided a pleasant experience while using the app were included in more recent versions, consequently enhancing engagement and usage. The inclusion of gamification elements was prioritized by the owners, as they believed instead of just being an obligation, donations should propitiate pleasure.

Sponsors valued the additional features of the Ribon platform, for example, the efficiency of the structure and processes, the ability to increase the amount of donations received by sponsors, and the ability to apply them for the benefit of reliable and competent NGOs.

In order to increase the confidence of its users in the app's donation system, the application published monthly proofs of donation, and users could verify in their profile the exact number of ribons donated for each selected cause and numerical information about the impact of the assistance provided. But there was no detailed follow-up about the organizations and projects funded by Ribon, nor information about the long-term impact on the lives of the people helped by the sponsors and app users.

Ribon's website explained the app's goal was to "actualize the target of eliminating poverty by 2030" (Souza, 2022). Ribon's dreams were bold, but so were its challenges. Ribon's platform work had impacted almost 220,000 people, with more than US$200,000 donated by 318,000 users by March 2022. Ribon was ready to continue to grow, but to reach this goal it needed to increase its client base and also its donor base. As important as increasing the number of users and sponsors was to keep Ribon's stakeholders informed about the impact of the social projects funded by Ribon.

During the first years, Ribon was so small that the growth was exponential. However, in order to continue to have a sustainable expansion it needed to be able to clearly communicate its social impact, targeting each stakeholder individually, according to their specific interests. It needed to know the opinions of their clients, and the success stories of the NGOs funded. Rafael, Juju, and João decided that they needed help in identifying the most effective ways to quantify and communicate Ribon's social impact to all relevant stakeholders.

7.   THE CHALLENGE OF CONNECTING VIRTUAL ACTIVISTS WITH IN-PERSON SOCIAL PROJECTS

Ribon's owners perceived the need to strengthen company ties with its stakeholders, being able to efficiently communicate the positive impact their involvement with the app had on people's lives. They found Business Model Canvas (BMC) to be very informative and an important resource to communicate the value proposition of an organization to different audiences (Osterwalder & Pigneur, 2010). BMC has been widely used and Upward and Jones (2016) subsequently adapted the model for organizations that focus on sustainability. This "flourishing" BMC seemed to be suited to social organizations such as Ribon.

They also perceived the difficulties associated with measuring the impact of investment in social projects where each stakeholder, and specifically each group of clients, had differentiated interests. Despite having a workforce of talented people, the Ribon entrepreneurial team knew they would need the help of external and unbiased consultants to accomplish these tasks. They invited consultants to present proposals to help Ribon better communicate its business model to its stakeholders and propose a system of indicators of impact evaluation that would reflect Ribon's social initiatives. Krocil and Pospisil (2018) proposed such a model to evaluate the social return on investment that is composed of 13 phases. The first six phases of this model focused on collecting information. This information would be used to choose the best indicators that would be important to all the relevant stakeholders.

Your consulting team has been chosen. You have a meeting next week with Ribon's owners (Rafael, Juju, and João) to present a proposal for the company. Your assignment is to work together to analyze the available information, collect additional data if necessary, and present a proposal of a system of indicators to evaluate Ribon's impact on the initiatives supported based on the six first phases of Krocil and Pospisil's method. You should also identify all relevant stakeholders and elaborate a BMC appropriate for a social enterprise that could inform its stakeholders in a clear and responsive way about the strengths, uniqueness, and differentials of its business model. You intend to use the Flourishing Business Canvas (FBC) tool, the adapted version of BMC, as FBC includes the concept of sustainability in its architecture, a very important aspect for social enterprises. You have a challenging task to accomplish, so get your team together to prepare the material for the proposal presentation next week. Owners also asked for proposals from two of your competitors, and you must work hard in order to prepare the best proposal and win a new client!

ACKNOWLEDGMENTS

We would like to thank João Moraes, Carlos Menezes (Juju), and Rafael Cordeiro for all the information they shared with us and their support for the development of this case.

REFERENCES

Buildfire. (2021). Mobile app download statistics and usage statistics. Retrieved April 21, 2022, from https://buildfire.com/app-statistics/

Evan, W. M. & Freeman, E. R. (1988). A stakeholder theory of the modern corporation: Kantian capitalism. In Beauchamp, T. L. & Bowie, N. E. (eds), *Ethical Theory and Business*. Englewood Cliffs NJ: Prentice Hall.

Gentil, C. (2020). A Ribon Incentiva a Filantropia entre millenials com um aplicativo que permite doar sem gastar um tostão. Retrieved April 26, 2022, from www.projetodraft.com/a-ribon-incentiva -millennials-a-doar-sem-gastar-um-tostao/

Gomes, T. (2019). As 100 startups brasileiras para você ficar de olho. Retrieved April 26, 2022, from https://revistapegn.globo.com/Startups/noticia/2019/05/100-startups-brasileiras-para-voce-ficar-de -olho.html

IBGE. (n.d.). Portal do IBGE. Retrieved March 2, 2022, from www.ibge.gov.br/index.php

Ingizza, C. (2021). Brasileira Ribon é eleita uma das startups mais inovadoras do mundo pela fundação do Bill Gates. Retrieved April 21, 2022, from https://exame.com/pme/brasileira-ribon-e-eleita-uma -das-startups-mais-inovadoras-do-mundo-pela-fundacao-do-bill-gates/

Krocil, O. & Pospisil, R. (2018). Comprehensive measurement of social enterprise impact. *Ekonomski Pregled*, 69(5), 594–609.

Melo, M. (2021, February 1). Países que falam inglês no mundo: você sabe quais são? Retrieved April 21, 2022 from, www.ie.com.br/intercambio/paises-que-falam-ingles/

Mitchell, R. K., Agle, B. R., & Wood, D. J. (1997). Toward a theory of stakeholder identification and salience: Defining the principle of who and what really counts. *Academy of Management Review*, 22(4), 853–886.

Osterwalder, A. & Pigneur, Y. (2010). *Business Model Generation: A Handbook for Visionaries, Game Changers, and Challengers*. Hoboken, NJ: Wiley.

Pompeo, C. & Simonds, L. (2021). Brazilian socialtech Ribon is recognized among the most innovative in the world by the Bill and Melinda Gates Foundation. Retrieved April 21, 2022, from https://labsnews .com/en/articles/technology/brazilian-socialtech-ribon-is-recognized-by-gates-foundation/

Similarweb. (n.d.). Análise de Tráfego e Participação de Mercado ribon.io. Retrieved April 21, 2022, from www.similarweb.com/pt/website/ribon.io/#overview

Souza, A. (2022). The culture of giving: A remedy to poverty eradication. Retrieved September 12, 2023, from https://ribon.io/en/the-culture-of-giving-a-remedy-to-poverty-eradication/

Statista. (2021). Number of apps available in leading app stores as of 3rd quarter 2020. Retrieved April 21, 2022, from www.statista.com/statistics/276623/number-of-apps-available-in-leading-app-stores/

Upward, A. & Jones, P. (2016). An ontology for strongly sustainable business models: Defining an enterprise framework compatible with natural and social science. *Organization & Environment*, 29(1), 97–123.

5

Urban Foundry: a purposeful business model

Beth Cummings, Samantha Burvill, and Ben Reynolds

1.   INTRODUCTION

Urban Foundry is a creative regeneration agency forging great ideas to change the world for the better – improving people's lives, making great places and building business with purpose. They help people to make their good ideas happen, to make them last and to demonstrate that they are making a difference. The business is a creative thinking organisation, grounded in theory with an entrepreneurial approach. They offer a variety of consultancy services including workshops and training, events and pop ups, social enterprise services, marketing, research and evaluation, fundraising and consultancy services around buildings and places and arts and culture. The company was founded in 2004 by Ben Reynolds.[1]

The company is Swansea's first (Wales' second) B Corp – an independently accredited global standard, which shows that businesses are balancing purpose and profit. B Corps amend their constitutions so that they are legally required to consider the impact of their decisions on their workers, customers, suppliers, community and the environment.

The company has seven employees and a number of associates who work on a freelance basis. Based in Swansea, the organisation delivers projects predominantly in South Wales but also undertakes work across the United Kingdom (UK). Their client base is drawn from the public, private and third sectors. Their projects fall broadly under the heading of 'Regeneration'. Some of their projects they undertake on a consultancy basis whilst others they choose to undertake themselves, essentially operating under a purposeful business model. Urban Foundry has at its heart a moral and ethical commitment to making the world a better place and puts this above a focus on financial return.

In March 2020 the COVID-19 global pandemic occurred, impacting organisations and people all over the world. In December 2021 the organisation's B Corp certification was due for renewal. The founder and owner of Urban Foundry, Ben Reynolds, has to make a choice that has to be justified to the stakeholders (communities, local government, financial partners, customers, local businesses) – whether to stick to his B Corp registration principles during this difficult period, whether to change to a social enterprise or whether to simply have corporate social responsibility (CSR) policies. This decision is not about the survival of the company but is about whether the business should continue to invest time and resources into maintaining its B Corp status during this difficult period or whether it would be better redirecting those resources elsewhere. What should Ben do? Time is critical and Ben only has a few weeks before his B Corp registration expires.

2. THE INFLUENCE OF SOCIAL PURPOSE ON URBAN FOUNDRY

Urban Foundry is an organisation operating in a time where social purpose and businesses operating in a way that benefits not just the organisation but society, communities and the environment are extremely important. Urban Foundry, like many others, is influenced by social and political changes, and the organisation must make business decisions in light of changing social and global landscapes. Recognising the significant global challenges and the need to develop policy and practice across the developed and developing world, the 2030 Agenda for Sustainable Development was adopted in 2015 by all United Nations member states. The commitment by the United Nations members comprises 17 Sustainable Development Goals (SDGs). The SDGs' aim is to act as a call to action and increase global commitment to improve human lives and protect the natural environment. Recent literature builds on this phenomenon, referring to it as purposeful business (Wilson 2015). A purposeful business is one that combines selling a product/service with tackling a problem or challenge in the world. The sale of products and services enables this positive change. Purposeful business was a term coined by the British Academy (2019) in their 'Principles for purposeful business' report. In this they argue that 'businesses have the potential to profitably solve the problems of people and the planet and to prevent businesses from profiting from harm'. In order for organisations to consider their role within this and to actively align their activities to making positive change, there are a number of benchmarks, frameworks and certifications to support businesses to achieve these goals. Local-level application and monitoring of change can be seen through the adoption of B Corp accreditation, evaluation of the economy for the common good matrix and initiatives such as the Well-Being of Future Generations (Wales) Act 2015.

For an organisation that wishes to engage in social purpose initiatives so as to balance their profit with purpose there are a number of different options that they can choose from – having CSR strategies/policies, becoming a social enterprise or becoming a B Corp. *CSR* is a self-regulating business model that helps a company to be socially accountable – to itself, its stakeholders and the public. The European Union defines CSR as: 'The voluntary integration of companies' social and ecological concerns into their business activities and their relationships with their stakeholders. Being socially responsible means not only fully satisfying the applicable legal obligations but also going beyond and investing "more" in human capital, the environment, and stakeholder relations.'

Social enterprises on the other hand must meet the following principles: the business has a clear social or environmental mission that is set out in its governing documents; the business is independent and earns more than half its income through trading (or is working towards this); the business is controlled or owned in the interests of a social mission; the business rein-vests or gives away at least half the profits or surpluses towards the social purpose; and there is transparency about how the business operates and the impact that it has.

A *B Corp* is something that is considered to be closely linked to CSR (Andre, 2012; Hiller, 2013) but B Corp is something that takes purposeful business to the next level and enables this to be certified and branded. B Corps are defined as 'businesses that meet the highest standards of verified social and environmental performance, public transparency and legal accountability to balance profit and purpose' (B Lab Global, 2022). B Corp launched in 2007 and represents a shift in global culture away from a focus on purely monetary returns to a focus on sustainability and inclusivity. Organisations that achieve B Corp status use their profits and growth to enable positive impact for their employees, communities and the environment. The B in B Corp stands for beneficial. The B Corp 'Declaration of interdependence' (n.d.) states:

> We envision a global economy that uses business as a force for good. This economy consists of a new type of corporation – the B Corporation – which is purpose-driven and creates benefit for all stakeholders, not just shareholders. As B Corporations and leaders of this emerging economy, we believe that we must be the change we seek in the world. That all business ought to be conducted as if people and place mattered. That, through their prod-ucts, practices, and profits, businesses should aspire to do no harm and benefit all. To do so requires that we act with the understanding that we are each dependent upon another and thus responsible for each other and future generations.

In order to achieve B Corp certification, organisations are assessed by a not-for-profit organ-isation called B Lab, who assesses the company using the B Impact Assessment (BIA) Score. BIA assesses the organisation's overall impact on its stakeholders and the score indicates how a company creates a positive impact in five areas: the governance; the company's workers; the customers; the community; and the environment. To achieve B Corp status an organisation must achieve a score of 80 points on the BIA out of a possible 200 points and the organisation must recertify every three years. The governance dimension covers the organisational mission and policies and practices. The workers dimension covers pay gap, worker benefits, training and education, job flexibility and culture. The community dimension covers local involve-ment, diversity and inclusion, civic engagement and community practices. The customer dimension covers whether the organisation provides products and services for underserved populations. The environment dimension covers the environmental consciousness of the organisation's operations. The cost of the annual certification fee depends on the company's revenue but starts at £1000 per year.

B Lab argues that this enables consumers to make informed choices as to their purchasing decisions. Certified B Corporations have to achieve a minimum verified score on the BIA which undertakes an in-depth assessment of the impact of an organisation on its workers, cus-tomers, community and environment. They are legally required to consider the impact of their decisions on their workers, customers, suppliers, community and the environment (Gazzola et al., 2019; Stubbs, 2017a). Fifty-five per cent of respondents to a B Lab survey believe that being a B Corp has contributed to improving the resilience of the business. From March to

July 2020 only 20 per cent of B Corps postponed or abandoned projects or initiatives linked to their social and environmental impact. These statistics highlight why B Corp status would be attractive to investors. UK B Corps reported an average growth rate of 14 per cent, 28 times higher than the national average (Sustainable Brands, 2018). B Corp registration is also seen to be a way of contributing to the SDGs (Stubbs, 2017a; Tabares, 2020). It is argued that B Corps pursue profits to enable them to create positive social and environmental outcomes, making profit a means to an end (Stubbs, 2017b).

However, despite the literature and research pointing to the positive impact of B Corp and B Corp registration there is also some research that points to the drawbacks of this type of business model. For instance, Parker et al. (2019) found that organisations who had B Corp certification had an average 20 per cent short-term growth penalty, suggesting that initial registration does negatively impact growth. B Corp registration can also be costly and some argue that it is not well known enough amongst consumers to impact purchasing decisions (Moroz & Gamble, 2020). Koehn (2016) argues that B Corp certification focus on multiple stakeholders can mean that the management of these can be very difficult.

Urban Foundry must constantly assess their business model in light of these different ways in which they could engage in purposeful business initiatives. Every decision they make has an impact on their business in terms of time, money, resources and ultimately their ethical and moral standpoint.

3. THE FOUNDATION OF URBAN FOUNDRY

Urban Foundry was founded in 2004 by Ben Reynolds, who has a PhD in urban regeneration. The approach of the organisation is multi-disciplinary and collaborative and combines creative thinking with a pragmatic entrepreneurial approach. The organisation has expertise in what makes people and places tick and that informs everything it does. It believes that everyone has the potential to generate great ideas and as such it works with a wide range of stakeholders. These include businesses, social enterprises, charities and non-profit organisations, people in communities, funding bodies, universities and the public sector. The organisation works across Wales and England and its work ranges from small community projects and micro-enterprises through to multi-million pound countrywide initiatives.

Urban Foundry's work is extremely varied but is always based on strong ethical and moral principles of purposeful business. It offers workshops and training focusing on measuring change and impact, CSR, writing winning funding bids, undertaking organisational health checks and business and marketing planning. It offers event management, design and social media support and pop-up events. It specialises in assisting social enterprises to develop their business. They also offer marketing services as well as research and evaluation services, enabling organisations to analyse their impact for both themselves and their stakeholders. It offers community consultation and engagement services as well as regeneration strategies focused on place making and urban design. It assists businesses with fundraising and has a strong focus on arts and culture.

Ben Reynolds, founder and owner of Urban Foundry, classifies his business as being centred around urban and community regeneration. The following is Reynolds' view of this industry and his business as a whole in his own words:

Regeneration is a very broad term, and frequently poorly defined. We take it to mean the process of creating resilience (you might also say 'sustainability') in economic, environmental and social terms (some would add culture as a fourth element, though you might think of the third term as socio-cultural as the final element is intended to relate to people's lives and how they experience the world). Note that the 'environmental' element is both the natural as well as the built environment – the environment(s) that we as humans inhabit, which can take a variety of forms.

Regeneration is the notion that there are problems with the system that need to be resolved (or at least mitigated) and it is the process of addressing these issues that we are engaged with at a variety of scales.

Urban Foundry undertakes commissions for third-party clients to provide advice and support in a variety of forms to help them to address various economic, environmental or societal needs.

Our work falls into three broad areas (though these often overlap):

- Identifying problems and creating the solutions to them in the first place (making good ideas happen), e.g. we might undertake a feasibility study, advise on policy or strategy, assist in developing a business plan or directly create a mechanism to address a particular problem or problems.
- Identifying and addressing the resilience of the processes that we create or already have, which serve to address these problems (making good ideas last), e.g. we might undertake a health check of an existing organisation and identify areas where they could improve, we might support them with an already identified area where they are seeking help such as their marketing perhaps or they might be seeking to develop such as moving from rented accommodation to taking on their first building or perhaps developing the building they are already in.
- Articulating and demonstrating the impact of the above and how they might be improved (ensuring good ideas make a difference), e.g. assisting people to better understand and articulate what their purpose is and why, assisting various organisations to create meaningful ways of assessing their success or undertaking assessments of their impact for them.

We refer to ourselves as a 'creative regeneration agency' – what we do is multi-disciplinary, and combines social/urban theory with creative thinking and a practical socially entrepreneurial approach. Whilst there are many of our competitors who do at least one of these well, very few effectively combine all three elements – that is our 'USP'.

We have a core team of staff to assist in the delivery of our own projects, as well as to deliver for third parties. The way we win work is via public tender where work is advertised and competitions are held (usually by the public or third sectors), via direct referrals to us (some of it through developing our own networks), occasionally through direct sales and also by creating our own projects that have their own dedicated income streams (e.g. the street market projects or a pop-up venue).

By its nature, regeneration is eclectic – it requires a multi-disciplinary approach and there are no two projects that are exactly the same. But there are commonalities, which are what led to us forming the company, which are:

- inequality and deprivation in many communities;
- unsustainable places;
- a fledgling social economy with significant scope for growth;
- a third sector more generally that has varying degrees of resilience;
- lack of specialist knowledge of how places and spaces work to inform regeneration decisions;
- lack of capacity – resources, time, knowledge and experience to make change happen/ make it last (a lack of civic 'entrepreneurialism');
- relatively weak partnership approaches and an overriding 'state-first' approach to change;
- complex interactions between various issues/stakeholder groups that are not easy to resolve;
- causal relationships between people, place and prosperity that are relatively weakly addressed in regeneration and undertheorised/evidence-based where they are adopted;
- poor relation of need to desired impact guiding approaches; and
- relatively weak capacity for understanding and articulating the impacts of change-making projects.

4. URBAN FOUNDRY: IN PRACTICE

Urban Foundry undertakes some of their own projects (non-consulted) and consulted projects that are delivered for third parties. The following provides an example of each of these types of projects to give a sense of Urban Foundry's mission and core values.

4.1 Unit Nineteen – own project (non-consulted)

4.1.1 The idea

Transform a disused nightclub in Little Wind Street, Swansea into a pop-up events space and offer engaging and vibrant activities to new audiences. Wind Street is a part of the city that is very heavily focused on a pub and club late-night economy, catering to a specific demographic. The landlord wanted to broaden the offer and change perceptions of the area.

4.1.2 What happened

Unit Nineteen was conceived as a pop-up multi-purpose space with a series of socially enter-prising creative initiatives focused on attracting new audiences and changing perceptions of the area. Street Food Friday ran monthly and brought an array of delicious Welsh street food (with options for vegans and gluten-free diets), live music and a pop-up bar to Little Wind

Street from 5pm – 9:30pm. It was sponsored by Swansea BID and City & County of Swansea as part of their work to enhance Swansea's early-evening economy. An indoor park was created for two weeks to promote Natural Resources Wales' work on the ecological and social benefits of green spaces (particularly in urban areas). The park hosted wellbeing and yoga classes, a conference on green infrastructure and free play sessions for children. The project, initially designed for a short three-month run, was so successful that it ended up running for almost two years, featuring live music events, mini-festivals, workshops, launches and classes, sip and sketch painting sessions, exhibitions and a range of other activities.

4.1.3   The impact

The venue was incredibly popular, attracting large crowds every month, with the Street Food Friday events particularly attracting significant interest. The majority of attendees were people dropping in after work and families – people who would not usually visit the city centre in the early evening. Feedback was overwhelmingly positive, with people feeling that it met a real need in Swansea, and lots of demand was expressed for more activities and events. It also featured in the *Guardian* newspaper (2017) with innovative projects that were trialling 'pop-up' activities across the UK.

The aim for the landlord was to market a problem empty space to the market for a long-term use, and the project succeeded in doing that with a long-term user signing up.

We are exploring longer-term projects that extend this 'pop-up' approach and it has been used as an exemplar by others seeking to do the same, including forming part of the Welsh Government's considerations of how we 'build back better' from COVID-19. We have subsequently been commissioned by the Welsh Government to further explore developing a more standardised approach to 'meanwhile uses'.

4.2   Missing People – third party consulted

4.2.1   The idea

Missing People is a charity that searches for missing people – children and adults – on behalf of their family and friends, providing specialist support and including a free confidential 24-hour helpline. The charity also provides, and is further developing, support for people after they have been missing, and with this in mind the charity secured funding from The Big Lottery Fund for a Wales-based programme 'Aftercare'.

Added to the project was a new element – a Return Home Interview for adults that have returned from being missing, with the purpose of gathering more information and better understanding their circumstances and with the aim that this (and onward referrals from it) could reduce the chances of them going missing again. Missing People sought support both to implement a new approach, which had not been trialled previously in the UK, and also to evaluate its impact.

4.2.2   What happened

We assisted Missing People to establish the pilot with partner agencies – South Wales Police and Cardiff County Council – to establish the pilot in the Cardiff area and provided support as the project developed through the pilot phase. Towards the end of the pilot additional partner police forces were engaged in North Wales, Gwent and Lincolnshire.

We also delivered a Theory of Change workshop, developed an evaluation framework for the project to utilise and provided Most Significant Change training for Missing People staff to supplement their existing data-gathering processes. The project gathered data and we then collated and analysed that, providing our own supplementary data gathering through a series of one-to-one interviews with project partners and beneficiaries.

4.2.3   The impact

The project was successfully concluded and generated data, both in terms of the impact of the provision but also the process of developing and delivering it and the complexities of delivering such a service. That information has informed the development of the approach to supporting missing persons in future both for Missing People and, through their advocacy work, for supporting missing people more generally in the UK.

5.   COVID-19 AND THE BUSINESS MODEL DILEMMA

In 2020 the world as we know it changed forever with the emergence of the COVID-19 pandemic. As a result of the pandemic, people and organisations are more focused on social purpose, community and the environment than ever before. However, COVID-19 has also put a strain on many businesses around the world, with some thriving during the pandemic while others have left the marketplace. It has been a time when organisations have had to evaluate their business models at a faster rate than they ever have before, with some organisations being forced to completely change their ways of operating. It was during the pandemic that Urban Foundry's B Corp certification was due for renewal. For Ben, the decision as to whether to adhere to the core business model or amend it due to the pandemic is something that is critical to consider.

Ben has to decide whether to stick to his B Corp registration principles during the pandemic, whether to change to a social enterprise or whether to have CSR policies, justifying his decision to his stakeholders (communities, local government, financial partners, customers, local businesses). In order to make this difficult decision Ben has to consider the following:

1. The various ways in which Urban Foundry's practice reflects the B Corp criteria.
2. What makes Urban Foundry (as a B Corp) different to organisations who class themselves as having a CSR policy?
3. Could Urban Foundry be considered as a 'social enterprise' or not?
4. Ultimately, during the global crisis of the pandemic, should Urban Foundry maintain its B Corp status, or take a different approach?

ACKNOWLEDGEMENTS

We would like to thank Ben Reynolds for his contribution to this case study and his support for Swansea University School of Management.

NOTE

1. Ben Reynolds was interviewed in August 2021. All quotes from Reynolds in this chapter are from this interview, unless otherwise stated.

REFERENCES

André, R. (2012). Assessing the accountability of the benefit corporation: Will this new gray sector organization enhance corporate social responsibility? *Journal of Business Ethics, 110*(1), 133–150.

B Corp. (n.d.). Declaration of interdependence. https://bcorporation.uk/b-corp-certification/what-is-a-b-corp/

B Lab Global. (2022). B Lab Global's 2021 annual report. 18 May. https://www.bcorporation.net/en-us/news/blog/b-lab-global-2021-annual-report/

British Academy. (2019). Principles for purposeful business. www.thebritishacademy.ac.uk/publications/future-of-the-corporation-principles-for-purposeful-business/

Gazzola, P., Grechi, D., Ossola, P., & Pavione, E. (2019). Certified benefit corporations as a new way to make sustainable business: The Italian example. *Corporate Social Responsibility and Environmental Management, 26*(6), 1435–1445.

Guardian (2017). Underground circuses and real ale pubs: Your photos of empty city spaces transformed. 3 June. www.theguardian.com/sustainable-business/gallery/2017/jun/03/cities-transformed-derelict-urban-spaces-businesses-community-spaces-arts-housing

Hiller, J. S. (2013). The benefit corporation and corporate social responsibility. *Journal of Business Ethics, 118*(2), 287–301.

Koehn, D. (2016). Why the new benefit corporations may not prove to be truly socially beneficial. *Business and Professional Ethics Journal, 35*(1), 17–50.

Moroz, P. W., & Gamble, E. N. (2020). Business model innovation as a window into adaptive tensions: Five paths on the B Corp journey. *Journal of Business Research, 125*, 672–668.

Parker, S. C., Gamble, E. N., Moroz, P. W., & Branzei, O. (2019). The impact of B lab certification on firm growth. *Academy of Management Discoveries, 5*(1), 57–77.

Stubbs, W. (2017a). Characterising B corps as a sustainable business model: An exploratory study of B Corps in Australia. *Journal of Cleaner Production, 144*, 299–312.

Stubbs, W. (2017b). Sustainable entrepreneurship and B Corps. *Business Strategy and the Environment, 26*, 331–344.

Sustainable Brands (2018). B Corp analysis reveals purpose-led businesses grow 28 times faster than national average. 1 March. https://sustainablebrands.com/read/business-case/b-corp-analysis-reveals-purpose-led-businesses-grow-28-times-faster-than-national-average

Tabares, S. (2020). Do hybrid organizations contribute to sustainable development goals? Evidence from B Corps in Colombia. *Journal of Cleaner Production, 280*, 124615.

Wilson, C. (2015). *Designing the purposeful organization: How to inspire business performance beyond boundaries.* Kogan Page.

6

Sustainable innovation and 3D printing: Comme des Machines' digital craftsmanship in Spain

Zulima Fernández, Antonio Revilla, and Alicia Rodríguez

1. INTRODUCTION

As Aran Azkarate prepares to eat 12 grapes as the bell chimes midnight—a Spanish New Year's Eve tradition—she cannot help thinking that 2022 will be a pivotal year in Comme des Machines' short history. The COVID-19 pandemic has taken a toll on sales, interrupting years of steady growth, and it has put the company's expansion on hold. Now it is time to bounce back and set the future course for the business launched in 2016 by Aran and Jon Azkarate, Suso García León, and Andrés Iglesias, four young Basque entrepreneurs.

The founders of the company want to stay true to their identity as "digital artisans" and focus on exploring the potential of 3D printing as a versatile and sustainable manufacturing technology. The factory floor is, and will remain, the core of the business. They are developing innovative 3D-printed fabrics, still a nascent technology that they think can revolutionize the fashion industry. They are also receiving an increasing flow of commissions from other creative industries. In their growth plans, they are contemplating an extension of their Bilbao workshop, or even opening a second one in Morocco; this would mean hiring additional staff for the first time since the business was launched.

Some external investors that have taken an interest in the company, however, consider it should take a different approach in order to exploit its full potential. They believe that it should pursue a more aggressive growth strategy, proactively investing in sales and marketing and developing a distinctive brand identity. They also think they should expand their focus from manufacturing to design and other activities in the value chain. They think that the company should adopt a more comprehensive business-like mindset rather than focusing too closely on manufacturing.

Leading fashion brands are currently taking a great interest in 3D printing as a manufacturing technology, and the market is expected to boom in the next few years. This will probably translate into rapid sales growth, but also more competitors entering the market. In this context, should Comme des Machines stay on the path set for it by its founders and maintain its independence, or pivot to a different business model, perhaps backed by equity investors?

2.   THE BUSINESS ENVIRONMENT: SUSTAINABLE INNOVATION, 3D PRINTING, AND THE TRANSFORMATION OF THE FASHION INDUSTRY

The fashion industry that constitutes the core of Comme des Machines has been dominated in recent decades by the rise of the fast-fashion phenomenon: clothing that is made available quickly and cheaply for the mass market. Fast fashion has been a huge business success that has led the average consumer to buy 60 percent more clothing than they did 15 years ago and keep each item for half as long (United Nations Environment Programme, 2019). Fashionable garments are cheaper and more widely available than ever before.

This, however, has come at a steep environmental price, which is becoming increasingly apparent. Fashion is heavily reliant on low-cost mass production in low-cost labor countries and global transportation and logistics, making it one of the most polluting industries globally, second only to oil. It accounts for 10 percent of global carbon dioxide emissions, 20 percent of all industrial wastewater, and the consumption of 79 trillion liters of water per year (Niinimäki et al., 2020). An estimated 92 million tons of textile waste are created every year, with the equivalent of one rubbish truck full of clothing ending up in landfill sites every second (Beall, 2020).

There is growing awareness of the need for more sustainable fashion. The "slow fashion" movement promotes mindful and intentional consumption, in which the consumer develops an emotional and cultural connection with quality clothing that they keep for a longer time. Moving beyond fast fashion requires rethinking the industry value chain, with a focus on small batches, local production, and an appreciation of craftsmanship and the unique character of each item. The challenge is to leverage innovation and technology for more sustainable fashion, which should involve end-to-end digitalization of the industry. The digital transformation of the value chain would not only deliver benefits in terms of sustainability, but also create an industry that is more customer-centric, faster and more flexible, and ultimately more efficient in the long term (Hämmerle et al., 2020).

Comme des Machines believes 3D printing can contribute decisively to this new paradigm in the industry, changing the way products are designed, manufactured, distributed, stocked, and sold, and bringing new possibilities for innovation and creativity. According to Aran Azkarate, one of the co-founders, 3D printing "is pushing the industry forward because it forces both the suppliers of materials and equipment and us, the manufacturers, to think differently."[1] However, in order to become an actual force for change in the industry, the technology needs to gain traction as a large-scale manufacturing technique, beyond prototyping, tooling, and the creation of samples.

Additive manufacturing enables intricate and complex shapes and designs that would have been unfeasible or uneconomical otherwise. When it comes to 3D printing, complexity is free, and the "local and personal" come at a much lower cost than they used to. As Avi Reichental

(2018), Founder and Chairman of XponentialWorks, puts it, additive manufacturing is reviving craftsmanship as it is "empowering artists, designers, and makers with affordable, easily accessible tools, not just for dreaming up masterpieces of craft and design but also for creating, exhibiting and monetising them."

It is therefore unsurprising that top designers, such as Iris van Harpen—a global reference in 3D-printed fashion—are pushing the envelope in order to create unique and exclusive designs and collections. Simultaneously, mass-market firms are also becoming increasingly aware of its benefits; the revolutionary potential of additive manufacturing lies precisely in its ability to bridge craftsmanship and industry, creativity and efficiency, while enabling sustainable, efficient, scalable, and flexible manufacturing processes:

- Production methods that print exactly the amount of product needed, eliminating waste. When combined with recyclable, reusable, and biodegradable materials, the sustainability benefits become apparent.
- New possibilities in terms of personalization of pieces to the specific needs of customers. Along with other digital tools for mass customization, it can bring design, manufacturing, and consumers closer together.
- Low fixed costs, so firms can produce efficiently in small batches while also being able to scale up and deal with large orders. "We are often told that we cannot compete with offshore production in China in terms of cost. We look at it the other way around; China cannot compete with us for small batches," Aran Azkarate argues.
- Quick and responsive production processes with local suppliers, enabling nimble supply chains that reduce inventory needs and time to market.

Rigid materials traditionally used for additive manufacturing, however, have limited applications in fashion. Beyond "architectural" designs aimed for fashion shows, their use has been largely confined to jewelry, accessories, ornaments, and small pieces. This is rapidly changing thanks to novel flexible materials and printing techniques; the "Holy Grail" of 3D-printed fashion is the search for digital fabrics that can match, if not exceed, the performance of traditional textiles. NASA is currently working on 3D-printed "space fabrics" that can be made into astronaut spacesuits, among other potential uses. Polymaker, a well-regarded manufacturer of 3D-printing materials, and Covestro, a large German chemical company, announced in 2020 a major development for producing 3D-printed textiles, combining innovative hardware, materials, and software. Researchers at the Massachusetts Institute of Technology are using a technique called under extrusion—ultimately, a defect in the 3D-printing process—to create tulle-like "quasi textiles." These are only some of the many projects currently ongoing.

3.   A BRIEF HISTORY OF COMME DES MACHINES

By the time Comme des Machines was established, in 2016, its founders had already been working on 3D-printing projects in their workshop in Sondika, near Bilbao, Spain for two years. None of them is an engineer or has a technical background. Aran and Andrés worked for the fashion industry, where they had been involved in digital projects for years. Jon Mikel worked as a 3D illustrator, and Suso was graphic designer and DJ (Figure 6.1). The name of the new enterprise was inspired by the fashion brand Comme des Garçons by the Japanese designer Rei Kawakubo.

Figure 6.1   Comme des Machines' founders

The vision behind Comme des Machines is ambitious: using additive manufacturing (widely referred to as 3D printing) to disrupt the value chain of the fashion industry and create innovative, locally produced, sustainable, and customizable clothing and accessories. The founders of the company never doubted the potential of the technology; still, they could hardly anticipate the immediate impression their innovative project would make in the industry.

Comme des Machines defines itself as a factory that exploits the innovative potential of 3D printing to bridge craftsmanship and traditional industry. It creates novel forms, textures, materials, and finishes at any scale, from one-off projects to large production runs. Although additive manufacturing is not a new technology, its use at large scale in manufacturing, particularly in the fashion industry, is in the nascent stage. Comme des Machines aims to tap into this potential and "explore new horizons for 3D printing," according to its founders.

Their innovative approach to fashion manufacturing made an almost immediate impact in the industry. In 2015, they collaborated with the Belgian designer Bruno Pieters—a reference in sustainable fashion—to create the first-ever collection of downloadable fashion accessories that customers could 3D print themselves. They have worked with domestic and international firms, such as Helena Rohner and Angel Schlesser (jewelry), Loreak (shoes), and Sur/Sac and Mércules (handbags), among others. They have also worked with larger customers such as Nike, Reebok, and the Guggenheim Museum.

Their growing reputation in the industry led Mango to knock on their door in 2020. This presented Comme des Machines with a huge opportunity, but also with the immense challenge of rapidly scaling up their production in order to work with a major international fashion retailer.[2] Was that the kind of client they wanted to work with? They stepped up to the challenge, creating the first collection of 3D-printed jewelry for Mango between September and October 2020. This commission pushed the manufacturing capacity of Comme des Machines beyond any previous project, and proved the scalability of 3D printing as a manufacturing technology. "It was the first time that a mass-market fashion brand launched an entire collection using this technique. Media around the world reported the achievement," Azkarate recalls (El Correo, 2021). In 2021, a collection of flexible accessories followed; they had to be as sustainable and artisanal as possible. "We are one of the very few workshops that can print pieces with these properties," Comme des Machines claim. While relying heavily on technology, when it came to postproduction and dyeing of the pieces, "we did it the old-fashioned way, but we knew that this technique would give our flowers the artisanal flair the client [Mango] wanted" (El Correo, 2021). This blend of cutting-edge digital technologies and craftsmanship is a hallmark of the Comme des Machines approach.

The use of flexible materials brings a wealth of opportunities for additive manufacturing in fashion, in particular the creation of 3D-printed fabrics, which may well be the next frontier in textile manufacturing. Comme des Machines is heavily committed to developing these "textiles of the future" as a keystone of sustainable textile production. In order to overcome the many challenges that digital fabrics—a nascent technology— pose, the company is working incessantly on internal research and development projects, as well as collaborating with its suppliers, in order to develop and test new materials and techniques. The effort is starting to pay off; Nina Ricci just launched a "zero-waste" collection of shoes and handbags using 3D-printed mesh mules entirely manufactured at the Sondika workshop by Comme des Machines. Looking further ahead, Burberry has picked Comme des Machines as one of the leading manufacturers of future textiles as they make the best pleated fabric using 3D printing.

In terms of recent developments and future projects, Comme des Machines is also moving beyond the boundaries of the fashion industry, originally its core market. They are exploring the potential of 3D printing in a range of creative industries: interior design, architecture, music, cooking, etc. Additionally, as the 3D-printing market itself evolves, and the company grows, they are incorporating new materials to their portfolio: clay, bronze, cement, ceramics, wood—the possibilities are almost limitless.

Table 6.1   Key operating principles according to Comme des Machines

Yes	No
Digital inventory	Physical inventory
Produced on demand	Stock requirements
Any order size, no job too small or too big	Minimum order required
Diversity	Uniformity
Custom designs and productions	Collections of samples
In between crafts and industry	Crafts or industry
Simplicity	Flamboyance

Source: Adapted from *Comme des Machines'* Instagram profile with permission.

4.   VALUE PROPOSITION AND COMPETITIVE STRATEGY

Digital technologies can be employed to create exclusive and highly differentiated products as well as to improve the efficiency of manufacturing processes. For Comme des Machines, this is not an either/or situation; they aim to capture the best of both worlds. They adapt their approach to the specific needs of their customers, using different approaches, from the most technological and automated to those that combine technology and craftsmanship.

Let us take as an illustration the handbags they produced for two small Spanish firms. For Mércules they created a "jelly bag" that is printed entirely in one go in an automated and streamlined process. Meanwhile, they also collaborated with Sur/Sac in the creation of a series of unique, numbered pieces; the handbags, with a classic inspiration, were 3D printed and subsequently postproduced, polished, and waxed by hand with painstaking attention to detail, bringing technology and craftsmanship together in a complex process.

Commes des Machines works to order; it does not have a product catalog, but develops customized proposals for every client. It works on a flexible production schedule, allowing clients to restock as required, without minimum orders or production runs. Every commission is unique and starts off as a blank sheet—or, to be more precise, a blank digital screen. The original design is refined in iterations until it is ready for production. The whole process, which typically takes from 6 to 12 weeks, depending on the project, is remarkably agile and flexible. Low fixed costs mean it is also efficient, regardless of scale (Moda, 2020). They manufacture small batches, even one-off pieces, at competitive prices, while automation allows them to also scale up and take on larger orders with the same machines. The process redefines traditional rules linking scale with efficiency and cost reduction (see Table 6.1).

5. DEFINING A BUSINESS MODEL FOR COMME DES MACHINES

A business model refers to the way an enterprise creates, delivers, and captures value or, in simpler terms, "how we make money in this business." It is shaped by a number of interrelated decisions on areas such as target customers, revenue streams, resources, processes, and configurations of the value chain, among others. The business model followed by Comme des Machines to date is the result of three interlinked choices consciously made by the entrepreneurial team.

5.1 Resources and key activities

The company is run entirely by the four founders. True to their identity as "digital craftspeople," they are in charge of the whole production process, including digital modeling, printing, and postproduction. They have never had any apprentices, despite numerous requests. The only facility is the Sondika workshop, measuring 150 square meters and home to 14 printers. They never outsource work, but they sometimes rent additional machines to cope with demand peaks, if needed. This allows them to operate with low and fixed costs, as well as to incorporate new technology (printers, software) as it hits the market, without needing large investments.

Their website is extremely simple and minimalistic, and they do little to no proactive marketing, beyond their Instagram account, which has around 13,000 followers. However, their innovative work has received significant publicity in the media. Client acquisition relies heavily on word of mouth. They have not pursued an aggressive growth strategy. They have taken no external investors, and the four founders remain the only stockholders of the company.

However … not surprisingly, Comme des Machines has been approached repeatedly by prospective investors, attracted by a unique combination of cutting-edge technology, an emerging market, and a top client portfolio. External investors could fund new avenues for the expansion of the business, ensuring that it would be able to cope with growing demand and not fall victim to its own success. However, the investors wanted to pivot the business model and implement formalized organizational processes and bureaucracy. After long hours of conversations, Comme des Machines declined the offer. A second investment fund approached them a couple of years later, but it soon became apparent that it was not the proper match; the investors did not buy into the philosophy of the business—they wanted to pursue aggressive growth and pursue a start-up management model.

Thus far, the business has relied on bootstrapping and retained earnings for growth. They do not rule out having equity investors in the near future, particularly if the market grows as much as they expect, but only if they feel they are a perfect fit for the company. Those that have approached them to date "feared that, perhaps, our discourse was too bold, too defiant. And we thought they were too bound by inertia and prejudice," Aran argues.

In terms of physical and human resources, Comme des Machines may hire its first employees in 2022, if growth continues as planned. It has also considered opening a second workshop, possibly in Northern Africa, which would offer both proximity to Spain and access to the largely untapped African market, facilitated by the African Continental Free Trade Area that came into effect in 2019. Comme des Machines strongly feels that any expansion must only happen if it is fully aligned with its ethos and discourse. The owners believe that this cautious and controlled approach to growth is key to preserving the essence of the business, but some might suggest that the rapidly evolving nature of the marketplace calls for a more aggressive expansion strategy.

5.2   Focus on manufacturing and sustainability

Comme des Machines focuses on the fabrication stage of the value chain, with a business-to-business model in which it works for and collaborates with a wide range of brands in order to create and manufacture an equally wide range of products. The driving force behind the business is the urge to explore the potential of 3D printing for customized, local, flexible, and sustainable manufacturing. In their own words, "we do not consider ourselves a startup. In essence, we are just a workshop, a factory, and proud of it." First and foremost, they see themselves as "digital craftspeople." As such, the factory floor is the core of the business, and flexibility its essence. They are happy to be involved in all phases of the manufacturing process, from design and 3D modeling to postproduction. However, they have never shown an interest in developing and marketing their own brand, or their own separate design studio. Meanwhile, they work on a commission basis with a wide range of clients, creating anything from unique products for small designers to large series for mass-market brands, mostly—but not exclusively—in the fashion industry. It is fair to say that, while they are becoming horizontally diversified, they remain vertically specialized.

Their operational approach focuses heavily on the sustainability benefits that 3D brings in terms of reduced waste—to the point of totally eliminating it, green materials, and proximity manufacturing, greatly reducing the environmental footprint of the fashion supply chain. For example, for the flexible pieces they produced for Mango, they created their own natural dyes using organic materials such as red onions, spinach, turmeric, and indigo in order to expand the chromatic possibilities of PLU filaments. Meanwhile, for rigid pieces, they typically resort to PLA, a biodegradable and compostable biopolymer obtained from natural ingredients such as potato, coffee, sugar cane, and wheat, among others.

However … some of the prospective investors that approached them argued that this might not be the most profitable and realistic business model for the company. In their view, they should adapt the way they operate, combining their disruptive technology with a more business-oriented mindset: they should specialize in the most attractive products and markets, and pursue a proactive sales strategy in order to capture as much demand as possible. This would be supported by heavy marketing investments in order to promote the brand identity of Comme des Machines as an innovative startup, and make the most of its growth potential. In terms of human resources, the company would hire interns and apprentices for the factory floor, freeing the founding team to focus on management, public relations, and new product design. In other words, they would pursue a vertical strategy while becoming more horizontally specialized. Venture capitalists and business angels would provide the funding needed to fuel the expansion of the business. Needless to say, regardless of its potential merits, this approach collides head on with the vision that the founders had for their enterprise, as it might shift the focus away from technology, fabrication, and, ultimately, sustainability.

5.3   Commitment to 3D-printed fabrics

When we started working in the fashion industry, we quickly became aware that lab-created fabrics were the future. Natural and organic fabrics that are so fashionable today are just a transitory solution. They need more land and more water than we can afford in a world with growing population and demand ... Lab-created food and fabrics may sound artificial and hostile today, but this is where we are headed. (Aran Azkarate)

Comme des Machines has shown an interest in 3D-printed textiles from the onset, before they were even able to print them. Digital fabrics not only expand the applications of additive manufacturing in fashion, but they offer several advantages. First, they are printed following a pattern, eliminating waste and the need for cutting. Second, they offer incredible design flexibility, so that different textures and thicknesses can be printed within the same piece, for example, in order to reinforce it exactly where needed. Digital fabrics can even be printed on natural ones, such as silk. Finally, the manufacturing process is fully automated and scalable as there is no need for manual postproduction. As a result, Comme des Machines claims that fabrics can be up to ten times more profitable than rigid pieces. In the wake of the COVID-19 pandemic and the subsequent global supply chain crisis, fashion firms are showing an increased interest in flexible materials, and demand for digital fabrics seems to be finally gaining traction.

However ... the technology and the market for digital fabrics are still embryonic and, as with most emerging technologies, substantial uncertainty remains. There is a limited selection of materials—which are typically recyclable but not biodegradable—and suppliers. Moreover, existing 3D printers are not designed to manufacture large pieces of fabric with the required accuracy and reliability—the slightest error in printing may spoil a whole piece. Comme des Machines had to work with one of their suppliers to "hack" their printers for their first textile pieces, and they may need to further redesign their machines and develop new technical solutions in the future. It is also unclear to what extent—and at what rate—the market will adopt this new technology. Current market trends still privilege natural and organic fibers; "we all relate more easily to natural stuff," Aran admits. "When clients called us, they showed interest in the fabrics but they did not totally trust them. Besides, their marketing departments pushed a different storyline: it was all about organic materials. We wondered if we were getting it all wrong." In summary, the potential pay-off of betting on digital fabrics is substantial, but so is the uncertainty; comparatively, rigid pieces made with PLA filaments are less revolutionary but more technologically mature and easily marketable.

6.   SHAPING THE FUTURE OF COMME DES MACHINES: IS THE BEST YET TO COME?

As Aran swallows her last grape and toasts to a great 2022, she looks back at the last few years and smiles. It has been a fascinating journey for Comme des Machines thus far! She knows Jon, Suso, and Andrés feel the same way. They have followed a well-defined path, firmly grounded in the beliefs and values of the founding team, and their conviction seems to be paying off. Moreover, they can look ahead to the future with confidence. They are convinced that the market for 3D-printed fashion—in particular, digital fabrics—is about to boom, and they will be ready when it does, bringing with it exciting new opportunities along with fresh challenges. How they will seize the former and confront the latter is still unwritten, though.

When they meet up in the Sondika workshop on Monday, the four entrepreneurs will, once again, be shaping the future of Comme des Machines. Should they stick to their current—and so far successful—path, or should they consider alternative business models? Should they reconsider the possibility of bringing in external investors? How can they know if the time to change course ever comes? Staying true to their original vision could be a gamble. Will the current path, focused on technology, fabrication, and sustainability, be as successful as it has been in the past, or should they balance it out with other activities in the value chain? Will they be able to scale up their operations to cope with increasing demand for 3D printing, or will they fall victim to their own success?

Perhaps most importantly, will they still be able to set the best course for the company, from a business perspective, without compromising on their values and beliefs? There is sometimes a fine line separating conviction from stubbornness. The entrepreneurs feel strongly against changes in the business model that may compromise the vision and purpose behind Comme des Machines; they want to keep focused on exploring the innovative potential of 3D printing, which demands they remain in close control of the operations, rather than aggressively pursuing growth. They are also wary of external investors who do not embrace the culture, management style, and radical entrepreneurial independence of the founding team. After all, for them, as for many entrepreneurs in analogous positions, Comme des Machines is much more than a business. It is a workplace, a life project, the realization of a vision.

Only one thing is certain: as 2022 takes its first steps, an exciting road lies ahead.

ACKNOWLEDGMENTS

We would like to thank Aran Azkárate and Andrés Iglesias jointly with the rest of the team at Commes des Machines for their contribution to this case study. This work is part of projects TED2021-130042B-I00, funded by MCIN/AEI/10.13039/501100011033 and by the European Union NextGenerationEU/ PRTR; and PID2019-106874GB-I00/AEI/10.13039/501100011033, funded by the Government Research Agency of Spanish Ministry of Science and Innovation. This work is developed with the support of the Madrid Government (Comunidad de Madrid-Spain) with the project Excellence of University Professors (EPUC3M20) in the context of the V PRICIT (Regional Programme of Research and Technological Innovation).

NOTES

1. All quotes in this chapter, unless otherwise stated, are from an interview held with the founders on December 17, 2021.
2. Mango had just reported sales of 2.37 billion euros in 2019.

REFERENCES

Beall, A. (2020, July 13). Why clothes are so hard to recycle. BBC. Retrieved from www.bbc.com/future/article/20200710-why-clothes-are-so-hard-to-recycle

El Correo (2021, May 22). Mango se une con una firma vizcaína para crear las sandalias más deseadas. Retrieved from www.elcorreo.com/bizkaiadmoda/moda/mango-sandalias-pendientes-bolsos-3d-comme-des-machines-sostenibles-coleccion-accesorios-moda-bizkaia-laboratorio-sostenibilidad-artesania-digital-20210518185511-nt.html

Hämmerle, V., Mühlenbein, C., Rüßmann, M, Gauger, C., and Rohrhofer, S. (2020, January 30). Why fashion must go digital—end to end. Retrieved from www.bcg.com/publications/2020/why-fashion-must-go-digital-end-to-end

Moda (2020, March 6). Comme des Machines, el aliado "techie" vasco que lleva el 3D a Mango o Moisés Nieto. Retrieved from www.modaes.com/equipamiento/comme-des-machines-el-aliado-techie-vasco-que-lleva-el-3d-a-mango-o-moises-nieto

Niinimäki, K., Peters, G., Dahlbo, H., Perry, P., Rissanen, T., and Gwilt, A. (2020). The environmental price of fast fashion. *Nature Reviews Earth & Environment*, 1(4), 189–200.

Reichental, A. (2018, June 1). How 3D printing is reviving craftsmanship across the globe. Forbes. Retrieved from: www.forbes.com/sites/forbestechcouncil/2018/06/01/how-3d-printing-is-reviving-craftsmanship-across-the-globe/#23afac3e1bda

United Nations Environment Programme (2019, March 14). UN Alliance for Sustainable Fashion addresses damage of "fast fashion." Press release. Retrieved from www.unep.org/news-and-stories/press-release/un-alliance-sustainable-fashion-addresses-damage-fast-fashion

PART II
GROWTH PATHWAYS: DISSECTING ENTREPRENEURIAL DECISION-MAKING ALONG THE CONTINUUM OF STARTUPS, CORPORATIONS, AND PUBLIC POLICY MAKERS

7

Three Colombian entrepreneurs in search of the next great business opportunity

Mario A. Manzi-Puertas and Isabella Gomati de la Vega

1.   INTRODUCTION

The management team of the Zoom-Up entrepreneurship mentorship program (EMP) met in the afternoon of November 26, 2021, in Bogotá, Colombia, to select one of the three entrepreneurs who had advanced to the program's final stage as the winner. The three finalists were Carolina Trujillo, founder and chief executive officer (CEO) of GoTok Music, a digital music platform company, based in Bogotá, Colombia, which planned to grow and settle its business in other countries; Gustavo de la Vega, founder and CEO of NativApps, a company located in Barranquilla, Colombia, which provided software development services and wanted to strengthen its growth in Latin America; and Javier Villota Paz, founder and production manager of Probionar, a company based in the region of Nariño, Colombia, which produced biodegradable cleaning products and needed to expand its business to new regions.[1]

The main goal of Zoom-Up's EMP was to support and coach high-potential entrepreneurs as they explored new business opportunities to enter new markets. The program lasted six months and it provided the winner with free mentoring, training, technical support, two trips to potential markets, and networking opportunities for six months so that they could find business opportunities in new markets. In its brief existence since its launch in February 2019, Zoom-Up has aided eight entrepreneurs in realizing their ambitions and breaking into new markets. For entrepreneurs, participation in this program was free because it was funded by several companies and non-governmental organizations. But there were extremely strict criteria for being chosen as a winner. The entrepreneurs and their businesses had to demonstrate that they (1) solved an important need in the market, (2) had validated solutions, (3) had a working team, which was leading with passion and resilience to achieve the proposed changes, and (4) had a long-term vision, reflected in the future business and market perspective. Although all three entrepreneurs are grand finalists, only one can be the winner.

2.   CAROLINA TRUJILLO: "I ALWAYS KNEW I WOULD BE AN ENTREPRENEUR"

Carolina was born in the city of Ibague, Colombia, into an entrepreneurial family; her father, Antonio Trujillo, and the majority of her paternal relatives were also business owners.[2] When Carolina was in school, she received an allowance from her father but she preferred to have her own income, so she organized raffles and sold a large number of items, which her friends would buy from her because they were always looking to buy new things. After completing high school, Carolina moved to Bogotá, where she attended Politecnico Grancolombiano and earned a degree in marketing and advertising. She combined these studies with her music career at the Conservatory of Tolima and EAFIT University. During her studies she worked as a model and salesperson for a financial company. At the age of 24, Carolina felt she was an expert in the modeling industry and found it lucrative, so she launched her own modeling agency in May 2005. Until 2009, she managed not only models but also artists, actors, and musicians, as her agency quickly expanded. She said, "The business grew because I knew the market and where I was, and you should stick to what you know." Carolina had many contacts, good relationships with her staff, and market knowledge, so she decided to make a new career move in October 2010 when she decided to launch a marketing agency with a friend.

Carolina was very happy with this new business because of how well it performed. At this time, Carolina welcomed Salomon, her son. From 2010 to 2013 she worked hard to attract clients like Coca-Cola, Hewlett-Packard, MTV, and Lucky Strike. At that time, Carolina faced the breakup of her relationship with her son's father and also the deterioration of her personal relationship with her business partner. She eventually made the offer to sell her share, which her business partner gladly accepted. Carolina experienced her first period of unemployment, which caused her a lot of anxiety and worry. What will I do? was a daily thought for Carolina. She asked herself, "Should I launch a new business? Or should I look for work?" Her best friend Ximena Erazo remembered those times, describing Carolina as a "visionary, risky, and innovative person who could make the right choice."

2.1   Exploring and discovering the market

After sending her CV to apply for two vacancies and reflecting on what she really wanted to do with her life, Carolina decided to follow her instincts, or her "genes," as she calls them: what she really wanted was to be a successful entrepreneur. By leveraging her expertise, connections, and knowledge, she started an events and marketing business in late 2013 that was exclusively dedicated to cultural issues. She was able to take advantage of the underdeveloped creative and cultural industries in Colombia and South America.

One day in early 2014, Carolina was chatting with her friend Omar Pucciarelli, whom she had first met 20 years earlier. Omar was from Argentina and had spent the last 30 years at EMI Music and Universal Music. Despite the fact that Colombia's economy was doing well and the music business was promising at the time, Carolina explained to Omar that there were no digital strategies for promoting artists. Omar was shocked because, despite his extensive knowledge of the digital music distribution business, he could not believe that there was nothing similar in Colombia. He was also surprised that other international companies such as Cd Baby and The Orchard, already operating in important European and United States (US) markets, were not in Colombia. Omar was aware that "on a global scale, it was observed that many Colombian artists were touring, traveling throughout Europe, and they were very well received, and there were no artists from other Latin American countries as interesting as Colombians." Furthermore, Marcela Palacio, an expert copyright lawyer, noted that Colombian artists faced challenges in international markets: "If a Colombian artist, who resides in Colombia and whose works are exploited in the local market, decides to hire an aggregator[3] to distribute their works on digital platforms and collect the corresponding royalties for such uses, it would create a difficulty to know which rights are being collected" (Palacio, 2017), since there were no Colombian aggregators. Carolina and Omar understood that they might be the first to benefit from that scenario.

In June 2014, Carolina used the tools at her disposal in her event and marketing firm to design a market study to learn more about the music market. Many of her friends and acquaintances who worked in the music industry admitted that they felt abandoned and occasionally scammed, that payments were very low, that they did not trust music businesspeople and labels, that the music business was extremely closed, and that in order to succeed, they needed to have friends in the industry. On a global scale, Carolina and Omar discovered that while several labels were in charge of the digital distribution of music in the US and Europe, they were absent from Colombia. As part of the strategies for promoting artists, they also looked at the various digital music monetization platforms and market trends. Although UNESCO and BOmm, a new platform to boost sales of the Colombian music industry, had just named Bogotá "The City of Music," they found that there was no regulation for the digital distribution of music at the local industry level (UNESCO, 2017). Carolina and Omar came to the conclusion that it was time to get creative because, despite the great talent of Colombian musicians, there were no commercial platforms outside of concerts that sought to reach new markets. Omar found it difficult to launch this company in Colombia with Carolina because "neither the artists nor the private entities or companies that sponsored the departure of Colombian artists abroad had any professional structure."

Carolina made the thoughtful choice to sell her event and marketing firm so she could launch a new enterprise that would concentrate on the local music industry. Carolina recalled that moment:

> I saw that I could work with music, which was something I was really passionate about, and combine it with my marketing career … I came to the realization that I could make a living playing the music I really loved! I realized it was time to start the company while working on this aspect of the business, which allowed me to support myself.

Carolina had been searching for something like this for a very long time, and her best friend Ximena encouraged her to take on the challenge.

Carolina and Omar designed a business model, for which they used different methodologies, including a SWOT analysis and the CANVAS Business Model methodology. GoTok Music was chosen as the name of the new business, which would concentrate on digital music distribution and promotional strategies for artists. Because of his substantial savings, Omar offered to be the capitalist partner. He would lend GoTok Music money as part of his investment, with the understanding that GoTok Music would begin repaying the loan as soon as it broke even.

2.2   The birth of GoTok Music

In order to validate their plans and procedures, Carolina, Omar, and a few of their musician friends ran pilot studies in the final months of 2014. GoTok Music was officially launched in March 2015. They were prepared to make their artists' music available to listeners around the world on digital platforms like iTunes, YouTube, Spotify, Amazon, Deezer, Google Play, and 60 more. Surprisingly, after 11 months, Carolina and Omar believed they would have to close their business because profits had fallen by 90 percent, mainly due to the drop in sales due to the arrival in the Colombian market of a large number of rivals, including Sony Music and Universal Music, which offered a similar service. The question of whether this venture was worthwhile was raised, and Carolina responded, "I am not going to throw away everything we have achieved so far. We do not have money to pay the bills, but because the company is positioned, within the market, people recognize us and look for us."

2.3   GoTok Music consolidation

From 2015 to 2017, GoTok Music had already collaborated with 60 or so up-and-coming musicians, with annual sales of around USD200,000. In order to attract new customers and artists, in 2016 the company started providing management services for artists. This service included branding, booking, management services both locally and internationally, production of concerts and tours, and management in compliance policies. The company also expanded its target market to include festivals, theaters, universities, and cultural institutions.

By March 2021, GoTok Music was defined as "a digital music platform focused on the development, promotion, and positioning of Latin American artists and labels globally, through the design and execution of digital marketing strategies, booking and management, cultural exchanges, festivals, tours, and the production of public and private concerts" (GoTok Music, 2018). It collaborated with a variety of artists, including Susana Baca Afrotronix from Chad, Piero and Miguel Mateos from Argentina, Liniker e os Caramelows from Brazil, and Celso Pia and Lila Downs from Mexico. To do this, Carolina handled the booking and management for Colombia and Mexico and Omar oversaw the distribution, digital marketing, and tour and concert production in the US. They were both in charge of the European and Canadian markets. Carolina and Omar were assisted by a team of seven people, which included an administrative assistant, an accountant, two bookers, a programmer, a community manager, and a graphic designer. Due to the COVID-19 pandemic, part of the business was on hold for several months in 2020, waiting for artist tours and concerts to reactivate. Carolina spearheaded a strategy to push artists through digital platforms, which allowed them to navigate during those months.

With all these new lines of business, Carolina knew that she still had to consolidate her company in Colombia, face new competition, and continue to innovate, but at the same time she wanted to strengthen her company as an international business by entering other Latin American markets.

According to the Recording Industry Association of America®, in 2020, Latin music revenues in the US experienced growth for the fifth year in a row, despite the challenges posed by the COVID-19 pandemic, such as the cancellation of live shows and restrictions on physical retail stores. US Latin music revenues saw a remarkable 19 percent increase in 2020, reaching an estimated retail value of USD655 million. This growth rate was significantly higher than that of the overall US music revenues. Streaming formats played a crucial role in this growth, with a 20 percent increase to USD630 million, accounting for 96 percent of the total Latin music revenues in 2020 (RIAA, 2021). Carolina was unsure whether she should decide to continue working in the Colombian market or try to expand her business overseas. Despite her extensive entrepreneurial experience, she was overcome by uncertainties about her skills.

3. GUSTAVO DE LA VEGA: EVOLVING TECHNOLOGY

Gustavo was born in 1977 in Cartagena, Colombia, and from an early age, he claimed to have an entrepreneurial vocation.[4] When he was in elementary school, his mother designed his name using adhesive paper of different colors and motifs to mark his notebooks, and since all his classmates liked it, Gustavo used to sell those notebooks to his classmates. Years later, in 1997, while he was enrolled in the Systems Engineering program at the Universidad de Los Andes in Bogotá, Gustavo launched Design +OnLine, his first website. Gustavo attempted to sell webpage development services via this venture. He said, "The internet was quite precarious, and nobody really understood what a website was at that time," after having little success.

After completing his undergraduate studies, Gustavo started working at General Motors as a systems auditor. He was later transferred to the human resources department to work on a technology project based on the PeopleSoft platform. In response, Gustavo created a procedure for the recovery of technology projects which could help solve one of the most common issues the company had. He once came across a report called CHAOS that assessed global technology projects. When Gustavo saw that 84 percent of these projects had failed, he reasoned that there must be a sizable market for solutions since so many businesses had failed. Gustavo was actually considering how to use the project recovery methodology he had created. He left his job with the intention of starting his own consulting firm, out of both fear of the unknown of doing something new and the conviction that something better lay ahead.

3.1 The challenge of becoming independent

In June 2003, Gustavo founded ProActive Consulting. After the business was established, he made the decision to sell the advisory service he had developed, which, in his opinion, was a remedy for all the companies that were having trouble with their technology projects. Unfortunately, it took a long time to complete the mission of selling his idea successfully.

There were no technology managers at any company who wanted to acknowledge that they had projects to recover or improve, despite the fact that the product was good, because it effectively allowed technology projects and systems to be better implemented or recovered. After realizing how difficult this would be, Gustavo decided that ProActive Consulting would focus on the implementation of enterprise resource planning, as other businesses in the industry were doing. Gustavo perceived that he was learning a lot during this process from his interactions with customers.

From 2004 to 2007, Gustavo leveraged his professional contacts to work in Puerto Rico and Costa Rica. By late 2007, during a work trip to Silicon Valley along with his wife, Olga Lucia Borrego, Gustavo noticed that the mobile development market was going to start growing exponentially. Gustavo saw that Apple had launched its first iPhone, and he saw how the technology market was beginning to adopt that technology. ProActive Consulting has always had a mobile product development unit. When mobile phones were known as personal digital assistants, they had a wireless internet connection, and ProActive Consulting developed software for the mobile platforms of Palm, Hewlett-Packard, and Blackberry. With the launch of the iPhone, Gustavo decided to focus on the development of applications for mobile devices.

3.2   Making important decisions

In early 2008, Gustavo promoted the idea that ProActive Consulting should focus its work on the development of applications for cell phones and personal digital assistants. He received a call from HP in March 2009 asking him to create and market WebOS, an operating system for mobile devices, in Latin America. The Palm operating system, which at the time dominated the market, evolved into this software. In Gustavo's eyes, this would be the company's future. Gustavo's wager on WebOS lost its appeal because the financial results for the period 2008–2011 were less than favorable. Leo Apotheker, the CEO of HP, decided to halt the WebOS project in August 2011, which resulted in ProActive Consulting's demise in 2012. "Proactive Consulting finally went out of business," said Gustavo in reference to this. "Bankruptcies do not happen overnight but are a process that can take several months, if not years."

3.3   Creating a new vision

By November 2012, after learning "not to put all your eggs in the same basket" and after many conversations with friends who had supported him, Gustavo decided to create a new company called NativApps, a tech company in the talent business (NativApps, 2019). He wished to concentrate on offering mobile users software development services. Gustavo had a general understanding of the business and the Colombian market, but it was still unclear to him how to make the new segmentation strategy of the company work more consistently and successfully than the old one.

In order to learn and apply this knowledge to his new company, he made the decision to travel to India in April 2013 to see what was being done there and how it differed from what he was doing in Colombia in terms of market approach. Olga, his wife, offers the following insight into his travels: "Going to India and being able to observe not only another culture, but different ways of doing and managing technology business, allowed Gustavo to bring better practices and implement them with his team back in Colombia. He learned about the value of multiculturalism in business from Indian culture."

Gustavo decided to focus solely on service development software, for which he could guarantee quality, deadlines, and, in some cases, the possibility of sharing risks with his customers, and to remove the development of fixed-price products from ProActive Consulting's portfolio. These decisions were influenced by the learnings from that trip as well as the ongoing search for business features in Colombia. NativApps started growing steadily in 2014 and continued to do so until 2018. In that year, it changed tack to become a "technology company in the talent business." It started by providing three different service types: "You Manage," "We Manage," and "Co-Manage," following the suggestion of Maria Alejandra Cotes, its marketing director.

The first service, called You Manage, was developed to give the client access to the developer of the required software and/or technology while leaving the client in charge of administration. After putting this service in place, Gustavo observed that while many customers were knowledgeable about their own businesses, there were surprisingly few who were knowledgeable about technology, necessitating the addition of more teams to handle the demand for technology development.

The company's second service was called We Manage. This service was more comprehensive than You Manage and consisted of assessing the needs of the companies' challenges in terms of time, personnel, and knowledge, and putting them at the service of the company, while also controlling the budget and the execution of the projects. Gustavo thought this new service had many advantages. First, using this service from NativApps meant having a team of subject-matter experts on hand. Second, it would allow for only paying for hours used, and third, it would allow managing the budget and individual roles in accordance with requirements.

Gustavo developed a third service called Co-Manage. This service was created as a result of a partnership between NativApps and other businesses to create new investment opportunities in Colombian tech firms. Gustavo was in charge of marketing this project because of its size and target audience.

NativApps had been consolidated as a business by the end of 2018 and was rapidly expanding. Gustavo then realized that the winning formula was You, We, and Co. Samir Arana, the IT manager at SYKES Colombia, claimed that NativApps' internal tracking tool was more than capable of overseeing the creation of reliable deliverables and that clients could count on NativApps to be an easy-to-use partner. That could only mean one thing to him: everything he had been doing in terms of market research, competitor analysis, and prototyping finally made sense. With that worldview, in 2020, NativApps built a team of 500 people, including more than 100 developers. It also partnered with Jumio Corp to run the first identity validation center in Latin America, which was constructed in Barranquilla using the Co-Manage model. According to Mike O'Callaghan, vice president of global operations at Jumio, choosing Barranquilla as the operational base of Jumio in Latin America with NativApps as a local partner was made possible by the city's talent, infrastructure, location, and environment. According to his wife, Olga, Gustavo's pursuit of more and better advancements and growth within the business was one of the key factors in NativApps' success: "He made the most of every opportunity he had, whether it was a meeting, a trip, or a single moment. It gave him a chance to think about where he wanted the business to go and how he could strengthen both its social capital and its growth strategy."

NativApps had increased sales by 500 percent since the company's founding in 2012, reaching USD2 million in annual sales. However, Gustavo's desire to advance persisted. Since the growth of the digital economy in this region was predicted to be 1.3 percent by 2019 and 4.8 percent by 2020, being one of the main growth sectors globally and with a positive trend for the coming years, he sought out new technology-based businesses that would enable his company to consolidate and expand (IDC, 2019). Gustavo felt that he could not leave Colombia without being the captain of his ship, though. Gustavo was troubled by these worries because, despite taking many risks when he first began developing NativApps, he no longer believed that he possessed the tools and abilities required to take on a new task. He believed that his desire to pursue new business opportunities would cause him to jeopardize everything he had worked so hard to achieve.

4.   JAVIER MAURICIO VILLOTA PAZ: "I HAVE AN ENTREPRENEURIAL FAMILY"

Javier was born on January 4, 1994, in the city of Pasto, Colombia, to a family made up of his father, Luis Alfredo, his mother, Liliana, and his sister, Ana Carolina. Javier's parents have encouraged him and his sister to run a family business ever since he can remember.[5] The example set by his parents, particularly that of their mother, whom Javier cited as his greatest role model, helped to reinforce this message: "We try to keep up with her pace, which is occasionally a little accelerated, but that is the hard and continuous work that we do as a family. My mother is a woman who represents Colombian mothers. She is the one who gets up first in the house, she is ready before everyone else."

The Villota Paz family was aware of the economic and social conditions in the Nariño department and Pasto, its capital. Among the 27 departments evaluated for the Departmental Competitiveness Index, Nariño was ranked nineteenth (Private Competitiveness Council and University of Rosario, 2018). This ranking was partially a result of the lack of roads and other transportation options that would have allowed for better connections with the rest of the country. The Villota Paz family frequently discussed this situation because they believed their region only produced raw materials that could not be given any added value and that this was not tapping into the creative abilities of the people of Nariño.

Early in 2011, when Javier was in his final year of high school, his family was concerned about the pollution their home's use of soap and detergent was causing. One day, they made the decision to start making their own dish soap and laundry detergent. They started making them by hand in the yard of their home, experimenting with the ingredients and processes while using various plastic containers. They used some of what they made at home and gave the rest to their uncles and cousins, who gave them feedback on the effectiveness of the products, such as how much foam they produced or how well they removed grease and stains. Javier described this situation as follows: "At the time, my family and I just wanted to improve our cleaning routine, but it was also important to have a positive impact on the environment, however, we lacked evidence that the product was indeed environmentally friendly."

The family made the decision to go out and sell their goods in supermarkets and convenience stores in the city because they believed they were more effective than those on the market. Ana Carolina, Javier's sister, claimed, "Customers asked us to negotiate with supermarkets and convenience stores to sell our products there because they wanted our products to be more easily accessible. We learned a lot during the negotiations, but because they were local goods, we got a lot of support." Although these local businesses expressed some interest, they soon realized that obtaining a license from the National Food and Drug Surveillance Institute (INVIMA) was necessary in order to sell these products. However, this process was time-consuming and expensive.

The Villota Paz family had the idea to start a family business that specialized in environmentally friendly detergents and wanted to call it Probionar, but they did not have enough savings or access to loans at the time. Ana Carolina said this: "We are a very close-knit and resourceful family. Even though we didn't have the money we needed, we went ahead anyway because we were sure of the quality of our product."

4.1   Getting started is never easy

Javier was worried about the slow-paced process. He remembered thinking, "Was that idea really our thing? Or should we have generated some other kind of idea?" The fact that his sister Ana Carolina gave birth to a daughter, however, prevented them from giving up on the project and encouraged everyone to work together to see Probionar through. They persisted in learning more about environmentally friendly inputs, raw materials, and biodegradable detergents. In 2013, a family they knew advised them to apply for the Fondo Emprender (Entrepreneurship Fund) from the National Learning Service, a government agency that facilitated access to seed money and additionally offered consulting services. However, Probionar was not selected for the funding.

While Javier was studying process engineering at Mariana University in Pasto, he also acquired some knowledge about chemical engineering, which he applied to improve their products, particularly in regards to viscosity and density, in order to obtain a gel-like appearance and not a liquid one. He was trying to prevent the toxic ingredients present in conventional powdered detergents, pastes, creams, and soaps from consuming the oxygen from the bodies of water they had contact with and affecting the survival of the species that lived in the habitats where the waste ended. The family started incorporating biodegradable raw materials and supplies into the detergents and soaps at that point. As Ana Carolina recalled, "Although challenging, starting a family business is also fascinating and very special. Being an interdisciplinary team was very beneficial to us, which is how we were able to create innovative products that were good for the environment." In June 2014, the family decided to reapply to Fondo Emprender after making these improvements; this time, they did so with engineer Angela Sofia Parra's advice. In contrast to their previous application, they were chosen and received two different types of assistance. Probionar received a conditional credit of COP94,280 as well as mentoring from Diana Fuertes. The family started to make the investments necessary to begin production at an industrial level under all necessary regulations. Diana first asked them to conduct a market analysis aimed at identifying potential customers. They obtained a database from the Pasto Chamber of Commerce that contained details of 26,000 registered businesses, but Javier noted that "it is very common that if you enter a commercial establishment in Pasto, that same establishment will recommend you to another; thus, a chain is being made." So, what they did was to start visiting establishments and getting to know their needs to see if they could become their customers. "We did not have much trust in the survey."

At the beginning of 2015, Probionar already had the financial resources it urgently required; the production plant's construction, however, was the next significant step. Finding the land was the first challenge; it was eventually found in the village El Palmar, 15 kilometers outside of Pasto. Even though construction was already under way, the family soon encountered a new issue: between 2014 and 2015, the Colombian peso lost 30 percent of its value against the US dollar. This led to an inadequate budget for the purchase of equipment and machinery, most of which had to be imported, and forced the family to delay their plans to begin production until the necessary funds could be raised.

In order to begin the production process at an industrial level, INVIMA visited the Probionar plant in February 2016 and approved the sanitary notification and permit after inspecting the finished facility. In May, the plant officially began to produce its first product line, which was focused on the institutional market, managing to count as their customers 216 educational institutions in Nariño and some hotels and restaurants in just a couple of months.

4.2   Growth and innovation

In January 2017, Probionar was strongly impacted by the value-added tax increase from 16 to 19 percent due to a Colombian tax reform. However, in June 2017 the company received some good news that boosted its forecasts: Fondo Emprender had completely forgiven all existing debt. The business started offering three product lines: one for cleaning vehicles; a second for cleaning homes, which included window cleaners, liquid cleaners, dish soap, bio degreasers, and a bio multi-purpose liquid cleaner (this was Probionar's flagship product); and a third for Tidylac, a detergent for milk tanks. None of these products contained toxic inputs, and it took 28 days for the active ingredients to decompose. Ivonne Paz, a client of Probionar, said: "Their customer service is outstanding, and their products are excellent. Great business! An illustration of success and entrepreneurship in our area."

By 2018, every member of the Villota Paz family had become actively involved in the business. Ana Carolina, a graphic designer, was the general manager and also in charge of the commercial area; Javier, a process engineer, was in charge of production; his father, Luis Alfredo, was a public accountant and the chief financial officer; and his mother, Liliana, a fashion designer, was in charge of the plant. In addition, friends like engineer Jaime Quijano and other experts and practitioners helped them out. In August 2018, Probionar won second place in the Latin America Green Awards, in the category "Responsible Production and Consumption." With this award and the vision to continue growing, Javier hoped to develop his business lines and reach new markets. The Chamber of Commerce of Pasto highlights this startup because "its products are characterized by offering greater performance, since by dissolving with water a greater quantity of the product can be obtained, which represents savings for its customers."

Probionar had managed to reach an annual turnover of USD80,000, and the family wanted to expand to more cities in Colombia or even Ecuador, even though it still needed to investigate new distribution channels in Nariño. In the period 2020–2024, sales of household cleaning products were expected to increase by more than 7 percent annually in Colombia, reaching a total of more than USD34 million (ProColombia, 2020). Javier and his family believed that internationalization to Ecuador was a crucial decision they had to make, but they also understood that they could not risk losing all the money they had invested in Probionar. As the head of the family, Javier had doubts about his ability to make the best decision and implement the new growth strategies that these opportunities could bring to his business.

5. THE CHALLENGE

The Zoom-Up EMP management team gathered in the late afternoon of November 26, 2021, to choose the winner of their most recent call. The three entrepreneurs who had reached the final phase were Carolina Trujillo, the founder and CEO of GoTok Music; Gustavo de la Vega, the founder and CEO of NativApps; and Javier Villota Paz, the founder and production manager of Probionar. The winner would receive networking opportunities, technical support, mentoring, training, and two trips to potential markets for no additional cost over the course of the following six months. The management team had to make a decision based on the following criteria: the entrepreneurs and their businesses had to demonstrate that they (1) solved an important need in the market, (2) had validated solutions, (3) had a working team, which was leading with passion and resilience to achieve the proposed changes, and (4) had a long-term vision, reflected in the future business and market perspective.

ACKNOWLEDGMENTS

We thank Carolina Trujillo, Gustavo de la Vega, and Javier Villota for their interest and support in the development of this case.

NOTES

1. With the pedagogical purpose of giving cohesion to the three stories of Carolina Trujillo, Gustavo de la Vega, and Javier Villota Paz and to frame these three cases in the same challenge, the authors created Zoom-Up. The Zoom-Up EMP is based on the consulting experiences of the authors and the reality of the Colombian entrepreneurship ecosystem.
2. An interview was held with Carolina Trujillo on February 22, 2022. All quotes from Carolina in this chapter are from this interview, unless otherwise stated.
3. In the music industry, aggregators are intermediaries between independent artists and digital music platforms, who facilitate the distribution of their music by negotiating licenses

and verifying the ownership of musical works. In the case of artists who have contracts with record labels, the latter are in charge of these tasks.

4. An interview was held with Gustavo de la Vega on February 26, 2022. All quotes from Gustavo in this chapter are from this interview, unless otherwise stated.

5. An interview was held with Javier Mauricio Villota Paz and Ana Carolina Villota Paz on January 10, 2022. All quotes from Javier and Ana in this chapter are from this interview, unless otherwise stated.

REFERENCES

GoTok Music. (2018). *About*. Available at: https://gotokmusic.com/acerca-de/ (Accessed: January 20, 2020).

IDC. (November 20, 2019). *IT industry in LA will grow 1.3% in 2019 and 4.8% by 2020*. Available at: www .idc.com/getdoc.jsp?containerId=prLA45665419 (Accessed: January 21, 2020).

NativApps (2019). *Our Services*. Available at: https://nativapps.com/ (Accessed: May 12, 2020).

Palacio, M. (2017). Los artistas colombianos y las plataformas de música digitales: algunas dificultades. *Revista Derecho Privado*, *33*, 111–133.

Private Competitiveness Council and University of Rosario. (2018). *Departmental Competitiveness Index 2018*. Available at: https://compite.com.co/wp-content/uploads/2018/11/LIBRO-CPC_IDC_2018 _FINAL.pdf (Accessed: September 12, 2019).

ProColombia. (May 15, 2020). *The growth of the cleaning and cosmetics sector in Colombia continues*. Available at: https://procolombia.co/noticias/covid-19/el-crecimiento-del-sector-de-aseo-y -cosmeticos-en-colombia-continua (Accessed: January 22, 2020).

RIAA. (2021). *Year-end 2020 RIAA US Latin music revenue report*. Available at: www.riaa.com/wp -content/uploads/2021/04/Year-End-2020-RIAA-U.S.-Latin-Music-Revenue-Report.pdf (Accessed: May 2, 2023).

UNESCO (2017). *Bogotá city of music: 2012–2017 report*. Available at: https://en.unesco.org/creative -cities/sites/creative-cities/files/monitoring_reports/Bogotá_uccn_2012_-_2017_monitoring_report _.pdf (Accessed: June 14, 2020).

8
Playground energy: fun, health, and education on the playground

Veneta Andonova, Juan Pablo Soto, and Jana Schmutzler

1.   INTRODUCTION

One hot day in May 2012, Hristo Aleksiev, a serial entrepreneur, and Ilian Milinov, an industrial designer, were sitting in a pub in downtown Sofia, having a beer and discussing possible new initiatives together.[1] Rocking back and forth in their chairs following the rhythm of the music, they started wondering whether they could take the energy of the moving chairs and charge their mobile phones, which kept blinking with a "low battery" icon. After brainstorming for a while, they concluded that whereas using the energy from the chairs in office buildings would not be necessary since there is always electricity in the office, if the idea was applied somewhere in the open air, it could have value. Listing human activities in different open-air venues, they concluded that most energy is freely generated at children's playgrounds. They felt this as a Eureka moment and agreed to explore how the energy produced by kids on the playground could be turned into a business model that could create value for parents and kids alike.

Hristo and Ilian had strong engineering and design knowledge but did not have in mind a specific technological solution that could be suitable for the playground concept. The biggest challenge, however, was the business strategy of the venture, whose core was to capture the energy that kids spend on the playground and turn it into value someone would be willing to pay for. What would a successful entrepreneurial strategy in this case look like?[2]

2.   TRENDS AND INDUSTRY ENVIRONMENT

2.1   Green technology

Green technology started to surge in the 1960s. Green technology is an encompassing construct that refers to various methods and products – from generating energy to non-toxic cleaning products – and relates to energy, green building, environmentally friendly purchase of products, green chemistry, and green nanotechnology. The declared goals of the green tech-nology movement include sustainability, understood as meeting the needs of society without the depletion of resources; resource usage reduction; regeneration, understood as creating an economic activity around products and processes that benefit the environment; innovation; and cradle-to-cradle design, which implies the reuse of products.

According to data from the Bureau of Labor Statistics, United States (US), from August 2011, 75 percent of businesses reported the adoption of at least one practice related to green technologies. The two most common business practices were energy efficiency and waste reduction. Information and educational services were among the industries with the highest incidence of green technologies and the adoption of related practices.

Around the world, more and more companies were including sustainability practices in their annual reports. In Mexico, 66 percent of companies reported their sustainability per-formance in 2011, compared to 17 percent in 2008. In Brazil, 88 percent of the companies in 2011 reported their sustainability performance compared to 78 percent in 2008, and for South Africa, the percentages increased from 45 to 97 percent during the same period.

During the Rio+20 Summit in 2012, a coalition of 24 large companies, including Coca-Cola and Nike, was formed and announced a common commitment to green business. Moreover, a coalition of institutional investors, led by Aviva, a British insurer, was brought together with the common aim of lobbying governments to pressure companies in favor of releasing regular reports on environmental and social performance by publishing data about greenhouse gas emissions, use of water, employee satisfaction, and others (*The Economist*, 2012).

There was a lot of expectation to see how green technologies were about to transform con-sumption patterns and business practices, but some experts had serious reservations regarding the speed of change. It had taken 12 years for Fortune Global 250 companies reporting their sustainability performance to increase from 35 to 95 percent (United Nations Development Programme, 2012). A few dissident voices questioned the desirability of the green transition on the grounds of poverty increase and unclear cost and benefit merits.

2.2   Public health concerns

In early 2013, the Rockwool Foundation Research Unit, a Danish independent research center, studied how children spent their time and how this affected their well-being. The results, published in a newsletter, showed that children between 7 and 11 years old spent around seven hours of a weekday in school, two hours watching screens, and only 20 minutes exercising. During weekends, the same age group spent 3.5 hours in front of the screen but only half an hour doing physical exercises. Almost 35 percent of the boys between 7 and 11 years old spent at least five hours watching television or playing computer games on a weekend day. Around 37 percent of the boys in this age group exercised daily, and the percentage for the girls was even lower – only 30 percent. Younger children were also less likely to exercise outside than older children (12–17 years old). Furthermore, the study showed a relationship between the amount of time kids spent in front of a screen and the parents' education and the family's status – whether the parents lived together or separately. The research revealed that for every hour a parent spent in front of a television or computer screen, their child spent 10 minutes doing the same. An additional 10 percent of the children who lived with both their parents spent over three hours daily watching television or playing computer games more than children who lived with a single parent (Tranæs and Jensen, 2013).

Researchers believe that the results prove that parents' behavior was a significant factor in determining a child's eagerness to spend time at the playground. The technological advancements had led companies to a computerized paper system, which made parents spend more time in front of a computer inside their home than they did in previous decades. This role modeling could explain the tendency among children to spend more time playing video and computer games rather than outdoor games.

Some argued that playing video and computer games altered the mindset and behavior of children. Swedish National Institute of Public Health researchers conducted experiments with children who often played games in front of the screen. The results showed an increase in children's aggression in play but also the presence of other aggressive feelings and behaviors. Additionally, there were more cases of overweight girls who played computer games (Lager and Bremberg, 2005).

In some countries, obesity has become a serious health problem. In the US, for example, it was the second leading cause of preventable disease and death, and childhood and adolescence were considered to be the critical periods for obesity development (Morris, 2007). A particular concern was attributed to obesity in the early years of childhood because of its effect on children's psychological development, mortality, and morbidity in the long term (Wang and Lobstein, 2006). Thus, preventing obesity among children has become a priority for health institutions in many economically advanced countries.

2.3 Power generation industry

The power generation industry was a capital-intensive industry that provided a vital commodity – energy – to all citizens, entities, and organizations. The industry structure of power generation was determined by the fact that these companies were natural monopolies, whose enormous market power accrued from the great economies of scale that characterized the traditional power generation technologies. As a result, companies had enormous market power and were subject to complex regulations.

The regulators established an acceptable rate of return on the expensive assets used in the process of power generation and trading in the market. The cash flows in this business were stable and institutional investors chose the industry in their long-term holdings. Among the largest power companies in the world in 2012 were Enel (Italy), Eon (Germany), General Electric (US), State Grid (China), Engie (France), and Iberdrola (Spain).

2.4 Video game console industry

The video game industry was a multi-billion dollar entertainment industry that represented "the cutting edge of entertainment" and was dominated by a few global players (Discovery Channel, 2012). According to Nolan Bushnell, the founder of the first successful video game company Atari, video games had a more complex structure than good movies and this was exactly what caught kids' attention. The key attribute of games was that children could influ-ence their characters' ability to make a choice that would influence the development of the game.

The industry of game consoles grew in the early 1970s and, throughout the years, encoun-tered frequent and rapid changes in sales growth and industry leadership. Atari was the company to create the home video game industry with its first games *Pond* and *Space Invaders*. Since then, Nintendo, Sega Enterprises, Microsoft, and Sony have been competing for the leader's position in the market. Consoles such as PlayStation, GameCube, and Microsoft Xbox differed in technological advancements and image quality but became an enduring part of children's entertainment in the last decades (Hagiu and Halaburda, 2009).

Including public health concerns in the technological parameters and value proposition of its Wii console led Nintendo to unprecedented success in 2006. Even though it was technolog-ically less advanced than Microsoft's Xbox 360 (2005) and Sony's PlayStation 3 (2006), Wii had an innovative and user-friendly appeal. It offered something new to the audience – wireless, motion-sensing controllers that allowed gamers to dictate the movement of their characters with their own actions. These features attracted users from age 9 to 65, both female and male, and thus led to the expansion of the profile of the typical gamer.

The family-friendly game console allowed parents to play together or compete with their children in front of the screen. Versions of the game included Wii Sports and Wii Fit, which were used even in hospitals for rehabilitation purposes. The game targeted not only the physical movement but also the mental agility of the players – it developed skills for visual recognition, logic, and analysis besides precision of movement. As a result, the Wii became a desirable video game that made parents more likely to allow their children to stay and play inside in front of the screen (Adams, 2013).

2.5   The energy-generating playground equipment industry

There were a few companies whose value-added was at the intersection of energy generation and transformation and some level of entertainment.

The Scandinavian company Octavia produced a device called Son-X-Octavia, which was attached to a swing. It was powered by solar panels and had a motion sensor. The product included interactive audio games that kids could play when they reached a certain height: Applause, Concert, and Beat. When the kids were swinging, the device made noises (e.g., clapping during the first stage) that motivated them to swing even more energetically. This product, however, did not convert the energy of the kinetic movement and had the disadvan-tage of being entirely dependent on sunlight (HAGSGlobal, 2013).

Empower Playgrounds was a US non-profit organization that focused on enhancing educa-tional opportunities in rural African villages. The company produced and installed playground equipment that converted the energy created by children while playing into power for portable lighting. The platform was a type of merry-go-round. The entire platform was attached to a hub. A drive shaft from the hub was attached to a helical gearbox, which served as a speed increaser. The electricity generated by the mechanism was transported through underground wires to a power enclosure, where it could be immediately converted into electricity and used to charge a large storage battery.

The Empower Playgrounds system also contained "smart" LED lanterns, with a battery pack of over 40 hours, which were supplied by Energizer Battery Corporation, an Empower Playgrounds sponsor. One specific feature that differentiated these lanterns was an inside chip that allowed recharging from the large storage battery and power to the LED bulbs. In addition to the existing mechanism, a solar panel was connected to the equipment to prevent battery discharging during school breaks. As children played on the merry-go-round, their energy was collected and used to charge the portable LED lanterns. Those lanterns were then used to power the classroom lights during the day and were given to kids in the evening when they had to do their homework. Many school-aged children in Africa had to go to work after school to support their families, and they could only study at night. Thus, they needed light during the late hours in order to prepare their lessons for the next day.

In 2010, Empowering Playgrounds formed a partnership with playground manufacturer Playworld Systems and the science kit company Loose in the Labs, to begin the production of a crate full of electricity-generating playground equipment and science kits for shipments around the world.

At the low end of the spectrum were the small mechanical torches that were sold for only 99 cents in Southeast Asia, which if wired with ingenuity and connected to traditional playground equipment could produce electricity and offer opportunities for entertainment.

3.   TEAM AND BUSINESS IDEA ANTECEDENTS

Ilian Milinov and Hristo Aleksiev had been close friends for more than 20 years. They met when they both attended the University of Forestry in Sofia, Bulgaria. While Hristo discontinued his studies, Ilian graduated in 1996 with an interior and furniture design degree.

Ilian was one of the best industrial and furniture designers in Bulgaria. His professional portfolio consisted of a broad range of creative designs, from wristwatches to concept cars. He was the winner of numerous international design awards, such as Top Ten, Best of Neocon (for the most innovative product), Grand Prize Winner – Buildings Innovations Award, Prize of the National Center for Contemporary Art for High Achievements in the Field of Design, and Beck's Prize. He was a two-time winner of the Red Dot Design Award for his design concepts Hang Stool (2012) and Hug Chair (2010) (see Figure 8.1). His signature designs were acclaimed for their practical side that enhanced the user experience.

Hristo accumulated experience in five companies that he co-founded, one of which was the world's largest producer of climbing walls, Walltopia. Prior to becoming the co-founder of Walltopia, he had spent eight years in the supply department of IKEA as the manager in charge of product quality assurance.

Apart from their friendship, Hristo and Ilian shared previous business experience. In October 2009, they launched a Dutch-based user-generated website for mobile citizen journalism called MaYoMo (short for Map Your Moments). After four years of dedicated time

a. Hug Chair (2010)	
b. Hang Stool (2012)	

Source: www.ilian-milinov.com/Ilian_Milinov_Studio.pdf.

Figure 8.1   Ilian Milinov Red Dot Design Award winning design concepts

and effort to the venture, they finally reached the desired 100,000 visitors per day. This was the exact moment when their startup venture ran out of resources and closed.

4. THE IDEA: FUN, HEALTH, AND EDUCATION ON THE PLAYGROUND

From the very beginning, Hristo and Ilian agreed that they did not aspire to compete with companies in the energy generation industry. They remembered the outdoor playgrounds from their childhood as the gaming platform of the time and felt nostalgia for the game-related innovations and socialization among kids, who used to liberate an enormous amount of energy while having fun. These memories contrasted with the current concept of games that took place in the digital universe from a console placed in a living room. Ideally, the energy spent in the playground could be stored or directly used for the illumination of surrounding elements for kids' entertainment, such as sounds or lights, for supplying electricity to street-lamps near the playground so that kids could continue playing in the evening, and for Wi-Fi hotspots that would allow parents to work online outdoors. The concept looked promising, and Playground Energy was born.

Playground Energy aimed to make outdoor playgrounds more interactive and engaging, so that kids wanted to play longer in the open air. Hristo and Ilian imagined that sometime in the future online gaming platforms and original outdoor playground equipment manufacturers could become complementary, thus ensuring a healthy lifestyle for the youth and alleviating the problem of child obesity. One possible venue for experimentation they envisaged was to connect playground equipment to an online game experience so that children could earn rewards for their physical activities in the form of virtual tokens, which could be redeemed online. The more energy a kid spends in the open-air playground, the more virtual tokens he or she would earn, which could lead to an upgrade to the next online gaming level. If such a scenario could be validated, Playground Energy could stimulate children to switch from their computer or console for a while and go outside and play in the open air instead. One important driver of Playground Energy's founders was to help kids have a more balanced play style combining online and outdoor entertainment.

Given that the technological base of Playground Energy consisted of transforming the kinetic energy that kids spent at the outdoor playgrounds and converting it into a pleasant or entertaining stimulus, such as light or sound or energy to charge mobile devices or Wi-Fi hotspots, there also existed an educational element that could be brought into the core of the future business model. The founders imagined that Playground Energy could bring learning opportunities regarding energy use and transformation alongside the entertainment and health benefits.

At the beginning of the prototyping and validation process, Hristo and Ilian experimented with attaching a generator to a swing and used it to harvest the kinetic energy from the motion. This design could power up lights in different colors. However, Hristo and Ilian reached the conclusion that since models of swings vary too much around the world, customization could

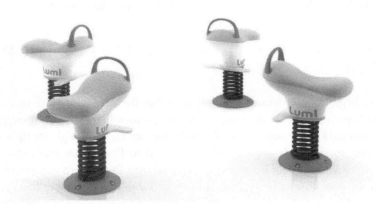

Source: Taken with permission from www.playgroundenergy.com.

Figure 8.2   Lumi 1 playground

Source: Taken with permission from www.playgroundenergy.com.

Figure 8.3   Lumi 2 playground

be a challenge for scaling up a swing generator. Therefore, the entrepreneurs decided to create a unique design for their playground equipment. Lumi 1 was the first product of Playground Energy. It was a spring toy made of high-impact translucent plastic. All of its components were produced locally in Bulgaria. Lumi 2 came soon after that, which was an upgraded version of Lumi 1 as it had a more powerful generator and a slightly different design (see Figures 8.2 and 8.3).

5. PITCHING FOR FUNDING AND QUALITY NETWORK

Once the value proposition of Playground Energy was formulated, Hristo and Ilian decided to apply for seed-stage funding at Eleven – a EUR11 million acceleration venture fund that focused on early-stage technology-based ventures. It worked as a combination of an accelerator and investment fund. The European Investment Fund had selected Eleven to manage the seed financing under the JEREMIE Holding Fund in Bulgaria (Eleven Ventures, n.d.). JEREMIE was an initiative of the European Commission and the European Investment Bank. It aimed at developing high-impact entrepreneurship by improving access to financing for micro, small, and medium-sized enterprises in the European Union for the period from 2007 to 2013 (JEREMIE, n.d.).

Eleven used an incremental investment approach alongside iterative development. As a new investment fund, it started with many small seed-stage investments and distinguished failures from successes relatively early. In the first stage, the venture fund provided up to EUR50,000 during the six months of the acceleration program. The capital was divided into two equal installments: the first covered the initial three months, and Eleven received 8 percent equity participation; the second was released during the fourth to the sixth month, and Eleven got 5 percent additional equity participation. After these six months, the startups had the opportunity to apply for an additional EUR150,000 of follow-up funding, provided that new private investors were attracted.

At the end of August 2012, when the first investment window of Eleven opened, Playground Energy applied for funding. It received seed funding of EUR33,000 twice – on September 1, 2012 and February 3, 2013. On June 6, 2013, the company received additional seed funding of EUR196,500.

From September 2012 until January 2013, the company operated under the co-working space of Eleven and was entirely focused on developing its first prototype. In January 2013, during one of the demo days, Hristo and Ilian presented their prototype, and John Bradford, a partner of Eleven, was impressed by the two entrepreneurs. He invited them to join the Springboard Hardware Accelerator in Cambridge between March and May 2013. This opportunity helped the startup advance fast in the development process and connect with possible future investors, partners, and clients. After investing in Playground Energy, Springboard also received a small percentage of the company's equity (see Figure 8.4).

Springboard was a 13-week European startup accelerator supporting Eleven, which combined investment capital and mentorship. It was based at Google Campus in London and ideaSpace in Cambridge. It provided seed capital of up to USD150,000 in the form of free services and onsite support for entrepreneurs, investors, and mentors. At the end of the program, startups pitched their ideas in front of angel investors and venture capitalists from London and beyond. Over half of the companies participating in the Springboard accelerator programs raised additional investment funding (Bryant, 2012). The co-founders of Playground Energy believed networking was key to a successful business and embraced the opportunity that the Springboard accelerated program offered.

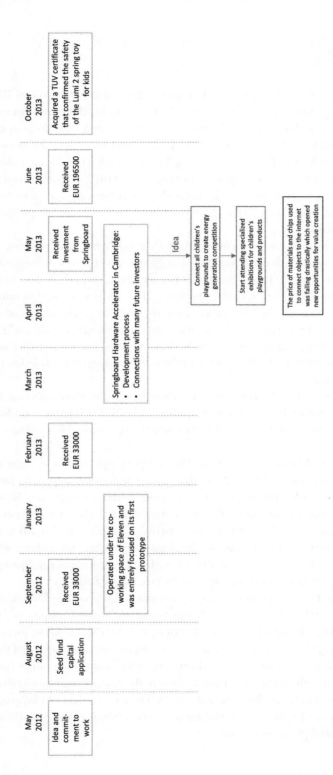

Figure 8.4   Company timeline

"It would have been much harder if we had stayed in Sofia," stated Hristo after returning from the three-month accelerator program in Cambridge. The program focused on ventures immersed on the Internet of Things technologies and trends. The price of materials and chips used to connect objects to the internet was falling drastically, opening new opportunities for value creation. One such opportunity the Playground Energy founders identified after the Springboard program was to connect all children's playgrounds that used the company's equipment, creating small competitions in energy generation among different neighborhoods and regions.

Attending specialized events and exhibitions for playground equipment and products became a priority of the Playground Energy founders as such venues started to reflect a myriad of new trends that went beyond the Internet of Things.

6.   BUSINESS STRATEGY FOR SUSTAINABILITY AND GROWTH

The first product of Playground Energy was Lumi 1, a spring toy (*Wall Street Journal*, 2013). The end users of the product were children and their families. Playground Energy's initial paying clients were both private (shopping malls, private kindergartens, foundations, non-profits, and families wanting to buy the toys for their backyards) and public (local municipalities and some central governments).

From the very beginning, Ilian and Hristo did not consider broadening the portfolio with an oversized offering of playground equipment. They did not plan to engage in a head-to-head competition with the producers of traditional playground equipment, either. They focused heavily on developing a unique generator mechanism that stored and converted kinetic energy with very little resistance. With Lumi 1 and Lumi 2 (see Figure 8.2), Playground Energy decided to bundle the unique power transformation mechanism into very attractive and carefully designed outdoor spring toys for fun, health, and education. Potentially, the product could be unbundled, and the generator installed on equipment designed by other companies. Even though such unbundling was feasible, the founders decided not to pursue it. Public-sector clients were expected to be key to the new venture's success. The co-founders expected to convince public officials to invest in the "fun, health, and education" promise of Playground Energy and anticipated stronger public-sector interest as a result.

"Gratitude would be later expressed in the votes in the next election cycle when parents vote for mayors and local councils," said Hristo. Because local elections were held every four years, no actual validation of this anticipated positive effect on the election results of the governing teams was immediately available. In general, the idea behind the Playground Energy value proposition was perceived as innovative and people normally reacted to it with enthusiasm and curiosity, which was essential for positive word of mouth-based marketing.

7.   PLANS FOR THE FUTURE

In October 2013, Playground Energy acquired a TUV certificate that confirmed the safety of the Lumi 2 spring toy for kids. Thus, the company could start production and distribution to the first buyers. The company could not reach breakeven the year after receiving the first seed investment. The expectation was that this important benchmark could be achieved in a few more months after product shipments had started.

Iliyan and Hristo had the ambition to operate globally. Due to logistic reasons, they decided initially to focus on Europe. Playground Energy had its first contracts with municipalities in Bulgaria. It was also part of the SmartCity project in England. Hristo and Ilian saw this as serious progress towards global recognition that could leverage a more ambitious global strategy of which they already had a vision.

According to this vision for the future, once the company achieved global acceptance and playgrounds worldwide were equipped with Playground Energy's spring toys, the interaction between kids at every level could be constantly improved. For example, spring toys in playgrounds could be connected to a central hub that lit up in different colors depending on the location where the energy was generated. Furthermore, when two kids swung simultaneously, their spring toys could produce light of the same color, indicating the synchronicity of the movement. Competitive games as well as collaborative events, such as the Simon Game, could also be possible. Strategic partnerships with global brands such as Lego were seen as possible venues for future development.

"In my experience, companies frequently fail not because their idea is bad but because they do not have a focus," said Hristo. Ilian and Hristo were determined to turn their venture into a sustainable company with a positive impact that could not save the world but would make it better. What was the right scale-up strategy ahead now that the prototype was validated and the first paying customers were secured?

8.   TEN YEARS DOWN THE ROAD: NEW CHALLENGES AWAIT

In 2013, when Playground Energy was created, a low-intensity conflict between two neighboring European countries began to manifest: Ukraine and Russia. Ukrainian President Viktor Yanukovych did not sign an association agreement with the European Union. Pro-Western protests eventually forced Yanukovych to leave the country and an interim government was established. The removal of President Yanukovych in 2013 was the trigger for Russia's annexation of Crimea and the establishment of separatist entities in eastern Ukraine. This conflict persisted until October 2021, when Russia began moving troops and military equipment near its border with Ukraine in response to the possibility of Ukraine joining NATO. On February 22, 2022, Russian President Vladimir Putin signed a decree recognizing the self-proclaimed Donetsk People's Republic and Luhansk People's Republic as independent. Following this, on February 24, 2022, Russia proceeded with a special military operation on Ukrainian territory. In parallel, significant developments regarding energy availability affected the world.

Between 2003 and 2013, Germany closed its nuclear facilities and shifted to a strategy of energy generation from more environmentally friendly sources. The Netherlands established strict regulations to stop using natural gas as a source of energy to meet net-zero targets. This trend has been followed for years by all countries of the Organisation for Economic Co-operation and Development that declared their intention to control and prevent environmental deterioration and global warming. In the US, on January 20, 2021, President Joe Biden revoked the permit for the Keystone XL pipeline on his first day in office with the aim of moving away from fossil fuels.

Russia, which had become one of the principal gas suppliers of the world, reduced its supply to Europe dramatically, leading to an increase in energy prices across the continent. Between 2021 and 2022, energy prices grew by 15 percent and natural gas prices grew by 34.37 percent. Under this new scenario, alternative sources of energy became a priority for the entire world.

By 2023, Hristo and Ilian had successfully completed projects in 30 countries and sold playground equipment that harvested children's energy on five continents. They had developed a portfolio of 22 different products (see Figure 8.5). They believed there was room for growth for the company, either within the same industry or in related ones. Their aim was to have at least 100 playground sites per country and to start generating a significant positive impact on kids' lifestyle around the world. Part of the initial vision, which included the deployment of playground equipment that could be connected to digital games, was still a prospect. In the public arena, municipalities changed their priorities. The global COVID-19 pandemic also affected the firm's international growth, as children were not allowed to go outside to open playground spaces, while public spending was redirected towards health-related expenses.

 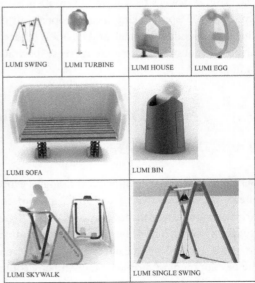

Source: Taken from www.playgroundenergy.com/ with permission.

Figure 8.5 Current playground energy portfolio

Also, at a wider level, there has been a surge of movements towards more extreme right- and left-leaning political parties, with a growing global tension in a highly uncertain environment. Although this has improved since the pandemic period, the global economy has been showing signs of weakness.

Despite selling hundreds of units of playground equipment, Playground Energy was still to achieve mass adoption. The company, which in 2023 consisted of a team of six, received additional external funding of EUR425,000 from the Bulgarian fund Eleven and UniCredit Bulbank, which was used to develop, produce, and export six new products. The playground equipment market was estimated to be USD4.2 billion globally in pre-pandemic 2018. One major challenge Playground Energy was facing in its operation was that many projects were publicly funded and required complex approval processes, expanding additionally the sales cycle.

Playground Energy operated through local partners and distributors, who were companies specialized in building playgrounds. These partners were responsible for sales, installation, and maintenance of Playground Energy products. The model was successful in helping the company export to numerous markets as Playground Energy took care not to compete with their distributors as they limited their direct offerings to individual items rather than complete sets or playground designs. However, since 2012, at least four other companies in the same industry segment have started incorporating an energy transformation component into their products (Empower Playgrounds, Peachy Keen, Berliner Seilfabrik, and RotoGen Reactions Totem).

In the middle of this uncertain environment, Playground Energy was approached by a local agent who said that the Government of Colombia was looking for power generation playground devices to deploy in remote areas of the country that had intermittent electricity supply. Despite having initially opted out of the power generation industry in 2012, the altering geopolitical, social, and business landscape has given rise to a distinct scenario, where diversification was expected to increase its strategic significance for doing business in a world of flux.

9.   TRENDS AND INDUSTRY EVOLUTION

9.1   Green technology

Between 2013 and 2023 green technologies evolved significantly. The shift towards renewable energy accelerated, with solar and wind power becoming more affordable and widespread. Advances in battery technology also enabled greater adoption of electric vehicles and energy storage systems. The Internet of Things and artificial intelligence were applied to optimize energy usage and reduce energy waste. New materials and manufacturing processes enabled the development of more efficient and environmentally friendly products. Governments, corporations, and consumers alike were increasingly recognizing the importance of sustainable practices, and there was a growing trend towards adopting circular economy principles. While there were still challenges to overcome, such as scaling up green technologies and reducing the environmental impact of production, the progress made over the last decade generated optimism for a more environmentally sustainable future built on alternative sources of energy.

9.2   Public health concerns

Public health concerns had been growing. According to the World Health Organization, the number of overweight or obese children under the age of five rose from 32 million globally in 1990 to 41 million in 2016. In developed countries, this issue was fueled by a combination of factors including unhealthy diets, sedentary lifestyles, and lack of access to healthy food choices. The COVID-19 pandemic exacerbated the problem, with many children becoming even less active due to social-distancing measures and remote learning. This led to concerns about long-term health consequences such as diabetes, heart disease, and other chronic illnesses. The rise of technology and digital devices increased children's time in front of a screen. With the widespread use of smartphones and tablets, children had access to a multitude of digital distractions, leading to potential difficulties in managing their time effectively. There was also a growing awareness of the importance of limiting screen time and promoting healthy habits for children's overall well-being.

9.3   Power generation industry

The global renewable energy market grew 11.1 percent between 2017 and 2022, reaching a total of USD941.7 billion in 2022. According to the Economist Intelligence Unit, global energy consumption grew by just 1.3 percent in 2023, amid a slowing economy and high energy prices. Waning gas supplies, geopolitical tensions, and extreme weather events forced many countries to fall back on fossil fuels, delaying the green energy transition. The industry was still capital-intensive with almost the same companies dominating different national markets. EDF (France), ENEL (Italy), and SPIC (China) are some of the most powerful entities in the world, owning significant assets and operating on a multinational scale. The armed conflict between Russia and Ukraine created pressure for energy supply in Europe where citizens started facing high variability and increases in energy costs.

In 2022, the global supply of renewable energy from solar, wind, hydro, geothermal, and ocean sources experienced a remarkable growth of nearly 8 percent. As a result, the collective share of these technologies in the total global energy supply increased by nearly 0.4 percentage points, reaching 5.5 percent. Additionally, modern bioenergy's share also saw a significant rise, increasing by 0.2 percentage points and reaching 6.8 percent.[3]

This surge in renewable electricity capacity additions, coupled with the increased availability of hydropower, contributed to non-bioenergy renewables achieving their second-highest share growth in history, after the exceptional year 2020 with the pandemic impact.

9.4   Video game console industry

The game console market grew by 12.7 percent between 2017 and 2021, with a peak during 2020 in the COVID-19 pandemic period. Home entertainment accounted for 73.6 percent of the total market. The game software market grew by 4.6 percent during the same period. There was a stable trend for children to spend most of their time playing video games and interacting in social networks, dedicating less time to activities in the open air.

9.5   The energy-generating playground equipment industry

Since 2012, other companies have entered the energy-generating playground equipment industry. Companies such as Berliner Seilfabrik, founded in 1865, found in the energy-generating devices a new avenue for their consolidated industry. Others such as Empower playgrounds, a US-based non-governmental organization, were also pursuing a global market share. Peachy Keen from the United Kingdom and rotoGen Reactions Totem, producing energy playground products, were new to the market.

10.   COLOMBIA: A COUNTRY OF BIODIVERSITY

Colombia, situated in the northwest of South America, is a diverse and dynamic nation known for its unique blend of cultural influences. It holds the distinction of being the second most biodiverse country on the planet. For over five decades, Colombia has grappled with various forms of violence stemming from political causes and has been significantly impacted by drug trafficking, leaving vast territories stripped from proper provision of public services, among which is electricity provision.

In August 2022, a left-wing party won in the presidential elections for the first time. The new leadership is driven by a vision to implement progressive social and environmental policies, aiming to address the pressing issues faced by the nation. Since 2015, several efforts have been made to promote peace and stability through various peace agreements with armed groups. However, political challenges persist, including corruption, income inequality, and regional disparities.

Colombia has a mixed economy characterized by abundant natural resources, including oil, coal, and coffee. With 50 million people, it is one of the largest economies in Latin America. The territory of Colombia accounts for an area of 1.141.748 km² (equivalent to the territory of France, Spain, and Portugal together), with most of the population being located around the Andes mountains. However, this vast extension makes it difficult to have complete coverage of essential services such as energy or paved roads in many areas of the country. Many of these areas lack a formal presence of government.

Previous governments promoted foreign investment and trade, resulting in a diversified economy with sectors such as manufacturing, agriculture, services, and tourism. However, economic growth has experienced fluctuations due to external factors and internal challenges. Some recent policies are perceived as creating additional barriers for foreign companies.

Colombia is a country rich in cultural diversity, with various indigenous and ethnic groups contributing to its vibrant society. However, it also faces social issues, including poverty, income inequality, and limited access to education and healthcare, particularly in rural areas.

Social programs and initiatives have been implemented to address these challenges and improve the overall well-being of its citizens.

In terms of technology and digital infrastructure, Colombia has made significant achievements. Major cities boast well-developed information technology industries and successful digital startups. The government has invested in expanding broadband access and promoting innovation through research and development incentives. However, there is a deep infrastructure and digital divide, with rural and remote areas lacking adequate access to technology.

Colombia's natural beauty is unparalleled, with diverse ecosystems ranging from rainforests to coastal regions. The country faces environmental challenges, including deforestation, illegal mining, and threats to biodiversity. Conservation efforts have been made, and the government is actively promoting initiatives towards sustainable development practices to preserve its unique natural heritage.

Colombia's legal system is based on civil law, and the rule of law is upheld. However, issues like corruption and slow judicial processes can hinder legal enforcement. The country has implemented reforms to enhance transparency and tackle corruption, aiming to improve the overall business and investment climate.

11.   DECISIONS TO MAKE

In January 2023, Playground Energy was contacted by an agent that said that the Government of Colombia was considering submitting an inquiry about the possible production of several spring toys that could support the government strategy for educational inclusion in remote areas of the country. In many remote regions of Colombia, it takes days to bring petrol to the power plants, which generate electricity for daily needs. Most of the time, the petrol supply is interrupted and insufficient and is mainly used for essential activities such as water pumping. A special, more powerful version of the spring toys produced by Playground Energy was needed to produce energy for school playgrounds. The company needed to decide if it was worth working on a solution that would fit the requirements of the remote areas with electricity shortages. The decision had to be made quickly.

1. If you were in the position of Hristo and Ilian, would you consider diversifying Playground Energy activities into the business of energy generation?
2. Did the contextual factors that the company considered in pursuing its strategy for the past 10 years change so much to make them shift the company's strategy towards energy generation?
3. Should Playground Energy rethink its strategy and expand its internal resources to diversify into the energy generation domain, or is it better for the company to delve deeper into its current business model?

ACKNOWLEDGMENTS

We greatly acknowledge the research assistance of Dilyana Dobrinova, Temenuzhka Panayotova, and Vasil Sariev.

NOTES

1. An interview with Hristo took place in October 2014. Some parts of the interview are available on YouTube: www.youtube.com/watch?v=oPS5Z-8dXM0
2. This case was prepared by Veneta Andonova, Juan Pablo Soto, and Jana Schmutzler as the basis for class discussion rather than to illustrate either effective or ineffective handling of a business situation.
3. Data from the International Energy Agency website: www.iea.org/

REFERENCES

Adams, Georgie (2013). Nintendo Wii games download: Obesity can be fought with Nintendo Wii. *Published*, November 10. www.published.com/b-Nintendo-Wii-Games-Download---Obesity-Can-Be-Fought-With-Nintendo-Wii_7948.aspx

Bryant, Martin (2012). Springboard partners with ARM, Unilever, Neul and Raspberry Pi to launch Internet of Things accelerator. https://thenextweb.com/news/springboard-partners-with-arm-unilever-neul-and-raspberry-pi-to-launch-internet-of-things-accelerator

Discovery Channel (2012). Rise of the video game: Level 1. November 4. www.youtube.com/watch?v=3u3Hc13wzHE

Eleven Ventures (n.d.). https://www.11.vc/. Accessed May 2023.

Hagiu, Andrei, and Hanna Halaburda (2009). Responding to the Wii? Harvard Business School Case 709-448.

HAGSGlobal (2013). SonXOctavia. April 29. www.youtube.com/watch?v=hjmny2cu7ZE

JEREMIE (Joint European Resources for Micro to Medium Enterprises) (n.d.). What we do. www.eif.org/what_we_do/resources/jeremie/index.htm

Lager, Anton, and Sven Bremberg (2005). Health effects of video and computer game playing. Swedish National Institute of Public Health. www.fhi.se/PageFiles/4170/R200518_video_computer_game(1).pdf

Morris, S. (2007). The impact of obesity on employment. *Labour Economics*, 14(3), 413–433.

The Economist (2012). Rio 20 Summit: Green business. June 22. www.economist.com/blogs/schumpeter/2012/06/rio20-summit

Tranæs, Torben, and Bent Jensen (2013). Children spend five times as long in front of TV and computer screens as they do exercising. Newsletter, Rockwool Foundation Research Unit, June. www.rff.dk/files/RFF-site/Publikations%20upload/Newsletters/Engelsk/Newsletter%20June%202013%20(2).pdf

United Nations Development Programme (2012). Green economy in action: Articles and excerpts that illustrate green economy and sustainable development efforts. November 10. www.undp.org/content/dam/aplaws/publication/en/publications/environment-energy/www-ee-library/mainstreaming/Green%20Economy%20in%20Action/Green%20Economy%20Compilation%20Report.pdf

Wall Street Journal (2013). Harvesting energy from kids. June 11. http://blogs.wsj.com/tech-europe/2013/06/11/harvesting-energy-from-kids/?KEYWORDS=playground+energy

Wang, Youfa, and Tim Lobstein (2006). Worldwide trends in childhood overweight and obesity. *International Journal of Pediatric Obesity*, 1, 11–25.

9
Jumia, the Amazon of Africa: its quest for combining growth and profitability

Lourdes Casanova and Anne Miroux

It was the right time and the right place to take the firm to a higher level, bring it increased visibility and enable it to access a new group of shareholders and investors.
(Jeremy Hodara, Jumia co-chief executive officer)

1.   THE ORIGINS OF AN AFRICAN E-COMMERCE PIONEER

Jumia, often dubbed the "Amazon of Africa," is Africa's largest e-commerce player and the first unicorn[1] in the continent. Offering an e-commerce marketplace, logistics services, and a payment platform, Jumia operates in 11 countries, an area of about 600 million people accounting for almost 70 percent of Africa's gross domestic product. Since its inception, the company has pursued a strategy focused on growth, registering ever increasing revenues. Jumia has been a source of pride which rode the technology boom in Africa. However, after ten years of existence and significant moves in its growth strategy, Jumia has not yet turned a profit. Admittedly, it is often the case that e-commerce startups are not profitable in their early years, but a decade is a long time. How much longer will investors be willing to wait? A few major and historical investors have already left, possibly signaling more trouble ahead. In early 2022, the two founders and chief executive officers of Jumia, Sacha Poignonnec and Jeremy Hodara, face the following question: How to turn the tide and bring Jumia to profitability? And under what time horizon should they operate? It is a question of survival.

Jumia is headquartered in Lagos, Nigeria. It was founded in 2012 by Tunde Kehinde from Nigeria and Raphael Afaedor from Ghana, along with two Frenchmen Jeremy Hodara and Sacha Poignonnec, who remained at the helm of the company after Kehinde and Afaedor stepped down. It became the Jumia Group in 2016. Initially operating in Nigeria, the company quickly expanded and, by the end of 2018, it was operating in 14 African countries. Having risen at a remarkable speed, it had become the largest e-commerce firm on the continent. As of 2022, Jumia is active in Algeria, Cote d'Ivoire, Egypt, Ghana, Kenya, Morocco, Nigeria, Senegal, South Africa, Tunisia, and Uganda. The countries are all over the continent.

Its robust growth in gross merchandise volume (GMV),[2] total orders, annual active customers, and total payment volumes (TPV) on its digital payment platform (JumiaPay) impressed Jumia's investors from the beginning. The company was originally backed by the German platform and company builder Rocket Internet and was criticized at times for not being a "real African company." Established venture capitalists and high-profile investors such as the French insurance group Axa, the telecoms groups Orange in France and MTN in South Africa, and the United States (US) firms Summit Partners and Goldman Sachs later joined Rocket Internet through several rounds of financing. By the end of 2018, Jumia had raised the most among African e-commerce businesses (Casanova, Miroux, and Finchelstein, 2021).

In April 2019, Jumia went public in New York, thereby becoming the first startup from Africa to list on a major international exchange. Its shares, originally listed at USD14.50, reached a high of USD50 just a few days after its initial public offering (IPO) (Figure 9.1). Since then, however, Jumia's share value has been on a rocky path. Faced with allegations of fraud regarding the information provided for the IPO as well as fraudulent sales by its "JForce" sales team, and with lower-than-expected financial results, the share price tumbled to a low of USD7 by the end of 2019; it did not recover until late 2020. As of May 2022, public ownership was 23.6 percent (Orbis database; accessed April 2022).

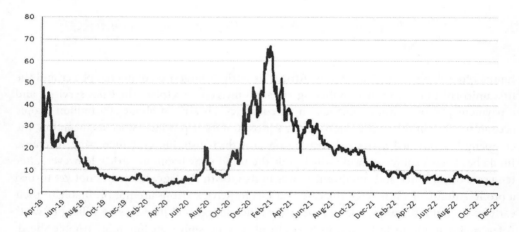

Source: Taken from Yahoo Finance: https://uk.finance.yahoo.com/quote/JMIA?p=JMIA. Permission as per Yahoo rules given.

Figure 9.1   Jumia's share price in USD since initial public offering, April 2019–December 2022

By October 2019, Rocket Internet – Jumia's historical investor – began reducing its participation in Jumia and, in April 2020, it announced that it had completely pulled out. In October 2020, South Africa's MTN, Jumia's largest shareholder with 30 percent ownership, also announced it had sold its stake in Jumia.[3]

2. JUMIA'S EVOLVING BUSINESS MODEL, PRODUCTS, AND SERVICES

Over the years, Jumia evolved its business model. First, the company transitioned from being a first-party retailer to becoming a third party-focused marketplace. After 2020, it changed the focus of its product portfolio towards less expensive, more day-to-day items. In addition, to overcome some of the acute problems that e-commerce firms face in Africa such as tricky logistics, security risks, low bancarization, and low credit card penetration, Jumia developed its own logistics network and payment systems. The following examines in more detail the evolution of Jumia's business models, products, and services.

2.1 From online retailer to marketplace

Confronted with the African population's lack of familiarity with online shopping, and a lack of trust, Jumia made customer satisfaction a key element of its growth strategy. The firm innovated to address such problems. For example, Jumia opened customer adoption centers, enabling users to place orders on Wi-Fi-connected laptops and tablets and helping them become familiar with online shopping. It developed a force of sales agents (the JForce) who, going door to door, would acquaint customers with Jumia's website and products and help them place orders. It also put in place a system whereby, once an order was placed, customers received a confirmation call within 30 minutes. Very early on, it incorporated a mobile app into its digital products, as well as a chatbot functionality, giving customers the ability to continually stay connected within its ecosystem (Casanova et al., 2021). Its introduction of Black Friday sales, the first to do so on the African continent, offering huge discounts to customers, also contributed to the visibility and increased acceptance of online shopping in Africa. Since 2014, the Jumia website has received millions of page views per day during the November Black Friday period.

Initially, Jumia operated as a first-party seller of phones, electronics, and other expensive items to consumers. In 2016, it began transitioning to become a more third party-focused marketplace, enabling sellers to connect with buyers for e-commerce transactions – a shift that has further strengthened since 2020. Third-party sales are important because they offer better margins to e-commerce companies than first-party sales where the firm must buy, store, and sell the goods itself. Supplementary services (such as advertising) offered to sellers for a fee are also an additional source of revenue. Today, its marketplace is at the core of Jumia's activity; more than 50 million items are listed for sale on its platform, and 90 percent of items are sold by third-party sellers (Jumia company presentation, April 2022). By the end of 2021, third-party revenues accounted for more than 60 percent of Jumia's total revenues, compared to less than 50 percent two years before (see Table 9.1).

The shift to a third party-focused marketplace is in line with the trend set by other major e-commerce firms. Amazon, for instance, has put significant efforts into growing its third-party GMV. It is estimated that about two-thirds of the USD600 billion of Amazon's total GMV in 2021 was third-party sales, up from 57 percent in 2018 (see Table 9.2).

Table 9.1   Jumia's revenues: Marketplace and first-party revenues, 2019–2021 (USD million unless stated otherwise)

	2019	2020	2021
Total revenue	179.5	159.4	177.9
Marketplace revenue	87.8	107.1	108.2
Commission	28	39.5	35.3
Fulfillment	30.1	37	36.4
Marketing and advertising	6.8	8.8	10.8
Value-added services	22.9	21.8	25.7
First-party revenue	90.9	50.4	65.1

Source: Own elaboration based on data from Jumia, company presentation Q4 2021–April 2022.

Table 9.2   Facts and figures on the largest e-commerce firms in the world, 2021 (USD billion unless stated otherwise)

Company	Country of origin	GMV	Market cap/ valuation	Revenue	Net income	Number of countries	Employees (thousands)	Mobile payment
Amazon	USA	578[a, b]	1232.94	477.75	21.41	14	1608.00	Amazon Pay
Alibaba	China	1239.00[a]	319.53	127.46	9.30	24	254.94	Alipay
Jumia	Nigeria	0.99[a]	0.81	0.19	(0.27)	11	4.48	JumiaPay
Mercado Libre	Argentina	28.40[a]	41.54	7.94	0.18	18	29.96	Mercado Pago

Notes: [a] Data as of December 31, 2021; [b] Amazon's GMV figure is estimated by Pitchbook.
Source: The authors and EMI team elaboration, based on CapitalIQ database, Pitchbook database, https://ir.aboutamazon.com/annual-reports-proxies-and-shareholder-letters/default.aspx, www.alibabagroup.com/en/ir/reports, https://investor.jumia.com/financialsfilings/default.aspx, https://investor.mercadolibre.com/financial-information/annual-reports, all accessed June 2022.

2.2   Moving to everyday category products

Since 2020, Jumia has been shifting more business towards *everyday category products* such as beauty, fashion, or fast-moving consumer goods – a major move in the firm's strategy. Mobile phones and electronics accounted for about 36 percent of Jumia's GMV in 2021, down from 56 percent in 2019 (see Figure 9.2), while beauty, personal care, fast-moving consumer goods, home food delivery, etc. was the company's fastest-growing category, accounting for about two-thirds of Jumia's GVM.

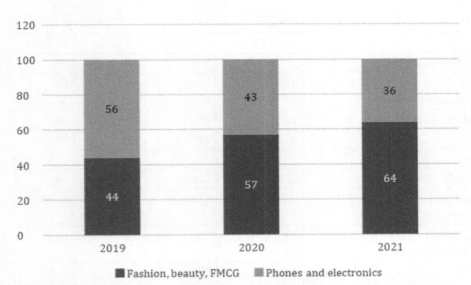

Source: Own elaboration based on data from JUMIA Company Presentation, 2022: https://s23.q4cdn.com/836376591/files/doc_presentation/2022/03/JMIA-Post-Q4.pdf.

Figure 9.2   Jumia's gross merchandise value breakdown 2019, 2020, and 2021

"Everyday" products have higher commission rates and are less promotionally intensive than, for instance, phones and electronics. In addition, being bought more frequently, they drive repeat consumers – which contributes to the visibility of the firm and its ability to extend its market. The transition to a third party-focused marketplace has also helped Jumia to diversify its product mix, since the firm no longer needs to hold all the goods in store (with all the associated expenses). The shift to the everyday category of products was also accentuated during the COVID-19 crisis.

Jumia has become a highly diversified business, offering a wide range of products and services. As of July 2021, it had 23 million website visits per month, the highest number of visits of all e-commerce players in Africa. Its number of active consumers continued to rise to reach 8 million in 2021, gaining almost 2 million active users in two years (see Table 9.3).

3.   MOBILE PAYMENTS AND LOGISTICS AS SOURCES OF INNOVATION AND GROWTH

Because of low bancarization in Africa (48 versus 75 percent in the world), Jumia first relied on the cash on delivery model, i.e., the customer would pay for the merchandise on delivery. Then, in 2016, following Alibaba's example, Jumia created its own payment system, JumiaPay. Besides facilitating safe and fast payments, JumiaPay bypasses the need for a bank account. JumiaPay is what PayPal was to eBay before the two companies split in 2015. Today, JumiaPay is one of the most important elements of Jumia's business.

Table 9.3 Jumia's summary table (in USD million unless stated otherwise)

	FY2017	FY2018	FY2019	FY2020	FY2021
Marketplace KPIs					
Annual active consumers (million)	2.7	4.0	6.1	6.8	8.0
Orders (million)	n.a.	14.4	26.5	27.9	34.0
GMV	576.7[a]	851.9[a]	1172.7[a]	955.5	990.6
JumiaPay KPIs					
JumiaPay TPV	n.m.	62.6[a]	141.0[a]	224.3	263.3
On-platform penetration		7.3%	12.0%	23.5%	26.6%
JumiaPay transactions (million)	n.m.	2.0	7.6	9.6	12.1
On-platform penetration		13.9%	28.7%	34.4%	35.6%
Selected financials					
Total revenue	104.9	152.3	179.5	159.4	177.9
Gross profit	27.2	44.2	84.9	106.0	110.5
Fulfillment expense	−34.4	−50.5	−86.6	−79.1	−88.7
Gross profit after Fulfillment expense	**−7.2**	**−6.3**	**−1.7**	26.9	21.8
Sales and advertising expense	−36.9	−46.0	−62.7	−37.1	−81.9
Technology and content expense	−20.6	−22.4	−30.5	−31.8	−39.2
General and administrative expense	−89.1	−94.9	−161.8	−132.0	−142.8
EBITDA loss	**−154.7**	**−169.7**	**−255.1**	**−170.3**	**−240.9**
Economics per order					
Gross profit after fulfillment expense	n.a.	−0.4	−0.1	1.0	0.6
Sales and advertising expense	n.a.	−3.2	−2.4	−1.3	−2.4
Technology and content expense	n.a.	−1.6	−1.2	−1.1	−1.2

	FY2017	FY2018	FY2019	FY2020	FY2021
General and administrative expense	n.a.	**−6.6**	**−6.1**	**−4.7**	**−4.2**
EBITDA loss	n.a.	**−11.8**	**−9.6**	**−6.1**	**−7.1**
Economics as % of GMV					
Gross profit after fulfillment expense	−1.2%	−0.7%	−0.1%	2.8%	2.2%
Sales and advertising expense	−6.4%	−5.4%	−5.3%	−3.9%	−8.3%
Technology and content expense	−3.6%	−2.6%	−2.6%	−3.3%	−4.0%
General and administrative expense	−15.5%	−11.1%	−13.8%	−13.8%	−14.4%
EBITDA loss	−26.8%	−19.9%	−21.8%	−17.8%	−24.3%

Note: [a] The data from FY2017 to FY2019 is converted from EUR to USD using the exchange rate as of December 31, 2021. Numbers in bold imply negative figures.
Source: Own elaboration based on data from Capital IQ database and Jumia company presentation (https://s23.q4cdn.com/836376591/files/doc_financials/20 20/q1/1Q20-Earnings-Presentation.pdf).

The growth of JumiaPay has been remarkable. JumiaPay had a breakout year in 2019 as its TPV more than doubled from about USD63 million in 2018 to USD141 million; TPV continued to rise significantly in 2020. In 2021, it reached USD263 million and more than a third of total transactions on Jumia were paid via JumiaPay and accounted for 27 percent of Jumia GMV compared with 12 percent in 2019 (see Table 9.3).

JumiaPay offers a variety of services, beyond paying on purchases on the Jumia platform. It can be used by consumers to get cashback on purchases, or pay for utility bills, phone bills, or online sport betting, among others. It has also started offering loan services to consumers and sellers through partnerships with financial institutions. Its transformation to become a "SuperApp" has been driving its growth. In 2020, the company added over 111 different services[4] to the JumiaPay app.

In June 2021, Jumia entered a partnership with Huawei that enables consumers in Egypt, Morocco, Tunisia, Algeria, Nigeria, and Kenya to directly and conveniently click through the Jumia online marketplace and buy instantly from their Huawei phones. It has also been added to the Huawei AppGallery.[5]

In addition, since 2021, Jumia has been working to start offering payment-processing solutions off-platform to third-party merchants. Egypt was the first market where such services were available, following the granting of the necessary licenses to process payments for third-party businesses by the Central Bank of Egypt.

JumiaPay is a marker of Jumia, giving the group a significant competitive edge over competitors. No other African e-commerce firm has developed such an advanced digital payment system. This service is present in eight countries in Africa: Egypt, Ghana, Ivory Coast, Kenya, Morocco, Nigeria, Tunisia, and Uganda. Offering a lot of growth opportunities; it remains to be seen if and how it will expand to other markets.

Besides payments, logistics infrastructure is one of the most challenging issues faced by e-commerce firms in Africa. This pushed Jumia to devote a lot of effort and resources to building its own logistic system, based on a hub-and-spoke distribution model, maintaining a network of warehouses – as Flipkart had done in India – and investing in a fleet of delivery vehicles. It invested in tech, developing its proprietary technology to optimize, track, and notify customers, and collecting a stream of data on vendors, buyers, consumption patterns, and other trade-related information. Such data tracking provides a significant competitive advantage, especially in countries with limited market information, as is the case in many African countries. Jumia has established over the years an extensive and diverse network of logistics partners including individual entrepreneurs as well as large enterprises. Jumia also developed a network of drop-off and pick-up stations (about 3,000 as of 2021), enabling a cheaper option for delivering packages.

In 2021, the company expanded its logistics arm to "logistics-as-a-service," delivering 8.3 million packages for 1,489 external clients, with revenue generated from this activity exceeding USD3 million. As part of its efforts to monetize its logistics infrastructure, Jumia signed in April 2022 a partnership with the American UPS that gives the latter access to Jumia's last-mile logistics expertise and infrastructure, including its extensive network of pick-up stations. Investments into its logistics service rose to USD25 million in 2022, up from USD7 million capital expenditure the previous year.

4.　　FROM GROWTH TO PROFITABILITY

Ten years after its launch, Jumia is still in the red and the management is increasingly faced with questions on Jumia's ability to generate profit. Like many other e-commerce firms, Jumia initially focused less on profitability and more on top-of-the-line growth. It is common for digital startups to not generate profits in their early years. For instance, it took the US giant Amazon nine years to turn its first yearly profit.[6] This "get big fast" (GBF) strategy has been widely studied in prior literature. Oliva, Sterman, and Giese (2003) suggested that GBF feeds early-mover advantages such as network effects, learning curves, complementary asset development, and standards setting. These allow companies to dominate the market and build up entry barriers to reduce competitive pressure (Tirole, 1988). However, a major shortcoming of this approach is that low margins together with high investments in the infrastructure needed for massive growth impair the company's ability to fund future growth and increase the company's dependency on external capital. As a result, the company becomes vulnerable to capital market turbulence. In addition, diseconomies of scale may arise if the entrepreneurial firm grows at a rate beyond what its capability allows it to handle (Glancey, 1998).

Table 9.4   Jumia's average order value in USD, 2019–2021

	2019	2020	2021
Average order value	43.5	34.2	29.1

Source: Own elaboration based on data from Jumia, Q4 2021 presentation (https://s23. q4cdn.com/836376591/files/ doc_presentation/2022/03/JMIA-Post-Q4.pdf).

Jumia's leadership began refocusing on profitability after the turbulence in the months following its IPO in 2019. As seen above, Jumia has expanded its third-party marketplace and enlarged its assortment of products with a focus on higher turnover and margin products. To cut costs, it shut down its activities in Cameroon, Rwanda, and Tanzania over 2018–2019. Reflecting these changes, after growing by 45 and 18 percent in 2018 and 2019, respectively, revenues declined in 2020 (Table 9.3). Revenues registered a slight increase of 11 percent in 2021. Average order value fell over 2020–2021 (see Table 9.4), but gross profits saw some improvement. Gross profits after fulfillment[7] began to turn positive, reaching USD26.9 million in 2020. Overall, however, EBITDA losses, after a slight decline in 2020, widened again in 2021, dragged down by higher operating expenses. For the full fiscal year 2021, Jumia's EBITDA loss rose to USD240.9 million, a 41 percent increase compared to 2020 (see Table 9.3). This was the result of a surge in sales and advertising expenses that more than doubled between 2020 and 2021 and were much above the amounts of the previous four years. In the same vein, technology and content expenses almost doubled in 2017–2021 while expenses regarding administration and other general costs rose almost every year during that period and, at USD143 million in 2021, were 60 percent higher than five years before.

5.   THE AFRICAN E-COMMERCE SPACE HAS BECOME CROWDED

Jumia was an e-commerce pioneer in Africa. It benefited in its early years from a favorable competitive environment on the continent with few competitors. In addition, some of its main competitors failed. The Nigerian Konga, its main contestant at the time, was bought back by a Nigerian firm[8] after firing most of its employees in 2018, while AfrikaMarket, another key player, went bankrupt in fall 2019 (Casanova et al., 2021). As of 2022, Jumia is still, by far, the frontrunner in the industry on the continent. With more than 20 million visits per month in 2021, it had twice the number of visitors registered by the next-in-line company, the South African Takealot (see Table 9.5). Competition, both local and global, however, is gaining ground (see Appendix 9A). As of 2022, Amazon (that has one Egyptian subsidiary, Souq) was considering expanding in the main markets in Africa: Nigeria and South Africa. Alibaba was available in many African countries and had two regional hubs in Ethiopia and Rwanda as of 2022.[9]

Jumia has several key advantages over most of its competitors on the African continent. Being a public company, one such advantage is its cheaper cost of capital. The other is the number of markets in which it operates: active in 11 countries in 2021 – as opposed to one or two for most of its competitors – Jumia can take advantage of the growing markets in this

Table 9.5   Largest e-commerce marketplaces in Africa, 2021

	Name	Region/ country	Product category	African visits per month
1	Jumia	Africa	General	23.3 million
2	Takealot	South Africa	General	10.5 million
3	Souq	Middle East	General	10.0 million
4	Konga	Nigeria	General	2.3 million
5	Bidorbuy	South Africa	General	1.9 million
6	Noon	Middle East	General	1.8 million
7	Zando	South Africa	Fashion	569,900
8	Amazon	Global	General	445,500
9	Kilimall	Africa	General	267,200

Note: Souq in Egypt is owned by Amazon; Zando is a subsidiary of Jumia specializing in fashion retail in South Africa.
Source: Own elaboration based on data from Webretailer (www.webretailer.com/b/online-marketplaces/#The_top_four_regions).

wide range of countries. In addition, most of Jumia's competitors don't have a mobile payment system like JumiaPay.

6.   LOOKING BACK AND SEARCHING FOR PROFITABILITY

E-commerce has exploded in Africa. According to Statista, the number of digital shoppers in Africa doubled between 2015 and 2021. Online shoppers represent between 1 and 9 percent of the population compared to 46 percent in China[10] and Africans want to catch up. It is estimated that by 2025, online sales may reach 10 percent of all retail revenues in the continent's largest economies. According to Statista (2020), Africa's e-commerce market is set to grow from USD33 billion in 2022 to USD46 billion in 2025.

In the pursuit of profitability, Jumia's leadership has reduced its geographical footprint, closing its business in three countries. Regarding business units, the company closed the hotel booking engine Jumia Travel and made the strategic shifts discussed above. This started to pay off, with Jumia's gross profit after fulfillment expenses turning positive by late 2020.

However, Africa offers a huge long-term opportunity in e-commerce, with massive potential rewards but also great risks. Challenges – especially logistical challenges – are immense. Jumia is an innovative company that has shown its ability to address many of those challenges. Will investors be patient enough to enable the company to capitalize on its long-term vision? For Jumia's chief executive officers, the existential question is: how soon can Jumia turn out a profit? Where are the next growth opportunities and sources of profit?

ACKNOWLEDGMENTS

We gratefully acknowledge the contribution of Noel Liu and Xingqi Ye, both research assistants at the Emerging Markets Institute at Cornell University.

NOTES

1. Unicorns are startups reaching a USD1 billion valuation.
2. GMV is the total value of the goods sold through an e-commerce platform.
3. As of June 2022, Jumia Technologies AG had 163 institutional owners and shareholders that had filed 13D/G or 13F forms with the Securities Exchange Commission. These institutions held a total of 32,118,502 shares. The largest shareholders included Baillie Gifford & Co, Vanguard International Growth Fund Investor Shares, Morgan Stanley, Renaissance Technologies, Susquehanna International Group, D. E. Shaw & Co., Goldman Sachs Group, Susquehanna International Group, Citadel Advisors, and Citadel Advisors. See https://money.cnn.com/quote/shareholders/shareholders.html?symb=JMIA&subView =institutiona
4. Jumia Presentation, Q4 2021, https://s23.q4cdn.com/836376591/files/doc_financials/2021/ q4/Q4.2021-Earnings-presentation-23.02.22-vF.pdf
5. See https://techweez.com/2021/06/11/huawei-petal-search-jumia-partners/; https:// techtrendske.co.ke/huaweis-petal-search-now-features-a-direct-link-to-e-commerce-site -jumia/; www.zawya.com/en/press-release/huaweis-petal-search-now-features-a-direct -link-to-jumia-africas-e-commerce-platform-g4mpdfmh
6. Amazon turned its first net yearly profit in 2003; its first net quarterly profit occurred in Q4 2001.
7. Order fulfillment costs are the total costs of storing inventory, processing orders and delivering orders to the end consumer. It also includes fees for processing returns, restocking fees and other costs, such as initial setup fees and account management fees, inbound shipping costs, receiving costs, pick and pack costs, box and packaging fees, custom labeling and order insert fees.
8. Although Konga was bought up (by the Nigerian group Xinox) and later merged with another retail outfit, the brand name was maintained.
9. See www.ispionline.it/en/pubblicazione/chinas-evolving-role-africas-digitalisation-build-ing-infrastructure-shaping-ecosystems-31247; https://fintel.io/so/us/jmia
10. UNCTAD, https://unctad.org/system/files/official-document/tn_unctad_ict4d17_en.pdf

REFERENCES

Casanova L., Miroux, A., and Fiechelstein, D. (2021). Digital companies driving business innovation in emerging markets: The cases of Alibaba, Flipkart, Jumia and Mercado Libre, in Cahen, F., Casanova, L., and Miroux, A. (eds), *From Copycats to Leaders: Innovation from Emerging Markets*. Cambridge University Press.

Glancey, K. (1998). Determinants of growth and profitability in small entrepreneurial firms. *International Journal of Entrepreneurial Behaviour & Research*, 4(1), 18–27.

Jumia, Results presentation Q4 2019, https://s23.q4cdn.com/836376591/files/doc_financials/2019/q4/ 4Q20-Earnings-Presentation.pdf

Jumia, Results presentation Q4 2020, https://s23.q4cdn.com/836376591/files/doc_financials/2020/q4/ Jumia-Q4.20-Earnings-Presentation-24.02.21.pdf

Jumia, Results presentation Q4 2021, https://s23.q4cdn.com/836376591/files/doc_financials/2021/q4/Q4.2021-Earnings-presentation-23.02.22-vF.pdf

Oliva, R., Sterman, J. D., and Giese, M. (2003). Limits to growth in the new economy: Exploring the "get big fast" strategy in e-commerce. *System Dynamics Review*, *19*(2), 83–117.

Statista (2020). E-commerce in Africa: Statistics and facts, April 5, www.statista.com/topics/7288/e-commerce-in-africa/#topicHeader__wrapper

Tirole, J. (1988). *The Theory of Industrial Organization* (3rd edn). MIT Press.

APPENDIX 9A

Table 9A.1   Jumia's competitors

	Takealot	Konga	Noon
Description	Developer of an online shopping platform intended to offer a wide range of consumer products	Provider of online shopping store – customer	Operator of e-commerce platform of consumer products
Primary industry	Internet retail	Internet retail	Internet retail
Location of headquarters	Cape Town, South Africa	Lagos, Nigeria	Dubai, United Arab Emirates
Revenue	$212 million, TTM December 2020	–	–
Employees	2,427, 2021	300, 2020	9,311, 2022
Total raised	$816 million	$75 million	–
Post valuation	$76 million, April 11, 2017	$35 million, February 5, 2018	–
Last financing details	Undisclosed amount, later stage venture capital, January 1, 2018	Undisclosed amount, accelerator/ incubator, March 2019	Undisclosed amount, corporate September 20, 2017
	Souq	Jiji	Zando
Description	Provider of online marketplace	Developer of online marketplace	Operator of online fashion store (fashion, home, and beauty products)
Primary industry	Internet retail	Information services	Internet retail
Location of headquarters	Dubai, United Arab Emirates	Lagos, Nigeria	Cape Town, South Africa
Revenue	$272 million, TTM December 2015	–	–
Employees	4,500, 2022	1,000, 2022	243, 2021
Total raised	$727 million	$50 million	$25 million
Post valuation	$583 million, May 12, 2017	–	–

Last financing details	$583 million, merger/ acquisition, May 12, 2017	$21 million, later-stage venture capital (Series C), December 9, 2019	Undisclosed amount, private equity growth/ expansion
	Loot Online	**Yuppiechef**	**Mall for Africa**
Description	Operator of online retail store in Tokai, South Africa	Provider of online kitchen and homeware platform	Operator of online shopping platform based in Nigeria
Primary industry	Internet retail	Household appliances	Other services (non-financial)
Location of headquarters	Tokai, South Africa	Cape Town, South Africa	Nairobi, Kenya
Revenue	$15 million, TTM December 2017	$1 million, TTM March 2013	$17 million, TTM December 2014
Employees	0	97, 2021	57, 2021
Total raised	–	–	–
Post valuation	–	$326,680, August 1, 2021	–
Last financing details	Undisclosed amount, merger/acquisition, March 1, 2015	$326,680, merger/ acquisition, August 1, 2021	Undisclosed amount, private equity growth/ expansion, July 1, 2013

Source: Authors based on data from Pitchbook, https://my.pitchbook.com/as-criteria/
COMPANY/s234675685/15732212.

10

Social capital and corporate growth strategies in the Spanish ceramic cluster

Luis Martínez-Cháfer, F. Xavier Molina-Morales, and Jesús Peiró-Palomino

1. TERRACAS AND MR. MONTORO

TerraCas was in 2023 a medium-sized company that operated in the Spanish ceramic tile cluster located in Castelló, a province in the region of Valencia.[1] Founded in 2000 by Javier Montoro, the main mission of the company was producing and selling high-quality ceramic tiles. Since the beginning of its operations, the company had grown by gaining a good reputation in the market thanks to the quality of its manufactured products and commitment to sustainability. During these 23 years, TerraCas had established strong relationships with clients and suppliers, expanding the business on a national and international scale. Due to its commitment to quality, investments had been made to keep up with the latest technological innovations in the sector and to provide the appropriate training to its employees. Some of these innovations, however, would have been unfeasible without a solid social capital endowment that enabled collaboration and knowledge sharing with other members in the cluster. In fact, in some cases, patents or other legal protections were not required for these shared innovations.

However, the ceramic cluster had undergone profound changes because of aggressive corporate growth strategies in the form of acquisitions as well as changes of firms' ownership. These developments had a strong impact on the business structure of ceramic companies. This had put TerraCas in a difficult situation as it faced increased competition and the need to adapt to an environment in flux. So far, the company has been able to remain competitive by exploiting its commitment to quality and sustainability. However, new structural dynamics are causing the optimal size of a ceramic company to increase. With this scenario threatening the company's continuity in business, Javier Montoro faces an important decision regarding the corporate strategy.

Montoro is a businessman with extensive experience in the ceramic sector in Castelló. Although his entrepreneurial journey began in 2000, his experience in the ceramic field goes back to 1987. Before founding TerraCas he was an employee of another important company in the sector. The ceramic tile sector was traditionally characterized by the territorial attachment of its entrepreneurs. In fact, the dense and closed network of local relationships was considered the basis of the success of the cluster companies. This territorial commitment facilitated the development of social capital as a driving force for business collaborations related to the technological development of ceramic products.

In early 2023, Montoro found himself in a tight spot as he had to made an important strategic decision. The main possible moves included organic growth of the company, growth by related acquisitions, or the sale of the company's shares to a corporate group or an investment fund. The choice was important since some of the options under consideration could break the territorial commitment acquired during his years in the sector and erode the endowment of social capital created after years of interaction and coordination with other actors in the cluster. Indeed, the possible sale of the company to international groups without territorial attachment posed a moral dilemma for Montoro. However, from a more pragmatic and less emotional standpoint, the financial muscle of these players could be of great help in facing the industry's new challenges.

By the end of 2022, an international investment fund showed its interest in TerraCas. The fund offered Montoro €60 million to acquire the firm. Montoro had one month to think about it, and this term was about to expire. Whatever the decision would be, Montoro was aware that he must decide the corporate growth strategy with urgency; otherwise, competitiveness and the future of TerraCas could be jeopardized. In this scenario, Montoro was sitting in his office thinking about this important decision to make. He had an excellent knowledge of the ceramic tile cluster and was well aware of the different processes of corporate growth strategy that were taking place. Moreover, he had strong embeddedness in the territory and a notable endowment of social capital based on solid relationships with the main actors in the cluster. He had arranged a meeting with the board members to explain the corporate growth strategies that TerraCas could consider.

2.   THE SPANISH TILE CERAMIC CLUSTER

TerraCas operates in the Castelló ceramic cluster, located in the region of Valencia, in the east of Spain (see Figure 10.1). The cluster is spread over 40 km² and is located in an area with a long-standing ceramic tradition. Castelló's ceramic tile industry had its origins in the start-up of the Real Fábrica de Loza, L'Alcora in 1727. The promoter of this initiative, the Count of Aranda, located this porcelain and fine chinaware factory in an area rich in the necessary resources for this activity, as well as a long tradition of pottery making (Molina-Morales et al., 2008). Other business initiatives soon emerged that imitated the practices developed in the L'Alcora factory. During the nineteenth century, the industry began to specialize in the production of floor and wall tiles, with many production centers in the town of Onda, where the size of the pieces was reduced in response to the increase in demand and technical advances (Molina-Morales, 2002).

Source: Own elaboration based on Budí-Orduña (2008).

Figure 10.1   Spatial location of the ceramic tile cluster in Spain

With the introduction of electric power and friction pressing, the sector developed intensively in the twentieth century, especially since 1960. Ceramic tiles spread rapidly as a construction material, and its use became popular. On the industrial side, advances aimed at improving processes and reducing costs. During the 1960s and 1970s, the demand was predominantly national. The 1980s saw the international expansion of companies which were more concerned with volume than product quality. Towards the 1990s, international competition grew, and countries such as Italy and Brazil began to rival Spain in terms of production. In addition, new ceramic tile-producing countries, such as China, Turkey, Mexico, and Indonesia, competed with Spanish factories. In that decade, the gap in terms of product quality was narrowed with respect to Italy, and it was also the time of consolidation of advances in tile-shaping processes and, above all, the introduction of single-firing and energy cogeneration processes that made companies more efficient (Albors-Garrigós et al., 2008). Companies began to be concerned about quality standards facing international competition, producing improvements that put Spanish products on a par with Italian tiles, their main competitor (Molina-Morales & Martínez-Fernández, 2009).

In the 2020s, Spain was one of the world's top five producers of ceramic tiles and derivative products and the world's second biggest exporter of these products, which could be

Table 10.1   Types of firms and outputs in the cluster

Actor (type of firm)	Output
Tile manufacturers	Wall tiles
	Floor tiles
	Outdoor tiles
Frits and glazes	Frits and glazes
	Pigments
	Granulated glazes
	Additives
	Inks
	Engobes
	Technical assistance
	Product development services
Machinery and equipment	Press machinery
	Atomizers
	Convection belts
	Dryers
	Kilns
	Decoration lines
	Packaging machinery
	Classification machinery
	Digital printers
	Technical assistance
Atomized clay producers	Atomized clays
Complementary tile manufacturers	Decorated complementary tiles
Chemical additive providers	Additives for ceramic tile manufacturing

found in more than 190 countries. A key feature of the Spanish ceramic sector was its high concentration. The cluster accounted for more than 94 percent of the Spanish production of tiles and related products, and it was a leader in terms of technological development, design, and quality. There were in 2021 about 180 companies in the cluster, and the main industrial process was based on the elaboration of ceramic tiles. However, there were other companies that had developed complementary activities (ASCER, 2021). These are described in Table 10.1. As can be observed, the composition of the cluster was quite heterogeneous, although the tile producers predominated (about 50 percent of the firms).

In addition, there was a scientific environment, mainly formed by research groups belonging to universities alongside public and private organizations that were dedicated to these tasks. The role of the Universitat Jaume I stands out (Molina-Morales & Martínez-Cháfer, 2016). Some of its departments developed important lines of research for the ceramic sector in various fields, such as ceramic technology, chemistry, environmental pollution, and ceramic design, among others. Finally, there were other institutions and associations of firms, e.g., Asociación Española de Fabricantes de Azulejos y Pavimentos Cerámicos and Asociación

Nacional de Fabricantes de Fritas, Esmaltes y Colores Cerámicos, which provided support to the companies in the cluster (Martínez-Cháfer et al., 2021).

In 2021, companies in the cluster generated about 17,180 jobs in the region, being one of the big industrial engines. Rising competitiveness was crucial to maintaining employment levels and the generation of value added for the territory (ASCER, 2021). In that regard, the cluster had traditionally been a center of innovation in the area, with a ratio of patented inventions far above other sectors in the region (Corma-Canós and Corma-Buforn, 2018). Indeed, innovation was crucial for the companies to survive and keep competing against other traditional foreign competitors such as Italy or Turkey, or more recent ones such as India, Brazil, or China, which in the 2020s largely dominated certain segments of the market and forced companies in the more traditional markets such as Spain to push innovation to remain competitive in a much more globalized environment.

The success of the companies in the cluster and, in general, the positive performance of the industry cannot be understood without the benefits of intense and long-lasting collaboration links between the clustered firms. These relationships are formally known as social capital. In a more general sense, social capital facilitates cooperation and coordination within a society or a group of companies or individuals. It is mainly composed of networks of collaboration and exchange, norms, and trust mechanisms that act as the "glue" that holds the group together. In general terms, social capital can be seen as an element that positively affects productivity, cohesion, and, most importantly, innovation, thus being essential for competitiveness. In the context of a cluster such as the ceramic tile industry in Castelló, the influence of social capital in the form of cooperative relationships, long-lasting collaborations, and trust had facilitated the diffusion of knowledge and ideas, reduced transaction costs, and had been key to the development of technological innovations (Boari et al., 2017; Molina-Morales et al., 2008). These innovations had made ceramic sectors such as Castelló in Spain and Sassuolo in Italy the main leaders in terms of both product and process innovation, as shown in Table 10.2. As a cluster member, TerraCas has also benefited from social capital. In fact, the company holds strong links with other members in the cluster and this has been essential to push the innovation potential of the firm.

The impact of the ceramic sector was notable in the region of Valencia. Considering data for 2019, this industry generated an impact equivalent to 2.7 percent of the region's gross domestic product. In fact, the total contribution of tile manufacturers in 2019 was €2,811 million. This contribution was direct (43 percent), indirect (41 percent), and induced (16 percent), as shown in Figure 10.2 (PwC, 2021).

In terms of employment, the figures are also revealing (see Figure 10.3). In 2019, the employment generated by the ceramic industry accounted for 2.1 percent of the region's employment. A relevant part of the sector's impact on the region came from the indirect impact, which was quite significant (44 percent). In addition, the induced impact, derived from the additional consumption that was produced because of the wages and salaries generated both directly and indirectly, accounted for 21 percent of the total (PwC, 2021). The employment generated was characterized by its stability, since the ceramic sector had shown high resilience in crisis years (ASCER, 2022).

Table 10.2   Innovation in the ceramic industry since 1960

Innovation	Year	Product	Process	Marketing	Organization	Origin
Tunnel kiln	1960		✓			Italy
Friction press	1960		✓			Italy
Glazing line	1960		✓			Italy
Melted glazes-frits	1960	✓				Spain
Hydraulic press	1970	✓	✓		✓	Italy, Spain
Gas-based energy	1980		✓		✓	Italy
Single-layer roller kiln	1980	✓	✓		✓	Italy
Spray dryer	1980	✓	✓		✓	Italy
Single-fired stoneware tile	1980	✓	✓	✓	✓	Italy
Automatic tile classification	1980	✓	✓		✓	Italy
Single-fired porous ceramic tile	1985	✓	✓	✓	✓	Spain
Direct tile selling	1985			✓	✓	Italy
Design provided jointly with enamels	1985			✓	✓	Spain
Granulated glazes	1985	✓	✓			Spain
Guided tile transport	1990	✓	✓		✓	Italy

Innovation	Year	Product	Process	Marketing	Organization	Origin
Technical porcelain tile	1990	✓	✓	✓	✓	Italy
Cogeneration	1990		✓			Italy, Spain
Picking tile loading	1990			✓		Italy
Roller printing technology (Rotocolor)	1995	✓	✓	✓		Italy
Full-range typology of enamels	2000	✓		✓		Spain
Glazed porcelain tile	2000	✓	✓	✓	✓	Italy
Inkjet printing technology	2005		✓	✓	✓	Spain
Artificial vision for QC	2010	✓	✓		✓	Italy

Source: Own elaboration based on Corma-Canós and Corma-Buforn (2018).

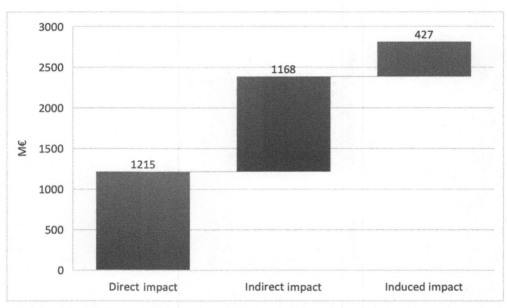

Source: Own elaboration based on PwC (2021) with data from INE (www.ine.es) and ASCER (2022).

Figure 10.2   Impact of the ceramic industry on the gross domestic product of the region of Valencia

Furthermore, regarding exports, the data reveal that the ceramic floor and wall tile manufacturing sector was the main exporter in the province of Castelló in 2019. Table 10.3 summarizes the information. The total value of ceramic exports reached 33 percent in this province, surpassing other important industries such as the chemical industry, cokeries and oil refining, agriculture and livestock, the manufacture of machinery and equipment, and the manufacture of motor vehicles. In the context of the region of Valencia, which besides Castelló includes two more provinces, the relative volume of ceramic exports corresponded to 8.7 percent, occupying fourth place at the regional level (PwC, 2021).

As reported in Table 10.4, the destination of the exports was diverse. Of the €2,818 million exported, 49 percent was destined for a European country (88 percent were European Union members). Among them, France stands out as the main destination for exported Spanish ceramics, with 11 percent of the total exports. Outside the European Union, the United States was the main market, with 10.8 percent of the total exports in 2019. The total for the rest of the world was 51 percent, which is equivalent to €1,443 million (PwC, 2021).

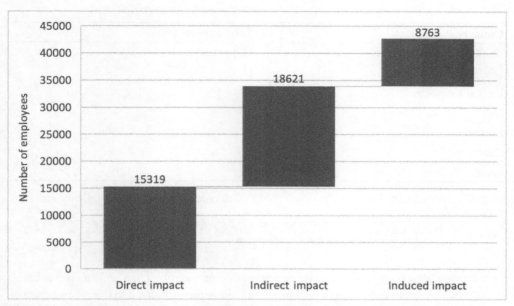

Source: Own elaboration based on PwC (2021) with data from INE (www.ine.es) and ASCER (2022).

Figure 10.3   Impact of the ceramic industry on the employment of the region of Valencia

Table 10.3   Sectoral weight in Castelló's exports, 2019

Sector	%
Manufacture of ceramic tiles and floor coverings	32.9
Chemical industry	24.8
Petroleum coking and refining	11
Agriculture and livestock farming	10.7
Manufacture of machinery and equipment	3.3
Manufacture of motor vehicles	2.6
Manufacture of other non-metallic products	2.2
Manufacture of metal products	1.8
Manufacture of rubber products	1.3
Rest	9.3

Source: Own elaboration based on PwC (2021) with data from INE and DataComex.

Table 10.4   Main destination countries of ceramic sector exports, 2019

Country	Total exports (%)
France	11.4
United States	10.8
United Kingdom	6.3
Italy	3.9
Morocco	3.7
Germany	3.6
Israel	3.3

Source: Own elaboration based on PwC (2021) with data from INE and DataComex.

3.   RECENT CORPORATE GROWTH STRATEGIES IN THE CERAMIC CLUSTER

From 2000 to 2020, the Spanish ceramic cluster underwent plenty of changes. On the one hand, there was a significant reduction in the number of companies dedicated to the manufacture of wall and floor tiles, despite the total growth of the cluster. Figure 10.4 shows the evolution of the number of these companies between 1985 and 2020. The maximum number of companies was reached in 2005 (180), while the minimum was registered in 2020 (81), which represented a remarkable decline. The cluster, however, had continued to grow, as shown in Figure 10.5 (Molina-Morales et al., 2021).

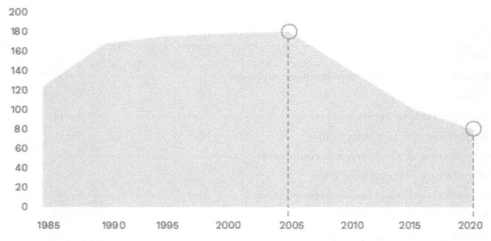

Source: Own elaboration based on Càtedra de Transformació del Model Econòmic (Molina-Morales et al., 2021).

Figure 10.4   Evolution of the number of producers, 1985–2020

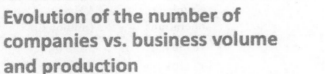

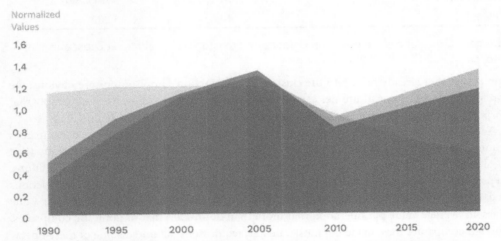

Source: Own elaboration based on Càtedra de Transformació del Model Econòmic (Molina-Morales et al., 2021).

Figure 10.5 Evolution of the number of companies versus business volume and production, 1990–2020

The ceramic tile sector was also involved in an intense process of mergers and acquisitions. This caused significant changes in the structure of the cluster, which saw very frequent changes in the ownership of companies. Table 10.5 provides information on the number of companies involved in the acquisitions process and the total and average value of the operations (Molina-Morales et al., 2021).

In mergers and acquisitions, a relevant issue consists of knowing the origin of the buyer companies. It is pertinent to distinguish between foreign companies and native or local

Table 10.5 Acquisitions, general description, 2010–2020

Number of operations	61
Number of companies involved in acquisitions (as a buyer)	43
Number of companies involved in acquisitions (as a seller)	46
Total value of acquisitions	€3,28 million
Average value of the operations	€52,9 million

Source: Own elaboration based on Càtedra de Transformació del Model Econòmic (Molina-Morales et al., 2021).

Table 10.6   Acquisitions by buyers' origin

	Number of operations	Value (million €)
Investment funds	18 (30%)	2,128 (65%)
Multinational companies	12 (20%)	592 (18%)
Local companies	31 (50%)	562 (17%)
Total	61	3,282

Source: Own elaboration based on Càtedra de Transformació del Model Econòmic (Molina-Morales et al., 2021).

companies that already belong to the cluster. The distinction's implications are obvious; the foreign investments constitute net capital inflows to the territory; however, they imply that corporate control may move outside the cluster's limits (Molina-Morales et al., 2021).

Table 10.6 distinguishes acquisition operations performed by foreign-owned companies from those within the cluster by 2021. There were more foreign-owned operations than local-owned. This is particularly noticeable in terms of the economic value of the operations. In percentages, purchases by foreign companies accounted for 30 percent of total transactions and 65 percent of the total value of transactions during the period. In fact, this higher value gives an average value per operation that more than quintuples that of domestic companies. Foreign companies have made the most valuable acquisitions, although some of these operations have been carried out with companies in the cluster that were already owned by foreign capital. In fact, when considering the ownership of the companies, even those with a relatively long period of activity in the cluster are considered foreigners (Molina-Morales et al., 2021).

In addition, regarding internal and external acquiring companies, there were three types of acquiring companies: (1) related and local companies, which are firms that carry out the same activity as the acquired company; (2) companies belonging to multinational corporations, which are mostly industrial group multinational companies, i.e., groups that have companies that belong to various businesses and industries more or less related to the ceramic tile industry; and (3) investment funds that manage a portfolio of investments in various businesses and that pursue basically financial strategies (Molina-Morales et al., 2021).

The entry of foreign capital was characterized by the presence of two main types of operations. On the one hand, there were foreign capital inflows from industrial groups or investment funds, which generally carried out large-scale investment purchase operations. These international operations focused mainly on companies that produce tiles and on companies that produce glazes and ceramic colors. On the other hand, there were also many sales transactions between local companies. These transactions were of lower investment value but quite numerous and usually focused on tile manufacturers, the same industrial activity that TerraCas carried out. In some cases, buy-outs have sought to take advantage of the financial difficulties of one of the companies. However, the overall process of the cluster did not seem to indicate that buyout prices, on average, were below market. Furthermore, some transactions made by investment funds showed high volatility, with resales in the short term that had been the result of financial speculation.

The institutions representing the cluster companies, such as trade associations, continued to perform the same functions. In any case, these processes, which were still in force by 2023, had important implications for the future of the cluster and had been received positively by the representative institutions and organizations linked to the cluster. From the point of view of these institutions representing the companies, the arrival of this type of international investment group or fund was viewed favorably. They valued very positively the fact that international groups or funds were targeting the ceramics sector, as this showed its potential profitability. Moreover, it is important to highlight the strong financial muscle of these investors. To a certain extent, this financial capacity could guarantee the continuity of many companies in the sector and the preservation of crucial jobs for the region in terms of their direct and indirect impact on the economy. Emphasis had also been placed on the contribution of financial funds to the sector, the generation of economies of scale, the increase in efficiency, and internationalization, among other advantages.

Finally, the cluster's evolution also had consequences for other important aspects of business operations. The entry of foreign capital together with business concentration produced a change in the optimal size of tile companies. This had serious implications for those companies below this size. They had to either increase their size or specialize in very select niche products to be competitive. Increasing size means acquiring advantages through economies of scale that have become more relevant in this new context. Larger companies can thus access more resources and capital to enable them to invest in research and development, marketing, and other activities that are important for business development. In addition, the increase in size and the resulting economies of scale also improve bargaining power with suppliers and in the markets. Increases in business size were also associated with certain risks. Such is the case of the increase in fixed costs, bureaucracy, the complexity of decision making, or even its slowness, to give a few examples.

In this context, and regarding ceramic tile manufacturing companies, an interesting range of strategic possibilities was opening up, also for TerraCas, which is directly affected by these changes in the industry. Looking at the main changes in the business structure of the sector over the past decade (2010–2020) four main types of strategy emerge. Table 10.7 describes the implications of these strategies for different business aspects.

3.1   Type 1

Local companies that grow and diversify their business through acquisitions of other companies within the cluster. This is known as related diversification or horizontal integration. Pamesa is an example of this type of ownership. In other words, Pamesa is a company that is part of the cluster and has grown and expanded its business by acquiring other companies within the cluster. This type of growth strategy allows the company to add new products or services to its portfolio and potentially increase its market share.

Table 10.7   Summary of corporate growth strategies and their features

Strategy	1 Acquisition by related companies	2 Acquisition by industrial groups	3 Investment funds	4 Internal growth
Example	**Pamesa**	**Victoria**	**Lone Star Funds**	**Porcelanosa**
Local perspective	Internal Share capital, exchanges of information and knowledge (informal) Use of local institutions	External Acquisition of external knowledge Internationaliz-ation momentum	External Acquisition of external knowledge Internationaliz-ation momentum	Internal Share capital, exchanges of information and knowledge (informal) Use of local institutions
Diversification	Related, multi-location Decentralization	Semi-related Related industries	Unrelated Portfolio investments	Related Brand focus
Integration activities	Vertical/ horizontal	Horizontal	Horizontal	Vertical/ horizontal
Growth rate (internal/ external)	External via acquisitions	External via acquisitions	External via acquisitions	Internal via direct investment
Operational synergies	High operational synergies	Low operational synergies	Non-operational synergies	High operational synergies
Commercial	High market	High market	Low market	Low market

Strategy	1 Acquisition by related companies	2 Acquisition by industrial groups	3 Investment funds	4 Internal growth
Management	High managerial synergies	High managerial synergies	High managerial synergies	Low managerial synergies
Social capital	High, preexisting links are maintained Possibility of additional links	High, if preexisting links are maintained and the external group shares the firm's business model Low, if the external group imposes a different business model and breaks the previous links	Low, preexisting links can be lost Low probability of creating new long-lasting links	High, preexisting links are maintained

3.2   Type 2

Companies that are not part of the cluster but have grown through acquisitions of companies within the cluster. This type of growth is known as semi-related diversification, as the company diversifies its business by acquiring companies in a related field but not necessarily within the same cluster. Vitoria is an example of this type of ownership. In other words, Vitoria is a company that is not part of the cluster but has grown its business by acquiring companies within the cluster. This type of growth strategy allows the company to enter a new market or add new products or services to its portfolio and potentially increase its market share.

3.3   Type 3

Companies that are not part of the cluster but have grown through acquisitions of companies within the cluster that are unrelated to their existing business. This type of growth is known as unrelated portfolio diversification, as the company diversifies its business by acquiring companies in different fields. Lone Star Funds is an example of this type of ownership. In other words, Lone Star Funds is an investment fund that is not part of the cluster but has grown its business by acquiring companies within the cluster that are unrelated to its existing business. This type of growth strategy allows the company to enter completely new markets and add a diverse range of products or services to its portfolio, potentially increasing its market share and minimizing the risk associated with relying on a single industry or product line. Investment funds are also known for their interest in obtaining profits from their corresponding investments. So, their final objective is to sell back the acquired companies to obtain an interesting return on their original investment.

3.4   Type 4

Companies that are part of the cluster and have grown through vertical integration. Vertical integration is a growth strategy in which a company expands its operations to include businesses that are related to its existing products or services but at different stages of the production process. For example, a company that produces raw materials might acquire a company that uses those raw materials to manufacture finished products. Porcelanosa is an example of this type of ownership. In other words, Porcelanosa is a company that is part of the cluster and has grown its business through vertical integration, expanding its operations to include businesses related to its existing products or services at different stages of the production process. This type of growth strategy allows the company to increase its control over the production and distribution of its products and potentially reduce costs and increase efficiency.

4.   TERRACAS TILES

After a long period of 15 years in charge of the operations management of one of the largest companies in the sector, in 2000 Javier Montoro decided to start a new venture as a ceramic entrepreneur. His initial commitment was based on simplifying production processes and maximizing efficiency. This resulted in the first catalog of quality products but with few references and designs for its customers, mainly in the domestic market.

In the first years, Montoro's activity proved to be successful. However, because of the 2008 global crisis, the company began to suffer from the low demand of the domestic market, whose construction sector and main customers were deeply affected. Montoro knew that the key to success was to produce high-quality ceramics that were made with the best materials and techniques available. To achieve this, he invested in state-of-the-art equipment and trained his team in the latest techniques and technologies. In this context, Montoro decided to bet on an incipient technology, inkjet printing, which would allow him to expand the references of his catalog and open up to other international markets.

In addition, Montoro established solid relationships with different actors in the ceramic cluster, including suppliers, support organizations, public entities such as the University Jaume I, associations, and even competitors. These connections created a dense network of social capital that facilitated the circulation of knowledge, cooperation agreements, and a shared vision that have been as important as economic resources to boost innovation, a key element to remain competitive in a turbulent scenario. As a result, the company overcame the 2008 real-estate crisis and began a new phase, increasing the quality, design, and prestige of its products. This was reflected in the company's exports, which increased during the period 2008–2014 to account for 70 percent of the company's total sales.

International markets, however, were more demanding in some respects, such as sustainability. In this sense, Montoro's commitment was total, and he adapted his production processes to maximize their sustainability. In 2015, the company was certified in the ISO14000 environmental standard and was awarded for its good practices in this area. He implemented eco-friendly production processes and invested in renewable energy sources to reduce the company's carbon footprint. This focus on sustainability helped differentiate the company from its competitors and resonated with consumers looking for environmentally friendly products. As a result, the company's sales increased, and so did its profits.

As the company's reputation grew, so did its customer base. More and more customers began to choose TerraCas for their home and business needs, and the company's profits soared. By the end of 2022, Montoro's ceramic company had become a well-respected and successful business known for its high-quality products and commitment to sustainability. Montoro is proud of the company he has built and grateful to the dedicated team that has helped him achieve his vision.

However, Montoro faced a difficult decision. Demand for the company's products reached an all-time high, and Montoro knew that in order to keep up with the demand, he would need to invest in expanding the company's production capabilities. In January 2023, the situation of the Castelló ceramic cluster was clearly dominated by a context of concentration and sale of companies. Montoro was aware that all options were open for TerraCas. The company's financial situation was unbeatable, and TerraCas could afford to invest in purchasing other companies in the sector. On the other hand, Montoro was in the twilight of his professional career and was aware of the succulent offers coming from foreign investors in the sector. In December 2022, an international investment fund offered Montoro €60 million for TerraCas and he had only a few days to decide. The idea of a peaceful retirement with the money obtained after selling his company was appealing. At the same time, some of the operations in the sector had been purely speculative and caused some fear and instability for the workers. Montoro's commitment and attachment to the territory were very strong, and this was a moral dilemma. Furthermore, he would like the company to preserve the social capital generated after years of cooperation with local institutions and other members of the ceramic tile cluster.

In this context, at the beginning of 2023, Montoro decided to bring together his entire management team to make the best possible decision for the company. He asked: Which is the best alternative? Should I sell the company? What is the most suitable next step?

ACKNOWLEDGMENTS

This work was supported by MCIN/AEI/10.13039/501100011033/FEDER, UE under grants PID2021-126516NB-I00 and PID 2020–115135 GB-I00, and the Generalitat Valenciana under grant PROMETEO CIPROM/2022/50.

NOTE

1. This case is based on secondary data only.

REFERENCES

Albors-Garrigós, J., Hervas-Oliver, J. L., & Marquez, P. B. (2008). When technology innovation is not enough, new competitive paradigms, revisiting the Spanish ceramic tile sector. *International Journal of Technology Management*, *44*(3–4), 406–426.

ASCER. (2021). Asociación Española de Fabricantes de Azulejos y Pavimentos Ceramicos (ASCER). El Sector. https://portal.ascer.es/el-sector/

ASCER. (2022). Asociación Española de Fabricantes de Azulejos y Pavimentos Ceramicos (ASCER). El Sector. https://portal.ascer.es/el-sector/

Boari, C., Molina-Morales, F. X., & Martínez-Cháfer, L. (2017). Direct and interactive effects of brokerage roles on innovation in clustered firms. *Growth and Change*, *48*(3), 336–358.

Budí-Orduña, V. (2008). El distrito de la cerámica de Castellón. *Mediterráneo Económico*, *13*, 383–407.

Corma-Canós, P., & Corma-Buforn, P. (2018). ¿Cuál será la siguiente innovación disruptiva en el cluster cerámico? In Castellón Chamber of Commerce, Industry, and Navigation (ed.), *Qualicer 2018*. Castellón.

Martínez-Cháfer, L., Molina-Morales, F. X., & Roig-Tierno, N. (2021). Explaining technological innovation of the clustered firms: Internal and relational factors. *Journal of Small Business Management*, 1–32.

Molina-Morales, F. X. (2002). Industrial districts and innovation: The case of the Spanish ceramic tiles industry. *Entrepreneurship & Regional Development*, *14*(4), 317–335.

Molina-Morales, F. X., & Martínez-Cháfer, L. (2016). Cluster firms: You'll never walk alone. *Regional Studies*, *50*(5), 877–893.

Molina-Morales, F. X., & Martínez-Fernández, M. T. (2009). Does homogeneity exist within industrial districts? A social capital-based approach. *Papers in Regional Science*, *88*(1), 209–229.

Molina-Morales, F. X., Martínez-Fernández, M. T., Ares, M. A., & Hoffmann, V. E. (2008). *La estructura y naturaleza del capital social en las aglomeraciones territoriales de empresas*. Fundación BBVA.

Molina-Morales, F. X., Martínez-Cháfer, L., Valiente-Bordanova, D., del Corte-Lora, V., & Serbanescu, A. (2021). *Concentración y adquisiciones de empresas en el clúster cerámico durante el período 2010–2020*. Informe Càtedra de Model Econòmic.

PwC. (2021). Resumen Ejecutivo: Impacto socioeconómico y fiscal del sector de azulejos y pavimentos cerámicos. https://transparencia.ascer.es/media/1039/informe-impacto-socioeco-sector-cerámico_ascer.pdf

11
POKEMON: Ethias' corporate entrepreneurship initiative

Frédéric Ooms and Fabrice Pirnay

1.   INTRODUCTION

As the twilight hues of a typical 2018 fall evening descended over Liège, Belgium, the headquarters of Ethias was slowly emptying of its employees.[1] In his office, Nicolas Dumazy, the recently appointed Chief Strategy and Data Officer, ponders the company's future. This HEC-Liège graduate, who had steadily climbed the ranks over a span of 12 years, was thinking about a major challenge Ethias was facing: staying relevant amidst the rapidly evolving landscape of Insurtech.[2] In this rapidly transforming market, startups were gearing up, ready to carve out their niche and possibly upsetting the existing market equilibrium.

Ethias, a well-established Belgian insurance company, had been a major player in the industry for years. However, the disruptive wave of innovative startups threatened to eclipse its traditional business model. The cautionary tales of once-dominant giants like Kodak, Blockbuster, and Nokia echoed in Dumazy's mind, a stark reminder that even the most successful, long-standing companies could stumble and be disrupted if they failed to adapt. For Dumazy, it was a clear signal that Ethias needed to accelerate the go-to market of its most innovative projects. Dumazy sought ways to foster internal innovation and encourage entrepreneurial initiatives within the company as a proactive strategy against these burgeoning disruptions.

2.   THE RISE OF INSURTECH

Dumazy was acutely aware of the emerging Insurtech startups that were progressively revolutionizing the insurance industry. By ingeniously intertwining traditional insurance methodologies with cutting-edge technologies, these startups were marking their presence across various sectors, such as health, life, property, and casualty insurance, among others.

A case in point was Lemonade, an Insurtech startup based in New York that had caught Dumazy's attention. Within five years, Lemonade had successfully disrupted the United States home insurance market with its entirely digital insurance system (Box 11.1). On the other side of the Atlantic, Discovery, a South African firm, offered a gamut of health insurance products and services, along with technology-driven healthcare solutions. These included its flagship Vitality wellness program, which uses data and analytics to encourage healthy behavior, and its connected health platform, which provides consumers with digital health services and resources.

BOX 11.1   LEMONADE 5 YEARS, 5 NUMBERS

And so, despite (to spite?) skeptics, cynics, and competitors—and with due reverence for the trials and tribulations that lie ahead—we're incredibly grateful for what team Lemonade has accomplished in these 5 years.

5 stats capture what a difference 5 years can make.

1.   Growing with our customers:

- 50% of the customers who bought Lemonade in our first 30 days are still our customers 5 years later, and …
- they spend more than 2X on Lemonade now than they did then.

2.   Time is relative:

- 3 years to go from zero to $100 million of in-force premium.
- 14 months to get from $100 million to $200 million.
- 8 months to go from $200 million to $300 million!

3.   Maya is getting the hang of things:

- Maya generated over 8 million insurance quotes in 5 years.
- 2 years to generate the first million.
- 2 months to generate the most recent million.

4.   Expanding family:

- 1 line of insurance for our first 4 years (homeowners).
- 4 lines this year (homeowners, pet health, term life—and we're on the cusp of launching Lemonade Car!).

5.   Giveback grows 40X:

- $4,278,340 donated to 154 nonprofits by the Lemonade community.
- 4,232% growth between our first and our fifth giveback.

Source: Schreiber (n.d.). Permission granted.

Closer to home, Dumazy was following the aggressive growth strategy of Luko, a French Insurtech startup. Additionally, Alan, another Paris-based unicorn startup, was making waves in the health insurance sector with its fully digital offerings. These startups were not just knocking on the doors of the insurance industry. They were paving the way for a new era of technology-based insurance, posing significant challenges and opportunities for traditional insurance companies like Ethias.

3.   ETHIAS: A BRIEF BACKGROUND OF THE COMPANY

In 1919, the Société Mutuelle des Administrations Publiques was founded in Liège, Belgium, in the aftermath of the First World War. Many uninsured public buildings had been destroyed during the war. While Europe was thinking about its reconstruction, a handful of Belgian cities decided to launch a company inspired by the Swiss mutual insurance model to insure buildings against fire, lightning, and explosions.

After more than a century, this historic company, renamed Ethias, encompassed all aspects of life and non-life insurance. Ranking within the top 5 insurers in Belgium, Ethias boasted 1.2 million individual clients, 40,000 community clients, and a dedicated workforce of nearly 1,850 employees, capturing a 9 percent market share (see Table 11.1). The company, with

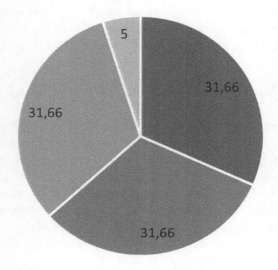

- Federal State   ■ Walloon Region   ■ Flemish Region   ▨ EthiasCo

Source: Adapted from www.ethias.be/invest/investors_relations/company-profile.html and www.euresa.org/en/members/ethias/.

Figure 11.1   Ethias' shareholding structure

Table 11.1   Market share of insurance companies in Belgium, 2015–2018 (%)

	2015	2017	2018
AG Insurance	20.80	21	21.70
AXA	14.20	12.50	12.10
KBC	8.70	9.40	8.80
Ethias	9	9.10	9.30
Baloise	4.80	5	4.90

Source: Author's own elaboration based on data from Statista.

its public shareholding, held financial stakes in dozens of companies across various sectors including insurance, finance, industry, environment, and social economy (Figure 11.1).

Ethias has always been a frontrunner in embracing technology, as demonstrated by its early adoption of a company website in the mid-1990s, online subscriptions in 2000, and the facilitation of online claims submissions in 2005. Nevertheless, the rigid organizational structure, required in the highly regulated insurance industry, had inadvertently fostered an environment of inertia. This inertia and a prevailing culture of risk aversion hindered the company's ability to adapt swiftly and seize emerging opportunities. To address this predicament, Ethias initiated an ambitious technological and organizational transformation plan. This plan involved the restructuring of its innovation division into two primary departments: a commercial department aimed at enhancing existing products and services and a corporate department focused on future positioning. While this seemed like a promising strategy on paper, many innovative ideas struggled to take off and languished in their nascent stages.

4.   CULTIVATING AN ENTREPRENEURIAL MINDSET

Confronted with the company's inertia, Dumazy believed that the solution lay in nurturing an entrepreneurial spirit within the company. He was convinced that by doing so, Ethias could shed the constraints of its entrenched organization structure, spur disruptive innovation, and compete more effectively against emerging Insurtech rivals. Yet, he was keenly aware that for such a transformative shift to occur, the company needed a skipper—someone possessing not only the requisite expertise and an innate passion for entrepreneurship but also an ingrained entrepreneurial mindset. Crucially, it was essential to have someone who also knew the company well, understanding its culture, strengths, and weaknesses, as this would be pivotal in navigating the complexities of large organizations.

His search for this entrepreneurial leader led him to recall a recent conversation with William Poos, Head of Innovation at Ethias' subsidiary, NRB. Poos praised Fabian Delhaxhe, a former colleague whose profile was marked by a strong drive for innovation and a keen entrepreneurial mindset.[3] Delhaxhe's eclectic career journey, which included DJing, consulting, community management for a gaming startup, and digital marketing for the Royal Opera of Wallonia, demonstrated his versatility and adaptability. His passion for digital innovation and an intimate knowledge of Ethias gleaned from his roles at NRB and another subsidiary, Afelio, made him a compelling candidate for the task at hand.

Prompted by this potential opportunity, Dumazy reached out to Delhaxhe, eager to leverage his unique blend of expertise and entrepreneurial mindset. In their ensuing discussions, the duo delved into the intricacies of digital transformation, the pace at which it was evolving, and how Ethias needed to adapt to keep up. They both concurred on the importance of fostering an entrepreneurial culture that prized creativity, adaptability, and speed. As their conversation unfolded, the idea of a fully digital tenant insurance emerged. Intrigued by this concept, Dumazy asked Delhaxhe to explore this idea further and devise a plan to explore its feasibility.

Weeks later, brimming with curiosity, the entire Ethias innovation team gathered. Aware of the changing landscape in the insurance sector, Delhaxhe advanced without ambivalence and unveiled the fruit of his idea (see Figure 11.2a, b, c and d):

> I am convinced that the company needs to be more active in the digital segment. For many months, I have been thinking about a 100% digital home insurance dedicated to tenants. From subscription to claim management, everything will be done online. No office, no phone line. Everything will be managed through an application animated by a chatbot. I have already found a name for this project that will change the way Ethias sells insurance. I call it POKEMON, in reference to the millennial target.

After the meeting, Delhaxhe swiftly received approval and was given three months to assess the business opportunity and develop a compelling plan. Drawing on the insights of French philosopher Emile-Auguste Chartier, who once said, "Nothing is more dangerous than an idea when it's the only one you have," Fabian recognized the crucial step of validating his concept before proceeding.

5.   FROM CONCEPT TO DISRUPTION: THE POKEMON JOURNEY

Delhaxhe recognized that his concept might not align with the market's needs. Were millennials truly prepared to transition to a purely digital insurance experience? At this point, being very curious about the world of startups and the new approaches advocated by serial entrepreneurs, Delhaxhe recalls:

> My priority was to validate the main assumptions of POKEMON. I met with potential customers in the street and shopping malls. I interviewed them personally. Some interviews confirmed my assumptions, but others surprised me. Price, for example, was an important element but not a determining factor. Another interesting finding was the negative comments commonly heard from the people I interviewed. Many considered insurance companies opaque, complex, useless, and even dishonest. I discovered that simplicity, speed, and transparency were key.

Figure 11.2a POKEMON first pitch

Interviews after interviews, the needs to address became clearer. Yet, one question lingered: Would an entirely digitally managed insurance deliver the simplicity, speed, and transparency the market craved? The innovation graveyard is full of failed innovations—Google Glass, Microsoft Zune, Apple Newton, and Amazon Fire are all cautionary tales that show that even the most meticulous planning and execution do not guarantee success. Delhaxhe knew that he had to validate his assumption at every stage of the process to prevent a similar fate for his project. Following the approach used by successful entrepreneurs, he crafted a landing page. But rather than simply launching it into the digital ether, he took a more hands-on approach. To directly engage with potential customers and ensure that his convictions did not shape

Figure 11.2b   POKEMON first pitch continued

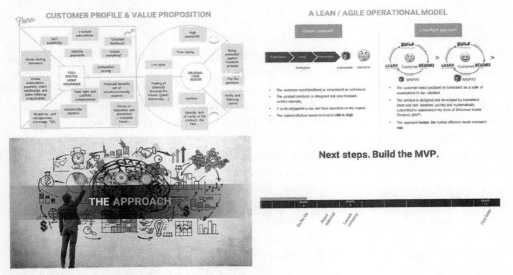

Figure 11.2c   POKEMON first pitch continued

POKEMON, he went again "out of the building" and set them in the following situation: "Imagine that you want to rent your first apartment. The landlord asks you to take an insurance. You search on Google, and you come across three offers. Look at the following three landing pages and tell me which offer you choose and why."

After several iterations, POKEMON emerged as the favored choice for an impressive 90 percent of respondents. This promising outcome paved the way for the launch of the online landing page. Marketing campaigns on Facebook and Google were rolled out to drive traffic,

Source: Courtesy of Ethias, images by Fabian Delhaxhe. Permission granted.

Figure 11.2d   POKEMON first pitch continued

testing the market's response and gauging traction for POKEMON. While these digital campaigns were ongoing, Delhaxhe had already taken the next step. In parallel, he marshaled a team from NRB's information technology staff to design a functional representation of POKEMON.

The objective was to create a working model of the concept within weeks (Figure 11.3a, b and c), offering both internal stakeholders and potential customers an opportunity to experience POKEMON first-hand. The culmination of these steps, underpinned by Delhaxhe's entrepreneurial mindset and clear vision, culminated in designing the initial business model for POKEMON (Figure 11.4). Having effectively validated several core assumptions, the stage was set to translate it into a detailed business plan, outlining the strategy operations, marketing, and financial projections. The creation of this business plan had a critical objective: obtaining approval from the board of directors. Delhaxhe was determined to illustrate that POKEMON was more than a shiny new innovative idea; it was a robust, validated promising business opportunity with potential for success. His goal was to win the board's endorsement, a critical stepping stone for the next phase of POKEMON's evolution—the execution and rollout of the platform on a larger scale.

6.   MOVING FORWARD

In the autumn of 2019, Delhaxhe presented POKEMON to a dozen directors with a mix of excitement and apprehension. Thesis, antithesis, synthesis. Delhaxhe's presentation resonated, yet a looming question remained unanswered: How could Ethias bring POKEMON effectively to life? As deliberations ensued within the boardroom, Delhaxhe, Dumazy, and the directors

VALUE PROPOSITION TESTING

'11 people out of 12 chose Flora vs. Ethias vs. Les AP'

Assurance locataire, telle qu'elle devrait être

L'Assurance Locataire

Assurance habitation pour les jeunes adultes

VALUE PROPOSITION TESTING

Mobile Application (Atello)

Quel est ton Loyer ?

550 €

7 Steps to Flora MVP
(Value Proposition Testing)

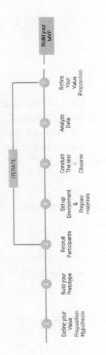

Build your MVP

ITERATE

1. Define your Value Proposition Hypothesis
2. Build your Pretotype
3. Recruit Participants
4. Set up Environment & Prepare materials
5. Conduct The test / Observe
6. Analyze Data
7. Refine Your Value Proposition

WHY DID THEY CHOOSE US?

DESIGN
"It's beautiful. The colors... everything."

STRUCTURE
"It's clear and well structured."

TONE OF VOICE
"They talk to me. I feel concerned."

Figure 11.3a   Value proposition testing

Figure 11.3b   Value proposition testing continued

(POTENTIAL) CUSTOMERS' FEEDBACK

- *"If it's that easy to get insured, I'll do it immediately!"*
  - ? – Renter

- *"Where can I register to a mailing list to get informed when it's available?"*
  - D. – Renter

- *"At least! Finally an insurer will offer a real app. It's not possible anymore in 2019 to manage all that on paper prints."*
  - ? – Renter

"It's my biggest issue. I have absolutely no idea if my renters are covered. Let me know as soon as it's available and I'll force all of my 18 renters to get insured at your company!"

Manu – Owner

"It has to be easy. If it's easy, I'll do it.

Virginie – Real Estate Broker

"And how much will that service cost? Oh, it's gonna be free!? Great!!!"

Delphine – Owner

Source: Courtesy of Ethias, images by Fabian Delhaxhe. Permission granted.

Figure 11.3c   Value proposition testing continued

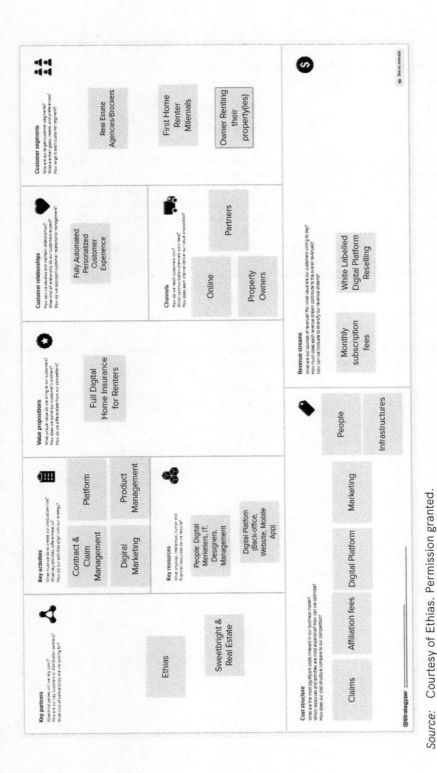

Source: Courtesy of Ethias. Permission granted.

Figure 11.4 Initial POKEMON business model for the exercise about pivots

weighed the pros and cons of their options. Each path had its distinct advantages and challenges, compelling them to ponder the most appropriate course of action. As they navigated this pivotal moment, their unanimous resolve was to make the right choice, a decision that could potentially catalyze disruptive innovation in their industry.

NOTES

1. This case was developed largely based on information provided by Jessica Lion, Fabian Delhaxhe, and Nicolas Dumazy. Other resources used are indicated accordingly.
2. Insurtech refers to using innovative technologies to create new insurance products, streamline the insurance process, and improve the overall customer experience. Insurtech companies often use data analytics, artificial intelligence, machine learning, and other advanced technologies to disrupt and transform the traditional insurance industry. The goal of Insurtech is to make insurance more accessible, affordable, and convenient for customers while improving the efficiency and profitability of insurance companies.
3. Several interviews were conducted with Fabian Delhaxhe between January and March 2021.

REFERENCES

Schreiber, D. (n.d.). How Lemonade Became a Precocious 5-Year-Old. Lemonade. Retrieved November 12, 2023 from www.lemonade.com/blog/lemonade-turns-5

12
Corporate intrapreneurship through start-ups: Atos' innovation ecosystem

Jonas Geisen, Rick Aalbers, Killian McCarthy, and Sebastian Schäfer

1. ATOS: STRATEGIC TURNAROUND THROUGH INNOVATION

Companies that undergo a radical change typically aim for an improvement and enhancement of their strategic market position. Such drive for improvement can be a bare necessity – when current methods falter – or rather originate in an ambition to innovate. Regardless of the motivation, such strategic change focuses on converting ideas into tangible improvements. For Rodolphe Belmer, both catalysts of strategic change have been evident since the beginning of his employment as Atos SE's[1] new chief executive officer (CEO) on January 1, 2022. After the first three months in his new role, Rodolphe realized that he could not wait to map out the company's future plan as the changing competitive landscape challenged Atos.

Atos, classified in the domain of "Computer Programming, Data Processing, and other Computer Related Services,"[2] had been struggling with issues stemming from its attempt to fundamentally change its business model since 2018. Moving from hardware-intensive services to consulting and technology services was a business model transformation that was complicated in itself. Problems multiplied as the transformation only took off slowly as new services had to compete with both incumbents that had positioned themselves with an early transformation and start-ups positioned at the technological forefront.

Amidst this context, Rodolphe was keenly aware that his appointment as CEO was to signal change in Atos' strategic direction. For a successful turnaround of the situation he had to create successful change and make it transparent not only for Atos' employees but for all stakeholders. Consequently, as a first important step Rodolphe had to implement a new innovation strategy serving the transformation of Atos' business model towards future-ready digitalization services accompanied by growth: "In view of the challenges facing Atos, we have appointed Rodolphe Belmer for his strategic acumen and his proven leadership and operational efficiency, as well as his ability to successfully lead complex transformations" (Atos, 2021a).

Although certainly challenging, this called for a leadership task not unfamiliar to Rodolphe. His 25 years of high-tech industry experience provided him with a wealth of experience and a solid international network, making him a business leader recognized in Europe, the United States, and Asia.[3] As the situation in which the company found itself had led to a tightening of internal funding, he envisioned a strategic framework that would foster innovation by allowing Atos' employees to take direct responsibility for turning novel ideas into profitable new products and services. Ultimately, this should lead to high-value, high-impact projects (further called *lighthouse projects*) that would serve and signal the transformation.

From a strategic perspective, there were two alternative pathways to build these capacities. The first was internally, through incubating new ventures (Chesbrough, 2002; Lerner, 2013). However, as this approach requires an extensive amount of time and financial resources that were both scarce, Rodolphe dismissed it. Instead, he favored the second approach centered around scouting and integrating emerging start-ups that pioneer technology. Enriching Atos' network would enable employees to meet, learn, work, and collaborate on new technologies and digital services, creating a buzz around new ideas and thereby rekindling genuine long-term market attention. Rodolphe knew that in the highly competitive high-tech industry such a positive external evaluation was relevant to stay ahead – as various tech trend watchers such as Gartner systematically pointed out (see Attachment 1[4]).

New emerging entities such as tech orchestrators were capitalizing on the momentum that start-ups trailblazing their way into established markets had generated. While start-ups force incumbents to recalibrate their strategies to safeguard their market position, tech orchestrators foster collaboration to jointly venture into new market domains. Rodolphe had always recognized the potential of start-up communities, yet he noted marked underutilization of such intermediaries across all of Atos' industries. To make matters more complex – despite a decade of knowledge, theory, and best practice related to innovation activities within Atos – history revealed that a large share of these programs either did not realize their founding objectives or failed entirely. This is a scenario not uncommon to many other growth-aspiring firms as innovation outcome hinges on the uncertainty in contrast to the initial expectation of input, associated risk, and motivation of the innovation program at hand.

2.   FAILING TRANSFORMATION?

Atos' necessity for strategic change is rooted in the imperative to bring fresh wind into the firm. The shift from a hardware-intensive service provider towards a provider of technology and consulting services followed a trend across various domains in information technology (IT). Atos' shift had been pursued heavily through the firm's recent acquisition history, leading to the necessity of cascading restructuring efforts since 2018. This, combined with repetitive changes of CEOs, left share prices continuously dropping, leaving Atos' market value behind its competitors. Rodolphe, due to his prior position as a member of Atos' board since October 2021, was painfully aware of this challenging context.

Founded in 1997 in France, Atos underwent multiple waves of mergers and acquisitions (see Figure 12.1) marking strategic shifts in the firm's value proposition. Initially, the corporation focused on hardware-intensive services such as IT outsourcing and system integration. The more recent acquisitions built a portfolio of technological assets and generated diversity in human resources, leading to the development of substantial tacit knowledge and explicit expertise in payment transactions as well as consulting and technology services. As a result, market penetration changed, providing Atos with a competitive punch in digital transformation with 109,000 employees, a total equity grossing over €6.8 billion, and annual revenue of over €11 billion (Atos, 2016). More precisely, the company's reorientation focuses on cybersecurity, cloud, and high-performance computing as well as a pioneering role in decarbonization services and products.

Yet, acquiring various targets, from differing subindustries and geographies (see Attachment 2 for a detailed overview), had multiplied Atos' scope and employee numbers without cutting loose from the old business model. While having had a historical focus in Europe, Atos' portfolio grew to encompass tailored end-to-end solutions for all industries in 71 countries. The ongoing sponsorship of the Olympic and Paralympic Games as the principal technology partner symbolically portrayed the global ambition of this IT giant. Amidst this context and to lay the foundations to (1) move from IT infrastructure to digitalization services and (2) enable further continuous adaptation of its value proposition, the organization faced a massive challenge: restructuring (see Attachment 3). Initialized in 2018 by Thierry Breton, CEO of Atos from 2009 to 2019, it proved difficult as creating new structures and service offerings required a vast field of expertise in processes and technology as well as transformational capabilities. "Following our recent acquisitions, we have prepared Advance 2021, a new and ambitious three-year plan for Atos. This plan will strengthen our position as the go-to partner for organizations who are looking to respond to the dilemmas of the digital world and navigate its challenges successfully" (Atos, 2018, p. 4).

As is usual with restructurings, Atos faced employee retention challenges and ruffled managerial engagement in the middle layers of the company. Due to such challenges, it was hardly surprising that the restructuring was neither an easy nor quick task. Therefore, in 2020 Atos realized that Advance 2021 would not be sufficient and kicked off its second restructuring wave, aptly titled "SPRING." This second wave was conceptualized as a process that encapsulated different subprocesses that jointly would snowball into a substantial corporate transition, a program with a keen eye for the human factor as a cornerstone to or a major disruptor of actual change.

> This profound and fast transformation also requires a change of scope for the Group. We will continue to intensify our bolt-on acquisition program – 3 more announced today – and we are aiming to augment the Group's capabilities with mid-size assets that will support our mid-term plan and growth agenda. (Elie Girard, Interim CEO 2019–2022, in Atos, 2021b)

When investigating Atos' position, it became apparent that the implementation of SPRING was stalling compared to the aims of its high-energy launch campaign. In total, Rodolphe inherited a firm whose share price was continually plummeting. Continued sales of shares by

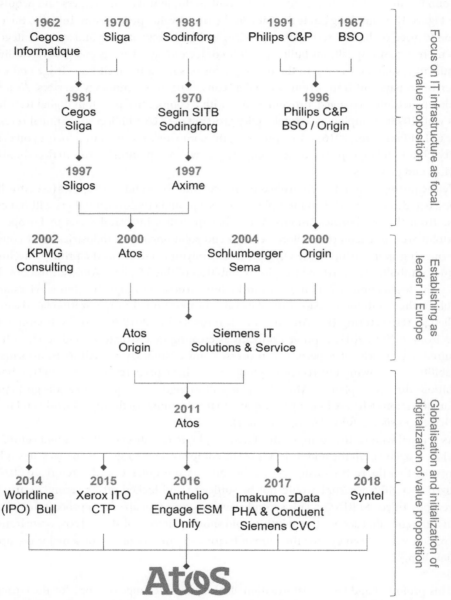

Source: Authors' own elaboration based on publicly shared information of Atos SE.

Figure 12.1   Development of Atos SE through successive merger waves over time

Atos' shareholders since 2018 as well as missing projections for revenue growth and margins in 2021 (see Attachments 4 and 5) depreciated the firm's market value. This development was highlighted and thereby reinforced by market analyst reports, e.g., those of NewsBites Finance (Attachment 6), one of the major financial information providers for investors worldwide.

The fall of Atos' market value was even more apparent when analyzing its share returns (the daily development of a share price) in context. Historically, Atos' share returns had been lower than that of its index, CAC 40,[5] and its direct competitor, Capgemini (see Attachment 7). However, its development co-varied until the beginning of 2021, when two thirds of the Advance 2021 restructuring had been under way. At this point, market valuations diverged. At the end of the first quarter of 2022, Atos' share returns had dropped by 72.58 percent. In comparison, its index, the CAC 40, had increased by 25.93 percent. Atos' competitor, Capgemini, had achieved an even higher increase in share returns: 104.55 percent. Accordingly, analyst reports deduced that the continuous downfall of Atos' share value since 2021 was not to be blamed on industry specifics but instead on internal turmoil.

It seemed that the shareholders, to some degree, had lost some of their trust in Atos' ability to strategically reposition itself as a digitalization partner. This, so the new CEO believed, had to be ascribed to the lack of progress achieved so far through the restructuring. For him, this implied two major long-term consequences. First, the decrease in market value tightened the financial situation, restricting internal budgets as expenses were subject to a high level of scrutiny and conditional on the prospect of positive returns. Second, the shareholders seemed to think that Atos lacked the ability to further secure and maintain its competitiveness and thus its position on the market. However, stock markets only factor in the information that its actors can lay their hands on. Therefore, in Atos' case, investors only assessed what was visible to them, pricing in information asymmetry, resulting in a negative valuation of Atos' current market value. Accordingly, it was necessary to shift the market's perspective of Atos, and the firm's current undertakings.

To do so, Rodolphe had to spring into action immediately. A strategic review of Atos' performance, including the current restructuring portfolio, was imminent for the next conference call on Atos' half-year results in July 2022. In this conference call, Atos management, spearheaded by Rodolphe, would have to face shareholders and analysts alike to announce and discuss the firm's financial results. So far, the outlook was not bright, but Rodolphe aimed to correct this to a more positive outlook. Time had come to reposition Atos onto its trajectory of success.

3. START-UPS: A STRATEGIC TURNAROUND FOR RESTRUCTURING

The severe issues Atos had been facing were mirrored in its financial performance (compare Attachments 4 and 5). Substantially decreasing funds for investment amplified the pressure for a quick turnaround. While the former restructuring waves had focused on the firm's governance structure, the board under the direction of Rodolphe wanted to focus on high-value, high-impact projects as the way ahead. Successful lighthouse projects needed to provide a portfolio of success stories to send a positive signal while being financially viable. By doing so, Atos would build upon the formerly achieved restructuring outcomes while facilitating the transformation towards its new business model. Rodolphe hoped to showcase how Atos was future-proofing itself, sending the necessary positive signals to reinstate shareholders' trust and secure its long-term market positioning.

Creating such lighthouse projects through internally developed capabilities seemed attractive, as it would provide intellectual property with a high degree of flexibility regarding its long-term exploitation. However, the IT giant was aware that the amount of resources necessary to do so and the associated high level of risk until a technology would reach the operational state of market readiness were factors which rendered the internal pursuit of all interesting technologies impossible.

In today's business environment, developing technologies and leading them towards a mature level for commercialization is often not achieved by big established companies. Instead, start-ups are usually a few years ahead regarding the application of emergent technologies. Usually, these small start-ups – FinTechs, InsurTechs, and HealthTechs[6] alike – are specialized to utilize technology to tackle a specific problem in an innovative way (Junior & Cherobim, 2020; Milian et al., 2019). Consequently, such start-ups possess knowledge and capabilities that are of utmost relevance to leverage emerging technologies. For this reason, Rodolphe had set his mind on embracing their technological and commercial energy for all of Atos' industry domains. Yet, how could Atos effectively monitor the start-up landscape? Rodolphe was aware that for this undertaking it would be easier to utilize best practices existing within Atos. After all, developing new routines is difficult and leveraging knowledge already in place can speed up transformation efforts. One best practice caught his eye as it had the potential to serve as a blueprint for an organization-wide rollout: the approach of Atos' Financial Services & Insurances industry (FS&I) to intrapreneurship. FS&I had set-up structures and processes that enabled them to scout FinTechs to work with on joint projects. Carol Houle, the head of consulting and marketing of FS&I, stated that leveraging these allowed FS&I to develop new projects that serve the "unprecedented acceleration of digital transformation across banking, financial services and insurance … seizing the opportunities for growth that digital differentiation presents" (Atos, 2021c).

Harnessing the power of start-ups through such scouting would allow the identification and selection of start-ups fitting each specific lighthouse project, enabling the development of new service offerings in an innovative way while providing the growth expected by the company's shareholders. Subsequently, at short notice, Rodolphe had to make two fundamental decisions about such a strategic framework to be reported at the conference call on Atos' half-year results in 2022. These decisions encompassed:

1. Was the FS&I strategy the right way to scout the best start-ups to fit the lighthouse projects?
2. Which governance mode should be chosen to work with the scouted start-ups?

3.1   Decision 1: The question of how to scout for the right start-ups

As Rodolphe had decided to focus on Atos' intrapreneurship through the utilization of start-ups, he first had to define a process for how these could be scouted. Rodolphe could either emphasize corporate scouting or he could play up orchestrated external scouting. Corporate scouting, on the one hand, was driven from within the firm and primarily built on exploiting existing relationships with start-ups. Orchestrated external scouting, on the other hand, made use of a third party to scout, thereby focusing on exploring new start-ups. These two scouting forms served different motives that have been found to be perceived differently by the market as well as impacting performance differently (Aalbers et al., 2021a, 2021b).

3.1.1 Corporate in-house scouting to exploit existing relationships

FS&I's primary focus was on corporate scouting. Their FinTech program aimed to make the most out of relationships with established FinTechs for lighthouse projects. FS&I based their FinTech program on three pillars (Atos, 2017): FinHub (engage); FinNet (thought leadership and research); and Atos Financial Services Sandbox (test drive):

- *FinHub*: FinHub acts as a dynamic bridge, connecting the aspirations of innovators and industry stalwarts, steering the ATOS FinTech program towards its vision of mutual growth and advancement. Consisting of a team of industry thought leaders and trend watchers who link into an active community of pre-vetted, quality-assured, and road-tested FinTechs, FinHub operates based on a stringent selection process. This process identifies, assesses, and partners with only those FinTechs that have the strongest possibility of delivering new value for Atos.
- *FinNet*: Geared up as a knowledge portal that integrates one of the brightest minds in the Atos FinTech community, FinNet stands as a comprehensive knowledge portal that delves into the cutting-edge realm of FinTech, encompassing a global perspective. It serves as a beacon to the ever evolving landscape of financial technology trends. FinNet functions as an empowering platform that facilitates the exchange of pivotal market advancements, nascent submarkets, and imminent innovations. Its role extends to curating and disseminating these transformative elements among a diverse spectrum of financial stakeholders, encompassing esteemed institutions in the financial services sector, dynamic FinTech companies, visionary InsurTech enterprises, and pioneering RegTech entities.
- *Atos Financial Services Sandbox*: Focused on completing end-to-end customer journeys by bundling FinTech services to demonstrate ways to challenge the status quo, this pillar is a cloud-based application programming interface platform for start-ups and their partners to create banking or insurance services in combination with Atos. As such, Atos' Financial Services Sandbox provides the technical blueprints and integration support to fast-track start-ups go-to-market propositions.

FS&I further stated that the FinTech program had only one central objective, namely to "exploit opportunities to survive and thrive in Financial Services" (Atos, 2017). In other words, it was set up to engage start-ups into the vertical FS&I industry, thereby positioning Atos as a chief integrator of FinTechs for its tier 1 and 2 customers. For Rodolphe, this clearly signaled an approach which required a comparatively low initial investment of financial and human resources while providing low levels of risk. Scaling up across the whole of Atos would be relatively easy as the knowledge about the necessary structures, practices, and infrastructure would reside in-house. Besides the lower effort for scaling, this approach would focus on creating a pull so that start-ups self-select into Atos' ecosystem. Accordingly, this strategy to build in-house would offer full control over the amount of resources input into the scouting, allowing to adjust it in a flexible manner whenever necessary.

However, on the downside, a purely internal solution could also lead to a higher degree of path dependency. Both the focus of existing internal knowledge as well as the focus on pulling start-ups into the firm would be more passive search efforts and therefore more narrow. In a fast-changing environment such as high tech this could be too little effort to innovate. Furthermore, there was another drawback observing the past development of the FinTech program. After a strong start the program had nosedived. To Rodolphe this seemed to be rooted in the higher-level managerial expectations that had gone hand in hand with the funding of the program. Apparently, there had not been enough tangible success stories to establish a positive return on investment, thereby raising questions about profitability. This assessment, however, seemed to be rooted in unrealistic expectations regarding the upper echelons of delivery through the program as well as a limited focus as it was diverted through the restructuring efforts. For Rodolphe, it was clear that this lack of managerial attention had reduced the availability of necessary resources and thereby the potential success. Accordingly, from his point of view, such a scouting strategy would take time to produce the necessary results to signal a turnaround in Atos' innovation efforts.

3.1.2   Orchestrated external scouting to explore new relationships

Rodolphe also learned about the "small partnership" that Atos Information Technology GmbH, the German entity of Atos, had formed with the German innovation hub FinTech Community Frankfurt GmbH (followingly called TechQuartier) (for a broad overview, see Attachment 8). TechQuartier was a cross-industry platform and ecosystem builder that connected start-ups and corporates to work, meet, learn, and collaborate on new technologies and digital business models. With a member-based community spanning more than 500 start-ups and hundreds of potential founders,[7] they seemed to be a prime partner to create opportunities for disruptive technologies, new ideas, and modern business models to thrive. As an ecosystem builder and orchestrator, TechQuartier's focus was therefore to bring together different parties to jointly contribute to a focal value proposition in an iterative manner (Kreutzer & Neudert, 2021). "The Frankfurt startup ecosystem has been one of the fastest growing ones we've measured globally in great part due to TechQuartier, a keystone organization that is a model we use when advising other agencies worldwide" (Jean-François Gauthier, CEO Startup Genome, Silicon Valley, in TechQuartier, 2022).

However, Atos' partnership was limited in its access to TechQuartier's offerings. The question hence arose as to whether this partnership should be extended to utilize TechQuartier in its capacity as a technology and ecosystem orchestrator. Joining forces with TechQuartier would allow Atos to fully access their vast network to explore start-ups and their value propositions to build on disruptive technologies. As a matter of fact, TechQuartier focused on the building of explorative partnerships through a cornerstone offering: TechMatching. TechMatching encompassed multiple different individual but combinable steps dependent on a customer's needs and thereby was a central building block of numerous innovation formats offered by TechQuartier (TechQuartier, 2022; see Attachment 9). Figure 12.2 presents an overview of these steps in the form of the TechScouting process.

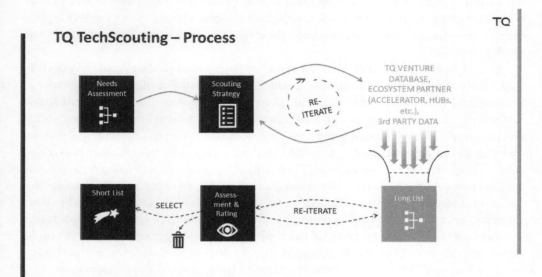

Source: TechQuartier. Permission granted.

Figure 12.2   TechQuartier scouting process

- Needs assessment: Processing the problem and the envisioned solution to the problem that a corporate, potentially Atos, is scouting for.
- Scouting strategy: Defining exclusion criteria that should ensure the best strategic fit for the corporate. In the past, TechQuartier encountered criteria as problem–solution fit, team size, the level of the start-up's maturity and product innovation capabilities, technical constraints, institutional certainty, geographical and industry relatedness, and ownership.
- Scouting by TechQuartier: Using both their direct and indirect communities – in the form of direct or indirect ties – as well as external means, promising start-ups are scouted for a long list.
- Assessment and rating: In bilateral communication with the corporate, based on the long list, the performance of the start-ups is measured against the selected criteria. TechQuartier develops a scaling and weighting of the factors in cooperation with the client.
- Short list: The outcome is a short list of interesting partners that is iteratively discussed and revised with the corporate and potentially extended by further services.

From Rodolphe's perspective TechQuartier and their service could provide a complementary view into the vast and ever expanding landscape of constantly newly founded start-ups, thereby allowing to discover and broaden the innovation funnel while eliminating blind spots.

Therefore, TechMatching was highly explorative as it not only allowed firms to leave their path dependency, created through firms' reliance on established ties and routines with start-ups, but also to keep up to date regarding technological innovation. Rodolphe was sure that, in comparison, this orchestrated external scouting would signal a proactive step towards exploring new opportunities. Hence, it could allow the creation of completely new service offers and lighthouse projects.

However, as he considered the prospect of further forging such an alliance, an array of challenges and intricacies unfolded, prompting contemplation about their alignment with the core business model and strategic objectives. The concept of collaborating with TechQuartier struck him as a decision demanding a substantial commitment of resources – spanning time, effort, and personnel – that were sparse given Atos' current situation. He was cognizant that such an undertaking could potentially divert crucial focus and energy away from the very bedrock of core offerings serving as Atos' cash cow. The resulting consequences of this diversion could hold notable weight for this endeavor to stand a chance of being successful. Nonetheless, the notion of investing in start-ups through an incubator such as TechQuartier introduced an element of uncertainty surrounding potential returns on investment – a risk profile that might not seamlessly align with the established risk appetite of a firm struggling financially. All in all, an amalgamation of factors that, he conceded, stirred a degree of reluctance prompting him to tread carefully and contemplate the viability of such a partnership with circumspection.

Given the two approaches, Rodolphe was aware that speed was of the utmost importance as he had to present results before the next conference call on Atos' half-year results. Therefore, a high diffusion rate and range of the scouting approach would be beneficial. To identify these properties for in-house corporate and orchestrated external scouting, he made use of Figure 12.3 to identify the respective (dis)advantages of the approaches. Ultimately, the information about the approaches at hand presented Rodolphe with an overview to consider how he should design a framework of start-up scouting for an Atos-wide implementation. Additionally, he faced the decision whether he should focus on one scouting form, and if so, whether this should be the corporate or the orchestrated external scouting, or even whether it should be a combined scouting approach.

3.2   Decision 2: The question of how to work with start-ups

Facilitating the work with start-ups also posed the question of how Atos should govern its ecosystem. As part of the strategic framework, Rodolphe had to provide clear guidelines as to how collaboration with start-ups should be governed. There were two potential governance modes in question that would allow Atos to utilize the external knowledge that start-ups provide:

1. The formation of an alliance with the start-up
   Alliances – a partnership between two firms – entail the trade-off between a low level of the investment and therefore a low level of control. A partnership maintains the independence of the start-up allowing for a quick process to align on the joint value proposition which reflects in a relatively low commitment of resources, both financially as well as temporally. Simultaneously, it provides flexibility as it allows to reshape the commitment – in different directions and actions – at any point of time. Consequently, the risk associated with an

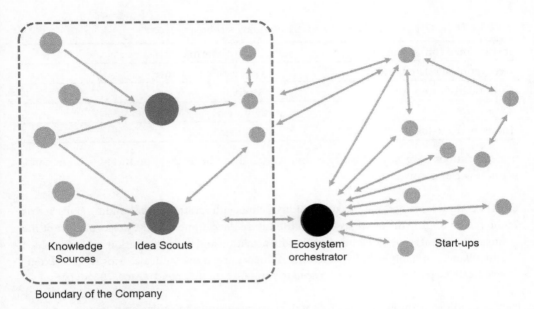

Knowledge   Idea Scouts   Ecosystem   Start-ups
Sources   orchestrator

Boundary of the Company

Source: Adapted from Whelan et al. (2011).

Figure 12.3   Knowledge network with and across the firm boundary

alliance is comparatively low, as roughly 50 percent of alliances turn out to be successful. The downside, however, is a loss of reduced long-term exploitative opportunities as the property rights of a joint-value proposition reside in both independent firms. While these can be used by both partners as a reference, the innovative, technological capabilities remain within the respective start-up and thus outside of Atos.

2. The acquisition of the start-up

    Acquisitions depict a significantly higher investment regarding financial and temporal means in comparison to the formation of an alliance with a start-up. This is due to the negotiations one also has to conduct for an alliance being extended by a detailed assessment of fit and finances, followed by the acquisition until completion of the post-merger integration. Independent from the comparison to an alliance, time for this process is of the utmost importance because the less time spent on it, the higher the chances are that the acquisition will fail. While being more resource intensive, an acquisition would nonetheless bring (dependent on how the start-up is integrated into Atos) both explorative and exploitative opportunities in-house. At the same time, it would be ensured that both technological capabilities as well as property rights would be owned by Atos. However, such a commitment is risky, as approximately 75–90 percent of mergers and acquisitions fail.

As pointed out by research, both governance forms follow different strategies weighting the associated risk with the underlying reasoning – in the form of the motive that aims to either explore or exploit innovation (McCarthy & Aalbers, 2022). Acquisitions are often exploitative as they are utilized to obtain the firm's capabilities, in the form of their employees, or consolidate the market by swallowing a competitor. Partnerships in the form of an alliance, on the other hand, are a prime means for explorative joint learning in a specific area. Both

Table 12.1   List of relevant factors backed up by strategy research

Institutional (un)certainty	Prior performance
Geographical relatedness	Ownership structure
Cultural distance	Motive
Target size	Founder
Industry relatedness	Business model

strategic actions have a long history within Atos and will be further conducted hand in hand, as Rodolphe announced himself:

> Atos completed more than 20 acquisitions in line with its strategy of building skills across the pillars of growth we see as core to the future development and transformation of the business: digital security, cloud, digital transformation and decarbonization … Partnerships and alliances, notably with hyperscalers, are becoming more strategic. Atos with its extensive strategic partnerships is well placed to capitalize on this trend. (Atos, 2021d, p. 5)

Each decision to form an alliance or conduct an acquisition to utilize start-ups would have to be made case specific for each lighthouse project. However, following the normal course of events within a corporation as large as Atos, the operational management would have to decide on the governance form. Therefore, Rodolphe's strategic framework had to incorporate a streamlined process for these decisions. Usually, such investments are assessed from an audit/controlling perspective, revolving around the financial outlook either governance form promises to generate. From a strategic perspective, there were more factors to be accounted for that prescribe the fitting governance form for a scouted start-up. Therefore, Rodolphe compiled a list of relevant factors backed up by strategy research (Hoffman & Schaper-Rinkel, 2001), shown in Table 12.1.

Strategy literature had informed Rodolphe that the factors in Table 12.1 were important to decide whether to ally or acquire. Therefore, it seemed reasonable to lean on such factors for the strategic framework. However, there also remained open questions that Rodolphe had to tackle to define this aspect of the framework. How should the factors be scaled and how should they be weighted? Also, what risk threshold should be set to determine if either an alliance or an acquisition is beneficial? Literature remained mute on these questions, however, Rodolphe had to answer these to provide a complete framework that would streamline intrapreneurship within Atos. Finally, he had to brood over the question as to whether the decision between an alliance and acquisition should be an exclusive one, or if this framework should incorporate a long-range planning approach (McCarthy & Aalbers, 2022).

4.   MOVING FORWARD

In summary, time was ticking for Rodolphe to implement strategic change to boost Atos' performance through intrapreneurship. A successful turnaround was important as the next conference call on Atos' half-year results, that would highly influence Atos' market evaluation, was imminent. Ultimately, he had to design a strategic framework, aimed to facilitate light-house projects that bolster intrapreneurship and transform Atos into an innovation power-house. Therefore, he needed to subsequently decide (1) how to scout the right start-ups and (2) which governance mode to choose to work with the scouted start-ups. These questions were important, as a credible solution that would allow a timely implementation could pave the way towards Atos' future success. Rodolphe had the possibility to signal a positive development towards investors, thereby reverting Atos' stock market value towards growth.

ACKNOWLEDGMENTS

As part of the FINDER program this project received funding from the European Union's Horizon 2020 research and innovation program under the Marie Skłodowska-Curie grant agreement No 813095. The funders had no role in the study design, data collection and analysis, decision to publish, or preparation of the manuscript.

NOTES

1. SE is the abbreviation for the Latin "societas Europaea," denoting a public company registered in accordance with the corporate law of the European Union.
2. Classified by the Standard Industrial Classification used by government agencies to define industry areas.
3. Before joining Atos he held the position of CEO of satellite operator Eutelsat Communications for six years following a 14-year career at Paris-based television giant Canal Plus, where he was appointed CEO in 2003 and served as group managing director from 2012 to 2015.
4. For Attachments 1–9, see the supplementary material for this chapter: http://dx.doi.org/10.4337/9781802204537
5. The CAC 40 is the French benchmark index of the 40 leading French stock corporations on which Atos was listed.
6. FinTech is a combination of two words: "financial" and "technology." From a broad perspective, FinTech is the integration of technology by financial services companies that aims to offer more efficient financial services to consumers. Similarly, InsurTechs integrate technology into insurance services and HealthTechs introduce technology into the healthcare industry.
7. Additionally, TechQuartier's continuously growing network encompasses 50 academic and corporate partners.

REFERENCES

Aalbers, R. H. L., McCarthy, K. J., & Heimeriks, K. H. (2021a). Market reactions to acquisition announcements: The importance of signaling "why" and "where." *Long Range Planning, 54*(6), 6.
Aalbers, R. H. L., McCarthy, K., Huisman, M., & Roettger, J. (2021b). Moving motives: How past and present strategy influence the market. *PLOS ONE, 16*(12), e0259660.
Atos. (2016, June 6). Company profile. https://atos.net/en/company-profile

Atos. (2017, June 21). Atos FinTech program: A catalyst for innovation in Financial Services. https://atos .net/fintech/home

Atos. (2018). Pioneering sustainable digital transformation. Integrated report.

Atos. (2021a, September 20). Rodolphe Belmer is appointed chief executive officer of Atos. https://atos .net/en/2021/press-release_2021_10_20/rodolphe-belmer-is-appointed-chief-executive-officer-of -atos

Atos. (2021b, July 27). *2021: Accelerating transformation in a year of transition*. https://atos.net/en/2021/ press-release_2021_07_27/2021-accelerating-transformation-in-a-year-of-transition

Atos. (2021c, November 22). Realization for change: Accelerating action now in financial services. https://atos.net/en/blog/realization-for-change-accelerating-action-now-in-financial-services

Atos. (2021d). Universal registration document, including 2021 annual financial report.

Chesbrough, H. W. (2002). Making sense of corporate venture capital. *Harvard Business Review, 80*(3), 90–99.

Hoffman, W. H., & Schaper-Rinkel, W. (2001). Acquire or ally? A strategy framework for deciding between acquisition and cooperation. *MIR: Management International Review*, 131–159.

Junior, I. C., & Cherobim, A. P. M. S. (2020). Academic production and technological emergence in finance: Bibliometric study on FinTechs. *Innovation & Management Review, 17*(2), 115–131.

Kreutzer, M., & Neudert, P. (2021). Ecosystem orchestration – much more than strategic alliance management. *EFMD Global Focus*, 11–15.

Lerner, J. (2013). Corporate venturing. *Harvard Business Review, 91*(10), 86.

McCarthy, K. J., & Aalbers, H. L. (2022). Alliance-to-acquisition transitions: The technological performance implications of acquiring one's alliance partners. *Research Policy, 51*(6), 104512.

Milian, E. Z., Spinola, M. de M., & Carvalho, M. M. de. (2019). FinTechs: A literature review and research agenda. *Electronic Commerce Research and Applications, 34*, 100833.

TechQuartier. (2022, December 23). Frankfurt's largest startup community. www.techquartier.com/ community

Whelan, E., Parise, S., De Valk, J., & Aalbers, R. (2011). Creating employee networks that deliver open innovation. *MIT Sloan Management Review, 53*(1), 37–44.

13
Reversing Nova Scotia's declining rural agri-food sector

Jahan Ara Peerally, Claudia De Fuentes, and Zainab Almukhtar

1. INTRODUCTION

Marah Schneider[1] came to Canada from the Netherlands seven years ago as a foreign student. In these seven years, her status changed from foreign student to immigrant to full-fledged Canadian. In that time, she also learnt French and polished her English while acquiring a bachelor's degree in business management, followed by a master's in innovation and development. Her master's thesis examined the contribution of immigrants to the Canadian economy. Two months ago, just weeks after her postgraduation, she was hired as a junior policy analyst at Nova Scotia's Department of Agriculture. Her duties are several, and include amongst others: (1) providing support, administration, quantitative and qualitative information and research to inter-ministerial and cross-jurisdictional projects and conducting research on sectoral development projects by assessing economic, labour market, employment and geographic indicators; and (2) preparing project products such as charters, work plans and draft status reports to support senior economic policy advisors in their various policymaking activities and processes.

Her first solo assignment in her new position is related to the problems of outmigration from Nova Scotia's rural regions, which has created chronic labour shortage and which in turn has led to a decline in the rural agri-food sector. Consequently, the declining agri-food sector in rural Nova Scotia continues to face the following problems:

- agricultural land and infrastructure being abandoned;
- aging proprietors within the traditional farming communities and businesses;
- poor succession planning; and
- agricultural production and agri-food processing labour market shortages.

Despite the several strategies implemented by Nova Scotia's provincial government to address these challenges, the shrinking of rural areas is still prevalent. Marah identifies two main tasks for completing her assignment. The first involves gathering the necessary information which will feed into the policymaking process. She will collect various quantitative and qualitative information and assess their relevance to the problems of outmigration. Marah decides to use the system of innovation framework, which she encountered during her master's studies, to guide her research. This framework will allow her to collect pertinent information on the roles and activities of all the actors in Nova Scotia's agri-food innovation system. In doing so, she will be able to evaluate: (1) the different actors who play an active role in the retention and settlement of newcomers[2] to the province, particularly those with expertise in the agri-food industry; (2) the projects and initiatives that these actors should champion to link newcomers possessing agri-food expertise with opportunities in the Nova Scotia agri-food sector; and (3) identify existing challenges for their integration.

Her second task involves providing an integrated analysis of the information collected, in the form of a written report, to a panel of senior policymakers, advisors and the Minister of Agriculture. Hence, the final report will propose actionable initiatives and solutions to the panel, on:

- linking newcomers and the agri-food industry;
- capitalizing on newcomers' knowledge to enhance innovation in the agri-food industry; and
- highlighting the key stakeholders who have the potential to promote the two above strategies and attract resources for revitalizing rural Nova Scotia and its local communities.

The panel will use the content of the report as a basis for devising the appropriate policies to redress the province's declining rural agri-food sector.

Marah is particularly keen on this project, because it resonates with her knowledge from her master's thesis and also because she fondly remembers the stories that her grandfather told her about their relatives immigrating to Canada after the Second World War. They were the Dutch settlers of Nova Scotia, and they brought with them a wealth of knowledge associated with farming techniques. Therefore, Marah feels especially connected to this project on a personal level, and she also feels that excelling at this first assignment will cement her position as a capable new hire within the Ministry.

2.   WHAT EXACTLY IS THE AGRI-FOOD SECTOR?

The agri-food sector includes different activities that range from primary agriculture (farmers), food and beverage processors, food retailers and wholesalers and food service providers. Marah realizes that in Canada, these activities contribute significantly to gross domestic product (GDP) and to employment, as indicated in Table 13.1.

Marah finds data on the 2016 contribution of the agriculture and agri-food sectors to the provincial GPD. In 2016, Ontario accounted for the largest share of the combined GDP for agriculture and food processing at 33.4 percent, while Quebec and Alberta accounted for 21.9 and 13.3 percent, respectively, as seen in Figure 13.1.

She also finds data on the share of provincial employment by the agriculture and agri-food sectors and information on the major agricultural commodity by province. As seen in Figure 13.2, Ontario has the largest employment share in the agriculture sector.

Table 13.1 The agri-food sector's contribution to GDP and employment, 2021

Activity	GDP (CAD billion)	Employment
Primary agriculture (farmers)	39.8	269,300
Food and beverage processors	32.4	288,800
Food retailers and wholesalers	32.9	637,200
Food service providers	21.1	809,100

Source: Adapted from Government of Canada (n.d.).

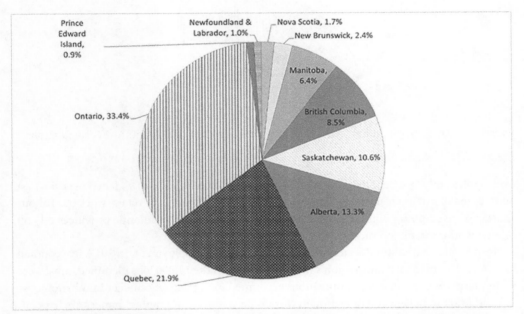

Source: Own elaboration based on Government of Canada (2017) and Agriculture and Agri-Food Canada (AAFC) calculations.

Figure 13.1 Provincial GDP for primary agriculture and food processing sectors, 2016

Figure 13.3 shows the distribution of major agricultural commodities across provinces.

3. ATLANTIC CANADA'S AGRICULTURAL SECTOR: TRENDS AND STATISTICS

Atlantic Canada includes four eastern provinces namely, Nova Scotia, New Brunswick, Prince Edward Island, and Newfoundland and Labrador. On average, Atlantic Canada's agricultural sector accounts for just 1 percent of the region's overall GDP. Its relative importance at the provincial level varies, ranging from 0.4 percent of total GDP in Newfoundland and Labrador to 4.0 percent in Prince Edward Island. On average, those employed in the agricultural sector

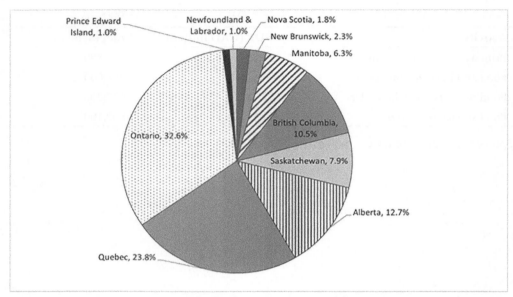

Source: Own elaboration based on Government of Canada (2017) and AAFC calculations.

Figure 13.2   Agriculture and agri-food system's share of provincial employment

earn significantly less than those in other sectors. This income gap has widened over the past decade, making it even more difficult for employers to attract and retain workers. Labour shortages are common in this sector and employers across all four Atlantic provinces rely on foreign workers to fill job vacancies.

Nova Scotia's agricultural sector is not a major source of employment. In 2017, it accounted for 1.3 percent of the Atlantic region's total workforce. Of the 14,800 jobs identified, most were within farms, while aquaculture operations accounted for a relatively smaller number of jobs.

In addition to the general reduction in workforce, major demographic changes are happening within the region's agricultural sector, namely, the aging of the existing workforce and the entry of younger workers.

Marah uses various tools available online to research the agriculture and agri-food sector in Canada, Atlantic Canada and Nova Scotia. These include, for example, the "Census of Agriculture: Mapping Tool"[3] and "Census of Agriculture"[4] both published by Statistics Canada, to collect information on the sharp decline in the number of Atlantic Canada farms. In total, there were 2,741 farms reported in Nova Scotia in 2021, as presented in Table 13.2.

4.   THE SPECIFICITIES OF NOVA SCOTIA'S AGRICULTURAL SECTOR

Using the same tools as above, Marah develops a clearer understanding of the specificities of Nova Scotia's agriculture sector. She finds from the 2021 census that the total number of farms reported in Nova Scotia decreased by 21.2 percent from the previous census. This was the

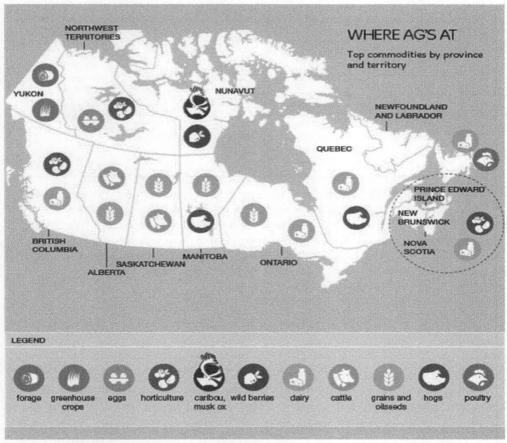

Source: Canada Action (2019). Permission granted.

Figure 13.3   Major agricultural commodity by province

largest decrease among provinces in Canada. By comparison, the number of farms reported across Canada decreased by 1.9 percent over the same period. Farms classified as hog and pig had the biggest percentage decrease. From 2016 to 2021, the number of pig farms dropped by 56.5 percent. These data can be seen in Table 13.3. Table 13.4 displays the composition of cropland for the province.

5.   ANNAPOLIS VALLEY: NOVA SCOTIA'S BREADBASKET

The Annapolis Valley is also known as Nova Scotia's breadbasket. This region is one of the most productive and diverse agricultural growing regions in Canada due to its unique microclimate, fertile soil and skilled farming community. The Annapolis Valley is home to

Table 13.2   Farms classified by operating arrangement in Nova Scotia

Operating arrangement[a]	2001	2006	2011	2016	2021
Total number of farms	3,923	3,795	3,905	3,478	2,741
Sole proprietorship[b]	2,600	2,452	2,492	2,091	1,611
Partnership	837	768	746	661	512
Family corporation	410	487	577	637	546
Non-family corporation	70	80	83	80	62
Other operating arrangements	6	8	7	9	10

Note: [a] In 1991 and 1996, respondents were permitted to report more than one operating arrangement. For presentation purposes in this table, each multiple response was assigned to a single operating arrangement. [b] The order and wording of the questions on operating arrangements were changed in 1996 primarily because in previous censuses individual or family holdings were being overreported. While previous censuses asked if the operation was an individual or family holding, the 1996 Census of Agriculture replaced this question with one asking if the operation was a sole proprietorship.
Source: Adapted from Statistics Canada (2022).

Table 13.3   Farm area by farm type, Nova Scotia, 2016 and 2021

	2016		2021		Change
	Acres	% of total	Acres	% of total	
Dairy and milk production	124,514	13.6	111,068	15.3	−13,446
Beef farming and feedlot	139,980	15.3	125,745	17.3	−14,235
Hog and pig farming	2,553	0.3	1,025	0.1	−1,528
Poultry and egg production	21,638	2.4	17,546	2.4	−4,092
Sheep and goat farming	9,076	1	10,535	1.5	1,459
Other animal production	51,330	5.6	36,290	5	−15,040
Oilseed and grain farming	25,334	2.8	23,164	3.2	−2,170
Vegetable and melon farming	20,890	2.3	67,438	9.3	46,548
Fruit and tree nut farming	232,201	25.4	160,600	22.1	−71,601
Greenhouse, nursery and floriculture production	88,050	9.6	61,301	8.4	−26,749
Other crop farming	200,091	21.9	111,026	15.3	−89,065
Total farm area	915,657		725,738		−189,919

Note: This table displays the results of farm area by farm type 2016, 2021 and change, calculated using acre units of measure (appearing as column headers).
Source: Adapted from Statistics Canada (2016a, 2021).

Table 13.4   Composition of cropland in Nova Scotia

Composition of cropland	Percentage of cropland		
	2021	2011	2006
Field crops	26.8	18.8	15.7
Hay		58.9	64.7
Fruits	18	18.7	16.3
Vegetables	2.1	2.4	2.3
Sod and nursery	1.2	1.2	1.1

Source: Adapted from Statistics Canada (2006, 2011).

Table 13.5   Farmland use in Annapolis Valley and Nova Scotia, 2001

Land Use	Annapolis Valley (acres)	%	Nova Scotia (acres)	%
Land in crops (excluding Christmas tree area)	76,811	37	294,596	29.3
Tame or seeded pasture	13,128	6	56,520	5.6
Natural land for pasture	17,335	8	81,215	8.1
All other land (including summer fallow and Christmas tree land)	101,559	49	573,502	57

Source: Adapted from Annapolis Valley Farmland Trust Society (n.d.).

the province's majority of Class 2[5] farmland. In 2001, land in crops accounted for 37 percent of total land use in Annapolis Valley. In the province, 26 percent of the crop land in use is in the Annapolis Valley. Table 13.5 shows the land use in Nova Scotia and the Annapolis Valley.

Agriculture in the Annapolis Valley is diverse, including dairy, poultry, beef and horticultural farms, such as apple orchards. In 2000, agriculture in the Annapolis Valley generated over $180.1 million in farm receipts, about 38.4 percent of all farm receipts for Nova Scotia. In the same year, farm operating expenses amounted to approximately $151.6 million.

Marah also realizes that farm businesses have a strong local orientation. They engage in direct marketing[6] and buy and sell in their local community. The Valley generates significant economic activity, such as through the creation of direct and indirect jobs associated with agriculture. Through linkages with other industrial sectors, an estimated 3,550 related jobs are created, or approximately 13 percent of all jobs in the local economy. Nevertheless, from 2006 to 2011, the total number of farms in Annapolis County only increased by six.

6.   DUTCH AGRICULTURAL SETTLERS TO NOVA SCOTIA BROUGHT NEW KNOWLEDGE ...

The Netherlands has a long history of commercial farming. Since the nineteenth century, the Dutch have developed capabilities in and modernized their agricultural sector. Agricultural advisors were on hand to advise farmers, and experimental farms were created. When the Dutch settlers arrived in eastern Nova Scotia, they found that most of the local farmers were engaged in subsistence farming, i.e., they farmed in order to sustain their day-to-day food consumption. Consequently, the Dutch settlers were well poised to introduce new farming techniques and methods for increasing capacity.

Dairy was the most common farming activity among the Dutch immigrants. Antigonish had the largest Dutch-owned dairy operations – 40 percent of all dairy farms in the county. The Dutch also engaged in the production of chicken, turkey, eggs, orchids, vegetables, apples and strawberries (Gerrits, 1996: 130). Initially, the success and prosperity that the Dutch immigrant farmers experienced caused fear of colonization among some of the subsistence Canadian farmers. Eventually, their new farming techniques and methods were adopted by Canadian farmers, especially in the dairy industry where the Dutch were the most active. Other Dutch practices related to the stabling and housing of dairy herds, soil management and crop management were also adopted by Nova Scotian farmers (Gerrits, 1996: 154).

7.   ... BUT THERE WERE SOME BUMPS IN THE ROAD

The road to settling into Canada was not always smooth for the Dutch settlers. While they brought new knowledge and they were very capable farmers, they nevertheless faced serious challenges when they first arrived in Canada. One of the challenges involved finding adequate and affordable housing. Not all local farmers who were interested in hiring immigrants were able to provide housing for the Dutch immigrant families (Gerrits, 1996: 29). Another challenge was the acquisition of loans. Dutch immigrants were only eligible for farm loans after spending at least two years within the sector. A third challenge was that some of the immigrants found local Canadian farming practices too unfamiliar. The farms in Canada were bigger than in the Netherlands. Commercial farming in Canada was extensive and highly mechanized. Dutch immigrants had to learn to operate different types of tractors and farming machinery. Some found that Canadians tended to do most farming activities and tasks themselves, while in the Netherlands, farmers hired workers and laborers to perform different farming tasks and activities.

In addition, many were unprepared for the culture shock that they would experience upon arrival. This was a result of the fact that many spoke little or no English. Distance was also another factor which contributed to the culture shock since they had to travel for long periods on unpaved roads to reach their final rural destinations. Another surprise for the Dutch settlers were the hills and rocks, and the long winters and short growing seasons. They also sensed a general negative attitude towards agriculture from the locals.

8.   THE ROLE OF LOCAL AND FOREIGN ACTORS IN DUTCH IMMIGRATION TO CANADA

During the 1940s, the Canadian government was concerned about the decline in farming and looked for ways to reverse this trend.[7] One way involved changing the immigration regulation, with preference for farm workers and other needed occupations. So, why the Dutch? The answer is that during the 1945 Permanent Migration Committee of the International Labour Office's meeting in Montreal, the Dutch government was the first to approach the Canadian government in providing surplus farmers and farm laborers to solve the problem of labor shortage. Thereafter, the Canadian and Dutch governments encouraged and coordinated the migration of Dutch farmers and laborers to Canada. They initiated an informal agreement known as the Netherlands Farms Families Movement or the Netherland Settlement Scheme. The number of immigrants was decided at the beginning of each year by the two governments. The agreement stated that the Dutch immigrants would accept employment on Canadian farms for one or two years or until they could buy their own farm. This eased the labor shortage and enabled farmers to be familiar with Canadian farming methods and acquire capital.

The Netherlands Emigration Foundation was granted the mandate of administering the Canadian government immigration policies and had the task of organizing the migration of Dutch agriculture human resources. It also provided other services such as passage for immigrants, and the Dutch government provided financial assistance for their travels. In 1953, the Foundation was recognized as the Netherlands Emigration Service, and the Emigration Council was created as an advisory body where different immigrant groups (secular, Catholic, Protestant societies) were represented. These societies would collect and distribute information about Canada. They maintained close contact and coordinated their activities with the corresponding immigrant societies in Canada.

Another way of encouraging Dutch immigration was to help them with farm ownership. One of the problems that Dutch immigrants faced was the currency restriction after the Second World War, which prevented them from taking large sums of money out of the Netherlands up to the 1950s. They therefore lacked the funds to purchase farms. So, the provincial government of Nova Scotia introduced a bill allowing the Nova Scotia Land Settlement Board to offer loans to farmers who were not Canadians for the purchase of farms. The Canadian federal and provincial governments were also responsible for finding employment and housing for the immigrants.

Religion and church affiliation played a role in Dutch immigration and settlement to Nova Scotia (Gerrits, 1996). The Dutch immigrants established churches which provided them with spiritual guidance and material support. These churches, in turn, established immigration societies to meet the needs of the Dutch settlers.

In the Antigonish Valley, for example, churches and related organizations were very important in attracting, sponsoring and settling immigrants. The Diocese of Antigonish, established in 1940, launched a land settlement program, which played a major role in attracting the Dutch immigrants to eastern Nova Scotia by providing them with financial aid. The program was discontinued in 1955.

To encourage Dutch immigrants as well as second-generation farmers to engage in the agricultural sector, the Diocese of Antigonish also established a fund from which qualified applicants could borrow, to add to their savings or to become eligible for loans from the Nova Scotia Land Settlement Board. The fund was later administered by the Extension Department of Saint Francis Xavier University.

The United Church and the Christian Reformed Church were also involved in the settlement of immigrants. The Catholic Church attracted Catholic immigrants from the Netherlands (Gerrits, 1996: 20–22). In fact, in 1953, the New Reformed Church played a strong role in attracting Dutch immigrants. It aimed to concentrate the immigrants in a number of rural neighborhoods so as to grow its rural congregations. The New Reformed Church did not provide financial loans, but it did provide limited financial support.

Moreover, many of the families who had settled in Nova Scotia came from other parts of Canada. One of the reasons that Dutch settlers moved to Nova Scotia from other parts of Canada was the relative ease of obtaining loans for purchasing farms. It was easier to evaluate the farmers who arrived from other Canadian provinces (Gerrits, 1996: 45). These settlers qualified for farm loans from the Nova Scotia Settlement Board since they had already accumulated two years of farm experience elsewhere in Canada.

Between the late 1940s to mid-1960s, a total of 230 Dutch immigrant farmers had purchased lands with loans from the Nova Scotia Settlement Board. This excludes farmers who purchased farms with the help of aid from non-governmental sources. The number of farms owned by Dutch Canadians in 1990 was 288, and this number represented about 7.25 percent of the provincial-owned farms (Gerrits, 1996: 119–120). These farms were distributed over about 18 counties in the province. Numbers varied from 113 in Kings Country to 1 in Queens County. Kings County accounted for about 36 percent of the farmers, and Antigonish county for about 14 percent (Gerrits, 1996: 120).

There were some other important factors which attracted the Dutch immigrants to Canada in the 1940s. This included the fact that there was already a significant Dutch population in Canada. Between 1846 and 1900, around 250,000 Dutch nationalists immigrated to Canada, due to perceived unfavorable religious and economic conditions in their native country. It is believed that these pre-war Dutch immigrants had established communities which later attracted their fellow agricultural immigrants to Canada. It is interesting to note that social factors and family ties were more effective in attracting immigrants than the information provided by local actors such as the provincial governments and informal immigration organizations (Gerrits, 1996). The liberation of Netherlands and of Princess Juliana – the heir to the Dutch throne – by Canada were additional pull factors which contributed to the immigration of Dutch farmers to Canada (Gerrits, 1996). Moreover, after the Second World War, the Dutch faced economic hardships in their native country and farmers were faced with unfit agricultural land, which acted as important push factors.

The Canadian political, economic and religious environment seemed suitable for Dutch immigrants. It allowed them to preserve their conservative ways which they perceived as being increasingly difficult to do in their native country, especially during the post-war period.

9.   THE CHANGING LANDSCAPE OF AGRICULTURAL IMMIGRANTS TO CANADA

Since the days of the arrival of the Dutch agricultural immigrants in Canada, other newcomer immigrants from different origins have settled across Canada and contributed to agriculture, bringing revitalization to different rural areas. Marah realizes that they also contributed significantly to the agricultural and agri-food sector.

Figure 13.4 indicates the agriculture-related immigration in Canada and differentiates between landed immigrants and temporary foreign workers. It shows a widening gap in the skilled immigrants who work in the Canadian agricultural sector. There are several programs which focused on agricultural temporary foreign workers. For example, the Seasonal Agricultural Worker Program, which was initiated in 1966 as a labor migration agreement between the Canadian and Jamaican governments, allowed Jamaican laborers to temporarily travel to and enter Canada to work in agricultural production (Budworth et al., 2017). This initiative was expanded to include 10 other Caribbean states and Mexico. Mexico joined in 1974 (ESDC, 2019; Preibisch & Binford, 2007).

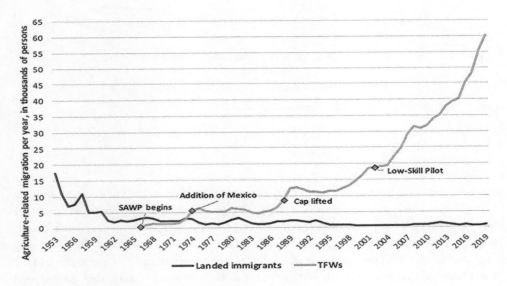

Source: Adapted from Falconer (2020).

Figure 13.4   Agriculture-related migration, 1953–2019

Some immigrants became farm operators, managing the day-to-day operations of their own farms. In 1996, immigrants made up 10.2 percent of Canadian farm operators, accounting for 39,620 people (Tam & Shumsky, 2019). By 2016, immigrants made up 8.7 percent of Canadian farm operators, accounting for 23,440 people (Statistics Canada, 2016a, 2016b).

The country of origin of these immigrant farm operators has evolved over time, shifting away from mostly European ones (Figure 13.5). In 2016, the United States and China emerged as the two most frequently reported countries of origin for immigrant farm operators. Immigrants who came to Canada between 2011 and 2016 represented 1.7 percent of immigrant farm operators in 2016. There are many differences between other immigrant, non-immigrant and Chinese and American immigrant farm operators who came to Canada between 2011 and 2016. These span from where they live to the type and size of farm they operate (Tam & Shumsky, 2019). Newcomer immigrants to Nova Scotia tend to be highly educated relative to the domestic population (Akbari & Haider, 2018), and according to the Nova Scotia Finance and Treasury Board (2019), they are more likely to create jobs through entrepreneurial activities.

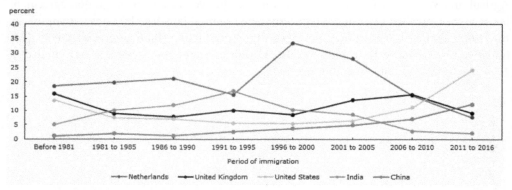

Source: Adapted from Tam and Shumsky (2019).

Figure 13.5   Select countries of birth for immigrant farm operators by period of immigration

Aside from immigrants, there is also an increasing number of diversified newcomers arriving in Nova Scotia. These include Canadians from other provinces and refugees who come from farming and agricultural production communities, and who bring with them existing knowledge, skills and experiences in agri-food-related activities. These newcomers have a strong background in agri-food production methodologies and processes and a desire to work in the sector. However, they are primarily settling in urban communities because they do not have access to adequate resources and support which would allow them to start their own farms or agri-food-related activities and businesses.

10.   CONCLUSION

Marah surveyed and processed all the information she had collected and combined it with her knowledge of the Dutch immigrants' experience. She now has a sound and solid understanding of the Nova Scotia agri-food innovation system. She has one week to write the final report of actionable initiatives and solutions for the panel of senior policymakers, advisors and the Minister of Agriculture. The pressure is high, but she is confident that all the tools and knowledge acquired during her master's degree program will help her in completing her first solo assignment with success.

ACKNOWLEDGMENTS

We would like to thank the Change Lab Action Research Initiative in Nova Scotia for providing financial support to collect the needed information for writing this case. We also thank the Sobey School of Business at Saint Mary's University in Halifax, Nova Scotia for their support. We thank all the organizations in Nova Scotia who volunteered their time and knowledge during the interviews.

NOTES

1. Fictitious protagonist.
2. Newcomers refer to both incoming immigrants and Canadians arriving from other provinces.
3. Available at www150.statcan.gc.ca/n1/pub/32-26-0003/322600032016001-eng.htm
4. Available at www150.statcan.gc.ca/n1/daily-quotidien/220615/dq220615a-eng.pdf
5. Class 2 soil has the least restrictions for agricultural production of all the land classes in Nova Scotia.
6. Direct marketing is the practice through which farms sell agricultural products directly to consumers for human consumption. Farms can sell unprocessed products, such as fruits, vegetables, meat cuts, poultry, eggs, maple syrup and honey, or value-added products, such as jellies, sausages, wine and cheese. Direct marketing represents an important means for connecting farms and communities and creates many opportunities for farmers to engage in novel ways for bringing their products to and create linkages with their communities.
7. Serious labor shortages were being felt in all the main industries, namely farming, mining and logging.

REFERENCES

Akbari, A. H., & Haider, A. (2018). Impact of Immigration on Economic Growth in Canada and in Its Smaller Provinces. *Journal of International Migration and Integration*, 19(1), 129–142.

Annapolis Valley Farmland Trust Society (n.d.). Our Mission. Available at www.avflt.ca/

Budworth, M.-H., Rose, A., & Mann, S. (2017). Report on the Seasonal Agricultural Worker Program. Inter-American Institute for Cooperation on Agriculture Delegation in Canada, 67.

Canada Action (2019). Agriculture Sector in Canada: By the Numbers. Available at www.canadaaction .ca/agriculture_sector_canada_by_the_numbers

ESDC (2019). Employment and Social Development Canada 2019–20 Departmental Plan. Available at https://publications.gc.ca/collections/collection_2019/edsc-esdc/Em1-10-2019-eng.pdf

Falconer, R. (2020). Family Farmers to Foreign Fieldhands: Consolidation of Canadian Agriculture and the Temporary Foreign Worker Program. SPP Briefing Papers, School of Public Policy, University of Calgary, 13(21). Available at www.policyschool.ca/wp-content/uploads/2020/08/Family-Farmers -Falconer.pdf

Gerrits, G. H. (1996). *They Farmed Well: The Dutch–Canadian Agricultural Community in Nova Scotia, 1945–1995*. Vinland Press.

Government of Canada (2017). Overview of Canada's Agriculture and Agri-Food Sector. Available from https://publications.gc.ca/collections/collection_2018/aac-aafc/A38-1-1-2017-eng.pdf

Government of Canada (n.d.). Overview of Canada's Agriculture and Agri-Food Sector. Available from https://agriculture.canada.ca/en/canadas-agriculture-sectors/overview-canadas-agriculture-and-agri-food-sector

Nova Scotia Finance and Treasury Board (2019). About Us. Available at https://beta.novascotia.ca/government/finance-and-treasury-board

Preibisch, K., & Binford, L. (2007). Interrogating Racialized Global Labour Supply: An Exploration of the Racial/National Replacement of Foreign Agricultural Workers in Canada. *Canadian Review of Sociology and Anthropology*, 44(1), 5–36.

Statistics Canada (2006). 2006 Census of Agriculture and 2011 Census of Agriculture. Available at www150.statcan.gc.ca/n1/ca-ra2006/index-eng.htm

Statistics Canada (2011). 2011 Census of Agriculture. Available at www150.statcan.gc.ca/n1/daily-quotidien/120510/dq120510a-eng.htm

Statistics Canada (2016a). 2016 Census of Agriculture. Available at www23.statcan.gc.ca/imdb-bmdi/instrument/3438_Q1_V4-eng.htm

Statistics Canada (2016b). 2016 Census of Population. Available at www12.statcan.gc.ca/census-recensement/2016/dp-pd/prof/index.cfm?Lang=E

Statistics Canada (2021). Canada's 2021 Census of Agriculture: A Closer Look at Farming across the Regions. www.statcan.gc.ca/en/census-agriculture

Statistics Canada (2022). Table 32-10-0158-01: Farms Classified by Operating Arrangement. Census of Agriculture Historical Data. Available at https://doi.org/10.25318/3210015801-eng

Tam, S., & Shumsky, M. (2019). Canadian Agriculture at a Glance: The Changing Face of the Immigrant Farm Operator. Statistics Canada, 96.

14

A pioneer without followers: a case of productive diversification from rice to aquaculture in Chaco, Argentina

Verónica Robert and Nicolás Moncaut

1.   INTRODUCTION

In early 2021, George assumed the position of Head of the Office of Productive Development in the province of Chaco, Argentina.[1] The main objective of the office is to achieve productive diversification of the province and increase private employment. George has two years to achieve progress in the productive area before the next elections in 2023, so action needs to be taken as soon as possible. He is a person with great experience as a consultant and knows the productive reality of the province and its entrepreneurs. He also has a highly qualified team for the implementation and monitoring of public policies and effective communication strategies.

Chaco is a province in the northeast of Argentina that represents 2.6 percent of the Argentine territory. According to provincial statistics, in 2018 Chacho population was 1.2 million people, around 2.5 percent of the Argentinean population, however, its contribution to the national gross domestic product was approximately 1.5 percent (ECLAC, 2022). This province specialises in low value-added primary products, which is not enough to generate sufficient employment for its population. In 2018, the province's unemployment rate reached approximately 8.5 percent. The employment in public offices predominates over private business employment. The number of employees in public offices over private-sector employment reached 103 percent, while this indicator for the country as a whole was 35 percent. In this regard, there were higher unemployment rates covered by employment in the public sector, introducing pressure on the province's fiscal accounts. In 2019, workers in the private sector in Chaco accounted for around 67,000 people and a similar number of employees were registered in public offices (Ministerio del Interior, Obras Públicas y Vivienda, 2019). In this regard, there are also a high number of people living in rural areas with self-employment/maintenance activities, with low income, and lacking access to health services and infrastructure. Some of these activities are wood handicraft, artisan fishery, and low-scale farms with pigs and poultry for self-consumption or selling at a very low scale. There are also bigger agricultural producers focused on large-scale rice and soybean production that employ few people and do not allow structural transformation.

George was able to observe over 10 years the process of growth and consolidation of a successful experience of productive diversification: Edward, a rice producer with 30 years of experience, carried out a massive productive diversification process, triggered by an environmental community claim on the use of herbicides and pesticides in his rice plantation (Figure 14.1).

Source: Taken from www.peakpx.com/599886/raw-rice-grains under the Creative Commons License.

Figure 14.1   Paddy rice

In order to show to the community that his activity was sustainable, he implemented a rotation scheme between rice and fish culture. As a result, he entered into a wide new set of activities including fish culture of pacú (an indigenous species of the northeast of the country), fish slaughtering and processing, the elaboration of fish-based agrifood products, logistics, and the commercialisation of those products through his own new fishery franchising that had extended all over the northeast of the country. Edward also entered into a series of downstream-linked activities, such as production of feed for fish (and then for pets), pre-germinated rice production, and culture of fingerling pacú (baby fish breeding; Figure 14.2). He also got involved in related infrastructure projects such as a river dock, electricity infrastructure, and rice silos developed with public funds with the goal of consolidating this new activity and expanding production and employment in the province (Figure 14.3).

Source: Taken from www.peakpx.com/459427/gray-pacu under the Creative Commons License.

Figure 14.2   Pacú

The arrival of a wide range of new activities and infrastructure should mean new opportunities for the local environment, since innovative firms face learning costs and pave the way for followers by reducing uncertainty and creating new markets. However, after 10 years from the first appearance of the pioneer, no followers have yet emerged. The policy maker, George, knows that the Office of Productive Development has supported with several instruments the emergence of this innovative company and promoted its growth from less than 50 to 250 employees. However, innovation remained encapsulated in this sole experience. Now, he thinks that while the diversification process started with an environmental claim and was supported by public policy, this did not guarantee a Schumpeterian process of imitation and diffusion that brings about structural change processes at the local level.

Today, George wonders why these followers have not emerged, as predicted by theory. In particular, he wonders what set of public policies should be implemented to take advantage of this successful experience of productive diversification. The literature shows that innovation problems are problems of private appropriation of new knowledge, and that policy instruments should be oriented to strengthen innovative entrepreneurs and help them develop their new businesses. Once innovation is achieved, the literature assumes that the uncertainties for potential followers are reduced (Hausmann & Rodrik, 2003), and imbalances are therefore produced that encourage the development of other links in the production chain associated with the new activity (Hirschman, 1958). However, after 10 years of starting this process of productive diversification, there are still no signs of these followers. So, the main question is: to what extent does the diversification process faced by a pioneer firm mean opportunities for followers, and what strategy should the policy maker take to promote territorial development based on the success of the pioneer? More specifically, is it enough to promote the development of a pioneer to induce the automatic emergence of followers, or is it necessary to implement policies that reduce the barriers to entry derived from the presence of a pioneer that dominates the new markets created? If not, what could be blocking the emergence of them? What should the policy maker do to achieve its objective of productive diversification of the territory based on the emergence of followers?

2.   DESCRIPTION OF THE COMPANY

Edward, the entrepreneur, comes from a rice producer family. At the end of the 1970s he settled at La Leonesa, a small town located in the east of Chaco. He was dedicated to the production of paddy rice: rice covered by its brown or black husk, a low-value intermediate product not suitable for human consumption. He has produced the same product for over 30 years, so he was not the prototype of a Schumpeterian entrepreneur. This is a generalised characteristic of local enterprises. This represents a great challenge for the Office of Productive Development. George, the policy maker, needs to promote new activities in the region that yield to the diversification of the productive structure and generate new sources of employment.

In 2008, Edward was involved in a controversy about agrochemicals used in rice production. Several local community actors and environmental associations presented a complaint against Edward for contamination of the soil and water derived from herbicide and pesticide use in rice production (endosulfan and glyphosate). He faced several lawsuits that enforced restrictions on agrochemical applications and compelled them to prove their activities did not harm the environment. He commissioned several technical reports on the environmental conditions and the possible implication of agrochemicals used in rice production in those conditions. Although the results supported Edward's position on non-contamination, the community's claims did not go away.

Edward needed to demonstrate to the community that responsible herbicide use in rice production does not necessarily entail environmental risks. Consequently, in December 2010, the firm decided to create an 18 hectare pond to culture pacú, near to the urban area, under the assumption that the presence of living fishes would act as proof of the low level of contamination.

In the beginning, the fish pond was built without any aim for profit, but then a business opportunity was identified by combining rice production (sowing pre-germinated rice) with fish farming, under a fish–rice rotation system.[2] The rotation project scaled up from 18 to 900 hectares. Pacú farming, although marginal compared with rice production, turned out to be interesting because of its potential applicability to rural areas where land is not suitable for other crops.

It attracted the attention and support of local government, development offices and local universities. George saw in Edward's story an opportunity to diversify the province's production and incorporate new activities to its productive profile. The immediate actions were to collaborate with Edward so that the province could overcome the problems it was facing (capacity building and infrastructure), with the objective that the demonstration effect achieved by his story would spread to other rice producers in the area and motivate them. The set of productive activities carried out by Edward results in an annual turnover of approximately USD4 million (according to the 2018 balance sheet).

Today the situation is very different from that faced by Edward. Rice production has been revalued as a sustainable activity, there is a new market for the consumption of frozen pacú-based products, and there is even infrastructure for fish processing (with a new slaughterhouse and fish-processing plant) and open distribution channels, not only for the final consumer, but also for hotels and restaurants in the area that increasingly identify pacú as a typical coastal dish, surpassing other river fish such as surubí. Also, new abilities have been developed among the population (Edward has employed around 250 people) related to fish culture, net fishing, water management, and other capabilities needed to implement the new rotation technique.

George wonders why all these advances have not been enough for the potential development of new entrants to the sector that would allow moving from this experience of productive diversification at the company level to an experience of regional diversification that enhances the productive development of the province. He wants Edward's story to spread throughout the province and promote other rice producers to enter into a diversification process which could help them to grow while at the same time expanding employment and structural change in the province. However, he knows this cannot happen automatically. He wonders what should be the policy mix that has to be implemented for this to happen.

2.1 Description of the industry and other elements of relevant context

Pacú culture and processing was a new industry in Chaco, therefore, there were no nearby specialised suppliers of inputs, machinery, or infrastructure (i.e. electric power). Until the emergence of the pioneer, the local demand for river fish was met by artisanal fishermen. Beyond inputs and machinery, this activity also required the development of specific capabilities related to: (1) the primary activity by itself (pacú–rice rotation, field and pond preparation, water management, etc.); (2) fish processing (elaboration of fish-based agrifood frozen products); (3) commercialisation and marketing, in order to open up new markets; and (4) logistics.

The rice–pacú rotation allowed the implementation of new techniques with less use of agrochemicals, which was the origin of the conflict. The rice–pacú rotation made the production of rice much more sustainable in terms of the contribution of fertilisers, herbicides, and tillage.

Compared to rice or pacú monoculture, the rotation allows greater economic, environmental, and energy efficiency, in particular in the use of water. A synergy between both activities is achieved: on the one hand, the rotation allows the rice cultivation with minimum tillage and greater sustainability. On the other hand, the use of the drainage infrastructure for sanitary emptying in the production of pacú prevents pathologies in the ponds; without this, the system would be idle until the next campaign. To make it profitable, large-scale production is needed. Previous experience had not succeeded because small-scale production does not justify the necessary water management infrastructure expenses. In the same vein, other activities emerge which are linked to this process as products that, when integrated, help in gaining efficiency. For instance, the lack of local suppliers leads to new entrants to vertically integrate several inputs and activities, like fish feed, which is elaborated with grain, fish flour, and oil that comes from the fish slaughterhouse and processing plant. Therefore, there are possibilities for integration and large-scale operation.

On the demand side of the business, the local market was underdeveloped. Although there was a culture of consuming river fish, this was linked to artisanal fishing activities and not to the consumption of a vacuum-sealed industrial product. Here again there is a challenge for a new entrant for developing markets, new commercialisation channels, and even new consumption practices. For example, introducing daily consumption from semi-finished frozen products (like fish burgers and pre-fried battered fish), vis-à-vis the traditional consumption of grilled fish by the river, typical of the culture of the coastal provinces. For the development of this market, a new entrant must also make investments in activities such as brand design, advertising campaigns, and others that bring the consumer closer to a new product. In this particular case, these marketing activities were also necessary to establish an image of a healthy product that was not associated with the agrochemicals to which rice production was linked.

2.2   Specific issue

When Edward started this diversification process, he was not sure why he was doing it. He knew that if he did not do something, his activity as a rice producer would be severely threatened. Community actions against his rice plantation were growing and the company did not have the capacity to respond because the scientific studies on the environmental impact they had personally commissioned would (rightly or wrongly) be criticised because of its origin bias. The company needed to make a radical change. It needed to demonstrate that its rice production was non-polluting and sustainable, but above all it needed social acceptance of its activity. So, pacú production began as an experiment, to demonstrate that live fish along with rice farming was a demonstration of non-pollution.

However, the development of this fish pond introduced Edward to a new body of knowledge that led him to seriously analyse the possibility of establishing it as a new productive activity. Obviously, this was going to require new investments and research and development efforts for the development of an entire new set of activities. Edward confronted the risk expenditures for two main reasons:

1. He faced the risk of disappearing as a rice producer.

2. The public sector channelled resources to set up infrastructure and to finance the main investments related to this new activity. In particular, they provided electricity infrastructure and subsidised credits to set up the fish-processing plant.

The specific knowledge about fish farming and related activities (from fish processing to commercialisation channels) was acquired by contracting a specialised consultant: an agronomist who had been working on small-scale fish farming in Clorinda (in the province of Formosa, near to Chaco). The agronomist had devoted a large part of his life to studying and implementing different models of inland aquaculture. The acquired knowledge was not constrained to the fish growth cycle and fingerling reproduction, but also to the optimum size for gastronomic purposes, including the removal of fish bones and the development of fish products (fish fillets without bones, whole fish for grilling, battered pre-fried fish, fish hamburgers, etc.).

Experience of more than 25 years in fish farming as well as the establishment of exploitation schemes for his own venture had endowed Edward with a deep knowledge of the activity, although without concrete experience in large-scale farms. That specific knowledge was provided by the rice producer, with experience in water management and different techniques in rice production – specially, pre-germinated rice that was key for the pacú–rice rotation scheme.

The implementation of the rice–pacú rotation scheme allowed them to use new techniques with less use of agrochemicals, confronting in this way the origin of the conflict that pushed Edward into aquaculture. The planting of pacú in the rice fallow, given its omnivorous characteristic, allows the fish to feed on the remains of rice and the snails that attack the rice crop in its first stage. Then, when draining the ponds after the pacú cycle, it is possible to sow pre-germinated rice on the saturated mud, free of snails and weeds, and flood them.

The scheme of semi-extensive pacú production introduced by Edward allows production with a low density of fish per cubic metre of water, which minimises the risk of disease without having to apply animal health products. However, this requires supplementary feeding, particularly in the fattening stage. Edward developed fattening circuits that allow capturing animals of optimal size for processing and marketing throughout the year. In fact, one of the usual problems of small-scale fish farming is the impossibility of providing a constant flow of product throughout the fattening cycle, and the need to empty the pond to avoid the appearance of disease.

The introduction of a new activity like pacú culture required the development of various types of specialised suppliers. However, in this case, Edward chose to (and had the capacity to) vertically integrate the main peripheral activities. Thus, he was able to implement a strongly interrelated process of harvesting, processing, and marketing pacú on a large scale.

In the case of balanced feed, given that this input represented 70 percent of the cost of production of pacú, it generated a strong dependence on non-specialised external agents. The volatility of the price and quality of balanced food represented a risk to the profitability of the new product. Therefore, Edward integrated vertical fish feed production, elaborated with grain, animal oil and protein, and alimentary supplements.[3]

At the same time, it was necessary to develop the pacú-processing stage. The company had to develop its own cold storage and processing plant to meet regulatory requirements. Edward obtained subsidised credits from public banks for funding this. The parts of the pacú that were not suitable for human consumption (head, spine, tail, skin) began to be used to produce fish flour and oils, which were, in turn, inputs in a new fish-feed production plant.

The fish-processing plant complies with the regulatory requirements[4] in which the entire production is processed and operates with a surplus of installed capacity. In the plant, trained personnel perform several specific tasks, from the cleaning of the animals, disinfection, processing of elaborated products, and packaging and freezing. The plant was expected to provide processing services to smaller fish farmers or artisanal fishermen. Industrialisation (fish-processing plant and cold storage plant) and marketing requires having an adequate volume of production that is difficult for a small producer to achieve on its own. Therefore, several public efforts to invigorate Edward's ventures were oriented to create a new infrastructure that may help smaller producers to emerge.

In terms of marketing, the company had to make a major effort to develop and position its own brand for pacú products. In addition, it established specific marketing channels that were not previously open. The consumption of pacú and other river fish in the town and surrounding areas was based on artisanal fishing and recreational activities, which were certainly valued, but only in a small way. In this context, the firm implemented a search to expand the local and regional pacú market, trying to reach families and encourage daily consumption. To this end, the company established a network of franchises with which it reaches different neighbourhoods and localities within the province and also neighbouring provinces, in an attempt to market the brand as a quality, innovative product.

This process of vertical integration fostered a greater horizontal productive diversification. In order to improve efficiency in the use of the installed capacity of the pacú food plant, and to use the fish oil that was previously discarded, the idea of producing balanced feed for pets (cats and dogs) arose. Thus, fish flour was used as a protein supplement for its own breeding of fingerlings, which require more animal protein than larger fishes.

The production of balanced feed today requires the purchase of soybean expeller. However, within the firm's plans, processing soybeans to obtain 'expeller' and transforming the oil derived from pressing into biodiesel. By 2021, this objective was on track to materialise from the purchase of equipment for the soybean extruder. The biodiesel plant is already in operation and the company has purchased shell burners for drying rice to replace LPG, a more expensive fuel.

For commercialisation, the company had to make an important effort in developing and positioning its own brand for the products derived from pacú. In addition, it established specific marketing channels not previously opened. The consumption of pacú and other river fish in the locality and in the surrounding areas was based on artisanal fishing and recreational activities. In this context, the firm implemented a search to expand the local and regional pacú market in order to encourage daily consumption. To do this, the company established a network of franchises with which it reaches different neighbourhoods and towns in the province and surrounding provinces, trying to ensure that its brand is identified with a quality product ready to prepare and bring to the table. This required significant learning efforts that had already been undertaken by the Formosenian consultant. A large part of the products offered by the firm had already been proven in the Formosenian market, although on a smaller scale. The key knowledge of the market highlighted the importance of: (1) offering a product without thorns, as pacú is known for being a fish with many thorns; (2) offering a frozen product in small portions; (3) identifying the optimum size for its presentation on the dish; and (4) optimising the size of the cut and reaching the market with a lean product. This learning allowed them to discard other options, for example, pacú hamburgers that they considered introducing in fast food chains.

Eventually, all this new activity demanded more infrastructure, which was developed with provincial capital and the private participation of the entrepreneur. In particular, Edward installed his own silos and, together with these, the province invested in the construction of river dock infrastructure, necessary for the commercialisation of rice (for the domestic market and for export) and potentially pacú (today only for the domestic market), which also required the opening of new roads. Finally, fish-processing activities and cold storage facilities required new power lines. Although most of this new infrastructure was of a public nature, the entrepreneur was involved in the various projects, and sometimes as a partner of the state.

In short, Edward was able to carry out a very successful process of productive diversification, which went far beyond the introduction of a new activity but rather created a dense web of interrelated activities and infrastructure generation in a process of vertical integration and public–private partnership. The company's image changed radically, from a production company questioned for its environmental impacts to a productive and cultural success. The company generated new investment, promoted public investment in new infrastructure, created new competencies for the territory, and expanded its capacity to generate employment by five times (from 50 to 250).

However, after 10 years of these developments, no followers have emerged. It would be expected that new companies would enter into any links of the new productive chain: from pacú culture, to fish processing, or the deployment of new commercialisation chains. On the contrary, Edward vertically integrated each of the productive links.

In part, this could be explained by the lack of capacity of local stakeholders. The poverty rate in Chaco reached 35 percent (for Argentina as a whole it is 30 percent) (Ministerio del Interior, Obras Públicas y Vivienda, 2019). Gross per capita income is around $5,000 (Argentina's is $10,000). Currently there are around 9,000 private companies located in the province (the national total amounts to 587,000). Of these, 90 percent are concentrated in commerce, services, and agricultural activities. Of the companies in the province, 85 percent have fewer than 25 employees (65 percent have fewer than five employees).[5]

Initially, when no one was doing the activity, market uncertainty, a lack of specialised suppliers, and insufficient infrastructure made the development of fish farming and pacú industrialisation unfeasible. However, once the new market had been developed, it is possible that its monopoly power as a supplier of balanced fish feed or its demand of fresh fish to be processed in the fish-processing plant may have created new barriers to entry. It is conceivable that the followers would have to replicate the vertically integrated structure in order to enter the newly created market, which requires the productive scale and organisational capabilities that local entrepreneurs do not have.

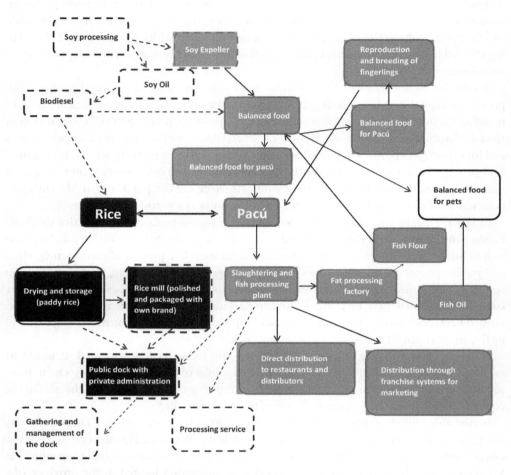

Dotted line : Activities and planned products (in different stages of execution)
Solid line : activities and products carried out by the firm
Gray background with white letter : diversification related to pacú
Black background with white letter : diversification related to rice
White background with black letter : unrelated diversification

Figure 14.3   Diversification map and relations between activities integrated by Edward

3.   CONCLUSION

This success story makes the policy maker very proud. He witnessed the ups and downs of all of Edward's story and was aware of the real risk that he ran in 2008 when he was sued for environmental damage. George feels that part of Edward's success is the success of previous management and is a triumph for the region. Now the company is targeting export markets which implies a new phase in its development. This will mean more scale, more employment, and foreign exchange earnings, improving the province's balance of trade and possibly better wages for the population. Undoubtedly, the Office of Productive Development has a role to play in this new phase for the organisation, but at the same time it cannot help but wonder why the Schumpeterian story of the imitating innovator is not being reproduced in this experience; why new players have not entered and why this success is encapsulated in a single company.

Undoubtedly, economies of scale constitute barriers to entry. George does not know what to do to improve the chances of new market entrants. Sometimes he thinks that this entrepreneur could be capturing public funds for the benefit of his own venture. The company vertically integrated all the complementary activities that triggered its entry as a pioneer in the pacú market. This gives the company a certain bargaining power vis-à-vis the local government, consumers, and potential entrants in any of the links of the production chain. However, in a lagging region like the province of Chaco, all opportunities for productive development could be concentrated in a few entrepreneurs. If public funds effectively encourage local productive development this should be considered a significant achievement. He knows that in the future he will continue to work together with Edward, which will bring new attractive projects to the region, but he wonders what other public policy actions he should take for followers to emerge. After all, can a pioneer be a pioneer without followers?

As George thinks this he receives two pieces of news in his office. The first, from the national government, is a new line for the funding of innovative activities in the province. He immediately thinks that this is an opportunity to channel those resources to the emergence of followers, which will allow consolidating this process of local productive development. At the same time, Edward calls him and tells him that he has just returned from a business trip to Bolivia and Peru and sees opportunities to export, but recognises that he should enter this market with another fish species, such as tilapia, which is more popular among consumers. This will require new investments and scale but the market analysis is very promising. There is an unstoppable growth in inland aquaculture in Latin American countries.

The policy maker will have to decide where to place the new resources: should he support Edward in its internationalisation process in the hope that this will open up new possibilities for potential followers as well, or should he promote the emergence of followers through capacity building of local actors and other types of support to enable them to insert themselves competitively in the new market initiated by the pioneer? As always, time is short. A productive development strategy has to be designed in the next two months.

ACKNOWLEDGEMENTS

We would like to thank the Escuela de Gobierno de Chaco for the approach to this case study and acknowledge their significant contributions to the research carried out. We also thank all the interviewees who gave their time and testimonies, key inputs for this case study.

NOTES

1. This case study is based on real-life experience with information collected in 2018 and analysed in: Robert et al. (2019). The real names were removed and the case was partially

adapted to highlight the elements of controversy and dilemma in order to contribute to a compelling narrative for pedagogic purposes.

2. The detail of the productive rotation process between rice and pacú can be found in Pontelli (2016).

3. Currently only expeller soy, corn, wheat, and vitamin mineral core is purchased.

4. In Argentina the National Service for Agrifood Health and Quality regulates the sanitary conditions of food products.

5. Observatorio de Empleo y Dinámica Empresarial: www.trabajo.gob.ar/estadisticas/oede/index.asp

REFERENCES

ECLAC (2022). Desarrollo productivo en la provincia del Chaco: Capacidades, recursos y potencialidades. CEPAL. www.cepal.org/es/publicaciones/48562-desarrollo-productivo-la-provincia-chaco-capacidades-recursos-potencialidades

Hausmann, R., & Rodrik, D. (2003). Economic development as self-discovery. *Journal of Development Economics*, 72(2), 603–633.

Hirschman, A. O. (1958). *The Strategy of Economic Development*. Yale University Press.

Ministerio del Interior, Obras Públicas y Vivienda. (2019). Información estadística para la planificación de estrategias de desarrollo provincial. Chaco. Sistema de Información para el Desarrollo Provincial Dirección Nacional de Políticas Regionales, Argentina.

Pontelli, C. (2016). Análisis tecnológicos y prospectivos sectoriales. Complejo arroz – peces. Programa Nacional PRONAPTEC, Ministerio de Ciencia, Tecnología e Innovación Productiva. www.argentina.gob.ar/sites/default/files/3.arrocero_acuicultura._carolina_pontelli.pdf

Robert, V., Moncaut, N., Perez, M., Miranda, G., Alegre, M., Balbiano, R., & Ossola, I. (2019). Capacidades organizacionales y competencias para la diversificación productiva: el caso de arroz y pacú en Chaco, Argentina. *SaberEs*, 11(1), 41–64.

PART III
NAVIGATING CRISES: ENTREPRENEURIAL RESILIENCE, WELL-BEING, AND ETHICAL IMPERATIVES

15
Pivoting to face COVID-19 in the mobility industry: the BusForFun case

Cinzia Colapinto and Vladi Finotto

1.   INTRODUCTION

It all started in 2015 on the Rialto Bridge in Venice. At the time, I was a manager in a transport company and Davide was on the board. For some time we have wanted to set up something of our own. We sat at a table, drank a Spritz and finally talked about it seriously. Luca's wife suggested that he show me the business plan. I read it, and I liked it. Then, he transformed the idea into a kilometer-long Excel spreadsheet.
(Davide Buscato, co-founder of BusForFun)

From the first moment, the two friends began looking for the first collaborators and opened an office in Venice. Luca Campanile, an engineer, and Davide Buscato, a key account manager in a large multinational, both in their 40s, left their permanent jobs in 2015 and teamed up to leverage on their specific skills and expertises. The former, employed by a private bus company, brought into the nascent venture competences related to the organization and management of transportation networks and data management; the second brought marketing and sales competences, together with a general understanding of the transportation business. Luca and Davide created a venture that distilled the results of all their previous professional experience. Luca worked for about 20 years in the transport sector, gaining a deep knowledge in the bus regulation that has proved to be crucial for setting BusForFun logistic and operation activities. In particular, Luca worked as a business manager at a passenger transport company in the province of Venice.

Davide worked as a sales manager for 16 years and his know-how was fundamental for the creation of a sales network. Davide described his career: "The companies I have worked with are mostly multinationals or large Italian organizations: I am therefore accustomed to continuous relationships not only with international Sales Divisions, but also with Engineering and Technical Divisions."

Observing and analyzing data on people's mobility habits, Luca envisaged creating a platform aggregating people who wanted to enjoy an event and who needed a ride to it (Figure 15.1). Luca commented on the process and the discovery of the idea:

The idea of BusForFun came about when I was working for the largest and most ancient transport company in Venice. At that time, I was in charge of managing the tourist transport for the Venice cruise terminal and for the top 20 tour operators in the world. Looking at quarterly data, I realized that the number of aggregators [associations or single people who put together groups of people for traveling], was declining over time. I thought it was the time for digital aggregators. After talking about FIT [For Individual Travelers] with a manager at Kuoni Gulliver, and Andrea Incondi, Country Manager at Flixbus, I came up with the idea of creating an aggregator of people who want to enjoy an event.

Source: Taken from www.busforfun.com/. © Busforfun.com. Permission provided.

Figure 15.1 BusForFun website/platform

Davide and Luca started with an initial investment that consisted of their savings and money raised from family and friends. Davide brought his experience as a sales manager in the mechanic industry and gave the company a strong commercial footprint from the beginning. They also leveraged their relatives and extensive professional networks in terms of human resources to staff the company with all the skills and capabilities. Being a startup in a mature sector, collective transportation, they could flexibly experiment novel ways of delivering services. A platform business model promised an opportunity to scale up. BusForFun started with a user-friendly booking system and an extensive route network, together with access to all the major entertainment events in the country.

The Italian Chambers of Commerce launched a support project for small and medium-sized enterprises willing to embark on digital transformation processes to spread and train businesses to exploit opportunities brought about by digital tools and to encourage the adoption of Industry 4.0 solutions. In particular, the project consisted of seminars, networking and training events to communicate basic knowledge on Industry 4.0 technologies, one-to-one meetings with companies and informative sessions on economic incentives, given by the chamber of commerce to SMEs willing to upgrade their IT systems. This governmental program allowed the two entrepreneurs to find connections, partners and mentors.

The company soon captured the interest of Italian private investors and financial institutions that supported the growth of its operations; in addition, the two managers could capture public funds to sustain the scaling up of the firm and the spin-off of a child company, ParkForFun. This spin-off focused on managing and booking off-street parking at stadiums, airports, and events; it did so by leveraging on the competences and technologies developed in the parent company. ParkForFun offers turnkey solutions to municipalities and local entities in Italy, Slovenia, and Spain.

2.   BUILDING BUSFORFUN

David and Luca developed the startup concept on the basis of integrating their knowledge, the recognition of the increasing success of new players in the transportation business (e.g., Flixbus), and an innovative approach to a market that was relatively unexplored: transporting large numbers of people to important events in Italy from different regions of the country.

> BusForFun's advantage is the simplicity of using the service. The user connects to our website, chooses an event, the bus stop which is more convenient to him/her, the date of the event and the number of tickets to be purchased. The booking takes place on our website [Figure 15.2]. We have created a network with more than 500 travel agencies in Italy to reach the important segment of users which prefers the offline channel to complete the payment. All the agencies are geolocalized and georeferenced: in this way, our passengers can choose the event on our portal and then reach the nearest travel agency to complete the payment. (Davide Buscato, co-founder of BusForFun)

The company did not own any buses and did not employ any drivers directly. It created a platform business model that coalesced owners of individual buses or fleets and several event-goers scattered around Italy. This was the trigger for the startup's rapid success, confirmed by the numbers in Table 15.1.

3.   STRETCHING COMPETENCIES: FROM DRIVING PEOPLE TO EVENTS TO MANAGING EVENT MOBILITY SOLUTIONS

The platform business model relied on the digital infrastructure that the company established in collaboration with an information technology partner that developed the platform: they opted to outsource the development of the platform architecture and code to a specialized sup-

Source: Taken from www.busforfun.com/listinoProdotti?destinazione=1974. ©
Busforfun.com. Permission provided.

Figure 15.2 BusForFun service

plier in the Venice area – Mapo Studio. Since the embryonic stage, BusForFun relied on this important technological partner. However, in the beginning the team grew mainly through friendship and family bonds: the founders delegated financial and operational activities and mainly focused on the brand and network creation, as well as dealing with public entities involved in event organization/authorization.

Event after event, BusForFun developed a strong reputation and expanded its network. In 2016 it supported the 73rd Golf Open of Italy, the 2016 Italian Grand Prix, concerts (i.e., Ligabue in Monza), and some corporate events (i.e., Wellstar in Rome). One of their clients, Anna Botter, International Vice President of Wellstar-Byas, said "the support of BusForFun was fundamental for the success of our events: a modern platform and an incredible availability." The two founders, who were active on the streets during these first events, were able to perfect their service and at the same time create new relations (Figure 15.3).

The epitome of the operational capacity of BusForFun and the prelude to ParkForFun, Vasco Rossi's concert in Modena in 2017, was the largest test the company had to face in its two years of life. Vasco Rossi is one of the most admired rock stars in Italy: active since 1977, he is famous among different generations. Hundreds of thousands of Italians flocked from all over the country to attend his concerts that were among the largest musical events in the country that year. As of 2023, the concert in Modena, with 227,000 tickets sold, still holds the world record of concert with the highest number of paying customers. Thirty-six thousand individuals reached Modena by train. The municipality made over 46,000 parking spaces for cars available and devoted 900 public buses to move people back and forth. Six hundred buses came from different Italian locations and BusForFun and similar companies were hired as service providers. ParkForFun directly managed 22 different parking lots, 7,000 cars, and 543 buses, totaling over 45,000 served customers.

Table 15.1 Financial profile (in euros)

	31 December 2015	31 December 2016	31 December 2017	31 December 2018	31 December 2019	31 December 2020
Revenue	0	135,118	316,473	479,573	853,215	244,891
EBITDA	−14,174	−5,407	89,624	259,771	74,501	−181,820
Net profit	−13,036	−18,678	14,353	59,019	−176,147	−200,23
Total assets	113,532	373,634	614,667	1,047,780	1,238,674	1,606,259
Net equity	96,964	78,285	92,639	151,659	89,312	380,918
Net financial position	n.a.	n.a.	n.a.	551,604	709,163	427,411
EBITDA/sales (%)	Not stated	−2.53	16.74	31.55	7.39	−57.8
ROS (%)	Not stated	−21.32	−2.66	10.13	−15.39	Not stated
ROA (%)	−15.83	−12.18	−2.31	7.96	−12.53	−11.32
ROE (%)	−13.44	−23.86	15.49	38.92	Not stated	−52.62
Debt/equity ratio	n.a.	n.a.	n.a.	4.06	8.21	2.28
Debt/banks on revenue (%)	n.a.	n.a.	n.a.	74.76	72.7	Not stated
Debt/EBITDA ratio	n.a.	n.a.	n.a.	2.37	9.84	−4.78
Turnover of capital employed (#)	0	0.36	0.51	0.46	0.69	0.15
Employees* BusForFun	8	9	9	9	6.75	5.625
Employees* ParkForFun	n.a.	n.a.	n.a.	n.a.	1.6166	4.175

Note: * Including part-time employees. EBITDA = earnings before interest, taxes, depreciation, and amortization; ROA = return on assets; ROE = return on equity; ROS = return on sales.

Source: Elaborated by the authors based on information from AIDA, 2022; BusForFun, 2023.

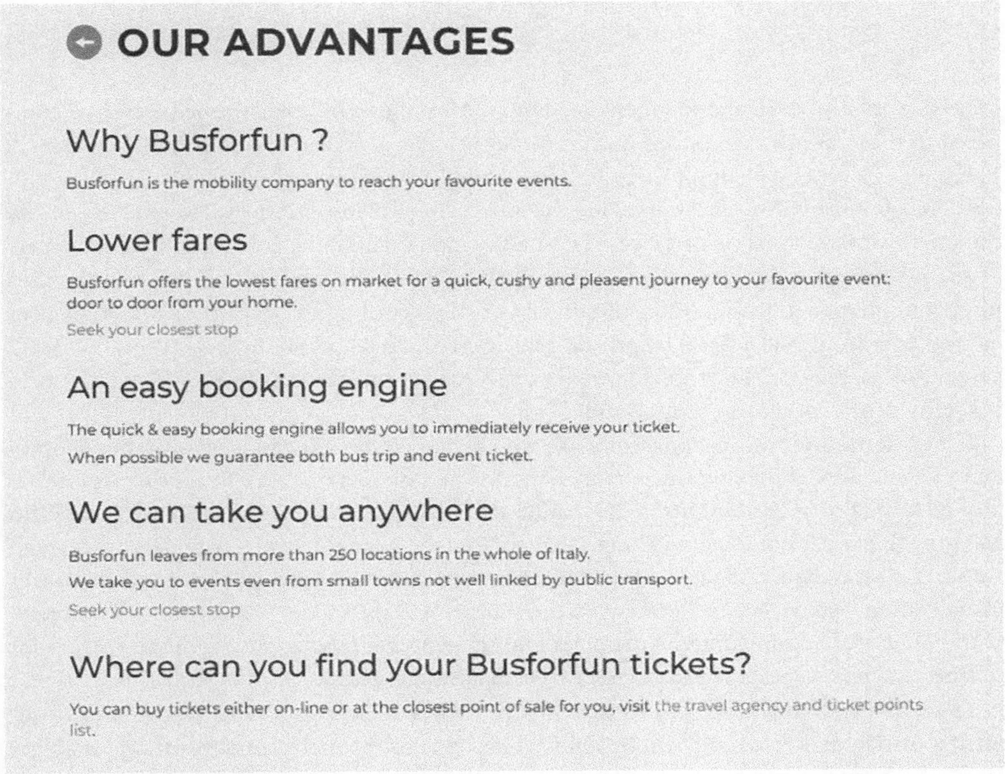

⬤ OUR ADVANTAGES

Why Busforfun ?

Busforfun is the mobility company to reach your favourite events.

Lower fares

Busforfun offers the lowest fares on market for a quick, cushy and pleasent journey to your favourite event:
door to door from your home.
Seek your closest stop

An easy booking engine

The quick & easy booking engine allows you to immediately receive your ticket.
When possible we guarantee both bus trip and event ticket.

We can take you anywhere

Busforfun leaves from more than 250 locations in the whole of Italy.
We take you to events even from small towns not well linked by public transport.
Seek your closest stop

Where can you find your Busforfun tickets?

You can buy tickets either on-line or at the closest point of sale for you, visit the travel agency and ticket points
list.

Source: Taken from www.busforfun.com/vantaggi? © Busforfun.com. Permission
provided.

Figure 15.3   BusForFun advantages

In November 2018, the two founders created a spin-off: ParkForFun, offering a variety of services related to the mobility around large events, both one-off and recurring. ParkForFun developed technology solutions to manage large parking spaces, to streamline the booking of parking lots, and the concession of permits to access limited traffic areas. Employing six collaborators, ParkForFun's turnover was over 200,000 euros in the first year and over 240,000 in 2019. It became profitable in its second year of life, with an EBITDA/sales ratio of 13 percent. Success in managing mobility around large events attracting hundreds of thousands of individuals in small cities in Italy represented the startup's most important credential that allowed them to become the provider of choice for Serie A (the major league of soccer in Italy), large motor sports events, and municipalities seeking technical partners to manage significant local events.

4.   THE CONTEXT: THE MOBILITY INDUSTRY IN ITALY

Italy is a very dispersed and fragmented country. Most cities are small or medium sized compared to those of other countries in Europe: 46 percent of Italian towns are smaller than 20 square km. Seventy percent of them have less than 5,000 inhabitants. Italy has 92 cities with over 50,000 inhabitants. These areas are the attractors of many citizens who commute to city centers to work or to access services. The Italian industrial fabric, composed of small enterprises, is scattered around the territory, especially in the north and center of the country, thus forcing numerous individuals to commute to work. According to ANFIA (2020), 80 percent of passenger traffic takes place by private vehicles (cars, that amount to 76 percent), while 9.7 percent of passengers resort to collective extra-urban forms of transport and 1.9 percent to collective urban means of transportation.

The national and regional governments, who assign concessions to local or national operators, regulate local public transport in Italy. In the last 10 years, the European Union has pushed for major liberalizations in the market for passenger transport, thus allowing the birth and growth of operators such as Flixbus that entered the market for interregional routes (both within a single country and across different European countries). While the effects of this liberalization were visible in Germany in the short run, Italy remained a conservative market, both because of administrative intricacies and the extreme fragmentation of the market for coaches and buses compared to Germany (Grimaldi et al., 2017).

The mobility sector is one of the most involved in establishing a model based on environmental, social, and economic sustainability. This adds to the increasing growth of "mobility tech," the development of novel technologies at the interface between transportation means and digital technologies. This innovation trajectory promises to combine freedom of movement with decreased social and environmental impact.

The fragmentation of the market for private coaches, owned by many small entrepreneurs operating one or a few vehicles, was one of the factors BusForFun made use of. The platform could mobilize a myriad of small enterprises serving a geographically dispersed demand and moving people to specific locations from several points of departure.

BusForFun leveraged on other contextual factors as well. The physical infrastructure of the country was a key driver: Italy offers few locations adequate for large events, such as concerts of international stars and prominent, international sporting shows. The demand to attend these events is high and distributed all over the country. Under such circumstances a coordination mechanism with pre-defined and capillary pick-up points made it easier for event-goers to plan their trips and avoid hours of travel by car.

The substitution of the individual car with shared rides by bus met an increasing attention of the public towards the need to reduce the impact of human activities (mobility being one of the most important) on the environment. The opportunity to attend concerts and events represented a relief both for youngsters and for their families as Italy has a sustained negative record in terms of fatal road accidents: 51 fatal accidents per million inhabitants, compared to less than 39 in Germany and France and less than 30 in Spain. Forty-five percent of fatal road accidents involve cars in Europe and 51 percent of victims are aged 0 to 49 (European Parliament, 2019).

The entertainment industry in Italy concentrates in a handful of places and cities: large concerts of international superstars or national musical icons take place in the north of Italy and in Rome, with Milan being one of the most active hubs for live music in the country. Italy is also home to two global events in the motor sports world: the F1 race in Imola and the MotoGP race in Mugello.

5.   COVID-19: ENTER THE BLACK SWAN

On the night of March 9, 2020, the Italian prime minister Giuseppe Conte appeared on every television set to announce that the virus that had been sweeping Asia and China was a real threat to the health of millions of lives in Italy. To fight it and avoid dramatic consequences, Italy had to declare a complete lockdown starting the day after. To "save every single life at all costs, Italy is becoming a protected zone. No movement is possible outside of regional boundaries except for those that are urgent and unavoidable." Fifteen days before, Italy had already entered a situation wherein different provinces were locked down. For the first time since the Second World War, Italians experienced a curfew and a drastic limitation of their mobility. The list of closures and lockdowns grew: schools, swimming pools, restaurants, cafes, shops, theaters, clubs, and more.

According to the first governmental decree, the lockdown should have lasted three weeks: authorities expected the end of the emergency on April 3. Actually, the lockdown lasted an additional month in its strictest form. During the rest of the year, continuous openings and closures of limited areas became the norm. Suddenly, two of the main elements behind the BusForFun business model viability – mobility and events – ceased to exist. Concerts and events were canceled or rescheduled for 2021 or 2022. The live entertainment sector experienced a prolonged period of uncertainty.

Trade fairs and commercial events saw a sharp decline, with the number of fairs being held in Italy plummeting by 83 percent in 2020. In the same year, dance clubs and live events lost their entire turnover, a full 100 percent decline. It was impossible for club owners and entrepreneurs in the live music sector to plan ahead. The enduring state of emergency made 2021 another dramatic year: dance clubs remained closed until April 2022, while live concerts didn't start until May 2022. Live sports events were limited in terms of attendance: the Italian major soccer league was played in empty arenas until June 2021 and started the 2021–2022 season in September 2021 with severe limitations in terms of capacity (50 percent until March 2022).

BusForFun's growth path (Figure 15.4), thus, was hit by a "black swan," an event that no one could predict and that had dramatic and widespread implications that propagated exponentially. Before the lockdowns the company had been enjoying a strong scaling-up phase. Many of their customers were loyal and satisfied. The burst of the COVID-19 emergency brought a violent halt to the firm's growth. COVID-19 also made evident some structural weaknesses in the mobility sector in Italy and changed the market, showcasing the limits of the existing Italian public transport system.

New rules for public transport, such as social distancing, impacted public mobility demand, leading people to reconsider the use of cars. In 2020, the Italian government promoted, through the Ministry of Transport, domestic measures to support mobility; for instance, the so called "Relaunch Decree" issued in May 2020 focused on enhancing the national mobility system and the Mobility Bonus for bicycles, micro-mobility electric vehicles, and shared mobility services (limited to up to 500 euros per person and only to applicants living in cities with over 50,000 inhabitants).

6. PIVOTING IN THE WAKE OF COVID-19: THE NEW CHALLENGE FOR BUSFORFUN

In the days following the announcement of the Italian Government, the two founders and their team were feverishly answering the phone and participating in hectic online meetings with partners, clients, and suppliers of mobility services. One after the other, all the main events that were scheduled, and that were indispensable for meeting the cash flow projections of the company, were canceled or postponed. Mobility in general, not only that related to mass entertainment and sports events, was becoming problematic. Limited to basic services, public transportation was subject to very strict rules of social distancing and a drastic reduction of carrying capacities to avoid the spread of infection.

The two entrepreneurs had two choices. The first was that of waiting for the ceasing of the emergency, while surviving on public subsidies with the only goal of enduring the sudden stop to operations and ensuring their employees a wage. Another option was that of responding to the crisis by pivoting and leveraging some distinctive assets the company had. Luca and Davide identified specific and valuable assets and capabilities that could be potentially redeployed:

1. Skills related to the design, management, and organization of complex multimodal transportations systems.
2. An advanced platform that enabled parties to match their respective interests, in particular owners of parking lots and buses, on the one side, and people who needed to move or park, on the other.
3. A relational capital developed thanks to client satisfaction with their services and positive goodwill related to the organization of mobility for large global events.
4. Several high-impact connections to decision makers in important cities in Italy, in particular, in Milan.

Luca and Davide understood that public funds were not a problem in the short run, but could finish sooner or later. The main challenge, in the first quarter of 2021, was that the evolution of the virus was unpredictable. Until the end of 2021, vaccines were not available on a large scale. After the summer people returned to closed indoor spaces and infections climbed rapidly, putting the health system under pressure once again. Such developments forced authorities to decree more or less strict lockdowns, to limit the attendance at events and occasionally to prohibit them altogether. No one could predict the duration of the state of emergency and the new market equilibrium in the mobility industry after; the future was highly uncertain but decisions needed to be made.

ACKNOWLEDGMENTS

We would like to thank Luca Campanile and Davide Buscato for their friendship, their enthusiasm in presenting the firm and letting us study it, and for their support in the development of the case.

REFERENCES

AIDA (2022). Analisi informatizzata delle aziende. https://login.bvdinfo.com/R0/AidaNeo

ANFIA (2020). Dossier trasporto passeggeri e mobilit. Focus trasporto su gomma. www.anfia.it/data/portale-anfia/comunicazione_eventi/comunicati_stampa/2020/Dossier_Trasporto_Passeggeri_Giugno_2020_DEF.pdf

BusForFun (2023, June 26). Our advantages. www.busforfun.com/vantaggi?lang=en

European Parliament (2019). Road fatality statistics in the EU. www.europarl.europa.eu/topics/en/article/20190410STO36615/road-fatality-statistics-in-the-eu-infographic

Grimaldi, R., Augustin, K., & Beria, P. (2017). Intercity coach liberalisation: The cases of Germany and Italy. *Transportation Research Procedia*, *25*, 474–490.

16

Feeding with love: Frisby's quest for a successor to preserve its legacy in times of sudden change

Julio Cesar Zuluaga and Beatriz Rodriguez-Satizabal

> *Nobody does it as Frisby does it.*
> (Company motto)

1. INTRODUCTION

Frisby is a leading family firm operating in the Colombian fast-food industry since 1977. The high-quality and service orientation of its workers, the presentation and packaging of the food, the decoration, and the motto "Nobody does it as Frisby does it" are differentiating elements of Frisby's business strategy. Husband and wife co-founders Alfredo Hoyos and Liliana Restrepo implemented a company culture and philosophy close to the values and beliefs they shared as entrepreneurs.

The management practices such as conscious capitalism and the founders' values and principles have allowed Frisby to build a differentiating organizational culture during the last four decades. Since its foundation, the firm has faced complex situations such as difficulties when the first franchise opened in Medellín in 1983, violence and security issues at the end of the 1990s, two major economic crises, and the challenges of a highly competitive sector with the entry of new local and international competitors who sought to win a share of the market from Frisby (Frisby, 2017). Despite all these difficulties, Alfredo and Liliana have successfully adapted to the industry's different changes and challenges, renewing their strategy to sustain growth based on creating and preserving a differentiating organizational culture.

The main legacy of Alfredo and Liliana is this unique organizational culture rooted in their lifestyle and ideology. As one of the founders said, "everyone who works for Frisby will be positively impacted" (Frisby, n.d.). Frisby is a company with effective human resource management based on conscious capitalism and governed by the principle of giving back to society. From the beginning, the business's core value was to "spread love" between co-workers and founders, promoting resilience and consciousness between one other, while their competitors were interested in just profit (Frisby, 2017). Frisby's strategy was successfully measured by positively impacting employees' well-being and health and making essential contributions to the company's growth.

Selecting the most capable successor to occupy the higher managerial position is the next step in the firm's growth and continuity of the founders' legacy. In 2018, Alfredo and Liliana began to lay the groundwork for succession as they were both close to retirement. The second-generation four successors, Alejandro Hoyos Bojanini, Carolina Hoyos Bojanini, Álvaro Hoyos Restrepo, and Catalina Hoyos Restrepo, have the education, management skills, and experience to assume total control and direction of the family business. All of them have been involved as franchise owners, divisional managers, and board members at Frisby for several years. Moreover, three of them have founded and managed other companies (Portafolio, 2021). Through family meetings, Alfredo and Liliana assured their four successors to socialize into and interiorize the values and principles of conscious capitalism that have guided the firm's strategy (Table 16.1).

Despite second-generation successors being prepared to take control, the generational succession in the company has continually been postponed because the founders expressed fears and doubts about the continuity of the legacy, values, and culture they had infused into the family business. As explained by one of the successors, "we are a family of five children, not only four. Frisby was born and grew as a brand side by side with the successors" (Posada Cifuentes & García Ríos, 2019). However, adding to the recent COVID-19 crisis that is changing the industry and business landscape radically, the death of Alfredo at the age of 74 (1946–2020) generated pressure to accelerate the succession process (Portafolio, 2020).

For now, Liliana, founder and matriarch, has assumed the company's leadership (Bernal Durán, 2023). Still, selecting a member of the second generation who can sustain the company's good performance and face the new challenges ahead is on the table. Liliana is clear about her desire and commitment to continue with the family and business legacy, making Frisby a company of which all its workers and Colombians are proud for its quality and commitment to the environment and society, under the idea of prosperity for all (El Diario, 2020). As a result, in 2023, the board of directors must make a critical decision regarding who should be the next chief executive officer (CEO) selected for generational succession.

First- and second-generation family members encounter the challenges of maintaining the organizational culture and navigating new market conditions. Therefore, the main criterion is selecting a family member capable of continuing the legacy while having the innovation orientation and mindset for adapting the family business to the next growth stage. Should Liliana continue as the president? If not, to whom in the second generation should succession be given?

2.   A LOVE (HI)STORY CALLED FRISBY

Frisby was born on June 17, 1977 as a pizzeria in Parque El Lago in the city of Pereira. More than four decades later, this family business that expanded under a franchise model has over 4,000 employees and about 270 points of sale nationwide (see Annex 1[1]). Family members and external managers know that the company's good performance is due to the principles and

Table 16.1   Profile of family members

Name	Generation	Education	Roles at Frisby	Roles at other companies
Liliana Restrepo	First	BSc Economics (Universidad Libre de Pereira) MSc Project Management (Universidad San Francisco de Quito)	President (2020–) Board member (2001–2019) Vice president (1994–2001) Co-founder (1977–)	
Alejandro Hoyos Bojanini	Second	BSc Engineering MBA (Georgia Institute of Technology)	Director of technology (1997–2000) Board member Owner and manager of five franchises (2000–)	
Carolina Hoyos Bojanini	Second	BA Management (Universidad de la Sabana)		Francorp

Name	Generation	Education	Roles at Frisby	Roles at other companies
Álvaro Hoyos Restrepo	Second	BA Industrial Engineer (Universidad de los Andes) MA Social Media Marketing (Universitat de Barcelona) Course in Blockchain Strategy (University of Oxford)	Board member (1984–) Owner and manager of three franchises (2000–)	Founder and chief executive officer Innova (2010–) Franchise owner Cinnabon Colombia (2009–2019) Founder Heaven Club (2007–2009)
Catalina Hoyos Restrepo	Second	BA Cell/Cellular and Molecular Biology (University of California Berkeley) MFA Filmmaking (New York Film Academy) Courses in business and management (Universidad Javeriana)	Board member (2005–2021)	Co-founder Fábrica de Experiencias SAS Wingz (2007–2019) Vice president of development Kree8 Productions (2014–2017) Founder Kayros (2005–2007)

philosophy of "conscious capitalism" that Alfredo and Liliana built as pillars of a differentiating organizational culture. This organizational culture has materialized in Frisby through different values that the founders synthesize in delivering a "unique flavor," "feeding with love" to all Colombian families, "since love is the force that inspires us to be the best in the category" (Frisby, n.d.; Fundación Frisby, n.d.).

To understand the success behind Frisby's strategy, it is crucial to know the story of husband and wife co-founders, Alfredo Hoyos and Liliana Restrepo (Frisby, 2017).[2] They always tried to implement a company culture and philosophy close to the values and beliefs they shared as entrepreneurs. Born in Pereira on May 17, 1946, Alfredo Hoyos was the son of entrepreneur Alfredo Hoyos Mejía born in Yarumal, Antioquia. He came to Pereira very young and started his poultry farming business. Alfredo Hoyos' father is one of the pioneers of the poultry industry in Colombia. Alfredo spent most of his childhood and teenage years in Pereira until 1962 when his father sent him to the Riverside Military Academy in Georgia, United States. There, he began to open up to the world and new experiences that led him at the age of 17 to Indiana, where he followed in his father's footsteps, studying and learning the fundamentals of the poultry business.

In 1964, he attended the Chicago Poultry Convention, where he met representatives of Dr. Salsbury's Laboratories, a veterinary pharmaceutical company offering veterinary products, vaccines, and poultry medicine. The company was looking to export its products to Colombia, and Alfredo Hoyos took this opportunity to make a deal with them. At the same time, he also met and agreed with Big Dutchman, a company realizing feeding systems and housing equipment for poultry production. He built up his own company, Importadora Avícola de Colombia, most commonly known by its acronym Impavicol. As he said, "Sometime later, I found out that what happened to me in Chicago was not a coincidence. Successful people call it 'synchronicity.' When you enter the adventure zone with the determination to find something, I assure you, it will appear" (Frisby, 2017).

Alfredo Hoyos moved to Pereira in 1965, with his company offering technical assistance to poultry farmers within the Colombian territory. Several years later, he took up a new challenge starting a poultry-processing business called Pimpollo. According to Alfredo Hoyos: "Pimpollo taught me a lesson: a good businessman is not the one who knows everything, but the one who knows people that know the path to lead a company to success" (Frisby, 2017, p. 32). From 1965 until 1972, Alfredo Hoyos founded several companies focused on the poultry business: Impavicol, the farm Santa Inés, Pimpollo, Avícola in the Colombian Pacific, and Procodes (a company treating chicken waste to manufacture dog food). Alfredo Hoyos also owned Pollo Loco, a restaurant chain based in Pereira, Manizales, and Palmira.

In 1973, the brand-new roast chicken chain Kokoriko based in Cali was looking for a supplier. After negotiations with Alfredo Hoyos, they decided to join forces, expertise, and capacities to establish Avinco. This alliance expanded Kokoriko's franchise in the Colombian coffee region and Antioquia; in the same year, Alfredo Hoyos met Liliana Restrepo. Jaime Aristizábal defined Liliana as a woman with solid entrepreneurial initiatives and an "overwhelming momentum." Alfredo and Liliana met, and then the history of Frisby started.

In 1976, Alfredo took some time off and sold his shares in Kokoriko and Pimpollo to come up with new ideas in the food sector. He decided with his wife to set up a pizza shop in Pereira, one of the main cities in southwest Colombia. The pizza shop was a hit; Alfredo decided to put the chef in front of the window so that people could watch the preparation of the dough and the baking of the pizza. Alfredo called his restaurant Frisby because the technique of spinning dough made him think of the game frisbee. The emblematic fried chicken of Frisby's restaurants came a few years later. Alfredo's brother, Fernando Hoyos, knew a distributor in California selling Henny Penny's pressure fryers. Alfredo saw huge potential and bought some fryers to start selling fried chicken.

Frisby's owners were always strongly committed to quality, "doing the best, whatever the cost." After several tests, they started their production of fried chicken. Between 1977 and 1989, ice cream, pizza, and fried chicken were found to be successful. Alfredo always involved his family in the company, particularly his children, Alejandro, Carolina, Álvaro, and Catalina. From an early age, his son Alejandro remembers that his dad got him involved in the family business, maintaining relationships with collaborators and learning about operation processes and equipment.

The company's growth and fried chicken were a hit, becoming increasingly successful. Alfredo started to expand his business to other regions, such as the coffee region and then in Medellín, with the opening of seven restaurant franchises. In the mid-1990s, there was an escalation of violence in Colombia and mounting insecurity in the cities. In this context, the construction of shopping malls emerged in the territory to protect entrepreneurial and business activities, highly impacted by the high levels of insecurity in towns. In 1995, Frisby partnered with Grupo Éxito, the biggest retailer in Colombia. With this new alliance, the brand started to sell fried chicken in shopping malls, thus making Frisby a success and increasing its sales between 1994 and 2013 significantly. Frisby started its expansion across the country in the Caribbean region in 1998, running several restaurants in Cartagena, San Andrés, Bogotá, Barranquilla, Santa Marta, Monteria, and Sincelejo.

In 1999, Colombia experienced a major banking crisis threatening business survival in several sectors of the economy. The CEO of Frisby, Liliana Restrepo, has always cultivated transparency with her collaborators toward the company's situation. A strong need for workers' partnership and job involvement was necessary to face the crisis, and people started working together to save the company. In the framework of this partnership, Liliana came up with "Plan 1000: One Thousand ideas saving one billion Colombian pesos without cutting staff." Plan 1000 was well received by employees, who even proposed being paid half their monthly salary to help the company during the crisis. The company did not choose this proposition and decided to maintain their salary, but this strategy had repercussions as employees did not receive a salary boost between 1999 to 2001.

The same year, Colombia faced a resurgence of violence and insecurity, thus impacting companies, as was the case for Frisby. Indeed, Liliana and Alfredo have been threatened and pressured by organized criminals claiming money multiple times. They immediately informed their collaborators of the situation and decided not to yield to threats, whatever the cost. In the words of Liliana: "This company is what gives us food at the table. Standing up to organized crimes is putting us in danger. We will completely understand if some of you want to leave the company. For those who stay, you must be aware of suspicious persons or situations" (Frisby, 2017). The support of employees was total as none of them decided to leave the company. For security measures, Liliana and Alfredo had to live abroad in 2001 while leaving the management of Frisby, for the first time, under the responsibility of a coordinating team. This team managed the company until 2003, when Alfredo and Liliana returned to Colombia and designated Francisco Guzmán as the company's general manager.

By 1990, Frisby counted 15 restaurants with a unique menu, but the crisis in 1999 and competitive fried chicken restaurant chains in the national territory led the company to rethink its strategy. The company created a research and development department and developed a set of fried chicken recipes such as the Frisbandeja, Frisnaks, Frisburrito, Frispicada, Frisandwich, Frisgranado, Frispecial, and the Frisparrilla. The restaurant decided to keep its authenticity, proposing fried chicken menus with Colombian flavors to its customers. One of the company's commitments was: "We are people serving people."

3.   FRISBY'S LEGACY: THE ORGANIZATIONAL CULTURE OF "NO ONE DOES IT AS FRISBY DOES IT"

Frisby's organizational culture also has its history. From the first day, the founders sought to develop a sense of family where the employees feel valued, invested, and happy (Frisby, 2017). While developing awareness amongst its employees about the importance of being part of the community, the founders provided clients with a quality experience, delivering excellent customer service and product quality. From the beginning, the slogan of the family business was "feeding people with love" (Frisby, n.d.), showing the importance and level of awareness that has developed in Frisby's employees toward the company and founders. Alfredo and Liliana's close friend and advisor, Jaime Aristizábal, commented on the company's culture:

> creating awareness and teaching ethical principles to all of the staff was at the beginning spontaneous, but great care and coherence later needed to be exercised to structure the business. Sometimes the owners were seen as crazy for doing meditation and relaxation exercises in the company. Still, now, other companies are contacting us to talk about our corporate culture and the issue of managing culture. (Posada Cifuentes & García Ríos, 2019)

Frisby's organizational culture has evolved over the years thanks to the guiding ethical principles of the owners. Alfredo has always been interested in psychology, philosophy, and sociology; this is undoubtedly the reason behind the company developing its first workshop activities in 1976, emphasizing live coaching and biodance (see Annex 2). Indeed, workshops focused on developing human skills rather than financial skills to support positive changes in employees' lives. Alfredo was looking for ways to become a better person and wanted to share experiences and techniques with his employees. He devoted himself to learning and applying the concept of conscious capitalism within the company, whose purpose is to operate ethically, considering all stakeholders involved, including its employees.

For her part, Liliana contributed to Frisby's organizational culture more emotionally, spreading the love at work and being in charge of the biodance activity during workshops. Liliana's son, Álvaro, said: "my mom always talks about love, which might sound weird in a workplace … but this makes all the difference." Liliana states: "The relationship with collaborators in a respectful, loving and inclusive way is fundamental. This type of relationship is based on respect, love and transparency, allowing us to work together on a common purpose" (Posada Cifuentes & García Ríos, 2019). New collaborators of the company were encouraged to follow the activities and philosophies applied by Liliana and Alfredo. They had to embrace Frisby's organizational culture and operate in it daily. As the human resources manager, Flor Elvira, mentioned, "I do think that principles, beliefs and ethics of a company have to be part of collaborator's personal values before you start working for them. I will make these values sustainable naturally and genuinely because this is in my DNA. I bring it from home and empower it in my professional activity" (Posada Cifuentes & García Ríos, 2019).

The company also provides incentives to employees, both monetary and non-monetary, and gives bonuses at the beginning of each year. Frisby's general manager, Francisco Guzmán, commented:

> The purpose of bonuses was to give our collaborators the possibility to spend a great time, going to Panaca or the Coffee Park without having to pay anything, using food vouchers and getting a 50% discount. We also offer discount-based birthday bonuses, and the company organizes a Children's Day at the end of each year, where gifts are given to children's employees. The most important for us is the Employees Fund which helps our collaborators if they need to purchase a home or even receive medical assistance, like going to the dentist. (Posada Cifuentes & García Ríos, 2019)

The company allows the employment of relatives and couples, considering that working with someone you know increases feelings of belonging and commitment to the team. Frisby offers professional development opportunities and a real chance to grow within the company. As mentioned by Francisco Guzman: "More than 87.5% of our collaborators have been taken on a higher-ranking role, and the vast majority of our executive directors won back their positions, working really hard." According to how leadership should be approached to impact the company positively, he commented: "positive leadership is when managers behave according to the company culture and look after their team members on how they follow the company's values. I call it healthy leadership, with a fundamental premise: as a leader, you must be a role model to others" (Posada Cifuentes & García Ríos, 2019).

Besides good financial performance, other important factors, such as staff rotation, are considered. According to Francisco Guzman, "in the United States, the staff turnover rate is close to 165% in operating positions and 60% in management-level jobs, while in Colombia, it rates between 98% to 105%. The employee turnover that our company handles is 43%, and we consider that this number is due to the relation between each other."

4.   FRISBY'S LEGACY: SOCIAL VALUES AND HIGHER PURPOSE

Frisby's organizational culture defends values such as commitment, respect, transparency, and quality that made the company highly valuable and respected despite the difficulties encountered (see Annex 3). To understand these pillars, it is essential to know Alfredo and Liliana's points of view: "We asked ourselves: How to improve society for the better? While other companies were focused on profit, we decided to do it differently. Starting with what we called a higher purpose: everyone who works for Frisby will be positively impacted." Alfredo and Liliana's son, Álvaro, also mentioned: "My parents always wanted the company's purpose to focus on the personal growth and development of its employees beyond the profit" (Posada Cifuentes & García Ríos, 2019).

For Alfredo, the concept of conscious capitalism was a way to achieve his mission and business philosophy (Semana, 2022). He commented:

> Savage capitalism should be replaced by conscious capitalism, as companies should be more aware and oriented towards people. For a long time, economics professors were teaching their students that profit was companies' unique concern while the government plays a role in social responsibility towards workers. But things have changed, and people now understand that we must be more involved in employee well-being.

5.   SOCIAL RESPONSIBILITY AND SOCIAL VALUE

Alfredo is the type of person who reflects on life and shares his way of seeing the world. As founder of a company, Alfredo believes that "paying tax is a way to help the society by providing better education, infrastructure and other services to people. By giving, you can receive more than you already have. Executive directors believe that their expenses will increase doing social activities whereas companies become more profitable" (Posada Cifuentes & García Ríos, 2019). Corporate social responsibilities within a company materialize value and ethical principles in business. Alfredo and Liliana decided to set up an initiative with the Frisby Foundation, created in 1979, where corporate funds were allocated to target educational initiatives for homeless children (Frisby, 2017). In 1995 the foundation was turned into the Technological Institute of Dosquebradas, which focused on food processing and agro-industrial business management. During the last years, the school welcomed more than 546 students, and 485 graduated. Frisby mainly financed the tuition and fees for the school, and students only had to contribute around 30 percent of the total costs. Recently, the company took a step towards creating the University of Frisby, giving access to training and promoting the professional growth of its employees.

6.   UNCERTAINTY AND PRESSURE FOR CHANGE AND INNOVATION IN THE CHICKEN RESTAURANTS SECTOR

The poultry industry will have the complex task of maintaining sustained growth this year and opening the doors to the international market (La Republica, 2023; Semana, 2021). Managing inflation will be one of the great challenges of the National Government (Pulzo, 2022).

Chicken is a dynamic and appetizing category in Colombia. According to Fenavi, the consumption of chicken in Colombia can be every 10 days or biweekly. "48% of Colombians eat out once a week. The chicken is there, but it's not necessarily roast chicken," says Fenavi's director of support programs, Luis Rodolfo Álvarez. The experts agree that the chicken category has boosted its consumption with innovation, not only because of the entry of wings or chicken tenders but also because of the protein's ability to transform into products that can become gourmet. "Chicken today is more competitive due to its ability to innovate, which is why it has positioned itself as the main protein. It is no longer just roast chicken; many restaurants have turned it into an attractive and appetizing product. In hamburgers, it is already an obligation to have the chicken option," adds Álvarez (Goula, 2022). "Colombians like chicken and many fast-food categories are aligning themselves based on this protein. In addition, the large chains move promotional themes that promote consumption and attract people. And finally, they have positioned themselves in delivery applications through guidelines and alliances," concludes Marisol Amaya from GIG Latam (Goula, 2022).

7.   IN SEARCH OF A NEW CEO

For 40 years, Frisby has been considered a role model for Colombian businesses (La Republica, 2017). Liliana and Alfredo's children now face the task of taking control of the family business and have the mandate to preserve Frisby's legacy and essence. Although they gained experience working in the company and know the values and organizational culture promoted by their parents, their profiles show they will bring different approaches to the management of the firm. Moreover, the industry landscape, market structure, customer preferences, and other cultural and social factors have rapidly changed over the last years due to the COVID-19 disruption, so they must react accordingly.

Alfredo Hoyos' two children, Álvaro and Catalina, have been assuming roles and functions in the company to be prepared for any eventual succession. Liliana did her best to raise her children according to her values and beliefs, such as cooperation between siblings, mutual respect, and considering the needs of others. Each year, the family met during the Family Council and with the board of directors to discuss the company vision and strategy and identify specific goals to reach without losing the essence of what has made the company successful. Additionally, the company turned its business into a franchise, allowing Liliana and Alfredo's children to have their own Frisby restaurants.

Since its creation, Frisby's organizational culture has been one of the most significant drivers of business performance and competitiveness (Semana, 2021, 2022). The board of directors has the mandate of preserving the essence and legacy of Frisby's corporate culture but readapting it to new business conditions that companies are facing in the fast-food industry. In the face of new competitive pressures derived from COVID-19 and the death of Alfredo, the family's second generation might be in a better position to adapt their strategy by innovating to stay competitive and sustain the company's growth. However, second-generation family members may not yet have the skills and experience to preserve the legacy to survive in such a turbulent period. Balancing legacy and innovation is difficult, so Frisby is on a double-edged sword.

In 2024, the board needs to choose a new CEO. By December 2023, the family had decided on a shortlist of their best candidates based on their achievements within the company. The finalists were Liliana Restrepo, Álvaro Hoyos Restrepo, and Catalina Hoyos Restrepo. The new CEO will face the difficult decision of preserving and maintaining the founders' legacy or innovating to adjust to the new business environment to keep the company's high performance. The following presents each candidate's CV profile and their vision for the future of the company:

1. *Liliana Restrepo (Co-founder, first generation).* Liliana is an economist who studied at the Universidad Libre de Pereira, Colombia, with a master's in project management from the Universidad San Francisco de Quito, Ecuador. She has trained in ontological coaching, neurolinguistic programming, and organizational and community transformation programs to approach her collaborators with a humanistic approach oriented toward developing conscience. According to Forbes Colombia, she was considered one of the 50 most powerful women in 2022. She states: "Frisby is a sample of conscious capitalism, as it is a company with a superior commitment to society and, above all, full of love, which is reflected in customer service and the well-being of the collaborators." She leads the Frisby Foundation and is a member of the board of directors of Businessowners for Education Risaralda. She also founded Biodanza SRT and is a co-founder of the Instituto Tecnológico de Dosquebradas. As the only first-generation member of the family, she sees herself as the guardian of Frisby's legacy:

   > All we have built with my husband must remain the same. Our values and strategies have functioned well in the past and allowed us to survive. My vision for the Frisby is to keep serving with love. Now, we are preparing to launch an investment plan focused on the modernization and technological updating of physical and digital points and resuming the opening of new stores. Recovering from 2020 will be a process. We adopt the 2019 figures as the budget base for this year, we want to return to that level of profitability, knowing that the uncertainty will continue.

   As a leader, she is risk-averse, highly trustworthy, and genuinely interested in preserving the values of the joint vision she built with her husband.

2. *Álvaro Hoyos Restrepo (board of directors, second generation).* Álvaro is an industrial engineer who studied at the Universidad de los Andes, Colombia with a master's in social media marketing from the Universitat de Barcelona, Spain and a course in blockchain strategy from the University of Oxford, United Kingdom. He has been a member of the board of directors since 1984. Regarding the family business, he claims, "they have always worked for a higher purpose. We do things that connect with a purpose, not for an economic result, but to give back to society and serve others." He founded Innova Social Marketing (ISM) in 2011, and his effective brand creation processes, advertising campaigns, and audiovisual content has positioned the company in the top 10 of marketing firms. Álvaro explains, "ISM was born in Frisby's headquarters. where my father's work always inspired me." He sees the company's future. Although he strongly believes in family values, he understands that customers change their preferences and competition is fierce; therefore revenues will fall. In his words:

   > the situation will inevitably lead Frisby to cut some jobs and close stores. Also, we need to start seizing business opportunities far away from the fast food sector. To do that, in the

medium run, we need to initiate some strategic changes to survive, refocus on improving the margin profits, and increasing shareholder value to attract outside-family investors.

As a leader, he is risk-tolerant, highly motivated to drive the business forward, and looking forward to investing in new business opportunities.

3. *Catalina Hoyos Restrepo (second generation).* Catalina is a molecular biologist who studied at the University of California, Berkeley, United States with a master's in filmmaking from the New York Film Academy, United States. She has been a member of the board of directors since 1990. She says, "Frisby was my life university where dad was the one who kept us informed about the latest in food technology. He was the visionary and mom the one that set ideas in motion." In a partnership with her husband in 2007, she founded Wingz, a successful fast-food restaurant. She mentioned the idea to Alfredo and Liliana, who supported the opening of the first restaurant by helping with the recipes, kitchen technology, and initial managerial tasks. After calls from potential buyers for both Frisby and Wingz, she claims, "seeing my parents giving everything into making Frisby, the answer will always be no. We can innovate, and at the same time, we need to preserve the legacy we inherited from our fathers: shared prosperity and serving our customers with love." As a leader, she has a clear direction in which she wants to steer the business, has good listening skills, and is able to change direction according to industry transformations.

As a board member of the company, which CEO will you choose? Will this CEO have the attitude and capability to maintain the legacy and introduce the necessary changes to adjust to the new business environment?

ACKNOWLEDGMENTS

We thank Alejandro García Rios and Mónica Posada Cifuentes, who authorized the use of the information gathered for their project under the guidance of Julio César Zuluaga at Universidad Javeriana, Colombia.

NOTES

1. For Annexes 1–4, see the supplementary material for this chapter: http://dx.doi.org/10.4337/9781802204537
2. We used several information sources to write this case, such as Frisby (2017), newspapers, Frisby's website and management and sustainability reports. All revised sources are publicly available on the internet. Julio Cesar Zuluaga-Jimenez and Beatriz Rodriguez-Satizabal thank Alejandro García Rios and Mónica Posada Cifuentes, who authorized the use of the information gathered for their project (Posada Cifuentes & García Ríos, 2019) under the guidance of Julio César Zuluaga at the Universidad Javeriana, Colombia.

REFERENCES

Bernal Durán, C. (2023, May 5). Liliana Restrepo: la mujer que llevó a Frisby a ser una de las mayores cadenas de restaurantes del país. Forbes. https://forbes.co/2023/05/05/forbes-women/liliana-restrepo-la-mujer-que-llevo-a-frisby-a-ser-una-de-las-mayores-cadenas-de-restaurantes-del-pais

El Diario (2020, December 13). Sensibles palabras para el señor Alfredo Hoyos, cofundador de Frisby. www.eldiario.com.co/temas/salud/sensibles-palabras-para-el-senor-alfredo-hoyos-cofundador-de-frisby/

Frisby (2017). *Una historia de amor llamada Frisby*, eds. L. Aguirre, P. Parra, & L. F. Arango. Panamericana.

Frisby (n.d.). Compañía: Nuestra historia. https://frisby.com.co/compania

Fundación Frisby (n.d.). Fundación Frisby. www.fundacionfrisby.com/

Goula (2022, July 29). Los colombianos están locos por el pollo y estas son las razones. https://goula.lat/los-colombianos-estan-locos-por-el-pollo-y-estas-son-las-razones/

La Republica (2017, June 6). A sus 40 años, Frisby planea la venta de congelados en almacenes de cadena. www.larepublica.co/empresas/a-sus-40-anos-frisby-planea-la-venta-de-congelados-en-almacenes-de-cadena-2518051

La Republica (2023, October 17). El plan de expansión de Frisby planea aperturas en el exterior a partir del próximo año. www.larepublica.co/empresas/entrevista-con-liliana-restrepo-presidente-de-frisby-sobre-el-plan-de-expansion-dentro-y-fuera-de-colombia-3728076

Portafolio (2020, December 14). Falleció Alfredo Hoyos Mazuera, fundador de Frisby. www.portafolio.co/negocios/empresas/fallecio-alfredo-hoyos-mazuera-fundador-de-frisby-547494

Portafolio (2021, April 1). Hijo de fundador de Frisby crea agencia de innovación. www.portafolio.co/innovacion/hijo-de-fundador-de-frisby-crea-agencia-de-550737

Posada Cifuentes, M. C., & García Ríos, A. (2019). *Alimentando con amor. La sucesión generacional y la gestión de la cultura organizacional en Frisby*. Pontificia Universidad Javeriana.

Pulzo (2022, November 4). Pollo de KFC, Frisby y más empresas será caro por impuesto de reforma tributaria. www.pulzo.com/economia/pollo-kfc-frisby-empresas-sera-caro-por-impuesto-reforma-tributaria-PP2180298

Semana (2021, February 27). "El pilar fundamental para enfrentar la crisis fue la comunicación": gerente general de Frisby. www.semana.com/economia/management/articulo/el-pilar-fundamental-para-enfrentar-la-crisis-fue-la-comunicacion-gerente-general-de-frisby/202121/

Semana (2022, July 1). Prosperidad compartida: el motor de Frisby para crecer. www.semana.com/100-empresas/articulo/prosperidad-compartida-el-motor-de-frisby-para-crecer/202200/

17

Sustainable talent development at Gray Global: deployment of corporate entrepreneurship for developing employee well-being in China

Susanna Chui, Kenneth K. Kwong, and Mary Suen

1. INTRODUCTION

Inspired by the enfolding harbour view of Hong Kong on a hot July day in 2022, Mary Chin, the human resources (HR) director of the southern region at Gray China, a subsidiary of Gray Global, was drafting, for the board, a pivoting and sustainable talent management proposal that could empower employees and ensure sustainable human capital development for the firm.[1]

As the HR director, Mary was given a mandate to construct a sustainable talent strategy at the upcoming autumn strategic retreat. The strategy should be launched in the first quarter of the following year. The fifth wave of COVID-19 had arrived in Hong Kong in February 2022. Its influence on talent well-being and retention had been widely felt and discussed. Mary understood that there was an urgency in creating a long-range talent management plan that placed a mental health policy at its core. One of its aims was to remove stigmatization associated with mental health amongst employees whose health and safety had been immensely impacted by the pandemic outbreak and the subsequent 'long COVID' effects.

What Mary also faced, as an added challenge, was the general misperceptions of mental illness in the China region. There was a strong perceived disapproval towards mental disorders that disincentivized individuals who had mental health issues from seeking treatment or peer support. In view of this cultural stigma, Mary realized that the social isolation brought by COVID-19 could deepen the potential adverse health effects associated with telework, warned by World Health Organization (WHO) studies over the last few years. With her entrepreneurial acumen, together with her compassion for mental health issues, Mary believed that exploring a more innovative approach to boosting employee wellness within Gray China in the future was the best way forward. Yet, she remained undecided in crystallizing a concrete recommendation for the board, which was due in two months' time.

2.   GRAY GLOBAL

Gray was a global professional service provider of audit and assurance, consulting, financial advisory, risk advisory, tax, big data analytics, and related services founded in the United Kingdom (UK) (see Figure 17.1). The firm was operating with over 68,600 employees, having nearly 36,000 professionals operating in over 35 countries in 2022, reaching clients in both the Global North and South. The regional operation was directed independently by a regional board. Professional consultancy organizations, which were knowledge-based firms, drew on specialized talent expertise as the core value creation and service delivery. The 'people connection' culture at Gray emphasized the components of leadership support and employee engagement at the heart of talent management.

Figure 17.1   Gray Global's service portfolio

3.   GRAY CHINA

Gray China boasted successes of its professional services and consultancy, which hinged strongly on its leadership and strong networks in China. The size of Gray China's workforce in 2021 was over 8,500. Out of its 8,500 professionals offering professional services, over 80 per cent served in Mainland China. The gender ratio of the professionals was 35 per cent male and 65 per cent female. The organization was proud of the diversity of HR policy they had pursued. Gray China had senior executives serving as National People's Congress deputies. Therefore, the organization was well positioned to serve over 10 provinces and municipalities, covering well over one-third of provincial-level administrative regions. Gray Global was a direct competitor of the Big Four accounting and professional firms, including KPMG International, Deloitte, PricewaterhouseCoopers International (PwC), and E&Y Global. Embraced by the Gray China leadership were the governing values of innovation, inclusion, well-being, integrity, and passion that had shaped the professional practice and culture.

Living out these values, Gray China endeavoured to sustain the efforts in building talent diversity and inclusion that underlay the 'people connection' corporate culture. According to the 2021 Gray China Annual Report, China's operation at Gray had been promoting women's leadership. The firm employed a balanced 4:6 ratio between male and female staff at levels below manager and as managers. The male and female ratio in the leadership team was 7:3. Its women leadership culture encompassed the Gray China governing board, China management team, Business Exco, and Region Exco. Gray China had been committed to leading diversity and inclusion in China, being ranked 110th in the Global Gender Gap Report 2020 published by the World Economic Forum.

To enrich employees' work lives and promote staff cohesion, Mary had created an internal employee network that fostered knowledge exchange and social connection in 2015 called the Staff Engagement Network (SEN). She had successfully organized knowledge interest groups and mobilized staff participation in community-building initiatives aligned with corporate social responsibility goals. To empower staff to embrace the extra role of managing the SEN autonomously, funding and venue support were offered. Therefore, the culture of community support had started to brew. While Gray had strived to build a supporting and empowering culture, its global operation had never lost sight of the rising challenge of mental health, which was most prevalently found in the younger generations, especially the Gen Zers. Since Gray recruited new graduates every year, in the China operation in 2022 35 per cent of the staff were new recruits. Being a strong advocate of building a helping culture in Gray, Mary boasted the firm was a responsible corporate citizen. On behalf of Gray China, Mary received an award a year previously that ranked Gray as one of the top 10 employers in China. Therefore, Mary had always identified with the Gray China values and leadership practices.

Mary started to serve at Gray China in 2005, at a time when the business growth of the firm was most rapid. Her strong identification with the firm's values aligned with her passion for facilitating the firm's growth in China. Nevertheless, she was also clearly aware of Gray's ferocious competition against the Big Four. Hence, Gray China, in her view, should prudently invest sufficient resources in preventing global challenges in undermining talent retention of the firm. She was aware that there was a strong expectation to uphold the exemplary employer brand of Gray. More importantly, she also found that employee well-being had been affected by the disruption of COVID-19. While Gray China had taken a proactive approach in protecting employees against COVID-19, the global trends of the 'new normal' work mode, 'quiet quitting', and the encroaching mental health issues had troubled Mary's consciousness. As a HR professional, she knew that there was an urgency to usher in an innovative measure to tackle emerging workplace challenges.

Reflecting on her days when she was studying corporate entrepreneurship for her masters, Mary recalled how HR management could be the turnkey function in promoting corporate entrepreneurship. Hence, subordinates could be empowered to develop new business or operational solutions. She still recalled case studies of 3M's 'Made to Stick' and Apple's 'Swipe to Unlock' as examples of bottom-up creative ideas that emerged from general employees. She also remembered how she was inspired by the call for collaborative efforts in solving systemic issues when studying social entrepreneurship. The spirit of co-creation with stakeholders both inside and outside a firm had always fascinated her. One of the examples she could still remember was the Grameen Danone yoghurt collaboration, a social–business co-creation that addressed the malnutrition of affected children.

Sitting back and considering a mental healthcare policy, Mary gradually saw that it might not be an internal HR matter that she had to address. She began to rethink mental healthcare as a systemic issue every employer was confronted with. Her natural instinct pushed her to commence in-depth research on the world's mental health issues and also how other professional competitors were handling this systemic problem. She was aware that one of Gray Global's competitors, Deloitte, had spent significant efforts in addressing the mental health stigma with a long-range planning perspective.

4.   WHY DOES EMPLOYEES' MENTAL HEALTH MATTER TO EMPLOYERS?

According to WHO statistics published in 2019 (Kestel, 2019), the productivity reduction caused by depression and anxiety, two of the most common mental disorders, was estimated to cost the global economy USD1 trillion each year. The combined factors of poor communication, inefficient management practices, limited participation in decision-making, long or inflexible working hours, and lack of team cohesion impacted employee mental health. The COVID-19 pandemic had further deteriorated workplace mental health amongst employees.

While COVID-19 pervaded, workplace environments were forced to evolve with advancing communication technology. Engaging employees in work processes through technology and telework became prevalent. However, 'leaveism', the growing tendency of individuals to be unable to 'switch off' from work, was also a rising phenomenon within the technology-enabled workplace culture. Together with increasing presenteeism, which means employees attending work whilst ill and not performing at full capacity, employee burnout had presented a worsening workplace well-being in the latest technology age.

According to a 2019 report published by the City Mental Health Alliance in Hong Kong (2019), the related costs directly and indirectly attributed by mental health illnesses were evidenced. The costs of absenteeism (HKD45–180 billion/USD5.7–23 billion); presenteeism (HKD4.7–10.0 billion/USD0.6–1.3 billion); turnover (HKD0.7–2.2 billion/USD0.09–0.3 billion); and employee assistance program (HKD130 million/USD16.7 million) in the professional service industry had presented a concern (see Figure 17.2). The report stated that there was a price in ignoring employee mental health, particularly related to professional service employees, and there were advantages in considering the prevention of employee mental hazards as a form of return on investment (ROI).

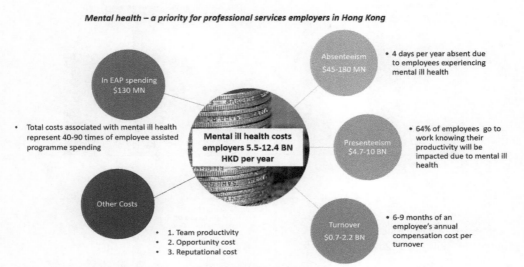

Mental health – a priority for professional services employers in Hong Kong

Mental ill health costs employers 5.5-12.4 BN HKD per year

In EAP spending $130 MN
- Total costs associated with mental ill health represent 40-90 times of employee assisted programme spending

Absenteeism $45-180 MN
- 4 days per year absent due to employees experiencing mental ill health

Presenteeism $4.7-10 BN
- 64% of employees go to work knowing their productivity will be impacted due to mental ill health

Turnover $0.7-2.2 BN
- 6-9 months of an employee's annual compensation cost per turnover

Other Costs
- 1. Team productivity
- 2. Opportunity cost
- 3. Reputational cost

Source: Adapted from City Mental Health Alliance (2019).

Figure 17.2   Costs of poor mental health in the Hong Kong landscape

In the UK, a Deloitte report (Deloitte, 2022a) showed that the annual costs of absenteeism, presenteeism, and labour turnover had increased by 25 per cent since 2019, reaching an estimated annual total of USD66–70 billion in 2020–2021 (see Figure 17.3). This cost range did not include additional costs from sickness absence and staff turnover. In general, burnout among employees, evidenced by exhaustion, mental distance from the job, and reduced job performance, had been more evident during the pandemic. More than one-third of UK working adults (36 per cent) said that in the past year (2020–2021) they had had to resort to some tools and resources to help them manage their mental well-being. Workplace mental well-being has become a strong business case of investment for employers. Similar statistics in China were not available, however, according to the latest WHO information shared on their website in 2022, 54 million people in China suffered from depression and 41 million suffered from anxiety disorders.

Furthermore, employee mental health could be considered a 'new cornerstone for ESG [environmental, social, governance] reporting', according to both the City Mental Health Alliance (Jowitt, 2022) and Deloitte (2022b). In a Deloitte report, it was stated that employee well-being, including mental well-being, would become an important reporting focus of the changing regulatory environment. In reality, it was already a legal obligation of United States (US) and UK employers to safeguard the psychological health of employees. This was enforced by the US Occupational Safety and Health Administration[2] and the UK's Health and Safety at Work etc. Act (1974). Mary was strongly aware that protecting employees from psychological hazards had legal, moral, and governance implications that any responsible employer had to manage with a sustainable and long-term policy.

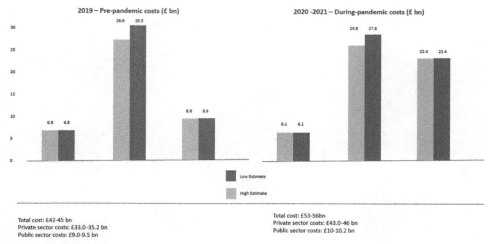

Total cost: £42-45 bn
Private sector costs: £33.0-35.2 bn
Public sector costs: £9.0-9.5 bn

Total cost: £53-56bn
Private sector costs: £43.0-46 bn
Public sector costs: £10-10.2 bn

Source: Deloitte (2022a).

Figure 17.3   Annual cost of poor mental health in the UK

5.   URGENT INVESTMENT AND EARLY SUCCESSES IN ADDRESSING A SYSTEMIC ISSUE

COVID-19 accelerated the emergence of mental health issues. Pandemic-related challenges that people faced included virus-related illnesses, financial concerns, and social isolation. Parents who worked from home faced increased stress and pressure during COVID-19 because they had to tackle the double demands of work while looking after their children within the same compact space in urban city homes. Moreover, other employees faced a plethora of challenges that posed a threat to their physical and mental well-being. Workers in jobs that required constant interaction with the public and high-density work environments were worried about exposing themselves to high risks of getting the virus. They were constantly under stress and suffering from anxiety. The concern was more serious for employees with chronic diseases.

Moreover, COVID-19 hastened the importance and urgency of introducing workplace mental health interventions to employers. A Deloitte report published in 2020 stated that workplace mental health interventions' ROI recorded positive results. It was found that the ROI range could be between 0.4:1 and 10.8:1, with an average ROI of 5.2:1. The study further examined the relationships between the type of interventions and the rate of returns.

Three categories of interventions were examined according to the Deloitte report. They involved the orientation of intervention, intervention types, and the size of the recipient groups. Organization-wide culture/awareness raising obtained the highest average ROI at 6:1 compared to proactive mental health support at 5:1 and reactive mental health support at 3:1. In terms of the types of interventions that employers found most yielding was screening individuals to provide personalized and early-stage support to prevent their mental condition from spiralling. As for beneficiary sizes, the highest average ROI could be obtained from group interventions, particularly for high-risk individuals, compared to individual and universal support.

Therefore, employers who treated mental health support as an investment and allowed employees to obtain early-stage treatment or awareness as prevention could reap high returns by saving costs on attrition and high turnover. Moreover, this investment could become a long-term talent management strategy for building a resilient workforce withstanding future uncertainties and grand challenges that could catch employers off guard. Nevertheless, different organizational cultures could foster just as much as fail to recognize the importance of mental health support.

6.   WHAT ARE THE BIG FOUR DOING TO SUPPORT MENTAL HEALTH IN THE WORKPLACE?

The Big Four started to develop strategies that supported the mental health of professionals long before COVID-19. In May 2018, Accountancy Age, the accountancy profession's leading source of news and analysis, which is part of the Association of Certified Chartered Accountants, reported that the Big Four were at different stages in making mental health issues stigma-free (Scoulding, 2018). The Big Four could serve as role models in employee care. This could put second-tier professional firms under pressure if they wanted to attract talent into their practices.

Both KPMG and Deloitte received a silver ranking in 2018 in the Mind Workplace Wellbeing Index, a benchmark of best practices and policies in the UK (Mind, 2018). Other than providing mental health initiatives, KPMG also offered training to managers to equip them to support professionals better individually and at a team level. Deloitte placed emphasis on conversations and talking about mental health. Deloitte's 'This Is Me' campaign allowed employees to share their own stories speaking about their mental health experience, which encouraged disclosure. E&Y Global professionals received training as 'Mental Health First Aiders' to identify and help employees who were mentally and physically struggling. PwC worked on raising awareness of mental health within the firm. PwC also developed a mental health app that employees could download on mobile devices. They worked closely with the Samaritans and the Lord Mayors Appeal team to pilot and develop mental health and listening skills.

Mary was interested in discovering how 'top-down' leadership and employee-driven initiatives could work together to create a supportive workplace. From her own desktop research, she found that Deloitte US and Deloitte UK set up coherent policies to create a future of work with both top-down and bottom-up approaches.

Deloitte's global chief executive officer, Punit Renjen, stated in a Forbes article on 7 October 2021 that it was important to achieve a future of work that embraced diversity, inclusion, and gender balance advancement (Renjen & Deloitte, 2021). Renjen was one of the world leaders that participated in the panel on mental health in the workplace during Davos Agenda Week 2021. Renjen had consistently advocated for creating a well-being culture in workplaces and appointed senior executives as stewards in promoting employee well-being. Jen Fisher was appointed as the first chief well-being officer after working at Deloitte for over 20 years. Kulleni Gebreyes was appointed as the chief health equity officer in June 2021 to lead the Deloitte Health Equity Institute in the US. Jay Bhatt was appointed as executive director of the Deloitte Center for Health Solutions and the Deloitte Health Equity Institute in February 2022. To Mary, Renjen, as the global chief executive officer, clearly set the agenda for Deloitte at the headquarters. She wondered how far top-down leadership was sufficient.

Deloitte UK's awareness of their employees' mental health had been put into implementation through a few initiatives. To balance life and work, four mechanisms were used:

1. The Deloitte Coffee Club helped employees to connect socially. To check on how Deloitte employees were doing, regular well-being pulse surveys throughout the pandemic, using the results to inform actions by management, were conducted.
2. As an internal support community, mental health champions volunteered from almost 100 employees across the business who were trained to listen and signpost help.
3. The 'My Wellbeing' app put all the well-being resources and initiatives onto an app platform. All employees were given a subscription to the mindfulness app 'Headspace'.
4. Deloitte UK collaborated with non-government organizations, including Mind (the mental health charity for England and Wales), in publishing mental health research and reports since 2019. This partnership not only placed Deloitte UK as a sectoral leader in raising awareness of mental well-being in the UK, but it also showed the commitment of Deloitte UK partners in addressing mental health issues for its employees.

Mary considered it most timely also to review measures for Gray China. Yet, the China context did not perceive mental health patients with sound understanding, hence posing as a rooted inhibitor in solving the systemic issue of stigmatization brought on by mental health.

7.   MENTAL HEALTH IN CHINA FACES ROOTED INHIBITORS: STIGMA AND FAMILY OBLIGATION

Scholarly discussions (Yu et al., 2018; Lancet, 2022; Xu et al., 2022; Huang & Wang, 2023) discussed issues of mental health faced in China. Being mentally ill was perceived as being abnormal by community members. Mental health patients expressed that they felt being perceived as 'incapable', 'crazy', or 'unfit'. When being discovered as mental health patients, opportunities such as employment or marriage could be drastically diminished. With this fear of stigma, patients struggling with depression were not willing to disclose their mental health status and kept it a secret. Moreover, family considered it a stigma and shameful to have family members suffering from mental illness. Patients often felt guilty about burdening family members in looking after them. As a result, they had to hide their mental illness.

Moreover, there was a strong misperception towards mental illness. The spiralling psychological effect drove mental health patients towards negative thinking. Lacking a sense of hope and confidence in recovery, these individuals believed that they had personal flaws and weaknesses because of their mental health issues. Their somatic symptoms, including fatigue and body pain, could affect patients' quality of life. As peer support for mental health patients became difficult to come by, whether it was within the family, one's friends' circle, or the community, mental health patients could suffer for a long time before recovery.

The stigma associated with mental illness in China was not unique. However, coupled with the strong sense of shame and guilt, which could be more prevalent in the Chinese culture, it could make patients lack the motivation to seek formal care and treatment. The collective culture in Asia could become a barrier for the mentally ill to seek informal family support. However, the opportunity to be socially accepted and cared for was crucial for recovery. Peer support was often considered the lifebelt of those suffering from depression and anxiety. However, good peer support systems with semi-trained volunteers were not so well developed in local communities in China. Furthermore, mental health resources and the professional workforce faced a serious undersupply situation (Xu et al., 2022).

8. THE FUTURE OF MENTAL HEALTHCARE: EMERGING DIGITAL AND ARTIFICIAL INTELLIGENCE-ASSISTED MENTAL HEALTHCARE SOLUTIONS AS ENABLERS

As early as 2000, WHO predicted that mental health issues would impact the world pervasively above cancer. COVID-19 further accelerated this prophecy and amplified the negative impacts of mental health issues. The cost of poor mental health was debilitating for families, employers, and national economies. Knowing that the integration of mental healthcare into management strategies would affect the future of operation efficiency, Mary conducted a quick scan of the latest mental healthcare interventions and related discussions to keep herself abreast of the latest trends.

8.1 WHO's advice for mental health at work

Employers were advised by WHO to improve mental health at work through a series of actions (see Box 17.1). Moreover, WHO advocated that mental health was an investment towards a better life and future for all. Investing in mental health for all advances public health in general. This claim was based on the grounds of reducing personal suffering, stopping human rights violations, enabling social and economic development, and facilitating the growth of communities.

BOX 17.1 WORLD HEALTH ORGANIZATION'S ADVICE FOR MENTAL HEALTH AT WORK

Employers were advised by WHO to improve mental health at work through a series of actions:

- Prevent work-related mental health conditions by preventing risks to mental health at work.

- Prevent work-related mental health conditions.
- Protect and promote mental health at work.
- Support workers with mental health conditions to participate and thrive in work; and create an enabling environment for change.

WHO advocated that mental health was an investment towards a better life and future for all. Investing in mental health for all advances public health in general. This claim encompassed the following grounds:

- Mental health sustainability can reduce personal suffering and improve individual general health, quality of life, functioning, and life expectancy.
- Investing in mental health is needed to stop human rights violations. This is because people with mental health conditions are frequently excluded from community life and denied basic rights.
- Mental health promotion can enable social and economic development. When people are mentally healthy and live in supportive environments, they can learn and work well.
- Collective well-being can benefit the growth of communities. Contrary to this, poor mental health creates a barrier on development with reduced productivity, straining social services.

Source: Adapted from www.who.int/news-room/fact-sheets/detail/mental-health-at -work

8.2   Experiments with digital mental healthcare resources and projects

The UK's National Health Service (NHS) shared a series of digital mental healthcare resources and projects online (see Box 17.2).

BOX 17.2   NHS EXPERIMENTS WITH DIGITAL MENTAL HEALTHCARE RESOURCES AND PROJECTS

- Online platform for virtual working with patients and carers supports self-management and more personalized care.
- Peer support-based e-health system to improve care and recovery.
- An electronic prescribing and medicines administration system in high secure services.
- Maximization of the benefits of mobile working when covering a large geographical area.
- Online consultations in mental health.
- Clinical dashboards and 'at-a-glance' information boards to improve in-patient care.

- Electronic prescribing and medicines administration in mental health in-patient wards.
- Video consultations for mental health services reduce missed appointments and improve user experience.
- Improved access to psychological therapies through online resources.
- A caseload management and supervision tool for community mental health services.
- Co-development of a mobile application with young service users.
- Communication enhancement between primary and secondary care mental health.
- The digital ward – using mobile technology in the in-patient ward environment.

Source: Adapted from NHS England (n.d.).

8.3 Studies examine the use of emerging digital mental healthcare through artificial intelligence-assisted interventions

A plethora of reviews (e.g. Graham et al., 2019; Zidaru et al., 2021) provided overviews of how far using artificial intelligence (AI) technologies in offering digital mental healthcare had presented both ethical concerns and opportunities. The jury was still out in judging the design justice of developing and adopting AI-assisted healthcare and the exploration of patient and public involvement in addressing diverse patient needs. However, there was clear and rapid development in AI-assisted mental healthcare tools, initiatives, and programmes that had been offering promising solutions. Examples of applying digital healthcare interventions in diverse cultural backgrounds, including Syrians (Cuijpers et al., 2022) and Korean students (Park & Kim, 2023), revealed that AI-assisted technologies had been widely deployed in addressing the systemic issues of mental health.

9. HOW SHOULD DIGITAL MENTAL HEALTHCARE BE INTEGRATED INTO A SUSTAINABLE TALENT MANAGEMENT STRATEGY?

In preparation for the Talent Strategy 2023, Mary started to explore emerging online mental health apps that provided resources, counselling, and support for employee well-being. She was reassured that the number of international online resources, together with local non-governmental organizations operators (see Table 17.1), had vastly increased to support the world's call for 'well-being' importance.

Between 2020 and 2022, Gray China has supported employees in China by providing hotline and medical consultations because of the COVID-19 pandemic. To release emotional stress, a 24-hour care programme was offered to employees in 2022, together with counselling hotlines. Moreover, regular webinars and wellness programmes, from stretching, breathing, yoga, and Pilates, are offered online. Yet, more sustainable mental health resources were yet to

Table 17.1   Online mental health resources offered by Hong Kong non-governmental organizations

Service name	Operators	Target beneficiaries
Open Up	Boys' and Girls' Clubs Association of Hong Kong	Youth aged 11–35
	Caritas – Hong Kong	
	Hong Kong Children and Youth Services	
	Hong Kong Federation of Youth Groups	
	St James' Settlement	
	Hong Kong Jockey Club Centre for Suicide Research and Prevention, University of Hong Kong	
	Hong Kong Jockey Club Charities Trust	
Counseline @MHAHK mobile app (Chinese version only)	Mental Health Association of Hong Kong	General population with mood disorder
Nite Cat online (Chinese version only)	Boys' and Girls' Clubs Association	Youths aged 24 or below
uTouch cyber youth outreach service (Chinese version only)	Hong Kong Federation of Youth Groups	Youths
Chatpoint	Samaritan Befrienders Hong Kong	People in need of emotional support and suicide prevention
eSmiley cyber youth support team	Hong Kong Children and Youth Services	Youths
Hong Kong Society of Counseling and Psychology free counselling Hotline information	Hong Kong Society of Counseling and Psychology	Students, parents, and other people who need crisis intervention

Service name	Operators	Target beneficiaries
Teens Online (Chinese version only)	Stewards Tsu Te Kian Charitable Trust	Youths aged 11–25
6PM cyber youth support team	St James' Settlement	Youths and their parents/ significant others

Note: This list was summarized through desktop research. It is not an exhaustive and most updated list.

be systematically offered and would be the key to defining a talent management strategy (see Box 17.3).

BOX 17.3 EVALUATION CRITERIA FOR DEPLOYING ONLINE OR ORGANIZATIONAL MENTAL HEALTH RESOURCES

Therapist credentials:

- price per session;
- weekly and monthly subscription plans;
- registration process;
- insurance options;
- availability of free initial consultations;
- therapist selection options;
- therapist availability;
- types of care available; and
- communication modes.

Source: Author's own elaboration based on monitoring and evaluation of mental health policies and plans, 2007, World Health Organization.

The aim of a new 2023 Talent Strategy was to elevate Gray China to a responsible and purpose-driven practice inspired by the market and through clients' eyes. Mary was under some pressure as she witnessed the accelerating efforts produced by competitors. As Gray China had over 10 per cent of employees of the whole Gray global operation, her strategic talent proposal would not only be a long-range investment proposition but also it would be pivotal to creating a competitive advantage for the firm in the China region. Further embedding 'purpose' in the firm's culture could improve the firm's ability to adapt swiftly. Employee well-being was considered the core of the solution to ensuring the sustainable development of the firm, not only in productivity but also in talent retention.

Mary believed that the healthy and resilient development of employee well-being would be the cornerstone of ensuring a sustainable future for the firm. Hence, if Gray China demonstrated itself as the market leader in steering transformative and sustainable change, it would develop strategic implications for the firm to become a prominent professional practice advising for a well-being economy. This strategic development would not only make Gray China a responsible organization, but it would also create a competitive edge for the firm. Mary only had less than six weeks to submit a strategy plan before the autumn strategic retreat.

How far could the top leadership (including herself) encourage a collaborative and supporting spirit in the name of corporate entrepreneurship along with the support of digital mental healthcare?

ACKNOWLEDGEMENTS

The development of this teaching case is partially supported by the Research Matching Grant Scheme of the University Grants Committee to the Hang Seng University of Hong Kong (project code: 700044).

NOTES

1. This case was based on a real organization and its mandate in removing the stigma of mental health illness. The post-COVID-19 environmental factors were supported by the evidence and analyses of reports with sources clearly provided. Originality was exercised in a few areas including the protagonist's profile (Mary Chin) and the situational deadline confronting the protagonist. The name of Gray Global, the main protagonist, and some details of the case are fictitious.
2. See www.osha.gov/

REFERENCES

City Mental Health Alliance (2019). The cost of mental ill health for employers in Hong Kong: City Mental Health Alliance Hong Kong in collaboration with Oliver Wyman. Retrieved from www.cmhahk.org/docs/research/2019-The-cost-of-mental-ill-health-for-employers-in-Hong-Kong_EN_WEB.pdf

Cuijpers, P., Heim, E., Abi Ramia, J., Burchert, S., Carswell, K., Cornelisz, I. et al. (2022) Effects of a WHO-guided digital health intervention for depression in Syrian refugees in Lebanon: A randomized controlled trial. *PLoS Med*, 19(6): e1004025.

Deloitte (2020). Mental health and employers: Refreshing the case for investment. Retrieved from: www2.deloitte.com/uk/en/pages/consulting/articles/mental-health-and-employers-refreshing-the-case-for-investment.html

Deloitte (2022a, March). Mental health and employers: The case for investment – pandemic and beyond. Retrieved from www2.deloitte.com/content/dam/Deloitte/uk/Documents/consultancy/deloitte-uk-mental-health-report-2022.pdf

Deloitte (2022b). Well-being: A new cornerstone for ESG strategy and reporting. Part I. Retrieved from www2.deloitte.com/content/dam/Deloitte/ca/Documents/human-capital/ca-consulting-human-capital-Eminence_Final_Paper_One_EN_AODA.pdf

Graham, S., Depp, C., Lee, E. E., Nebeker, C., Tu, X., Kim, H. C., & Jeste, D. V. (2019). Artificial intelligence for mental health and mental illnesses: An overview. *Current Psychiatry Reports*, 21, 1–18.

Health and Safety at Work etc Act (1974). Retrieved from www.hse.gov.uk/legislation/hswa.htm

Huang, R., & Wang, X. (2023). Impact of COVID-19 on mental health in China: Analysis based on sentiment knowledge enhanced pre-training and XGBoost algorithm. *Frontiers in Public Health*, 11.

Jowitt, H (2022). Putting the wellbeing of employees into the 'S' of your ESG strategy. City Mental Health Alliance and Mind Forward Alliance. Retrieved from www.cisi.org/cisiweb2/docs/default-source/

cisi-website/putting-the-wellbeing-of-employees-into-the-'s'-of-your-esg-strategy-final.pdf?sfvrsn
=89dd549a_2#:~:text=Our%20hypothesis%20is%20that%20mental,and%20initiatives%20to%20be
%20developed

Kestel, D. (2019). Mental health in the workplace. World Health Organization. Retrieved from www.who
.int/news-room/commentaries/detail/mental-health-in-the-workplace

Lancet, T. (2022). Mental health after China's prolonged lockdowns. *The Lancet*, 399(10342), 2167.

Mind (2018). Workplace Wellbeing Index 2018. Retrieved from www.mind.org.uk/workplace/workplace
-wellbeing-index/

NHS England (n.d.). Mental health digital playbook. Retrieved from https://transform.england.nhs.uk/
key-tools-and-info/digital-playbooks/mental-health-digital-playbook/

Park, D. Y., & Kim, H. (2023). Determinants of intentions to use digital mental healthcare content among
university students, faculty, and staff: Motivation, perceived usefulness, perceived ease of use, and
parasocial interaction with AI chatbot. *Sustainability*, 15(1), 872.

Renjen P., & Deloitte (2021). Creating stigma-free work cultures is key to tackling the mental health
crisis. Retrieved from www.forbes.com/sites/deloitte/2021/10/07/creating-stigma-free-work-cultures
-is-key-to-tackling-the-mental-health-crisis/

Scoulding, L. (2018, 17 May). What are the Big Four doing to support mental health in the workplace? Retrieved from: https://www.accountancyage.com/2018/05/17/what-are-the-big-four-doing-to
-support-mental-health-in-the-workplace/

Xu, Z., Gahr, M., Xiang, Y., Kingdon, D., Rüsch, N., & Wang, G. (2022). The state of mental health care
in China. *Asian Journal of Psychiatry*, 69, 102975.

Yu, S., Kowitt, S. D., Fisher, E. B., & Li, G. (2018). Mental health in China: Stigma, family obligations, and
the potential of peer support. *Community Mental Health Journal*, 54, 757–764.

Zidaru, T., Morrow, E. M., & Stockley, R. (2021). Ensuring patient and public involvement in the
transition to AI-assisted mental health care: A systematic scoping review and agenda for design
justice. *Health Expectations*, 24(4), 1072–1124.

18
Yogome's dramatic fall for alleged fraud

Francisco Sánchez and Alan Mella

1.   INTRODUCTION

On October 5, 2018, a Chilean angel investor was reading the news on an online newspaper. After a few minutes of reading, the angel investor's interest was piqued when he read the headline: "Blow to entrepreneurship: alleged fraud by Yogome" (Medina, 2018). This prompted him to look up the startup online to get an initial understanding of events. After this search, he crafted the following summary of what had happened at Yogome.

Yogome was a Mexican technology startup that designed educational mobile games for children and became a reference in Mexican entrepreneurship after it was founded in 2011 (Pineda, 2018). However, its co-founder, Manolo Diaz, was accused by employees of manipulating revenue reports delivered to investors. The allegations of fraud surfaced on September 18, 2018, when one of Yogome's employees provided an investor with a report based on financial data that did not match those they had previously received from the company (Meza, 2018). After this situation was disclosed, Yogome collapsed and shut down its operations (Giraldo, 2018).

The day before, the angel investor was analyzing a proposal to invest in a promising Mexican startup that offered English courses for children on mobile devices and whose founders were inspired by the success of Yogome. He wanted to invest in this startup and thus help finance the company's growth, but he grew wary when he found out about Yogome's alleged fraud. He started to wonder if the Mexican startup founders had also manipulated the financial data in the proposal to obtain funding. In particular, he had the following questions: What factors cause startup founders to manipulate financial data? How can fraud be detected? And how can we prevent fraudulent practices? He conducted further research on this case to address some of his concerns.[1]

2.   YOGOME AND THE EDTECH MARKET

The angel investor was intrigued and quickly searched for more information about Yogome. First, he inquired into Yogome's origins, founders, and business.

2.1   What was Yogome?

Yogome was founded in 2011 by Manolo Diaz and his friend Alberto Colin, both of whom were originally from San Luis Potosí (Liendo, 2017). The Mexican tech startup sought to develop educational games on mobile devices for children between the ages of 4 and 11. Through these games, users could learn about different subjects, including mathematics, science, geography, programming, languages, health, creativity, and sustainability. Yogome also produced educational apps, books, and videos (Giraldo, 2018), whose pedagogical qualities were validated by Yale University through its play2PREVENT program (Medina, 2018).

2.2   The educational applications market

Yogome's products belonged to the educational technology (EdTech) market. From a practical perspective, EdTech companies used applications (apps) and other types of technological tools (e.g., virtual reality, robotics, online courses, and artificial intelligence) to enhance learning (Galiana, 2021).

The global EdTech market grew sharply between 2010 and 2018, as reflected by the funds raised by startups in this sector. In 2018, China accounted for more than 50 percent of the funding and the United States accounted for approximately 20 percent, followed by India, Europe, and the rest of the world (see Figure 18.1).

Additionally, this market had high growth expectations. Venture capital investment in EdTech was projected to triple over the next decade. In particular, over US$87 million of funding was expected in this sector until 2030 (Holon IQ, 2020). The high growth expectations for this market were mainly based on six key trends:

1. Education spending would grow to US$10 trillion by 2030 (see Figure 18.2).
2. By 2025, there would be more than 500 million students. Therefore, new models and technologies would be needed to ensure scalability, educational quality, and innovation.
3. As of January 2019, digitization in education was rare, with less than 3 percent of budgets being spent on technology. Considering the scale of what was to come, this would represent a significant challenge going forward. However, given the expected growth in student numbers, this would likely need to increase.
4. Technology would be integrated into delivery and learning processes. Applications in education and learning would begin to bear fruit by 2025, when virtual reality/augmented reality and artificial intelligence become increasingly integrated into essential teaching and learning processes (see Figure 18.3).
5. In 2025, there would be more than 100 EdTech companies valued at over US$1 billion, while in 2015, there were only ten.

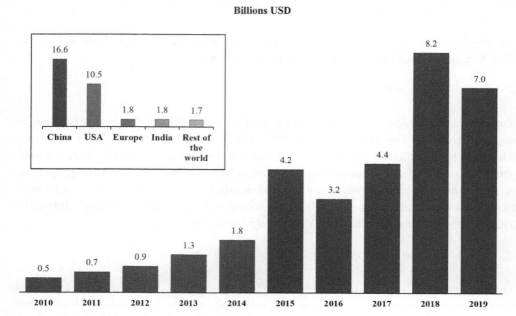

Source: Adapted from Holon IQ (2020).

Figure 18.1   EdTech startup funding around the world

6. Emerging markets in Africa, Latin America, and Southeast Asia were growing rapidly and had large, underserved populations. As a result, these regions were looking to move beyond traditional education systems to reduce costs and to improve access and outcomes by supporting students, teachers, and administrators with advanced technologies (Holon IQ, 2020).

In light of these findings, the angel investor thought that this was an especially attractive sector. Here was a business opportunity! As such, the angel investor began the second stage of his research. In this stage, he looked for information about Yogome's funding sources. These funds are another critical factor in a startup's success. First, however, he wanted to find out how Yogome's founders discovered this business opportunity.

2.3   The beginnings of the Mexican startup

The business opportunity was born when Manolo and Alberto created an educational mathematics video game to strengthen students' learning in an elementary school in San Luis Potosí in 2010 (Liendo, 2017; Medina, 2018). Manolo Diaz explained: "They loved the idea; we launched it with that school, and the parents were super excited" (Liendo, 2017). Nevertheless, Manolo and Alberto soon realized that their target audience entailed a long and tedious sales process. So, they decided that their next project would be aimed directly at

USD Trillions

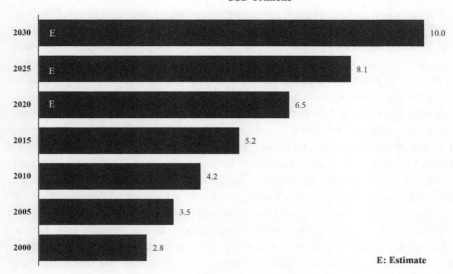

Source: Adapted from Holon IQ (2020).

Figure 18.2 Global expenditure on education and training

USD Billions

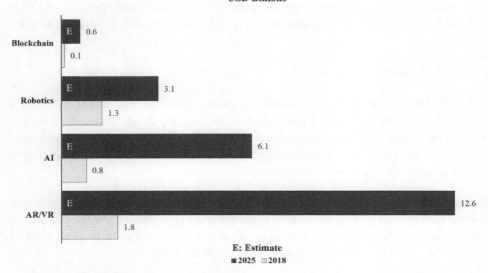

Source: Adapted from Holon IQ (2020).

Figure 18.3 Global expenditure on advanced technology for education

parents (Franceschin, 2016) and they created their first educational game demo. This marked the beginning of Yogome (Gómez, 2012).

In 2011, once their first demo was ready, they traveled to Silicon Valley in search of investment but failed to gain traction. Manolo Diaz said: "We went to Silicon Valley for the first time in 2011 … We invested the money we had in a demo, but when we presented it in the Ministry of Economy's office there, we received negative feedback. They were looking for bigger things" (Medina, 2017). After this disappointing trip, the entrepreneurs returned to Mexico to improve their products. Later, in their native country, they met Santiago Zavala, co-founder, and partner of an investment fund for entrepreneurs called Mexican.VC. Mexican.VC invested US$30,000 in Yogome, the startup's first investment (Giraldo, 2018). However, Manolo and Alberto felt that they needed greater access to funding, contacts, and mentoring from international experts to move their project forward. Manolo indicated: "We didn't have many downloads from the app stores, but we started to meet people from the competition, from the group of people who were creating quality games, and it was just a matter of connecting with someone important to access more money, incubators and investors" (Sánchez, 2013a).

Zavala recommended a venture into mobile applications and so Manolo and Alberto created an app and improved market possibilities and access to their content (Giraldo, 2018). Then, in 2012, they returned to Silicon Valley and things went differently. On this second trip to San Francisco, Yogome caught the attention of 500 Startups, a Silicon Valley seed capital investment fund, whose entity invested US$100,000 (Medina, 2017). Yogome became one of the first Mexican startups to enter 500 Startups' acceleration program, which proved vital for contacting mentors and other entrepreneurs across the Silicon Valley innovation ecosystem (Giraldo, 2018). Thus, Yogome began operations in the United States and Mexico with a team of 14 professionals and planned to make ten games available by the end of the year (Sánchez, 2013b).

2.4   Investment rounds

In 2013, the Endeavor accelerator recognized Yogome as one of the most promising startups in terms of job creation and wealth generation (El Empresario, 2013). Later, the company received its first significant investment in a round of US$750,000 from John McIntire and Juan Salaverria, both members of the OpenEnglish board of directors, thus consolidating its reputation as an up-and-coming company. For Manolo Diaz:

> The investment round had several objectives: to create 40 educational games, of which 60% devoted to mathematics, which is what parents are looking for. Somehow, they regard the iPad and these mobile technologies as an excellent way to strengthen knowledge. And we want to reach 10 million downloads next year. (Sánchez, 2013b)

According to company data, by the end of 2013, the application already had 600,000 downloads, leading to a total of 1.1 million hours of game play (Giraldo, 2018). At this point, Yogome was defined as a company that developed educational games compatible with mobile devices such as tablets and smartphones for children between the ages of six and ten. These games were created in different languages by pedagogy experts, a requirement that had helped place Yogome among the Apple Store's top ten apps (El Empresario, 2013).

At that point, Manolo Diaz had ambitious expansion plans. He commented: "We want to maintain the impact we have to reach more children. Our vision is to connect all the children in Mexico, China, and the United States, so that they can challenge each other" (Sánchez, 2013b).

In line with its success, in 2016, Yogome raised US$3 million in seed capital from Variv Capital, Topaz Capital, and 500 Startups (Giraldo, 2018). Everything pointed to the fact that the company was growing and doing brilliantly, or at least that is what Manolo declared to TechCrunch. He explained that although the educational games market was saturated, Yogome was successful because it focused on presenting children with a compelling story in which their knowledge was the key to saving the world. In the same interview, Manolo noted that 95 percent of the app's subscribers were based in the United States, Latin America, and Southeast Asia, and that it had expanded into more than 50 countries (O'Hear, 2017).

2.4.1 Series A and Series B

In May 2017, a Series A investment round was announced, and US$6.6 million was raised. The most prominent investors were Venture Capital, Seaya Ventures, Variv Capital, and Endeavor Catalyst (Giraldo, 2018). After the success of this investment round, Manolo Diaz was praised by the investors who trusted Yogome, mainly by Michael Kleindl, co-founder and managing partner of Seaya Ventures, who said:

> Manolo Diaz and his team have built a superb platform for kids' edutainment. As a result, Yogome has positioned itself as a global leader in this fast-growing market worldwide. We are extremely happy to have the opportunity to join Manolo and Yogome on this great challenge and look forward to supporting the company with our operational expertise in fast-growing, internationally expanding businesses. (LAVCA, 2017)

In June 2017, Yogome was a platform that stood out for its more than 500 mini-games, among which Epic Heroes of Knowledge was the most popular. This game could be downloaded for free from the app stores and came with 25 credits, or the equivalent of two hours of gameplay. A monthly or annual subscription granted unlimited access to the games (Cahun, 2017). Furthermore, in September of the same year, Manolo Diaz mentioned in an interview: "Yogome was working to bring its products to important markets in Asia, such as China, Japan, and Korea. The product was ready for the Chinese market, but the channels it used to acquire users did not yet exist there. We are specifically working on that" (LAVCA, 2017).

On March 7, 2018, Mexican.VC sold 25 percent of its stake in the company to Insight Venture Partners. For the fund's investors, this generated a return of more than 30,000 percent on their investment. Regarding the sale, Zavala pointed out: "This is historic because it is the first fund in Mexico to have generated returns for its investors, and the return has been extraordinary" (Pulsosocial, 2018). In addition, following this event, Diaz and Colin announced the launch of their own Mexico City-based investment fund to support entrepreneurs like themselves. The fund's name was Super Early Stage (Pulsosocial, 2018). This reflected the success that both entrepreneurs had achieved so far.

On March 12, 2018, Yogome announced its Series B investment round, in which it raised US$26.9 million. It was led by Exceed Capital Partners and also involved Seaya Ventures, Variv Capital, and Insight Venture Partners. These funds were earmarked for boosting the company's expansion into the Asian market. The plan was to establish a work team in China and to take the products to Japan, Korea, and the Philippines, while maintaining production in the United States and Mexico (Giraldo, 2018). Following the success of this investment round, Manolo Diaz said:

> It has always been our mission to create a better future for all children no matter what country they live in, and we know that making learning fun is a crucial piece of that puzzle. Exceed Capital also believes in that vision and shares our desire to expand globally and innovate at the forefront of educational technology. We are honored to be Exceed Capital's first investment, and working with Victor Hu and his team will be a phenomenal opportunity. (Martin, 2018)

Victor Hu, chief executive officer and co-founder of Exceed Capital, who was about to join Yogome's board of directors, said:

> Yogome's innovative educational games have already given millions of children an exciting start to their learning journey, and we are thrilled to join Manolo and his team in their mission to create the most powerful and engaging learning platform for children everywhere. Yogome's aspiration to empower learners and families aligns deeply with where we believe the global education sector is heading. We look forward to supporting them in their growth going forward. (LAVCA, 2018)

At this point, Yogome was considered the Netflix of children's learning, with more than 2,000 games, interactive books, and videos in six languages (English, Portuguese, Chinese, Spanish, Japanese, and Korean) on math, science, and emotional learning (Martin, 2018). The company reported more than 6 million active users monthly across 50 countries, mainly in the United States, Latin America, and Southeast Asia (Giraldo, 2018). As for Manolo Diaz and Alberto Colin, they were rockstars at entrepreneurship events; they won contests and Yogome was portrayed as a success story in industry magazines (Anderson, 2018).

The angel investor thought that the success Yogome achieved in 2018 did not suggest that anything was wrong with the Mexican startup. However, Yogome ceased operations at the beginning of the fourth quarter of that year. Therefore, he continued the search for information about the closure of the Mexican startup to find answers to his central question: What critical elements did investors not detect in Yogome's operation?

3.   THE BEGINNING OF THE END

Yogome's success ended on September 18, 2018, at a party held after a board meeting at its office. At the party, a company employee showed an investor revenue data they had not seen before (Meza, 2018). Specifically, the revenue figures shown by the employee were lower than those the company had officially shared with its investors, thus unleashing an investigation into alleged fraud from the end of 2016 (Pineda, 2018).

After this became known, Yogome investors decided to shut down the startup on October 4, 2018 (Adriano, 2018). Mariana Garcia, who served as the company's strategic partnership manager, announced the technology startup's closure without giving further details. However, a video leaked to Forbes showed one of the directors pointing out that the previous management had compromised the company's finances due to possible fraud and that the decision had been made to terminate the company for this reason (Medina, 2018). This video supported several Yogome employees' accounts that the company had allegedly closed due to embezzlement by Manolo Diaz (Adriano, 2018).

Manolo Diaz had allegedly concealed the embezzlement by manipulating the financial data he presented to investors, mainly by doctoring the downloads and revenue data (Pineda, 2018). In particular, a former Yogome employee said: "There were odd metrics. Manolo believed if he needed to reach a number of users to raise his next round of investment, he would buy them. He would talk up the company" (El CEO, 2018).

According to this former employee, Manolo was the one who manipulated the information. In the statements compiled by Expansión, a media outlet, Manolo Diaz took care not to disclose Yogome's financial data and made decisions without consulting his partner or his management team. Moreover, he allowed no one from the company to have contact with investors, thus, completely controlling the information that was disclosed to them. Therefore, Manolo built an entire system to mask the information provided by online stores such as the Apple Store about downloads and revenues. Similarly, other former Yogome employees revealed to online media outlets that the way financial data were manipulated was very sophisticated. It was on such a scale that no investor could have suspected it unless due diligence was performed for a merger of important companies (Pineda, 2018).

After announcing the closure of Yogome, other former company employees began to tell their stories on social networks, noting that manipulating figures was common practice at Yogome. For example, Jonatan Santos, a software engineer, tweeted: "We knew something was wrong. It just was not normal to receive so much money despite the fact the company was not growing. In the 5 years I spent there, Yogome never generated more than US$2,000 a month from its games and apps" (Giraldo, 2018). Along the same lines, Jeduan Cornejo, a web developer and the company's former chief technology officer, tweeted that every time Yogome raised money: "They indicated their market penetration in Mexico, US, and Southeast Asia. I was always surprised by the audacity of announcing the number of users purchased in plain sight, something that was well known" (Giraldo, 2018).

Finding this latest batch of information brought the angel investor's research on Yogome to a close. However, he could not find any information about whether any legal action was taken against Manolo Diaz. This surprised the angel investor, so he turned to Mexico's Federal Criminal Code for details about the definition of fraud in the country (see Box 18.1).

BOX 18.1   FRAUD IN MEXICO

The Mexican legislation applicable to cases of fraud is under Title Twenty-Two (Crimes against Individuals' Estate) of the Federal Criminal Code of Mexico, which states the following in Article 386:

> The crime of fraud is committed by anyone who, through deception or by taking advantage of a misunderstanding, unlawfully takes possession of something or obtains an undue profit. The offense of fraud will be punishable by the following penalties:

I.   With imprisonment of between 3 days and 6 months or of 30 to 180 days fine, when the defrauded amount does not exceed ten times the salary;

II. With imprisonment of between 6 months and 3 years and a fine of 10 to 100 times the salary, when the defrauded amount exceeds 10, but not 500 times the salary.

4.   THINKING ABOUT THE FUTURE

After delving deeper into the Yogome case, the angel investor thought aloud that in the absence of legal action and with only the details from the existing private investigations, it was impossible to assess the scale or sophistication of the deceit. However, if the accusations made by Yogome employees were true, he could infer that the fraudulent practices were widespread and intentional and that they were used to obtain financing and continued investment. Therefore, the angel investor decided to analyze the Mexican entrepreneurs' investment proposal in more detail. Specifically, he wanted to assess whether there were any signs that the financial data presented to him by the founders had been manipulated. Moreover, should he decide to invest in the Mexican startup, he needed to consider what internal oversight measures he could implement to prevent fraudulent practices in the future.

ACKNOWLEDGEMENTS

We thank Juan Pablo Torres and Miguel Cid for their valuable comments that helped develop this case.

NOTE

1.   This case was prepared exclusively based on public sources. The protagonist (the angel investor) of the case is fictional.

REFERENCES

Adriano, J.L. (2018, October 8). El último día de Yogome. El Norte. Retrieved from www.elnorte.com/aplicacioneslibre/articulo/default.aspx?id=1508397&md5=6764632592f4468da6db9d91ac98856e&ta=0dfdbac11765226904c16cb9ad1b2efe

Anderson, B. (2018, October 8). Yogome: del exceso de confianza al exceso de miedo. Milenio. Retrieved from www.milenio.com/opinion/barbara-anderson/nada-personal-solo-negocios/yogome-del-exceso-de-confianza-al-exceso-de-miedo

Cahun, A. (2017, June 5). YogoMe, la startup mexicana que desarrolla videojuegos educativos para niños. Xataca México. Retrieved from www.xataka.com.mx/aplicaciones/YogoMe-la-startup-mexicana-que-desarrolla-videojuegos-educativos-para-ninos

El CEO (2018, October 4). Yogome, la startup que engañó a inversionistas, empleados y usuarios. Retrieved from https://elceo.com/tecnologia/yogome-la-startup-que-engano-a-inversionistas-empleados-y-usuarios/

El Empresario (2013, March 20). Crece red de emprendedores de alto impacto. Retrieved from https://elempresario.mx/actualidad/crece-red-emprendedores-alto-impacto

Franceschin, T. (2016, July 7). Desde Edu4Me México: Manolo Díaz presenta YogoMe. Edu4.me. Retrieved from http://edu4.me/desde-edu4me-mexico-manolo-diaz-presenta-yogome/

Galiana, P. (2021, May 12). Qué es EdTech o Tecnología Educativa y sus beneficios. IEBS Digital School. Retrieved from www.iebschool.com/blog/que-es-edtech-tecnologia/

Giraldo, Y. (2018, October 5). Esta es la historia de Yogome, la startup mexicana que cerró sus puertas por caso de fraude. Pulso Social. Retrieved from https://pulsosocial.com/2018/10/05/startup-YogoMe-cerrara-sus-puertas-por-acusacion-de-fraude-contra-uno-de-sus-fundadores/

Gómez, J. (2012, April 21). La historia de YogoMe, empresa mexicana de juegos educativos en Silicon Valley. Webadictos. Retrieved from https://webadictos.com/YogoMe-silicon-valley/

Holon IQ (2020, January 28). $87bn+ of global EdTech funding predicted through 2030. $32bn last decade. Retrieved from www.holoniq.com/notes/87bn-of-global-edtech-funding-predicted-to-2030/

LAVCA (2017, September 19). Mexican EdTech startup Yogome targets Asia with series A (en español). Retrieved from https://lavca.org/2017/09/19/series-edtech-startup-yogome-sights-set-asia-en-espanol/

LAVCA (2018, March 12). Exceed Capital partners leads series B in Yogome. Retrieved from https://lavca.org/2018/03/12/exceed-capital-partners-leads-series-b-investment-in-yogome/

Liendo, O. (2017, August 6). Los videojuegos educativos de este mexicano van a la conquista de China. Univisión. Retrieved from www.univision.com/noticias/hispanos/los-videojuegos-educativos-de-este-mexicano-van-a-la-conquista-de-china

Martin, J. (2018, March 13). La startup mexicana Yogome levanta US$26.9 M para seguir conquistando el mundo. Pulsosocial. Retrieved from https://pulsosocial.com/2018/03/13/startup-mexicana-yogome-levanta-us26-9-m-seguir-conquistando-mundo/

Medina, A. (2017, July 20). Yogome: Juegos de clase mundial desde San Luis Potosí. Forbes México. Retrieved from www.forbes.com.mx/yogome-juegos-de-clase-mundial-desde-san-luis-potosi/

Medina, A. (2018, October 5). Golpe en el emprendimiento: presunto fraude en Yogome. Forbes México. Retrieved from www.forbes.com.mx/exclIlusiva-golpe-en-el-emprendimiento-fraude-en-YogoMe/

Meza, E. (2018, October 8). El fraude que llevó a Yogome a cerrar sus puertas. El Empresario. Retrieved from https://elempresario.mx/emprendedores/fraude-que-llevo-yogome-cerrar-sus-puertas

O'Hear, S. (2017, May 31). YogoMe, a Mexican startup that makes educational games for kids, raises $6.6m. TechCrunch. Retrieved from https://techcrunch.com/2017/05/31/YogoMe/

Pineda, A. (2018, October 5). Así se gestó el presunto fraude en la start-up YogoMe. Expansion. Retrieved from https://expansion.mx/emprendedores/2018/10/05/asi-se-gesto-el-presunto-fraude-en-la-start-up-yogome?utm_source=Hoy&utm_campaign=1e100f7fd8-EMAIL_CAMPAIGN_2018_10_05_01_16&utm_medium=email&utm_term=0_35f350be4e-1e100f7fd8-118635653

Pulsosocial (2018, March 15). Mexican.VC regresa más de 8x a sus inversionistas y abre una nueva era del emprendimiento mexicano. Retrieved from https://pulsosocial.com/2018/03/15/mexican-vc-regresa-mas-8x-inversionistas-abre-nueva-era-emprendimiento-mexicano/

Sánchez, J. (2013a). Las nuevas startups: Renovación de tecnología, creatividad y riesgo. Magis, N° 435. Retrieved from https://magis.iteso.mx/nota/las-nuevas-startups-mexicanas-revolucion-de-tecnologia -creatividad-y-riesgo/#menu-boton

Sánchez, J. (2013b, September 5). Yogome levanta inversión por 750,000 dólares. El Economista. Retrieved from www.eleconomista.com.mx/tecnologia/Yogome-levanta-inversion-por-750000 -dolares-20130905-0052.html

19
Clearview AI: ethics and artificial intelligence technology

Jason Rhinelander, Claudia De Fuentes, and Cynthia O'Driscoll

> *Morality cannot be legislated, but behaviour can be regulated.*
> (Martin Luther King, Jr.)

1.   CHARACTERISTICS OF FACIAL RECOGNITION

Biometrics, or biological measurements, are data that can be used to identify an individual. There are three types of biometrics: biological, morphological, and behavioural. Biological biometrics use biological samples to identify individuals, such as DNA, while morphological biometrics use one or more physical traits for identification. Retinal scanning, fingerprint matching and facial recognition are common examples. Behavioural biometrics are like morphological biometrics as they involve structure, but they also involve time. Some examples of behavioural biometrics include how a person talks or walks (e.g., gait analysis) (Kaspersky, 2022). As of 2022, biometrics had gained substantial interest by companies and investors as technologies were enabled by large data and faster and cheaper computing.

Facial recognition is employed in many different settings, but its use can be broadly categorized as either identification or authentication. Identification seeks to discover the identity of an individual within an image or video while authentication seeks to confirm a person's stated identity (Thales, 2021). Facial recognition can be carried out in two different ways. First, 1:1 facial recognition is when a captured image is compared against one or more images of the same individual that have been stored within the system. The use of 1:1 facial recognition is always applied to authentication and common examples include cell phone or computer access using the built-in camera. Second, the use of 1:N facial recognition can be found in both identification and authentication systems. 1:N facial recognition removes the need to know which individual the algorithm is trying to match. The captured image is compared to a gallery of N images, with the 'closest' match being the identified individual.

In the era of artificial intelligence (AI) and machine learning, 1:N facial recognition can be implemented at scale across large populations. Deep neural networks are capable of encoding, classifying, and segmenting individuals from unseen images. To create such an algorithm, it must be trained on photos and personal information of each person it may need to identify in the future. The acquisition of the training data can be problematic as it contains personal information, and because it is a system that can identify any individual, the data acquired must be at a global scale.

2. COMPANY CONTEXT

As a student, Hoan Ton-That had an aptitude for learning, was ranked first in Australia's Informatics Olympiad and took second place in guitarists under 16 years old in Australia's Eisteddfod Music Competition (Clearview, 2022a). In 2007, Ton-That moved to San Francisco to pursue a career in the tech industry. That same year, the first generation of iPhone was introduced and one year later Apple opened the App Store.

As of 2022, Ton-That had created over 20 iPhone and Facebook applications with over 10 million installations, with some apps being ranked in the App Store's top 10 list (Clearview, 2022a). Some of his previous works include: a video-sharing app which he subsequently took down after it was suggested as a possible 'phishing scam', an app that would apply a filter to photos that would modify a person's hair style to look like former United States (US) president Donald Trump, and a photo-sharing app (Hill, 2020). All three of the previous examples make use of photo and video data, and two of them use contact information in a type of social network environment.

It was in 2016 when Ton-That began reviewing academic papers about machine learning and image recognition. By the end of 2017, with the financial backing of politician Richard Schwartz, the two were able to set up a basic proof of concept that they called 'smartcheckr'. Ton-That described the system as a 'state-of-the-art neural net' that could convert a photo into a numerical descriptor or vector (Hill, 2020). The descriptor vector was then used for facial recognition.

2.1 Decision point 1: Ton-That decided what data were used and how they were collected in the development of Clearview AI's facial recognition algorithms

In 2017 Ton-That hired two engineers to help with the development of the facial recognition tool. One of the engineers created a web-scraping tool that could download photos and post information from various internet sources such as YouTube, Facebook, Twitter, and Instagram. Accessing publicly posted data violated the terms of service of the social media companies, however, Ton-That justified the collection of the data, and he was on the record as stating, 'A lot of people are doing it ... Facebook knows', when referring to the scraping of personal information from Facebook (Hill, 2020).

Clearview AI had repeatedly used the term 'public' when describing its dataset. The following excerpt was from a 2022 Clearview AI press release (Clearview, 2022b): 'Its platform of more than 20 billion facial images, the largest known database of its kind, is sourced from public-only web sources, including news media, mugshot websites, public social media, and many other open sources'.

Table 19.1   Growth rate of Clearview AI's facial image database

Year	Training set size (# photos)
2018	3 billion
2022	20 billion
~2026*	100 billion

Note: *Growth rate of 1.5 billion images per month assumed. Rate will be higher if Clearview AI receives additional funding as it seeks additional resources to grow faster.
Source: Adapted from Clearview (2022b).

Facebook's Data Policy (2022a) and Web Scraping Help Documentation (2022b) explicitly stated that people using Facebook or Instagram could send public information to anyone on or off their products. If an individual's Facebook page was set to 'Public' then anybody could use the Facebook platform to access photos and videos, posts, and information about the profile. The 'user' of Facebook in this case was not the owner of the profile, but the individual or organization accessing the data. To access the data, the user does not need to be logged into Facebook or provide any information to gain access. Facebook's statement on web scraping revealed that restrictions in the ability to access and transmit data from public profiles was viewed by Facebook as 'harming people's ability to use the respective apps and websites'. The motivation for Facebook to police the abuse of its platform did not include an ethical statement around the protection of publicly listed personal data on their platform. However, in the end, it could be argued that users of social media had a general expectation that their data would be used within the respective platform to which they originally submitted their information.

The decision to scrape social media accounts for imagery was made in 2017. At this time, the pace of research and monetization of AI was rapidly accelerating. Ton-That had a very limited amount of time to develop a unique state-of-the-art system, and his primary challenge was access to the vast amounts of data required to train the algorithms.

Clearview AI developed a general purpose, 1:N, a facial recognition system that was based on a state-of-the-art machine-learning system. In using photos that were posted online with public permissions (along with social-networking profile information, which was also public), Clearview AI could train their algorithms to identify any individual who was in the original training set.

Machine-learning systems rely on large amounts of data to function accurately. Early promotional material from Clearview AI stated that the database contained 3 billion (the N in 1:N) facial images (Hill, 2020). As of March 2022, Clearview AI Platform V2.0 contained over 20 billion facial images (Clearview AI, 2022). At the same time, in early 2022, a 'pitch' presentation that was obtained by the *Washington Post* illustrated that Clearview wanted to grow their database to 100 million photos (Harwell, 2022a). Table 19.1 illustrates the growth trajectory.

The human level of accuracy for facial recognition was approximately 98 per cent of tests. In 2015, Google produced FaceNet, which was a deep learning architecture that could identify individuals on a specialized dataset 99.63% +/− 0.09% of the time (Thales, 2021). The Information Technology and Innovation Foundation (ITIF) (McLaughlin & Castro, 2020) assessed the results of the National Institute of Standards and Technology (NIST) evaluation of over 200 algorithms (Clearview AI did not submit their algorithm for this study) for accuracy and the ITIF summarized the key findings as follows:

- 'Algorithms can have different error rates for different demographics but still be highly accurate.'
- 'The twenty [identification] algorithms that had the lowest false-negative identification rates for placing the correct individual … when searching a database that had images of 12 million individuals in NIST's September 2019 identification report have undetectable differences between demographic groups.'
- 'The most accurate verification algorithms as those that rank in the top 20 on NIST's FRVT 1:1 leaderboard on January 6, 2020 … have low false positives and false negatives across most demographic groups.'

Overall, there were differences in facial identification and verification algorithms, but in absolute terms, the differences were very low compared to overall accuracy (McLaughlin & Castro, 2020).

In the first year of the company's existence, when the facial recognition tool was still called 'Smartcheckr', Ton-That explored applications of Clearview AI's facial recognition technology in security, private use identification, and hospitality. There were also rumours of political groups in the US leveraging the technology. Ton-That had publicly stated that their technology was not offered to such individuals or groups. It was at that time that the company name was changed to Clearview AI and there was a decision to focus on using their tool for law enforcement purposes and thus began a marketing campaign that targeted various police forces inside and outside the US. Clearview AI also enlisted the help of current and former political officials to promote the software. Their most effective marketing strategy was to offer free limited-time licences to police officers and in turn get them to recommend the system to their procurement departments and colleagues at conferences and meetings.

There were numerous examples of Clearview AI's applications in the first couple of years of operation. Suspects involved in a shooting were identified by Indiana State Police from cell phone video recorded by a bystander. The criminal case was solved in 20 minutes. Clifton, New Jersey police were able to identify suspects in a matter of seconds in two different cases. One case involved identifying shoplifting suspects at a retail location while another case identified a good Samaritan who assisted during an attack involving a man with a knife. Investigators deemed Clearview AI's tool to be superior when identifying people who may not be looking straight at a camera, when a person was wearing sunglasses or a hat, or the face in the picture was partially obscured (Hill, 2020). The *New York Times* was able to access a marketing presentation where other cases were described, including a suspect accused of child sexual assault where the suspect's image was captured by a camera in the reflection of a changing room mirror, a suspect in a series of mailbox thefts, a deceased person found in a public setting whose identity was unknown, and other identity fraud cases at banks (Hill, 2020). Clearview AI also used their facial recognition technology to identify participants in the US Capitol riots on 6 January 2021.

2.2 Decision point 2: How Clearview AI expanded its customer base and grew market share

Following the *New York Times* investigative report in 2020 (Hill, 2020), Clearview AI stated that they had a client list of more than 3100 law enforcement agencies in the US alone, including contracts with the Department of Homeland Security, the Federal Bureau of Investigation, and the US Army (Harwell, 2022a). A *BuzzFeed News* report uncovered that Clearview AI was also offering its 30-day free trials to stores, banks, and other companies (Harwell, 2022a). In the very same presentation that illustrated Clearview AI's growth plans for the database of photos shown in Table 19.1, it also described how it intended to grow its client base. The company sought to expand into banking, health care, insurance, retail, financial services, the 'gig' economy, and real estate sectors. In fact, it stated that these new growth areas were much larger than government and defence contracts. Clearview considered that in the gig economy application, its facial recognition technology could revolutionize the screening process for apps that provided connections to babysitters, repair contractors, and even dating sites (Harwell, 2022a). In a May 2022 press release, Clearview AI announced a new consent-based facial recognition technology to integrate with an existing enterprise's workflow (Clearview, 2022c). The application of a consent-based method for data collection for the gig economy could be from the service provider's side. It could ask for profile photos to be uploaded from the service provider, or the client, or both. If photos were uploaded, it could state that consent was given in the terms and conditions of using its service. Ton-That was quoted stating that Airbnb, Lyft, and Uber were 'examples of the types of firms that have expressed interest in Clearview's facial recognition technology for the purposes of consent-based identity verification, since there are a lot of issues with crimes that happen on their platforms'. The *Washington Post* contacted the three companies in their investigative article (Harwell, 2022a) and representatives from all three companies stated they had no intentions to work with Clearview AI.

Other possible clients included babysitter service Sittercity, Tinder, and OkCupid parent company, Match Group. All companies publicly stated that they had no plans to engage with Clearview AI while Target and Walmart did not respond to requests for a comment (Harwell, 2022a). Internal documents obtained by *BuzzFeed News* revealed that Clearview AI had already shared or sold access to its facial recognition technology to a variety of companies as well as to some individual employees within companies (many through a 30-day free trial), numbering more than 200 as of 2020. Some of these companies included Kohl's, Walmart, Wells Fargo, Bank of America, Madison Square Garden, Eventbrite, Las Vegas Sands, Pechanga Resort Casino, National Basketball Association, fitness company Equinox, cryptocurrency platform Coinbase, Best Buy, Macy's, Albertsons, and Home Depot (Mac et al., 2020). The internal Clearview AI documents which revealed this information were leaked server logs from an unnamed Clearview AI insider (Mac et al., 2020).

The logs contained information about how many searches were performed, how many times the account was logged into, and the date of the last search. The corporations that appeared on the list had established at least one account and performed at least one facial recognition search. Many of these accounts were part of a 30-day free trial that Clearview AI offered to individuals to promote the tool to their employer or peers. At the time, Clearview

AI's Code of Conduct stated that individual users had to be 'authorized by their employer' to use the tool, but it was unclear whether Clearview enforced this rule. In fact, when a Home Depot representative was asked to comment on Clearview AI, they responded with, 'We don't use Clearview AI … curious why you thought we were a client' (Mac et al., 2020).

Clearview AI's promotional strategy was focused on making contacts to individuals within corporations without the knowledge of senior management. In its drive to increase the number of clients, its reach went well beyond law enforcement and public safety applications and included educational institutions. There were Clearview AI registered accounts at more than 50 educational institutions across 24 states in the US (Mac et al., 2020). In many cases these accounts were registered to campus police while school administration was unaware that employees were evaluating the software (Mac et al., 2020).

In 2020, Clearview AI expanded across multiple continents, even though the company stated at the time that it was focused on customers in the US and Canada predominantly. According to the leaked account logs, law enforcement agencies and government bodies in at least 26 foreign countries, some of which have been accused of human right violations, have used Clearview AI's software. Ton-That stated that Clearview AI would not sell their software to countries 'adverse to the United States', such as China, Iran, and North Korea.

In 2020, there was broad use of Clearview AI's facial recognition software in Canada. Over 30 law enforcement agencies across Canada used the software, with the Royal Canadian Mounted Police (RCMP) listed as a paying customer (Mac et al., 2020). The Toronto Police performed over 3400 searches across 150 free-trial accounts (Mac et al., 2020) and, although they initially denied using the software, in early 2020 they publicly stated they had used the technology. It was later, in 2021, that the police force detailed the software's use from October 2019 through to February 2020. It employed the software for 2827 searches, uploaded 115 officer photos for searches, 84 separate criminal investigations, which resulted in 12 victims identified, 4 suspects identified, and 2 witnesses identified (Brockbank, 2021).

The use of Clearview AI's tool to aid policing was questioned. A lawyer practising in Toronto was quoted as saying, 'If police violated the law as part of their investigations, this could make those investigations vulnerable to charter challenges'. By the end of 2021, the Toronto police indicated they had no plans to use Clearview AI facial recognition technology. A spokesperson for the force stated, 'The Toronto Police Services Board is currently developing a policy for the use of artificial intelligence technology and machine learning following public consultation'.

Canada's privacy commissioner, Daniel Therrien, investigated the RCMP's use of Clearview AI's software. In his report submitted to Parliament in 2021, Therrien stated:

> The use of facial recognition technology by the RCMP to search through massive repositories of Canadians who are innocent of any suspicion of crime presents a serious violation of privacy … A government institution cannot collect personal information from a third-party agent if that third-party agent collected the information unlawfully.

The RCMP initially denied it was using Clearview AI and did not agree with Therrien's conclusion that it violated the Privacy Act. The investigation determined that approximately 6 per cent of RCMP searches were related to incidents involving children (e.g., exploitation), but approximately 85 per cent of the searches had no explicit rationale for the use of the technology (Tunney, 2021).

The Office of the Privacy Commissioner of Canada conducted a joint investigation with three other provincial counterparts of Clearview AI's operations in Canada. The investigation found that Clearview violated both federal and provincial private-sector privacy laws by scraping images from the internet without permission. During the investigation in 2020, Clearview AI ceased operations in Canada but continued to collect personal data or delete data that it had previously collected (Office of the Privacy Commissioner of Canada, 2021).

In 2022, Clearview AI offered to supply its software to the Ukrainian government following the Russian invasion of the country. In a *New York Times* article (Hill, 2022a), Ton-That explained why Clearview was supplying its software: 'I remember seeing videos of captured Russian soldiers and Russia claiming they were actors … I thought if Ukrainians could use Clearview, they could get more information to verify their identities'. In its offer letter, Clearview gave various case examples, such as using the tool to aid in the identification of spies as well as casualties, by accessing Clearview AI's database of 20 billion faces from the public internet, including photos from Russian social media sites (Hill, 2022a). In less than a month of making contact, Clearview provided over 200 accounts to five separate Ukrainian government agencies that had conducted over 5000 searches. Clearview identified dead soldiers and prisoners of war, but also used it as a surveillance tool for travellers in the country by comparing search results with their travel documentation, as there was heightened fear about spies and infiltrators entering the country (Hill, 2022a).

In 2022, Ton-That stated that he didn't want Clearview AI's tool to be used in violation of the Geneva Conventions (Dave & Dastin, 2022). Albert Fox Cahn of the Surveillance Technology Oversight Project in New York gave his opinion on the technology's use within a war zone (Reuters, 2022). He stated: 'We're going to see well-intentioned technology back-firing and harming the very people it's supposed to help … once you introduce these systems and the associated databases to a war zone, you have no control over how it will be used and misused' (Dave & Dastin, 2022). Clearview AI shared emails from three branches of government in Ukraine, including the National Police, the Defence Ministry, and a third organization that did not want to be identified. These emails contained some details regarding the use of Clearview's software, but Clearview did not provide details of the remaining two government organizations to which it had given its software (Harwell, 2022b).

The decision to expand into new markets and to acquire new customers was a key driver behind Clearview AI's business strategy. Once the technology was developed, Ton-That's promotional strategy was to attract media attention and create a narrative that placed Clearview AI at the centre of need for various organizations and governments.

3. CLEARVIEW AI'S FUTURE IN THE FACIAL RECOGNITION INDUSTRY

Clearview AI faced legal battles in various jurisdictions in the US and internationally. There were several lawsuits in the US and the use of Clearview's web-scraped photo database was deemed illegal in Britain, Canada, France, Australia, and Italy (Hill, 2022a). It was levied a US$9.4 million fine by the United Kingdom's privacy watchdog (Hart, 2022) and a €20 million fine in Italy (European Data Protection Board Press Release, 2022). Clearview AI also faced deletion orders in many of the countries in which it was banned from offering its software and web-scraped database.

In 2022, Clearview lost a significant court battle in the US federal court in the state of Illinois. The lawsuit was filed by the American Civil Liberties Union alleging that Clearview AI had broken an Illinois law banning companies from sharing people's face photos, fingerprints, and other biometric information without their consent (Harwell, 2022c). Clearview AI was not the only company to have breached the 2008 Illinois law. Facebook was required to pay a US$650 million settlement because of its own use of facial recognition technology. Clearview agreed to the following terms as part of the settlement (Harwell, 2022c):

- To stop selling or offering free access to its facial recognition database to most businesses and other private entities nationwide (US).
- To stop working with all police or government agencies in Illinois for five years.
- Pay US$50,000 worth in advertising to notify Illinois residents about an opt-out form that would prevent their photos from showing up in Clearview AI searches.

Clearview AI saw increasing resistance to its facial recognition database, but facial recognition technology was relatively easy to implement based on publicly published methods and algorithms. The growth of facial recognition was significant when considering countries and regions outside of North America and Europe. China was quick to adopt facial recognition and in the list of top 10 cities globally that had street cameras were Chongqing, Shenzhen, Shanghai, Tianjin, and Ji'nan, representing the top five. Other projects in China included facial recognition glasses and facial recognition towers. Other countries with ambitions in the facial recognition technology space were India, Cameroon, Burkina Faso, and Russia (Thales, 2021).

In 2022 PimEyes was another company providing facial recognition for a fee. For US$29.99 a month anyone could search for a photo of a face and find results of online postings of the same person. As opposed to Clearview AI, the source database used online sources such as news pages, wedding photography sites, reviews, and blogs, as well as pornography sites (Hill, 2022b). PimEyes stated that searches should be for the users' own faces or the faces of individuals who had consented, but there was no policing of the tool to ensure it was used according to its terms and conditions. Kashmir Hill of the *New York Times* tested PimEyes with some colleagues and the tool found (often unexpected) photos of the subjects online as well as erroneous results for women in the test group, which often matched to other individuals on pornographic sites (Hill, 2022b). PimEyes is owned by EMEA Robotics and registered in Dubai, United Arab Emirates.

3.1   Decision point 3: Clearview AI and ethical concerns when developing and deploying the technology

In 2023, Clearview AI and many other technology companies were among the key players in the age of AI. Legislation was under way in many countries to provide increased protections of individual privacy and copyright rights involving AI technologies. Clearview AI had a decision to make in terms of its future, regarding ethical considerations in the use and deployment of its technology and how it operated in relation to forthcoming legislative frameworks.

ACKNOWLEDGEMENTS

We would like to thank the Division of Engineering, Faculty of Science and the David Sobey Centre, Sobey School of Business at Saint Mary's University in Halifax, Nova Scotia, Canada for their support of interdisciplinary research and education.

REFERENCES

Brockbank, N. (2021), Toronto police used Clearview AI facial recognition software in 84 investigations. *CBC News*, 23 December.

Clearview (2022a), AI corporate profile: Hoan Ton-That, www.clearview.ai/leadership

Clearview (2022b, 25 March), AI press release, www.clearview.ai/clearview-ai-releases-2-version-of -industry-leading-facial-recognition-platform-for-law-enforce

Clearview (2022c, 25 May), AI press release, www.clearview.ai/clearview-ai-launches-clearview-consent -companys-first-consent-based-product-for-commercial-use

Dave, P., & Dastin, J. (2022, 14 March), Ukraine has started using Clearview AI's facial recognition during war. Reuters.

European Data Protection Board Press Release (2022), Facial recognition: Italian SA fines Clearview AI EUR 20 million, https://edpb.europa.eu/news/national-news/2022/facial-recognition-italian-sa-fines -clearview-ai-eur-20-million_en

Facebook (2022a), Data policy, www.facebook.com/about/privacy/update

Facebook (2022b), Web scraping help documentation, www.facebook.com/help/463983701520800

Hart, R. (2022, 23 May), Clearview AI fined $9.4 million in UK for illegal facial recognition database. Forbes.

Harwell, D. (2022a, 16 February), Facial recognition firm Clearview AI tells investors it's seeking massive expansion beyond law enforcement, *Washington Post*.

Harwell, D. (2022b, 15 April), Ukraine is scanning faces of dead Russians, then contacting the mothers, *Washington Post*.

Harwell, D. (2022c, 9 May), Clearview AI to stop selling facial recognition tool to private firms. *Washington Post*.

Hill, K. (2020, 18 January), The secretive company that may end privacy as we know it. *New York Times*.

Hill, K. (2022a, 7 April), Facial recognition goes to war. *New York Times*.

Hill, K. (2022b, 26 May), A face search engine anyone can use is alarmingly accurate. *New York Times*.

Kaspersky (2022), What is biometrics? How is it used in security? www.kaspersky.com/resource-center/ definitions/biometrics

Mac, R., Haskins, C., & McDonald, L. (2020, 27 February), Clearview's facial recognition app has been used by the Justice Department, ICE, Macy's, Walmart, and the NBA. *BuzzFeed News*.

McLaughlin, M., & Castro, D. (2020, 27 January), The critics were wrong: NIST data shows the best facial recognition algorithms are neither racist nor sexist. Information Technology and Innovation Foundation.

Office of the Privacy Commissioner of Canada (2021, 14 December), Clearview AI ordered to comply with recommendations to stop collecting, sharing images. www.priv.gc.ca/en/opc-news/news-and -announcements/2021/an_211214/

Reuters (2022, 14 March), Exclusive: Ukraine has started using Clearview AI's facial recognition during war.

Thales (2021, 24 June), Facial recognition: Top 7 trends (tech, vendors, use cases). www.thalesgroup
.com/en/markets/digital-identity-and-security/government/biometrics/facial-recognition#:~:text=
Facial%20recognition%20is%20used%20when,passport%20with%20the%20holder%27s%20face
Tunney, C. (2021, 10 June), RCMP's use of facial recognition tech violated privacy laws, investigation
finds. *CBC News*.

20
Bridging cryptocurrency and traditional finance businesses: the case of SpectroCoin–Pervesk

Jurgita Butkevičienė and Aušrinė Šilenskytė

1.   THE SLIPPING OPPORTUNITY TO CONQUER THE GLOBAL MARKET

In 2009, the world experienced the birth of the first cryptocurrency, Bitcoin, a digital currency built on public permissionless blockchain technology (Nakamoto, 2008; Bhutta et al., 2021). Since then, financial and other markets, as well as their incumbents, international business players, and governmental representatives, have received an immense number of new opportunities and challenges brought about by the so-called crypto economy. The crypto economy and public permissionless blockchain-based innovations were seen as institutional technology that decentralized authority and governance structures and shifted trust from humans to the code (Aste, Taska, & Di Matteo, 2017). Constantly evolving, it enabled the development of novel business models, organizational forms, fundraising practices, and decision-making processes of economic actors in different industries (Shirole, Darisi, & Bhirud, 2020; Lumineau, Wang, & Schilke, 2021; Šilenskytė et al., 2023). Moreover, the transformations brought by the crypto economy were challenging existing, as well as creating new, institutional regulative and normative elements. Within such emerging business and institutional environments, lucrative business opportunities could be captured by FinTech firms (technology-enabled financial innovation firms).

By utilizing the emerging opportunities described above, SpectroCoin, the Lithuanian-origin FinTech firm offering various cryptocurrency exchange services, has been successfully growing since its establishment in 2013. SpectroCoin was an early adopter of cryptocurrencies and operated in the global crypto market, which at that time was unregulated. In this entirely digital world, for a long time, the cryptocurrencies remained used and understood primarily by technology experts—a relatively small and specialized customer group. However, increasing awareness of the crypto economy among the wider public hinted at the forthcoming billion-dollar business to be captured.

Vytautas, the chief executive officer (CEO) and one of SpectroCoin's co-founders, realized blockchain's potential to enhance payment quality and the lucrativeness of bringing cryptocurrencies to the wide base of ordinary users. While these ideas seemed tempting, the regulatory limitations were obvious: the ordinary users were customers of regulated financial system firms and were neither trusting nor yet equipped to operate with cryptocurrencies. As a result of this divide, in early 2016, a second firm—Pervesk—was established with the goal of becoming a licensed payment institution, i.e., compliant with the regulated financial industry norms, which would offer traditional bank-type services for old and newly targeted customers and solve challenges related to online payments for noncrypto-market participants. The two firms—one operating in the unregulated crypto market and the other operating in the regulated traditional finance market—connected their services through the technological platform, bridging the two marketplaces and becoming the first entity in the world to capture this unique global opportunity.

Soon after this bridging was completed and the possibility of conquering the world felt so close, on the morning of October 10, 2017, Vytautas was shocked by reading the newly issued statement:

> According to the Bank of Lithuania's approved position, financial market participants should not engage in the sale of virtual currencies, provide conditions for customers to pay in payment instruments issued by them (e.g., debit or credit cards, etc.), execute any operations in virtual currencies, and engage in their exchange or similar activities. Moreover, in their means of communication (website, mobile application, platform, ATM, customer's electronic account, etc.), they should not link their services to virtual currencies and create an impression that such services are supervised and subject to the same security standards as those applicable to financial services are. (Bank of Lithuania, 2017)

Suddenly, five years of hard work felt meaningless. The brilliant business idea felt like becoming lost. Although this was an official opinion statement, it provided a strong hint about the upcoming potential regulations, which did not seem favorable to the newly established business setting. Vytautas realized that if the co-founders remained only with SpectroCoin's cryptocurrency exchange business, their success would be solely dependent on the highly volatile cryptocurrency market, limiting strategic diversification. However, if the co-founders dropped the crypto business and continued only with the newly licensed payment institution Pervesk, they would need to compete with the traditional banks and run the traditional finance business, in which they did not have much experience.

Was there a way to comply with the regulatory institution's pressure without abandoning the rewarding idea of connecting the divided financial worlds? Vytautas decided to weigh all the factors before taking any further steps.

2. A LUCRATIVE BUT RISKY BUSINESS ENVIRONMENT CREATED BY THE EMERGENCE OF CRYPTOCURRENCIES

For many years, financial markets had been secured through the operations of various institutions that worked to ensure financial stability and trust in value exchanges. For example, in economic units such as the European Union (EU), the European Banking Authority (EBA) was qualified to supervise and carefully regulate the European banking sector (Ferrari, 2020), and the European Central Bank ensured that banks followed the rules established by the EBA. The central banking authorities (e.g., European Central Bank or national banks) had a monopoly on the provision and control of fiat money (Velde, 1998). The fiat money issued by the central authority had a form of cash or electronic money and was strictly supervised (Vlasov, 2017). The fiat money in electronic form, i.e., electronic money, could be stored in either physical card-based products or in software-based digital wallets such as PayPal and Google Wallet, which were generally operated by nonbanking institutions. However, even in electronic form, they were under the supervision of regulatory institutions. Exchanges with fiat money in any form were rigorously regulated, licensed, and supervised by the governmental authorities and the National Central Bank. The later regulations and supervision were the key to warranting trust when value exchanges between individuals and/or legal entities occurred.

The regulated finance system was shaken by the 2008 Global Financial Crisis, in which it was revealed that financial institutions performed malpractices that led to the global crash of financial markets (Faria, 2019). In response to the mistrusted regulated financial market model, starting in 2009, the public permissionless blockchain was utilized to create new types of various virtual assets, such as cryptocurrencies, for value storage and exchanges (e.g., Nakamoto, 2008).

Cryptocurrency was perceived as a purely digital currency, which relied on cryptographic protocols and a distributed peer-to-peer network of users to mine, store, and transfer value without the need for a central authority or trusted third party.[1] This meant that anyone, with the help of the public permissionless blockchain technology, could issue a financial exchange unit—digital currency (e.g., token or cryptocurrency)—similar to electronic money and perform financial exchanges with others (individuals and/or legal entities) residing anywhere in the world on their own terms. Such application of technology shattered the long-standing finance industry norms, in which only central banks could issue money (e.g., national currency), define its value, and supervise the process of exchanges between individuals and/or legal units within and across countries.

Early in 2013, Bitcoin was the only popular cryptocurrency known to the general public, while by 2017, many other cryptocurrencies existed and gained popularity (Giudici, Milne, & Vinogradov, 2020). The rapid growth of the different cryptocurrencies made a handful of existing cryptocurrency exchanges into a billion-dollar business. For example, in 2020, Binance and FTX were making nearly USD1 billion profit (Kruppa, 2021).

Since the emergence of the first cryptocurrency in 2009, activities with cryptocurrencies have been neither regulated nor supervised (Faria, 2019; Ferrari, 2020). Cryptocurrencies emerged with the goal of eliminating intermediaries and central authorities supervising financial exchanges (Šilenskytė et al., 2023). Having no external regulations, the decentralized crypto community, rooted in an open-source culture, created and defined the novel rules of the game (Ryan, Macrossan, Wright, & Adams, 2021). For example, the technology-savvy community was comfortable executing financial transactions without verification of each other's identity because transactions on blockchain were immutable due to the technology features (Hassan & De Filippi, 2017). Furthermore, the emergence of smart contracts allowed the transfer of legal rules into technical rules ("Code is Law") and formalized contractual agreements and transactions with self-executing and self-enforcing rules (Hassan & De Filippi, 2017).

Consequently, the unregulated cryptocurrency operations and technology-enabled trust mechanism created a space for revolutionary developments, supporting both legal and illicit business activities. For example, for legal businesses, crypto-related operations revolutionized the remittance industry by reducing transaction fees compared with those charged by traditional financial service providers. Market participants, who had no or little access to the services provided by banks, were granted access to bank-type services and the possibility of making payments in cryptocurrencies using their mobile phones (Turner & Irwin, 2018). Cryptocurrency exchanges became one of the first services in crypto space, which enabled users to establish market prices and trade these currencies (Hileman & Rauchs, 2017). Cryptocurrency exchanges were online platforms in which users could exchange (buy or sell) cryptocurrencies or exchange cryptocurrencies for fiat currencies (e.g., EUR, USD). Later, lucrative crypto exchanges started to offer services such as cryptocurrency wallet, a software that enabled storing, sending, and receiving digital currency (Manski & Manski, 2018).

Regarding illegal businesses, cryptocurrencies were linked to the online drug industry (Martin, 2014) and cybercrime-as-a-service (Vigna & Rudegea, 2017), raising a number of concerns regarding money laundering and terrorism financing (Pflaum & Hateley, 2013). The crime investigation authorities had difficulties obtaining records for Bitcoin transactions and tracking the identity of suspicious anonymous users (Turner & Irwin 2018).

The list of threats further expanded by various crypto-market developments. The high volatility of cryptocurrency as a new asset class had significant price swings, creating fertile soil for speculation (Korauš, Kelemen, Backa, & Polák , 2018). The initial coin offering (ICO), a new corporate fundraising practice performed by issuing coins or tokens to fund new product development projects, fell out of the scope of the existing legal frameworks. Anyone could issue coins or tokens for funding new product development projects (Boreiko & Sahdev, 2018) without necessarily executing the project after the funds were collected (Huang, Meoli, & Vismara, 2020). These new possibilities often encouraged opportunistic behavior and fraud (Ferrari, 2020; Huang et al., 2020), which led to serious risks for investors and consumers, financial crimes, and diminished market integrity (Marian, 2018; Edwards, Hanley, Litan, & Weil, 2019).

Due to a number of negative developments within the crypto economy, risk-averse, conservative industry players, governments, and other regulatory institutions started promoting adverse positions towards cryptocurrencies and related operations (Martin, 2014; Marian, 2018). In 2013, the United States was a relatively early mover and the first country where different federal agencies started to regulate crypto exchanges (Bellavitis, Fisch, & Wiklund, 2021). In 2014, the United Kingdom clarified the taxation of income from virtual currency trading, and Singapore announced that cryptocurrency exchanges needed to verify their customers' identities by proposing know-your-customer frameworks.

Within the EU, institutions adopted a "wait-and-see" approach (Ferrari, 2020) and warned rather than sentenced crypto-market participants (Bank of Lithuania, 2013). Since 2013, the EBA has issued multiple warnings for crypto investors, which have been echoed by national regulatory bodies. For example, in 2016, Estonia, which was among the first countries in the world to legalize crypto-related operations, started to regulate cryptocurrency exchange by stating that Bitcoin exchanges shall be subject to its Anti-Money Laundering/Combating the Financing of Terrorism (AML/CFT) law (Badmus, 2019). Such developments within the EU added to the conflicting perspectives on the crypto economy.

Figure 20.1 briefly summarizes some of the key events in the crypto-economy development process. In summary, the regulatory framework for crypto- and blockchain-based business (BBB)-related activities was constantly changing, including countries' positions towards such activities (Šilenskytė, Butkevičienė, & Dhanaraj, 2022), creating much uncertainty and sometimes confusion for industry participants.

However, neither the diverse regulatory responses nor the negative opinions or risks related to the crypto economy scared entrepreneurs from lucrative new businesses (Šilenskytė et al., 2022). Many business opportunities were noticed by technology-savvy market participants, so the crypto-related community started to dramatically grow globally (EU blockchain forum, n.d.). In particular, cryptocurrencies and public permissionless BBBs were attractive to emerging countries (Kshetri, 2017; Lim, Wang, Ren, & Lo, 2019), traditional tax havens (e.g., Malta: Marian, 2018), and new economies (e.g., Lithuania, Latvia, Estonia: Kostrikova, 2021), where market participants were tolerant of various risks (Bellavitis et al., 2021). The new economies, such as Lithuania, had undergone significant financial crises multiple times during their transition period (Kiyak & Reichenbachas, 2012). This created a relatively unique environment for crypto-related businesses.

3.   PERFORMING CRYPTO-RELATED BUSINESS IN LITHUANIA

Since the restoration of Lithuania's independence on March 11, 1990, the country had seen hyperinflation (1993), internal banking crises (1995), and external currency and debt crises (1998) and was severely affected by the Global Financial Crisis (2008–2009) (Kiyak & Reichenbachas, 2012). The fragility of regulated financial institutions had been present in the country for at least 20 years. Moreover, for many years, Lithuania did not have an established identity in the global market. It was frequently associated with the post-Soviet countries that strove to reintegrate into the European economy. Later, in its transition towards a market economy, Lithuania's financial services industry was characterized by a highly concentrated banking sector dominated by three Scandinavian banks (OECD, 2017). In 2017, the Scandinavian parent banks controlled 89.5 percent of total banking-sector assets and 91.4 percent of total system lending in Lithuania (OECD, 2017). While investments from the Nordic neighbors were highly appreciated, the oligopoly in the financial sector within the

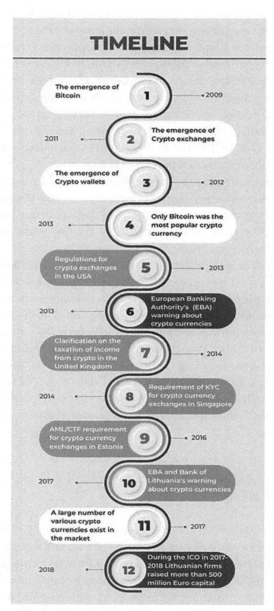

TIMELINE

1. The emergence of Bitcoin — 2009
2. 2011 — The emergence of Crypto exchanges
3. The emergence of Crypto wallets — 2012
4. 2013 — Only Bitcoin was the most popular crypto currency
5. Regulations for crypto exchanges in the USA — 2013
6. 2013 — European Banking Authority's (EBA) warning about crypto currencies
7. Clarification on the taxation of income from crypto in the United Kingdom — 2014
8. 2014 — Requirement of KYC for crypto currency exchanges in Singapore
9. AML/CTF requirement for crypto currency exchanges in Estonia — 2016
10. 2017 — EBA and Bank of Lithuania's warning about crypto currencies
11. A large number of various crypto currencies exist in the market — 2017
12. 2018 — During the ICO in 2017-2018 Lithuanian firms raised more than 500 million Euro capital

Figure 20.1 Regulatory uncertainty in the crypto-economy development process globally

country, previously greatly affected by multiple bank crises, raised a sense of cautiousness. To this end, regulatory institutions, entrepreneurs, and market participants were ready for alternatives.

Being an EU member state since 2004, Lithuania had to apply policies made at the EU level in addition to locally issued regulations that could not object to the EU's major legal principles (European Commission, n.d.). The EU directives typically formed part of national legislation, but countries had some freedom to choose how they would achieve the expected results (European Commission, n.d.). Within such a framework, the government and Bank of Lithuania took the initiative to develop a FinTech ecosystem and remove all the barriers to successful FinTech operations. One of the essential features of the later FinTech ecosystem was technical infrastructure and access (CENTROlink) to the Single European Payment Area (SEPA) for all payment service providers. Through CENTROlink, created in 2015, licensed FinTech firms had reduced barriers to providing international transactions and similar services across the entire SEPA (Toivonen, 2020; CENTROlink, n.d.). The other important advancement was the introduction of a remote digital identity verification method for clients, which enabled the identification of FinTech and traditional bank customers without the need for physical interaction or the need to operate a local physical office for receiving and verifying customers, as was previously required in the traditional bank system (Valcke, Vandezande, & Van De Velde, 2015; Ministry of Finance of the Republic of Lithuania, 2016).

Lithuania skyrocketed in developing a FinTech-friendly environment (EU Blockchain Forum, n.d.) and within four years took fourth place in the global FinTech 2020 rankings (GFICRR, 2020). With a population approximately one-third the size of London, Lithuania emerged in the financial service industry as a new player among the traditional markets and became a FinTech hub in the EU (GFICRR, 2020).

Among various FinTech ecosystem development initiatives in Lithuania, BBB initiatives and pro-blockchain attitudes were remarkable (EU Blockchain Forum, n.d.). In 2016, Lithuania hosted the first Bitcoin conference in the Baltics supported by the involvement of high-level politicians (Lithuanian Tribune, 2015). In 2017, many newly established BBBs by ICOs raised more than EUR500 million in capital (Enterprise Lithuania, 2018), with Lithuanian entrepreneurs capturing up to 4 percent of the entire world's ICOs (Kaal, 2018).

Despite the successful economic activity of BBBs and several pro-BBB steps, the Lithuanian government and the regulatory authorities were carefully observing market developments and balancing the national and EU positions towards crypto-related operations. For example, on July 16, 2014, the Bank of Lithuania, with regard to the EBA opinion on virtual currencies, suggested that "credit institutions, payment institutions and electronic money institutions refrain from the purchase, storage or sale of virtual currency in order to reduce the risk arising from the interaction of virtual currency schemes and regulated financial services" (Bank of Lithuania, 2017). At that time, the Bank of Lithuania did not forbid or strictly caution about crypto-related operations.

However, on October 10, 2017, complying with the EBA opinion[2] and making a shift in its initially pro-crypto national position, the Bank of Lithuania and the Ministry of Finance issued an updated position regarding crypto-related BBBs (Bank of Lithuania, 2017). In contrast to the softer 2014 statement, regulatory institutions warned investors and market incumbents to separate the exposure of investments in crypto assets from other investments and carefully evaluate the risk involved in crypto-related activities (Bank of Lithuania, 2017). Moreover, according to this position, if a market participant decided to engage in crypto-related activities, enhanced due diligence and compliance with AML/CFT rules had to be applied (Bank of Lithuania, 2017).

Such a shift in the position of national regulatory institutions posed enormous dilemmas for crypto-economy participants in Lithuania. Participants in the crypto economy strongly valued autonomy—the freedom to define the rules of the game in peer-to-peer interactions. While Lithuania's regulatory position was initially ready to embrace such emerging industry norms, the enforcement of AML/CFT directives and specifically the know-your-customer procedures in line with the EU's expectations drew BBB industries back to the traditional financial indus-try rules of the game, in which external institutions required verification of customers' identity and tracked information about the operation type and amounts transacted. Crypto-related firms faced unfavorable regulatory and normative pressures.

4. SPECTROCOIN AND PERVESK: LITHUANIAN-ORIGIN PIONEERS IN CRYPTOCURRENCY SERVICE AND PAYMENT MARKETS

Since 2009, Justas and Mantas have experimented with blockchain coding and the crypto economy, while Vytautas has explored finance trends in several universities and beyond. The young entrepreneurs ignored negative discourses floating around the crypto economy and dreamed about creating a digital bank that could operate with fiat and cryptocurrencies, ensur-ing fast and effective payments for both traditional finance and crypto communities. However, considering the novelty of this idea and the amount of funds needed for its implementation, a step-by-step implementation plan was needed.

In 2013, pioneering in the Baltic region, the friends co-founded SpectroCoin—the novel cryptocurrency exchange (Rekvizitai & SpectroCoin, n.d.)—and started cryptocurrency exchange and brokerage services (SpectroCoin, n.d.). Vytautas took the position of CEO, which meant that he decided to carry all the legal responsibility for the firm, operating in a very uncertain environment. The establishment of SpectroCoin allowed generating initial capital for further business development and growth, gaining invaluable experience in freshly emerged business areas, in which only a few entrepreneurs believed and worked.

However, Vytautas had to manage regulatory or regulation-related challenges multiple times. For example, SpectroCoin faced the derisking challenge, meaning that traditional finan-cial institutions were closing their accounts because crypto users were perceived as illegitimate and prone to money laundering or terrorist financing abuse (Durner & Shetret, 2015). The latter barrier of SpectroCoin business development was signaling that the traditional market was not yet ready to embrace the emerging crypto market and was not keen on accepting new business models. The motivation to innovate and lead the emergence of new finance market norms only increased.

There were a number of options by which Vytautas and the team could have addressed the derisking challenge. Not knowing which option was the best choice, the co-founder team started exploring all of them. The first option was to collaborate with the payment institutions and encourage them to consider cryptocurrency, as its market potential appeared promising. Thus, Vytautas began to search for pro-crypto-financial institutions. He tried collaborating with them to collectively create potential operation models that bridged the divided financial markets.

Then, Vytautas had the option to educate traditional financial institutions, regulators, and policy-makers by explaining the blockchain and cryptocurrency features, risks, and potential solutions for the crypto market. Vytautas was actively involved in public opinion formation by issuing various statements, commentaries, interviews, etc. in the public media and, in 2015, he started his PhD research on the crypto economy at KU Leuven. Additionally, SpectroCoin tried to imitate practices common in fiat currency operations and, in 2015, even offered debit cards for their customers. Existing AML/CFT requirements for fiat operations were also copied and applied for the crypto business, even if it was an expensive solution:

> Even before [AML5] regulation came into place, we were doing a lot of things, which we expected to be required in the future by law, just like fraud prevention. We knew that a lot of regulations come for a reason. In business, a lot of things we were doing, even if it was not required by law. We did it just because it made our business stronger, because we could look better in the eyes of our business partners; sometimes it was required by a business partner, and sometimes it was just a prevention to avoid fraud. (Vytautas, CEO, interview)

Consequently, despite sometimes adverse environments for crypto-related business, over the first three years, SpectroCoin released a cryptocurrency brokerage service, cryptocurrency wallets (for buying, selling, sending, receiving, and storing Bitcoins), solutions for crypto payments, and debit cards. Having succeeded very well in the crypto market, the firm soon became ready for further vertical growth and started recognizing other niches in the traditional financial market.

The e-commerce business was rapidly growing, but it continued to suffer from slow traditional remittance services, which were able to proceed with an international transaction only within one to three days (Eurostat, 2015). Thus, the adoption of blockchain technologies for instant remittance in cryptocurrencies seemed to be a perfect solution:

> We noticed that the bank services were not very friendly for online business payments because when the [online clients] made a small amount of payments, usually cross-border payments, they had to be settled instantly. If, for example, you bought advertisement, you wanted to go live now, not in two or three or four days. Therefore, that is why we were looking for options to pay online fast. The cryptocurrency at the time was one of the best technological offerings for this solution. That is why we decided to build our business around crypto. (Vytautas, CEO, interview)

In addition to slow payments, traditional financial institutions were not willing to serve crypto-related businesses due to various risks, leaving an increasing number of customers who needed traditional finance market services underrepresented. Vytautas realized that such an opportunity could be captured by transitioning a firm to a licensed payment institution. When having such a firm's status, they could have gained independence from traditional banks, reducing reliance on other financial institutions whose position towards crypto might have changed at any time. Moreover, entrepreneurs would have been able to serve both traditional fiat and crypto clients.

However, Vytautas was aware that such a transition to a licensed payment institution could be challenging due to the entirely new set of processes that the business would need to adopt. Additionally, business development such as this would require SpectroCoin getting a green light from the regulator. On the one hand, serving crypto-related customers was not explicitly forbidden in Lithuania or the EU, but the EU authorities and Lithuania's Central Bank had already warned market participants not to mix regulated and unregulated market activities (Bank of Lithuania, 2013). Such a warning became diluted among multiple institutional pro-blockchain/crypto-based business activities but retained the risk that a regulatory position towards such businesses might soon become more adverse.

Considering the risks and opportunities, Vytautas decided to search for a smart solution that would preempt potential future risks. Instead of implementing all business goals under one SpectroCoin, he was planning to establish a second legal entity, which would act as a separate traditional financial market participant:

> In payments' industry … competition was driven by price and speed of the payment. We always saw ourselves as being in the payments business: with SpectroCoin, we enabled a link between Bitcoin and later other cryptocurrencies and fiat. Cryptocurrency, in essence, required complying with a number of rules from technical—set by protocol—to legal—set by law. The fiat side required a relationship with a regulated financial institution, which was not guaranteed by just being compliant. The operations also depended on the views and perceptions of various stakeholders at the regulated institutions, from compliance officers to business owners. While cryptocurrency was more an exception by being distributed and having lower barriers to entry, most of the payment networks required financial license to operate and it was a rational choice for the future of our services to make a step up and get a license ourselves. (Vytautas, CEO, interview)

In February 2016, the new entity—Pervesk—was established in Lithuania to operate in the regulated financial market. In this way, the first stone in the foundation of bridging the unregulated and regulated financial industries was laid, slowly moving towards the implementation of the initial vision of becoming a digital bank that would connect the fiat and the cryptocurrency space. Next, the co-founder team submitted the license application and, in March 2017, the Bank of Lithuania granted Pervesk a Payment Institution License. After receiving the license, Pervesk was entitled to perform money remittances and debit/credit transfer services. Additionally, due to the existing advanced FinTech ecosystem in Lithuania, Pervesk gained access to the SEPA via the unique CENTROlink retail payment infrastructure operated by the Bank of Lithuania. Through this link, Pervesk had easy access to the entire EU payment area at a relatively low cost.

Being legally separate, SpectroCoin and Pervesk were connected via technological solutions, enabling the connection between the traditional and cryptocurrency markets. In this platform,

SpectroCoin customers had access to cryptocurrency-related services and linked applications to the more traditional bank-type services provided by Pervesk. SpectroCoin was able to provide an opportunity for their customers to use the International Bank Account Number (IBAN),[3] enabling customers to quickly and easily open an IBAN account at Pervesk and use it for SpectroCoin services by linking the account to their SpectroCoin wallet. This ecosystem created the first in the world unit, which served both the regulated fiat currency and the unregulated cryptocurrency markets.

From the business development perspective, SpectroCoin conducted an upselling to their existing customer base by offering an additional set of services. When Pervesk received the license in 2017, SpectroCoin was a well-established medium-sized brand with 500,000 registered users from the crypto community. The company had 20 employees, €3 million in sales revenue, and €0.51 million net profit (Rekvizitai & SpectroCoin, n.d.). Thus, a user base of 500,000 was readily available for Pervesk, as there were no other similar alternatives globally until 2018, when CoinBase received a license and was ready to offer similar arrangements (Zuckerman, 2018). The bridging was conducted in an extremely timely manner: the cryptocurrency prices were constantly increasing (Geuder, Kinateder, & Wagner, 2019), and the SpectroCoin–Pervesk tandem's services were in extremely high demand.

However, on October 10, 2017, the Central Bank of Lithuania issued an opinion on cryptocurrencies, stating: "Financial services must be clearly dissociated from activities related with virtual currencies. Banks, payment institutions and other financial market participants should not provide services associated with virtual currencies or participate in their release." While this was not an official ban, the media in the country interpreted it that way, and multiple publications with terminology indicating "ban of crypto" started popping up: "Bank of Lithuania bans banks from virtual currency activities" (King, 2017). The news shook the entire crypto and BBB community in Lithuania, especially Vytautas, whose years of hard work towards bridging the two worlds was shattered in one day.

Vytautas took a deep breath and managed to gather his thoughts for a few more minutes. He continued investigating the statement issued by Lithuania's National Bank, and after several rounds of reading, one note caught his attention: "Financial market participants that will provide financial services to customers who offer virtual currencies or are otherwise related to them will have to ensure strict compliance with the requirements for the prevention of money laundering and terrorist financing" (Bank of Lithuania, 2017). This was confusing. Could a small hope to hold on to their dream exist?

5.   ADDRESSING THE POWER OF INSTITUTIONS

For the last five years, Vytautas and the team were successfully navigating various formal and informal institutional pressures. They managed to find feasible ways to start an innovative cryptocurrency business within the old legal framework designed for the traditional financial market. Moreover, they found a technological solution that allowed them to comply with the two sets of very diverse market rules. Neither of the previous challenges stopped them from building new practices and, to some extent, creating new normative institutions. However, now, the situation felt very pessimistic.

Complying entirely with the regulatory opinion would leave Vytautas and the team with either the traditional finance or crypto business. This would mean either competing in the largely unfamiliar and concentrated market and dropping the ideals of the crypto economy grounded in decentralization and autonomy as well as the profit from the newly emerging opportunities or building business in volatile and risky crypto markets when leaving crypto customers without the traditional banking services they need. Compliance with the regulations by shifting the entire business into the crypto-friendly jurisdiction would allow securing both types of operations but would bring immense costs: changing the location would require starting the licensing process from the very beginning and losing the first-mover advantage to competitors. Going against regulatory opinion would entail facing negative public opinion, increased scrutiny from various regulatory institutions, and potentially a drawback to fighting the derisking challenge. In the long term, noncompliance would end up in various penalties and the withdrawal of the payment institution license.

The nature of the co-founders' vision—to bridge regulated and unregulated financial market operations—implied that the legitimization of the unregulated business part might require compliance with traditional financial market rules and norms. BBBs were constantly under pressure to fulfil traditional market players' demands, especially those coming from the need to know the beneficiaries and fulfil AML/CFT requirements. How could firms comply with the regulatory institution's pressure while maintaining both regulated and unregulated financial service activities? Should Vytautas engage in one more challenge and try to navigate conflicting isomorphic pressures?

ACKNOWLEDGMENTS

The preparation of this case would not have been possible without the extensive participation of the innovative entrepreneurs at Pervesk UAB and SpectroCoin Ou. We would like to sincerely thank Vytautas Karalevičius and Tadas Dapšys. We also appreciate valuable insights and input from the blockchain industry professionals in Lithuania, including Andrius Bartminas and many others.

NOTES

1. In 2013, the European Banking Authority explained the concept of cryptocurrency: "a virtual currency shall mean ungoverned and unregulated digital money, which may be used as a means of payment, but is issued into circulation and guaranteed by an institution other than the central bank."
2. The EBA was an independent EU authority, which worked to ensure effective prudential regulation and supervision across the European banking sector. The opinion was the instrument, through which it made a statement without imposing any legal obligation, however, the statement provided a strong signal about the regulator's expectations (directing both firms' and consumers' behaviors) and potentially upcoming legal obligations.

3. IBAN is an international number format, written in a standard and internationally recognized manner, which allows to identify an overseas bank account. IBAN is used across the EU for local and international money transfers (European Central Bank, n.d.).

REFERENCES

Aste, T., Tasca, P., & Di Matteo, T. (2017). Blockchain technologies: The foreseeable impact on society and industry. *Computer*, *50*(9), 18–28.

Badmus, G. (2019). A global guide to a crypto exchange regulatory framework. *Journal of Policy & Globalization*, *90*, 9.

Bank of Lithuania (2013, December 31). Įspėjimas dėl virtualių valiutų. Retrieved from: www.lb.lt/ uploads/documents/files/news/ispejimas_bitcoin.pdf.pdf

Bank of Lithuania (2017, October 10). Position of the Bank of Lithuania on virtual currencies and initial coin offering. Retrieved from: www.lb.lt/en/news/bank-of-lithuania-position-on-virtual-assets-and -initial-coin-offering-reflects-changing-market-realities

Bellavitis, C., Fisch, C., & Wiklund, J. (2021). A comprehensive review of the global development of initial coin offerings (ICOs) and their regulation. *Journal of Business Venturing Insights*, *15*, e00213.

Bhutta, M. N. M., Khwaja, A. A., Nadeem, A., Ahmad, H. F., Khan, M. K., Hanif, M. A. ... & Cao, Y. (2021). A survey on blockchain technology: Evolution, architecture and security. *IEEE Access*, *9*, 61048–61073.

Boreiko, D., & Sahdev, N. K. (2018). To ICO or not to ICO: Empirical analysis of initial coin offerings and token sales. https://papers.ssrn.com/sol3/papers.cfm?abstract_id=3209180

CENTROlink (n.d.). The Bank of Lithuania. Retrieved from: www.lb.lt/en/centrolink

Durner, T., & Shetret, L. (2015). Understanding bank de-risking and its effects on financial inclusion: An exploratory study. Retrieved from: www-cdn.oxfam.org/s3fs-public/file_attachments/rr-bank-de -risking-181115-en_0.pdf

Edwards, F. R., Hanley, K., Litan, R., & Weil, R. L. (2019). Crypto assets require better regulation: Statement of the financial economists roundtable on crypto assets. *Financial Analysts Journal*, *75*(2), 14–19.

Enterprise Lithuania (2018, May 10). Startup Fair 2018 about ICO boom in Lithuania. Retrieved from: www.verslilietuva.lt

EU Blockchain Forum (n.d.). EU blockchain ecosystem report. Retrieved from: www.eublockchainforum .eu/sites/default/files/reports/EU%20Blockchain%20Ecosystem%20Report_final_0.pdf

European Banking Authority (2013). EBA warning on virtual currencies. Retrieved from: www.eba .europa.eu/documents/10180/598344/EBA+Warning+on+Virtual+Currencies.pdf

European Central Bank (n.d.). Single Euro Payments Area. Retrieved from: www.ecb.europa.eu/paym/ integration/retail/sepa/iban/html/index.en.html

European Commission (n.d.). EU law and its application. Retrieved from: https://commission.europa .eu/law/law-making-process/applying-eu-law_en

Eurostat (2015). Eurostat regional yearbook 2015. Retrieved from: https://ec.europa.eu/eurostat/ documents/3217494/7018888/KS-HA-15-001-EN-N.pdf

Faria, I. (2019). Trust, reputation and ambiguous freedoms: Financial institutions and subversive libertarians navigating blockchain, markets, and regulation. *Journal of Cultural Economy*, *12*(2), 119–132.

Ferrari, V. (2020). The regulation of crypto-assets in the EU: Investment and payment tokens under the radar. *Maastricht Journal of European and Comparative Law*, *27*(3), 325–342.

Geuder, J., Kinateder, H., & Wagner, N. F. (2019). Cryptocurrencies as financial bubbles: The case of Bitcoin. *Finance Research Letters*, *31*.

GFICRR (2020). Global Fintech Index City Rankings Report 2020. Retrieved from: https://findexable .com/wp-content/uploads/2019/12/Findexable_Global-Fintech-Rankings-2020exSFA.pdf

Giudici, G., Milne, A., & Vinogradov, D. (2020). Cryptocurrencies: Market analysis and perspectives. *Journal of Industrial and Business Economics*, *47*(1), 1–18.

Hassan, S., & De Filippi, P. (2017). The expansion of algorithmic governance: From code is law to law is code. *Field Actions Science Reports: Journal of Field Actions*, *17*, 88–90.

Hileman, G., & Rauchs, M. (2017). 2017 global cryptocurrency benchmarking study. SSRN 2965436.

Huang, W., Meoli, M., & Vismara, S. (2020). The geography of initial coin offerings. *Small Business Economics*, 55(1), 77–102.

Kaal, W. A. (2018). Initial coin offerings: The top 25 jurisdictions and their comparative regulatory responses (as of May 2018). *Stanford Journal of Blockchain Law & Policy*, 1, 41–63.

King, R. (2017, October 13). Bank of Lithuania bans banks from virtual currency activities. *Central Banking*. Retrieved from: www.centralbanking.com/central-banks/financial-stability/fmi/3308211/bank-of-lithuania-bans-banks-from-virtual-currency-activities

Kiyak, D., & Reichenbachas, T. (2012). The impact of Lithuanian financial crisis for national economy: Comparative study. *Regional Formation and Development Studies*, 3, 92–105.

Korauš, A., Kelemen, P., Backa, S., & Polák, J. (2018). Economic security of business entities. *Innovation and Entrepreneurship*, 56.

Kostrikova, N. (2021, May). Studying adoption of cryptocurrencies and blockchain technology in the Baltic states. *Economic Science for Rural Development Conference Proceedings*, 55.

Kruppa, M. (2021 July 20). Crypto exchange FTX secures backing from venture capital and hedge funds. *Financial Times*. Retrieved from: www.ft.com/content/a3a90a4f-54e4-4b4f-b1df-2d9d8ca7712d

Kshetri, N. (2017). Will blockchain emerge as a tool to break the poverty chain in the Global South? *Third World Quarterly*, 38(8), 1710–1732.

Lim, C., Wang, Y., Ren, J., & Lo, S. W. (2019). A review of fast-growing blockchain hubs in Asia. *Journal of the British Blockchain Association*, 9959.

Lithuanian Tribune (2015, December 5). Vilnius to host largest bitcoin conference in Baltics. Retrieved from: https://lithuaniatribune.com/vilnius-to-host-largest-bitcoin-conference-in-baltics/

Lumineau, F., Wang, W., & Schilke, O. (2021). Blockchain governance: A new way of organizing collaborations? *Organization Science*, 32(2), 500–521.

Manski, S., & Manski, B. (2018). No gods, no masters, no coders? The future of sovereignty in a blockchain world. *Law and Critique*, 29(2), 151–162.

Marian, O. (2018). Blockchain havens and the need for their internationally-coordinated regulation. *North Carolina Journal of Law & Technology*, 20, 529.

Martin, J. (2014). Lost on the silk road: Online drug distribution and the "cryptomarket," *Criminology and Criminal Justice*, 14(3), 351–367.

Ministry of Finance of the Republic of Lithuania (2016, October 16). FinTech industry in Lithuania: More possibilities to remote identity verification. Retrieved from: https://finmin.lrv.lt/en/news/fintech-industry-in-lithuania-more-possibilities-to-remote-identity-verification

Nakamoto, S. (2008). Bitcoin: A peer-to-peer electronic cash system. *Decentralized Business Review*, 21260.

OECD (2017). Lithuania: Review of the financial system 2017. Retrieved from: www.oecd.org/finance/Lithuania-financialmarkets-2017.pdf

Pflaum, I., & Hateley, E. (2013). A bit of a problem: National and extraterritorial regulation of virtual currency in the age of financial disintermediation. *Georgetown Journal of International Law*, 45, 1169.

Rekvizitai & SpectroCoin (n.d.). SpectroCoin. Retrieved from: https://rekvizitai.vz.lt/en/company/spectro_finance/

Ryan, M. D., Macrossan, P., Wright, S., & Adams, M. (2021). Blockchain and publishing: Towards a publisher-centred distributed ledger for the book publishing industry. *Creative Industries Journal*, 1–20.

Shirole, M., Darisi, M., & Bhirud, S. (2020). Cryptocurrency token: An overview. *IC-BCT 2019*, 133–140.

Šilenskytė, A., Butkevičienė, J., & Dhanaraj, C. (2022). Digital entrepreneurs' strategic responses to the incomplete global policy framework for blockchain-based business, in J. M. Munoz (ed.), *Digital Entrepreneurship and the Global Economy*. Routledge.

Šilenskytė, A., Butkevičienė, J., & Bartminas, A. (2023). Blockchain-based connectivity within digital platforms and ecosystems in international business. *Journal of International Management*, 101109. https://doi.org/10.1016/j.intman.2023.101109

SpectroCoin (n.d.). SpectroCoin. Retrieved from: https://spectrocoin.com/en/about.html

Toivonen, T. (2020). A taxonomy of payment systems. https://helda.helsinki.fi/server/api/core/bitstreams/c6b834f6-efea-4349-9817-3f60a4ec24b9/content

Turner, A., & Irwin, A. S. M. (2018). Bitcoin transactions: A digital discovery of illicit activity on the blockchain. *Journal of Financial Crime*.

Valcke, P., Vandezande, N., & Van De Velde, N. (2015). The evolution of third party payment providers and cryptocurrencies under the EU's upcoming PSD2 and AMLD4. https://papers.ssrn.com/sol3/papers.cfm?abstract_id=2665973

Velde, F. R. (1998). Lessons from the history of money. *Economic Perspectives: Federal Reserve Bank of Chicago, 22*, 2–16.

Vigna, P., & Rudegea, P. (2017). Global cyberattacks prompt examination of Bitcoin's role. *Wall Street Journal*. Retrieved from: www. theaustralian. com. au/business/wall-street-journal/global-cyber-attacks-prompt-examination-of-bitcoins-role/news-story/c6af2866d078961512db591 cd87bd4a5

Vlasov, A. V. (2017). The evolution of e-money. *European Research Studies, 20*(10), 215–224.

Zuckerman, M. J. (2018, March 14). Coinbase receives e-money license for fiat activities from UK, its "biggest market." Retrieved from: https://cointelegraph.com/news/coinbase-receives-e-money-license-for-fiat-activities-from-uk-its-biggest-market